Alto Adige—South Tyrol

ALTO ADIGE—SOUTH TYROL

Italy's Frontier with the German World

by Mario Toscano

edited by George A. Carbone

The Johns Hopkins University Press

Baltimore and London

Originally published as *Storia diplomatica della questione dell' Alto Adige* (Bari: Editori Laterza, 1968).

Manufactured in the United States of America

The Johns Hopkins University Press, Baltimore, Maryland 21218
The Johns Hopkins University Press Ltd., London

Library of Congress Catalog Card Number 75–11349
ISBN 0-8018-1567-3

Library of Congress Cataloging in Publication data will be found on the last printed page of this book.

To my granddaughter Monica,
in the sunset of my days

Contents

Introduction

This volume is based principally on lectures given 1966–67 to senior year students in the School of Political Science at the University of Rome. It has, therefore, its origins primarily in teaching and is one of the required texts for examinations in History of Treaties and International Politics. Consequently, all the views expressed and the theses developed are exclusively the author's. Since this is a work dealing with diplomatic rather than general history, Italian domestic political activities relating to the Alto Adige are referred to only when they have international implications.

Aside from occasional references to certain antecedents that are useful to a better understanding of current events, the time span covered by this account begins with the proposal drafted in September 1914, by the Italian foreign minister, Marquis Antonino di Sangiuliano, stipulating the conditions for Italy's intervention in World War I. The period closes with the Austrian reply of March 30, 1965, to the "comprehensive outline of approach toward a settlement," developed by the Italian and Austrian foreign ministers in Paris in December 1964. This meeting was held in compliance with the U.N. Resolutions of 1960 and 1961 on the Italo-Austrian dispute over the application of the De Gasperi–Gruber agreement. If the choice of 1914 as a point of departure for this study is obvious, the reason for selecting 1965 as the terminal point is explained below.[1]

Additional research in the diplomatic history of the Alto Adige question during this period[2] has made it possible to fill in some of the gaps in the existent information and to more adequately evaluate later developments in this area. That portion of the investigation focusing on the period preceding the conclusion of the De Gasperi–Gruber agreement is based largely on archival material.

The dedicated collaboration of my two assistants and colleagues, Professors Gian Luca Andrè and Pietro Pastorelli, has been of inestimable value in the research and the preparation of this manuscript. Their cooperation has been laudable and their labors extensive in a project which we all agreed was not only stimulating but also valuable. I also wish to acknowledge the assistance of the superintendent of the Central State Archives, Professor Leopoldo Sandri; the superintendent of the Historical Records in the Foreign Ministry, Professor Renato Mori; the director of the Foreign Ministry Library, Dr. Renato Piccinini; and two other assistants, Professor Giustino Filippone and Dr. Franca Avantaggiato Puppo. I have also been assisted by former ambassadors Massimo Magistrati and Maurilio Coppini regarding specific problems relating to the period in which they served with the Italian diplomatic mission to Berlin and Vienna respectively. To all the above, I should like to extend my most grateful thanks.

My appreciation is also expressed to Signora Maria Romana Catti De Gasperi who graciously allowed me to consult the papers in the late Prime Minister's personal files. It would not have been possible for me to reconstruct the various phases of the negotiations leading to the Agreement of September 5, 1946, without these references and they form the primary and central focus of my work. Further, I wish to acknowledge the courtesy of Professor F. W. Deakin, warden of Saint Anthony's College in Oxford, for the photostat copies of those German and Italian Social Republic documents of which there is no remaining record in Rome. This source was of considerable value with reference to the material discussed in the latter part of Chapter III.

For the final chapters of this book I have also drawn on my own experience as delegate to the U.N. General Assembly meetings since 1956, having participated in some of the meetings between the foreign ministers of Italy and Austria, and on close scrutiny of subsequent developments. Such experience has enabled me to reconstruct and present a reasonably complete picture of the negotiations that took place following the 1960 and 1961 U.N. Resolutions, the origins of which I reconstructed and synthesized immediately after the conclusion of the various U.N. debates on the issues.[3]

The facts outlined in this book, based as they are on research and on recollections from my own experiences, were meant to provide the basis for a university lecture course, in much the same way as the courses that I offered in 1960 and 1961 on this problem, courses that are well known to students in Austria, Germany, and the Tyrol. Recently, however, a study has been published in Germany on the diplomatic history of the South Tyrol.[4] In this volume, use is made not only of the documents contained in the exhaustive and invaluable records belonging to the late Senator Ettore Tolomei,[5] but minutes of conversations between the foreign ministers of Italy and Austria or their representatives are also reproduced or amply summarized. A surprising procedure such as this, running entirely counter to international practice, has induced me to expand and publish my lecture material. In so doing, I have availed myself of the contents of these documents as well as of the records—also published in Ritschel's book—of the meetings that took place between Austrians, Tyrolese, and representatives of the Alto Adige after each Austro-Italian meeting.

The chronological scope of this volume, therefore, has to a certain extent been determined by that established by Ritschel. It has also been due partially to my desire to avoid following the same example, that of writing material that to some extent would represent a direct interference in the latest developments on the question of the Alto Adige. Accordingly, I have preferred to conclude this volume with March 30, 1965, the date of Vienna's failure to endorse "the first Comprehensive Outline of Approach toward a Settlement," to which both foreign ministers had agreed, with a view to settling the international controversy. Presently, in fact, the second comprehensive outline is being discussed, and in due course the opportunity will arise to describe the process that led to this latter proposal.

It is difficult to judge whether and to what extent this volume, essentially based on lectures for a university course, may favorably compare with a volume written by a correspondent on political matters. Perhaps a recollection of the facts will prove to be useful to all those who continue to believe that no force is as irresistible as the force of truth.

Rome   *Mario Toscano*
April 12, 1967

Editor's Note

As noted in the Introduction, Professor Toscano, in a subsequent edition, planned to describe the negotiations leading to the "Second Comprehensive Outline of Approach towards a Settlement" in the dispute between Italy and Austria. Toward this end, he had, after the publication of the present volume, worked on a supplemental text covering developments subsequent to March 1965. At the time of Professor Toscano's death, September 17, 1968, this supplement, albeit in rough draft, covered the negotiations down to January 21, 1967.

This new material was later published in *Rivista di Studi Politici Internazionali* (Florence), August–September 1968, pp. 536–654. Professor Giuseppe Vedovato, editor of this review, and Professor Toscano's daughter, Fabrizia Toscano Masutti, have kindly placed this material at our disposal, enabling us to include it in this edition as Chapter IX, further updating the second edition, published by Laterza, which has been used for this translation.

The positive accomplishments registered in the Austro-Italian negotiations by the end of 1969 have suggested the inclusion of an additional outline as Chapter X, in order to apprise the reader of the significant developments of the more recent period, providing as current a picture of the situation as is possible. Because of the additional materials and the limitations imposed in the matter of space, it has been deemed expedient to omit from this volume a number of passages dealing with matters of secondary importance and those dealing with purely Italian domestic problems where these have no determining effect on the primary issue in question.

Finally, it should be noted that the English translation was done by Professor Toscano's friends and colleagues in Rome.

March 1, 1975   *George A. Carbone*
Portland State University
Portland, Oregon

Alto Adige—South Tyrol

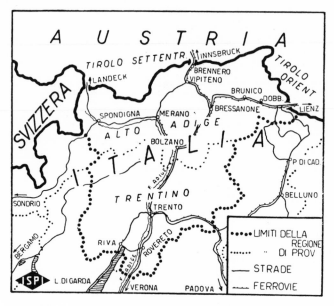

Regione Trentino-Alto Adige

Chapter I

Annexation
of the Alto Adige
to Italy

[1] Introductory remarks. Negotiations with Austria–Hungary and the Entente Powers prior to Italian intervention in World War I. [2] President Wilson and the Italian claims. The negotiations that preceded the armistices, and the reservations expressed by the government of Rome on Point IX of President Wilson's program. Developments in the American attitude: Colonel House's *aide mémoire* of October 29, 1918, and the findings of the *Inquiry.* [3] Opening of the Peace Conference. The memorandum of Signor Barzilai of February 7, 1919. Discussions in the Four-Power Council. The position of the Vienna government during the drafting of the Peace Treaty and the Austrian notes of June 16, July 10, and August 9, 1919. The negative reply given to Austria by the Allied and Associated Powers on September 2, 1919, and the Italian statement regarding treatment of the South Tyrol minority.

[1]

Due to its geographic position, the Alto Adige area has been subjected over the centuries to constant Germanic pressure aimed at acquiring possession of this Alpine region primarily for the military advantage it offered to facilitate access to the south. Only in the fourteenth century was the House of Hapsburg able to penetrate the region that had always been part of the life and political events of the Italian peninsula. But resistance to Germanization was such that the Alto Adige, then officially called the "Italian Tyrol," for a long time continued to maintain its Italian character. The Hapsburg monarchy retained possession of the territory until the Napoleonic era, when it was first assigned to Bavaria—by the Peace of Pressburg, December 26, 1805,[1] and later annexed, in part, to the kingdom of Italy, established by Napoleon and in accordance with the Franco-Bavarian Paris Treaty of February 28, 1810, which drew the new boundary slightly to the north of the city of Bolzano.[2] After the fall of Napoleon, the former possessions of the Emperor of Austria were restored through the Austro-Bavarian Treaty of June 3, 1814[3] and the Treaty of Vienna of June 9 of the following year.[4]

These events were destined to exert a considerable influence on the subsequent language pattern in the Alto Adige. The urban middle class, predominantly Italian, responsive to the liberal ideas introduced by the French, found itself in open conflict with the German-speaking peasantry, who opposed this trend. This provoked reprisals by the Austrian authorities, who induced a portion of the Italian population to leave the country: for example, between 1860 and 1913, the number of Italians living in Bolzano decreased by almost 50 percent.[5]

During this same period, the attitude of the German-speaking Tyrolese toward the demands of the Italian population in the Trentino also deserves attention. In 1848 the delegates from the Trentino refused to sit in the Diet of the Tyrol and incurred the opposition of the German-speaking delegates, who did not intend to disrupt the unity of the Tyrol–Trentino. A similar attitude was maintained by the Vienna authorities toward requests submitted by the Italians of the Trentino aimed at securing administrative provisions acknowledging the non-Germanic character of their region. On this point the Hapsburg government absolutely refused to make any distinction between the Trentino and the South Tyrol, insisting that the two regions constituted an economic unit that could in no way be separated without serious damage to both.[6]

After the Austro-Italian war of 1866, the attitude of the Vienna government toward the Italian minority became even more inflexible: the Emperor himself issued precise instructions to impede the Italians with "the utmost energy and having consideration for no one," with a view to progressively moulding territories containing Italian minorities either toward a Germanic or Slavic character, as the situation indicated.[7]

After the outbreak of World I, the Italian foreign minister, Marquis Antonino di Sangiuliano, though originally a supporter of the Triple Alliance, was soon moved to examine the possibility of Italy becoming an Entente partner. In this connection, on September 25, 1914, he asked the Italian ambassadors in Paris and St. Petersburg, Tittoni and Carlotti respectively, for suggestions on points and demands that the Italian government might advance in such an event, seeking their opinions on a series of eventual territorial claims, on some of which he appeared to have some uncertainty. However, he harbored no doubts as to the future northern frontier with Austria and formulated his proposed demand as follows: "In case of final victory, Italy shall be awarded the Italian provinces of Austria as far as the Alpine watershed, that is to say, as far as the natural boundary of Italy."[8] Though two ambassadors interposed various exceptions and reservations in connection with other suggested proposals forwarded by Sangiuliano, they raised no objections on this point.[9]

It should be noted that the precise definition of the natural geographic boundary between Italy and Austria has long been the subject of lengthy discussions, and even recently the Austrians have maintained that such a line runs slightly to the north of Trento, at the Salorno gorge, to the south of which the Alpine reliefs gradually become foothills and the plain begins. Even if the term used by Sangiuliano in his telegram may at first glance appear to be not very precise in that it referred to a natural boundary line over which there was some question as to the exact location, his reference to the Alpine dividing line leaves no doubt that he meant to refer to the Brenner Pass as the future frontier between Italy and Austria.

As a matter of fact, apart from disputes of a geographical nature, it had long been a well-known fact, at least in Vienna and Paris, that from a political standpoint, Italy identified her natural frontier to be the Alpine watershed at the Brenner Pass. During the negotiations of 1868–69 toward the eventual formation of an Austro-Franco-Italian alliance, Italy had, among other things, submitted a request for that portion of the Tyrol lying within her natural frontier as compensation for her entrance into a war against Prussia. This Italian request became more generally known when documents relating to these negotiations were published following World War I.[10] Further, since the publication of Volume XIII, First Series, of the Italian diplomatic documents, no doubt can now be entertained on the nature and extent of the Italian request.

In July 1870, in view of a possible resumption of negotiations, the Italian minister in Paris, Costantino Nigra, expressed himself as follows in a letter to the new foreign minister, Visconti Venosta, to bring him up to date on earlier alliance talks: "In case of victory, cession of the Italian Tyrol to Italy (Austria had only consented to eventually relinquishing the Trentino), Italy demanded the Tyrol lying to the South of the Alpine watershed, that is to say: . . . to the North of the main Alpine peaks in the area."[11]

A few days later, a more detailed report on the negotiations was dispatched to Lanza and Visconti Venosta by the former prime minister and foreign secretary, Menabrea, who also enclosed the latest version of the draft treaty as proposed by Paris, together with some remarks referring to explanations and amendments as discussed and agreed upon during the Italian cabinet meeting of July 3, 1869. According to Point 5 of the French draft: "In case of a successful war, Austria agrees to the annexation of the Trentino by Italy." In his observations, Menabrea pointed out that "Italy requested *the entire southern slope of the Alps, that is to say the Southern Tyrol from the Brenner southward.* But Austria opposed this and only consented to the cession of the Trentino," following a demarcation line to include "Rovereto and Trento as far as Lavis" and which, "following the ridge-line of the lateral bastions," merged with the then existing boundary "at Monte Cortellazzo (or, more correctly Castellazzo) to the East and Monte Piscanno (or, more properly Punta Pisgana) to the West." The Cabinet expressed the opinion that "the boundary rectifications in Italy's favor should, with regard to Austria, . . . at least include the Trentino."[12]

The above documents are of considerable importance. In the first place, they explain why the Marquis di Sangiuliano did not hesitate to request the Brenner frontier: this reflected a requirement that the Italian government had advanced and affirmed for decades. Second, the surfacing of this request during the first negotiations with Austria after the war of 1866, points out that the reason for claiming the Brenner frontier stemmed from the results of the Italian campaign in that war and the proven indefensibility of the existing Italian frontiers. It is worth noting that if strategic needs determined the Italian position on the problem of the northern frontier, the same requirements governed the Austrian position, as evidenced both by the boundary line established under the Vienna Peace Treaty of October 1866[13] and by the proposals subsequently put forward by the Austro-Hungarian government during the negotiations of 1868–69 and 1915. In fact, such proposals appeared consistently prompted by a desire to establish a boundary line with Italy which, without undue consideration for the ethnical factor, would contribute to insure a more successful offensive action in the direction of the Italian plain if need be. In this it clearly differed from the Italian requests, which were merely aimed at obtaining a defensible frontier. Third, the request for the Brenner frontier, with the consequent inclusion of a German-speaking minority within the Italian boundary, was voiced by men of the Risorgimento, that is to say, by those who had striven for Italian unification on the basis of the principle of nationality and who were still struggling to achieve such unity, with Rome as the nation's capital. Such an Italian request should not, therefore, be mistaken for a claim surfacing only when the defense of the principles of nationality frequently became confused with the postulates of nationalism.

It should further be noted that in 1869 Austria had already made the offer of a frontier line running 9 kilometers north of Trento, leaving within the Austrian boundary undeniable Italian territories, such as the Val Vermiglio, Val di Sole, Val Cembra, Val di Fiemme, and Val di Fassa. The Italian government, though not insisting at that time on their claim to the strategic frontier at the Brenner, did not consider the Austrian offer acceptable unless it were at least extended to include the entire Trentino.

Although such precedents had no influence on the conduct of the Austrian government during the negotiations of 1915, they were nonetheless remembered in Rome, and they should not be overlooked when considering the attitude then assumed by the Italian government. This also explains why in the Archives of the Foreign Ministry in Rome there is no trace of any paper or document which could lead one to infer that, before advancing the request for the Brenner frontier, the Foreign Minister had consulted with General Cadorna or other members of the latter's staff. Such a consultation did not occur, because it was general knowledge that the 1866 frontier with Austria had placed Italy in a position of marked inferiority. The absence of any military consultations and the widespread knowledge that such a frontier line placed Italy at a serious disadvantage, were facts already established. After half a century of military inferiority, Italy wanted to put an end to this situation, a psychological factor that should not be underestimated or ignored.

This position taken by Italian Foreign Minister di Sangiuliano is more important that at first appears. In fact, while putting forward his request for the Brenner frontier, he withheld making specific claims relating to Dalmatia. In the aforementioned telegram of September 25, 1914, to the ambassadors in Paris and St. Petersburg, di Sangiuliano also said he would appreciate receiving their opinion on possible Italian claims in Dalmatia. The absence of any direct connection between the request for the Brenner frontier and demands with regard to Dalmatia, certainly does not appear to lend support to recent arguments that the Rome government, when negotiating in London regarding an eventual Italian entry into World War I, did not really look upon the Brenner frontier as a definite war aim but rather as an undertaking in ultimate support of other claims and particularly in the Adriatic.

Equally clear were the views held on this entire matter by Marquis di Sangiuliano's successor, Baron Sidney Sonnino, who, on March 4, 1915, officially informed the three Entente governments, through Ambassador Imperiali in London, of Rome's requests relative to Italian intervention in the war. On the subject of the northern frontier, such requests included "the Trentino, Cisalpine Tyrol with its natural and geographic boundary (the Brenner frontier)."[14] The only Italian diplomat to express reservations on the matter was Tommaso Tittoni, then ambassador in Paris.

In a telegram dispatched to Sonnino on March 23, 1915, Tittoni acknowledged that, through annexation of the Trentino as far as the Brenner and of Trieste including Istria, Italy would secure "strategically excellent" borders, a subject on which the Entente Powers would not raise objections because it was not in their interest to do so. At the same time, however, he suggested that Sonnino also consider the extent to which it would be convenient, or otherwise, to annex territories inhabited by ethnically different populations that could become centers of irredentism.[15] Obviously, the tone of his remarks suggests that the Ambassador had given serious thought to the matter. Nonetheless, when he succeeded Sonnino as foreign minister in 1919, Tittoni not only approved without reservation the Treaty of Saint Germain, actually signed while he was in office, but was also intransigent in his opposition to attempts to restrict Italy's territorial acquisitions.[16] As noted, the Italian claims were the object of protracted negotiations with the Entente Powers,[17] but discussion of the northern frontier with Austria was in no way raised as an issue during the talks, and the wording suggested by Sonnino was embodied verbatim in Article 4 of the Treaty of London.[18] It was signed on April 26, 1915, and on this basis Italy entered the war, resulting in a sacrifice of men and resources far beyond any anticipation.

On the other hand, in the negotiations which took place simultaneously with the Central Powers, aimed at the maintenance of Italian neutrality on the basis of Article VII of the Triple Alliance Treaty, Sonnino requested that the frontier with Austria be moved further north so as to coincide with the border established under the Paris Treaty of February 28, 1810, and which, as noted, ran north of Bolzano and south of Merano.[19] The Austrian reply was negative, but in a last minute attempt to prevent Italian intervention the Vienna government offered, through a memorandum of April 16, 1915, the province of Trent as far

as the Salorno Gorge.[20] The request made to Austria by Foreign Minister
Sonnino was prompted by the same considerations that had moved di Sangiuliano.

[2]

Subsequent to Italy's entry into the war, some of the questions that had
already been settled under the London treaty were further discussed between
the governments of Italy and of the Entente. It should, however, be noted that
during the somewhat complex negotiations that ensued, the subject of the
Brenner frontier was never brought up for discussion by the Allies.[21]

In this respect matters became more difficult after the United States entered
the war. In fact, not only was America not a signatory of the London treaty and
consequently not bound by its provisions, but President Wilson had already
taken a stand against secret treaties and other agreements entered into among
the Allies regarding postwar settlement. To this end he had also made no secret
of his intention, at the Peace Conference, to encourage solutions that might well
be opposed to commitments already assumed between the powers.

Accordingly, when outlining his peace program in the well-known Fourteen
Points in January 1918, Wilson also touched upon the new boundaries to be
assigned to Italy in terms which caused considerable concern in Italian government circles and in public opinion generally. Wilson's Point IX in fact stated that
"a readjustment of Italian frontiers will have to be made along a clearly
recognizable demarcation line between nationalities." Now, since Italian claims
also extended to territories inhabited by Germanic and Slavic populations
(respectively in the Alto Adige and along Italy's eastern frontier), such a
statement was interpreted by some people who were familiar with the Treaty of
London as an indirect stand against Italy's territorial claims covered by that
agreement.

Actually, it appears unlikely that this was Wilson's intent. In particular, one is
led to rule out that under Point IX Wilson intended to oppose the strategic
requirements brought forward by Italy in claiming the Brenner frontier. When
drawing up the Fourteen Points, Wilson's ideas in fact were not very clear
regarding the Austro-Italian frontier, nor had the experts working on the *Inquiry*
provided him with unequivocal information on this point.[22] In all probability,
therefore, the wording he used was aimed simply at recognizing the necessity for
redrawing the Italian frontiers in accordance with certain general principles,
without wishing to indicate the precise pattern to which such a rearrangement
should conform.[23]

Nonetheless, the concept outlined by Wilson gave rise to explicit reservations
on the part of the Italian government.[24] Such reservations were confirmed and
further elaborated upon during the negotiations in the Supreme Allied Council's
meeting, held in Paris during the last days of October 1918, to discuss the
armistice conditions with Germany and Austria-Hungary. At that time, Sonnino
stated that Wilson's formula could not be considered satisfactory not only
because it merely mentioned boundary readjustments but also because it estab-

lished the ethnic criterion as the sole guiding line. On the other hand, the Italian Foreign Minister argued, it was also necessary to consider geographical and historical factors and, above all, the requirements of military security, which, incidentally, were also entirely in keeping with the principles which the Allies intended to apply toward Germany.

However, only a passing reference to these reservations was recorded in the minutes of the Supreme Allied Council's meetings.[25] The armistice with Austria-Hungary contained no reference to the conditions for peace as set forth by President Wilson. These were mentioned, however, in the armistice with Germany, though the reservations on Point IX were not recorded, on the grounds that they only applied to the future peace treaty with Austria. At the same time, the military clauses of the armistice of November 3, provided that Italy should occupy all the territories listed in the Treaty of London and, consequently, also Austrian territory as far as the Brenner.[26]

It was under these circumstances that Wilson's personal envoy, Colonel House, faced with criticism of the American President's program, drafted an explanatory comment on the Fourteen Points. On Point IX and in connection with the Brenner frontier, this comment ran as follows:

In the region of Trent the Italians claim a strategic rather than ethnic frontier. It should be noted in this connection that (Italy) and Germany will become neighbors if German Austria joins the German Empire. And if Italy obtains the best geographical frontier she will assume sovereignty over a large number of Germans. This is a violation of principle. But it may be argued that by drawing a sharp line along the crest of the Alps, Italy's security will be enormously enhanced and the necessity of heavy armaments reduced. It might, therefore, be provided that Italy should have her claim in the Trentino, but that the northern part, inhabited by Germans, should be completely autonomous and that the population should not be liable to military service in the Italian army. Italy could thus occupy the uninhabited Alpine peaks for military purpose, but would not govern the cultural life of the alien population to the south of her frontier.[27]

The importance of this document consists primarily in the fact that for the first time it expressed the concept of autonomy, to be accompanied by exemption from military service, on behalf of the German-speaking inhabitants. Thus, the idea of autonomy was of American origin and was stated even before the signing of the Villa Giusti armistice. At the same time, it was difficult to judge to what extent the concept of actually allowing Italy to occupy only the uninhabited Alpine peaks could turn out to be practicable.

The note, prepared by House and sent to Wilson on October 29, was immediately approved by the President. He however, remarked that "details of application mentioned should be regarded as merely illustrative suggestions."[28]

The document, which upon Presidential approval became the official expression of the American point of view, thus introduced an important exception to the principles embodied in the Fourteen Points and was to later serve as a guideline for the Washington government when the settlement of the Italian frontiers came up for discussion. In this connection, it is worth noting that Wilson approved the text without awaiting the results of studies still to be completed by the *Inquiry*. This commisssion, in fact, did not submit its report until January 21, 1919, and recommended that the new Austro-Italian border should be settled with due regard both to the ethnic factor and to the strategic necessities of Italy. In practice, the western part of the border would have followed the line established under the London treaty. The border would have veered to the south before reaching the Brenner and then followed a line similar to the one that had marked the boundary of the kingdom of Italy established by the Franco-Bavarian Treaty of February 28, 1810.[29]

Nevertheless, the opinion of the experts who exercised a profound influence on Wilson's attitude at the time the Italian–Yugoslav border issue was settled did not affect his decision concerning the Brenner frontier. Nor was this opinion taken into account in the delineation of the other frontiers established under the peace treaties of 1919–20.

In December 1918, Wilson arrived in Europe and was greeted enthusiastically by the people of all the friendly countries he visited. The impression was conveyed that he was vested with a direct mandate by public opinion in all countries. On that occasion he had no real or extensive preliminary talks with Orlando and Sonnino in Rome. According to an account given at that time by the Italian ambassador in Washington, Count Vincenzo Macchi di Cellere,[30] during his stay in the Italian capital the American President had had contacts almost exclusively with Bissolati, who had a few days before relinquished his post in the Orlando cabinet because of disagreement over the Italian claims. From this contact, Wilson derived the impression that not even the men governing the country were in agreement among themselves. Very little was apparently said at that time about the Brenner frontier, probably because Wilson had indicated from the beginning that he was disposed to accept the ruling of the Treaty of London on this point.[31]

[3]

When the Peace Conference opened in 1919, the Italian delegation submitted a memorandum on February 7, which had been drafted by Barzilai. This paper, without referring to the Treaty of London so as to avoid irritating Wilson, elaborated the motives prompting the Italian claims. Though they referred to the northern frontier, these claims also extended to incorporate the Sesto valley and the Tarvisio basin, which were not included in the London treaty. The memorandum reads as follows:

> The strategic value of the Upper Adige has always been recognized: in the upper valley of the Adige lies the centre of all the highways for a German invasion of Italy. With it, even if Italy had Trent, the Germans would still hold the gates of Italy in their hands. It is indispensable that Italy should reach beyond Bolzano in order that by owning the secondary line joining the two great railways of the Brenner and Toblach, the Germans should not continue to have the actual control also of the Italian side. An Austrian, General Kuhn, wrote:

"The Italians must conquer southern Tyrol as far as the Brenner, if they want to defend Venice."

Any other boundary more to the south would merely be an artificial amputation entailing the upkeep of expensive armaments contrary to the principles by which peace should be inspired. The boundary chosen by Italy ensures equal security also to the peoples living on the northern side of it, because the difficult and impervious nature of the ground makes it practically impossible to carry out military operations of any importance either from the north or from the south. The boundary, which we will call the "Brenner Frontier," is therefore indicated by the very conditions of nature, by the necessities of the people's life, and by reasons of peaceful security. It places the two neighbouring countries on a footing of a perfect equality in every possible way. By reverting to actual natural conditions and by identifying itself with reality, it acquires all the elements of stability.

Compared to the supreme necessity and practical advantage of such a frontier, the fact that it includes about 200,000 inhabitants of German nationality becomes a matter of no significance. Apart from the former historic relations between this region and Italy, commemorated by so many monuments and indelible memories which received eloquent military and political sanction by Napoleon the First's annexation of the Upper Adige to the Italian Kingdom; apart from the fact that the present national conformation of the Upper Adige is the result of violent intrusion and foreign invasions in a basin which geographically, historically, and economically belongs to Italy (even at the opening of the nineteenth century the region was predominatly Italian not only south of the Napoleonic frontier, but in the entire Venosta Valley, and partially in the districts of Bressanone and Sterzen, while the valley of Badia is still Italian at the present day, a total of not less than 45,000 Italians residing at present in the real and proper Upper Adige), it should be noted that the territory lying between the pre-war political frontier and the Upper Adige which forms one geographical whole, was a total population of 600,000 inhabitants, of which number even the Austrian statistics admit 380,000 to be Italian, while the correct figures reach 420,000. Even if the reasons of national safety and defence did not militate in favour of the inclusion of the Trentino and Upper Adige in the Italian Kingdom, the mere numerical prevalence of the Italian population (about 70 percent), in a region which for evident reasons is indivisible, would necessitate its return to its natural, economic, and national unity.[32]

Actually, Barzilai said nothing new or of particular import. On the contrary, viewing things in a historical perspective he could have said considerably more; but in reading this document today, one cannot fail to be struck by the ultimate considerations of the close links between the Trentino and the Alto Adige. Apart from the existence of such links having previously been repeatedly emphasized by Vienna and Innsbruck, the most interesting point lies in the fact that in assigning the Brenner frontier to Italy the Peace Conference itself should have at the same time implicitly accepted the concluding argument of the Barzilai memorandum.

The Italian claims were discussed in their entirety only on April 19, 1919. Though preliminary exchanges of views between the Italian and the United States delegations had revealed the existence of differences of opinion on the subject of the proposed Italian Adriatic frontiers insofar as the Austro-Italian border was concerned, President Wilson had declared himself in agreement with the frontier line as traced under the Treaty of London.[33] Moreover, even his advisors now appeared convinced that this was the best solution. Writing to Colonel House on March 16, 1919, Sidney Mezes of the *Inquiry* remarked that: "it would be equitable and advisable to assign to Italy the territory in the Trentino region between her frontier of 1914 and the line of the treaty of London, with generous[34] guarantees in the treaty of cession of autonomy, especially in the matter of language, of schools, and of freedom from military service, of the German-speaking population between the linguistic line and the treaty of London line."

Mezes justified his conclusion: "The treaty of London line in the Trentino gives Italy a security of frontier advantageous in the interests of disarmament, and probably necessary and expedient if German Austria should later on, as she well may, be united with Germany."[35]

Even more inclined to make concessions were the French experts, while the British ones, although favorable to a border drawn further to the south, stated their readiness to support the American point of view should it be decided to take Italy's strategic position into account.[36]

Therefore, on April 19, 1919, the Italian prime minister, Orlando, asked the Council of Four that the Peace Treaty assign to Italy the Alpine watershed in accordance with the provisions of the Treaty of London, with the addition of the Sesto valley and the Tarvisio basin. He did not deny the existence of a German-speaking language group in the Alto Adige, but he contested the validity of the census carried out by the Vienna government in 1910, the results of which were also to prove unreliable in connection with the Czech, Croatian, and Rumanian minorities. In all events, according to Orlando's statement, the ethnic factor became of secondary importance in view of the necessity of guaranteeing Italy the security of her frontiers.

Wilson promptly confirmed his willingness to accept Orlando's request, including the inclusion of the frontier line at Sesto and Tarvisio. Lloyd George and Clemenceau,[37] who were bound by the provisions of the London treaty, raised no objections. The discussion on this point was very brief, but it should be noted that it was agreed to delay decision on the Brenner frontier for the time being, with the obvious intent of exercising pressure on the Italian delegation while the question of the Yugoslav frontier was still under consideration. Not until May 29, 1919, after Orlando had accepted the Tardieu compromise as a basis for discussion on the eastern border, did Wilson agree to render the final decision on the Brenner.[38]

Austrian reaction to the Peace Treaty proposal drawn up by the Four was very vigorous. Locally there were repeated public demonstrations of loyalty toward Austria,[39] and at the diplomatic level the Austrian delegation submitted a series of memoranda to the Allied representatives to affirm Austria's right to the Southern Tyrol.

One of these documents, submitted on June 16, 1919, opened by refuting the

Italian argument on the military importance of the Brenner frontier. Accordingly, the Austrians proposed a demilitarization not only of the Southern Tyrol but of the whole Tyrol as a means of meeting Italy's desire for national security. Following some observations on the ethnical aspect of the question, the Austrian memorandum went on to stress the necessity of maintaining the various parts of the Tyrol united, both on a basis of historical precedents and for reasons of economic necessity.

In conclusion, the memorandum affirmed that: "as regards the annexation of Southern Tyrol to Italy, any argument is indeed of little weight in the force of the will of a people that disdainfully refuses to become united with its conquerors. This unanimous feeling at the moment of the nation's direct collapse renders it certain that this people, proud of its history and traditions, will never accept foreign domination."[40]

If the final part of this Austrian memorandum merited respect and consideration, the value of the document as a whole was somewhat lessened by its denial of a common bond in the relations of the Trentino and the Alto Adige, the strict safeguarding of which had repeatedly formed the basis of previous Austrian refusals to concede to the Trentino the administrative autonomy many times requested by its representatives in Vienna and Innsbruck.[41] Even the waving aside of Italian strategic arguments appeared to somewhat understate and oversimplify the question and was contrary to all the military literature of the time. The proposed expediency of neutralizing the area suggested a certain measure of casualness in the way a still recent past was forgotten by those who, as already noted (see note 34), on August 3, 1917 and May, 12, 1918, publicly and without a single dissenting voice had approved rather ravenous programs of annexation at Italy's expense, including denial of Trentine autonomy and projecting total Germanization of the "Italian Tyrol."

On July 10, 1919, a second Austrian memorandum referred to the principle of self-determination of peoples and proposed that a plebiscite be held, township by township, so as to trace a significantly precise demarcation between the different ethnic groups.[42] This proposal, probably prompted by a realization that the international position of the Austrian delegation at the Paris Peace Conference was deteriorating, was undoubtedly the basis of the speech delivered to the Chamber of Deputies by the Socialist leader, Filippo Turati, four days later. In all events, it should also be noted that in this same Austrian memorandum of July 10, the Vienna government representatives asked for a plebiscite in more than a thousand townships situated in northern Bohemia, the Sudeten district, Moravia, Silesia, southern Bohemia, southern Moravia, in lower Austria, German western Hungary, Styria, Carinthia, and Carniola.

Finally, through their memorandum of August 9, 1919, the Austrian delegation again emphasized that the Tyrol constituted an economic as well as an ethnical unit and insisted on the necessity for a plebiscite so as to eliminate any solution that would endanger peace. The document ended in an overtly threatening key:

One may take into serious consideration the entire disastrous scope of the decision by virtue of which the southern Tyrol would be incorporated in Italy. This people, struck with misfortunes and condemned to servitude, will be a disquieting element and a grave danger for peace and social tranquillity. As soon as the Tyroleans, for the moment exhausted and worn out, have been able to recover—and they will do it sooner or later, for the Gothic race, hardened by a struggle of centuries, has endured still greater miseries—they will feel only the sacred duty of not being unworthy of their heroic ancestors and of doing honor to the example shining in history of the "Sandvirt" of the Passeier valley, Andreas Hofer. It will then arise, the old spirit of the Tyrolean heroes, to shake off the yoke, the weight of which is an insult to the white crests of their mountains, raised as a symbol of an independent Fatherland. And then—at the expense of hundreds of lives, of valor, and of effort, that the price of peace has compromised—the Tyroleans will again see the dawn of their liberty breaking.[43]

This document appears significant and did not differ substantially, either in tone or content, from the remaining portions relating to the other Austrian frontiers. Nonetheless, the appeal to the desires of the populations concerned appeared worthy of respect and consideration. However, the delegates of the Rome government were well aware that a number of towns with an entirely Italian population and history were, for various reasons, destined not to be reunited to the fatherland. On the whole, the peace conditions then made to Italy were such as to be interpreted on the peninsula as a "mutilation" of victory, and they gave rise to the most serious political crisis that occurred in any of the victorious countries.

The various Austrian requests were rejected by the Allied and Associated Powers, and it is worth noting that the latter emphasized in their reply to Austria, on September 2, 1919, that the head of the Rome government had, in official statements before Parliament, expressed the intention of following "a generous and liberal policy toward Italy's new subjects of German race as far as concerned their language, culture, and economic interests."[44] The note referred in particular to the statement made by Premier Nitti to the Chamber on the preceding July 9: "In regards to the newly redeemed Italian territories, a new set of laws has been approved and we trust that many causes for discontent will soon be removed. The change-over of these territories to the fatherland must take place without sudden shocks and we must respect all the laws and regulations which are not absolutely necessary to abolish. No excess zeal for change must give rise to unnecessary crises."[45]

From a purely legal point of view, such a reference certainly could not be construed as the assumption of a strictly binding engagement, but its moral weight was considerable. It clearly revealed that though Italy had not had to sign a treaty for the protection of her own minorities, as had been the case with Poland, Czechoslovakia, Rumania, and Greece, she had nevertheless given verbal assurances on the matter. Such assurances were subsequently confirmed both in the statement made by the foreign minister, Tittoni, on September 27, 1919, and in the King's address at the opening of Parliament on December 1, 1919.[46]

The last two Austrian statements were received in Italy with varying degrees of attention. Generally, there was disappointment over the so-called "mutilated victory," and though political and social strife in the country reached heretofore unknown heights, both declarations received little notice from the majority of the Italians. Not so, however, in the Alto Adige and the Trentino, where they were destined to engender disappointments, delusions, and misunderstandings, and where one of the keenest observers was the future Italian prime minister, Alcide De Gasperi, a resident of the Trentino.

At this point, it might be well to consider carefully whether the decision of the Italian government to request the Brenner frontier did or did not have solid justifications. It should be emphasized that based on the contemporary military conceptions, great importance was attached to the possession of certain strategic positions. It is true that during the course of the war—as in the then famous case of Mount Lovcen—the control of certain positions considered as cornerstones to the control of entire areas, had proved to be considerably less significant than the general staffs had estimated. This, however, did not seem to apply to the Brenner Pass frontier, since experiences during the war in the Alps from 1915 to 1918 demonstrated that even a modest mountain relief could constitute a formidable bulwark. Therefore, the strategic value of the frontier requested by Italy was not open to question. Nor, to lessen its value, could it be maintained that once the Hapsburg Empire was dissolved, Italy was confronted merely by the small Austrian Republic along part of her northern border. An Austro-German Anschluss at that time appeared anything but improbable. In the event of such an Anschluss, the problem of an effective defense of the Alpine border would have been more worrisome than in the past because the place of the Hapsburg Empire, which had on the whole pursued a conservative foreign policy, would be taken by a Germany endowed with very much greater capacity for expansion.

The security requirements put forward by the Italian government, therefore, had a serious foundation and were also recognized by the Allied authorities including the Americans. On this specific point, the counterarguments contained in the Austrian notes submitted to the Peace Conference appeared distinctly weak. Historical experience, furthermore, had also pointed to the common and fatal destiny of all clauses concerning demilitarization of territory in any treaty. Consequently, the Austrian offer to demilitarize the Alto Adige had—not unjustly—been looked upon as lacking any real value. Undoubtedly, a less secure frontier would also have involved considerably greater military expenditures, with adverse effects on an Italian economy that had already been sorely tried by over three years of war and that had brought the country to the brink of an extremely severe economic as well as political crisis.

There was yet another political and psychological factor to be recognized. During the course of the 1915 negotiations, Austria-Hungary had offered to cede to Italy the Trentino as far as the Salorno gorge. It would now have been difficult for the Italian government to accept in the peace treaty the same conditions that could have been obtained by simply remaining neutral, without drawing upon itself justifiable criticism, especially from that sector of public opinion which, at the time of Italy's intervention, had been in favor of accepting the limited compensations offered by Vienna.

Further, it should be noted that much in the same way as in Great Britain, where memories of the mud-soaked trenches on the Somme exerted a decisive influence upon English policy between the two world wars, in Italy memories of the carnage on the Carso, a consequence of the close grouping of troops (necessitated in part by the difficulties of attacking in the Trentino) also exerted no small psychological influence. Under any circumstances, a second such experience should be averted. It was also feared that Vienna might harbor lasting resentment toward Italy's decisive role in the fall of the Hapsburg Empire.

Despite these considerations, however, Italy did underestimate—even then— the strength of the argument concerning the resistance to be expected from the majority of the Alto Adige population. Consequently, voices were raised in criticism of the decision to ask for the inclusion within the national territory of populations belonging to a different ethnic group (Bissolati's resignation from the Orlando cabinet was a typical example).[47] Even more trenchant, though less well-known, was the speech delivered before the Chamber of Deputies by the Socialist leader, Filippo Turati, on July 14, 1919.[48] In an Italy that had seen the birth of its own unity based on the principle of nationality, extending the frontier to the Brenner Pass and thereby including within its new boundaries a German-speaking minority that had repeatedly expressed a desire to remain with its fatherland could not fail to provoke certain negative reactions.

At the same time it should be noted that, unlike what was happening in other areas of Europe, this exception to the ethnic principle was neither due to expansionist aims nor to the spirit of revenge or designs of supremacy, but was in effect dictated by security reasons that no government anxious to safeguard the interests of its country could have neglected. It should also be recalled that the same strategic considerations relevant to Italy in the historical and political evaluation of her request for the Brenner frontier were later at the base of Hitler's decision to annex not only the Alto Adige but also the Trentino and the province of Belluno in September 1943. This decision, of which more will be said later, does not appear to have given rise to any complaint on the part of the responsible Tyrolese leaders, who were—between 1943 and 1945—clearly informed of its development.

In all events, after the exposition and evaluation of the diverse views advanced by all parties concerned, it should be significant that from a purely historical point of view, a fundamental event then did occur: the annexation of the Alto Adige to Italy. The Rome government asked for the Brenner frontier, this request was endorsed by the Allied and Associated Powers; the Vienna government resisted and the local population protested, but these objections were all turned down and the Brenner Pass frontier was definitely established under the Treaty of Saint Germain signed and ratified by the Austrian Republic.

It is this treaty that even today provides the pattern for the territorial demarcations of Italy's northern border.

Chapter II

From the End of World War I
to the Anschluss

[1] Italian administration in the Alto Adige in the period following the Villa Giusti armistice. The signing of the peace treaty and the setting up of the General Civil Commissariat. Conversations between the Nitti government and the Alto Adige leaders. [2] Policy of the Mussolini government in the Alto Adige. Senator Tolomei's program. [3] The question of the Brenner in the negotiations for the Treaty of Locarno. Held's speech of February 5, 1926, and Mussolini's reply. Stresemann's intervention. Lessening of tension in the relations between Rome and Vienna—the proposed custom's union between Italy and Austria, and the establishment of the province of Bolzano. [4] The rise to power of national socialism in Germany. Hitler's views on the Alto Adige problem. Changed attitude of the people of the Alto Adige after the advent of national socialism. [5] The question of the Alto Adige in Austrian politics. First soundings of the Viennese government toward obtaining concessions favoring the minority in the Alto Adige. The meeting between Dollfuss and Mussolini on April 12, 1933. Further pressure exerted by Schuschnigg and Dollfuss at the meetings in Rome and Riccione. Intensified Austrian activity after Schuschnigg becomes chancellor. His conversation with Mussolini on November 19, 1934. Mussolini's apparently more moderate attitude on the Alto Adige problem. Renewed pressure by Schuschnigg at the meeting in Venice on April 22 and 23, 1937. Overall evaluation of the Austrian government's action. [6] The Alto Adige question not initially discussed between Rome and Berlin. Goering's visit to Rome on January 15, 1937—his conversation with Mussolini and his statement to the German amabassador to Italy, von Hassell. Importance of this statement in connection with the origin of the 1939 agreement granting the option of citizenship to German-speaking inhabitants of the Alto Adige.

[1]

At the end of World War II, the Austrians claimed that even in the pre-Fascist period the Italian democratic governments had pursued a policy of oppression toward the German-speaking minority in the Alto Adige, and that consequently not even the promises of postwar anti-Fascist Italy could be given any credence.

Historically, such claims have little validity. Even in those years, of course, there were misunderstandings and mistakes on both sides. This was inevitable, particularly in the initial stages and in a situation such as the one present in the Alto Adige, complicated not only by a multitude of problems but also by psychological difficulties. Nonetheless, it is quite clear that on the whole, the

15

attitude of liberal Italy toward the problem of the German minority was inspired by principles of moderation and tolerance.[1]

The military administration installed in the Alto Adige following the Armistice of Villa Giusti quickly demonstrated its willingness to adhere to these principles. In his first proclamation to the local population, the commander of the First Army, General Pecori Giraldi, solemnly and publicly declared that Italy was opposed to any idea of oppressing the inhabitants of a different race and language, and with whom, indeed, she proposed establishing a brotherhood relationship. He also gave assurances that the use of German would be allowed in the schools, law courts, and administration, in the same way, by these principles, the people of the Alto Adige would be allowed to preserve their institutions and associations.

Certainly not everybody in Italy shared this attitude. Among others, there was Ettore Tolomei, a man from the Trentino, who advocated a policy of Italianization of the region and who eventually would exert considerable influence on the views of the Fascist government. Appointed commissioner for language and culture in the Alto Adige in July 1919, Tolomei did not hide his intention to impede any form of autonomy for the German-speaking population, but for the time being his activity had very limited effect in practice and did not prevent the military authorities from following a line of conduct inspired by the precepts that General Pecori Giraldi had outlined in his proclamation.[2]

In the first place, in carrying out the occupation, all possible care was taken to keep to a minimum any friction with the local population, avoiding, for instance, actions—such as the removal of Hapsburg coats of arms or the changing of local topographical names—which might be construed as gestures of intolerance. Such a guideline governed actions in all areas of activity and life in the Alto Adige. The authorities at the township and district level were maintained in office, even in cases where their behavior would have justified adopting punitive measures; justice continued to be administered by the former Austrian personnel and German remained the official language of the courts of law. Even the postal service and railway systems remained in charge of former Austrian officials, and in the field of education complete freedom was allowed in the organization and administration of the German-speaking schools.[3]

A rather singular proof of the spirit of tolerance characterizing the Italian occupation is given by the fact that on November 16, 1918, in response to a proclamation issued three days before by the Tyrolese National Council in Innsbruck, a group of Alto Adige delegates was able to convene at the *Rathaus* in Bolzano, where they solemnly proclaimed the Republic of South Tyrol to be one and indivisible. They then swore loyalty to the new government, voted on the union of the new republic with the Confederation of Austro-German countries and, on the same day, brought the relevant act to Innsbruck. On November 18, 1918, the "Republic of Südtirol" posted a large placard for the collection of taxes; banknotes and postage stamps were printed in Innsbruck for circulation in the new republic, to be presided over by the burgomaster of

Bolzano, Herr Perathoner. Printed ballots were also distributed for the purpose of obtaining a kind of plebiscite.[4] Not even when confronted with these incidents—events representing a rather obvious attempt to usurp political and administrative powers in a territory still under occupation and legally in a state of war—did the Italian authorities choose to adopt repressive measures. They merely confined themselves to asking the more influential members of the self-styled National Council to stop such activities, while the burgomaster Perathoner, who had been the moving spirit behind the entire plan, was allowed to remain in his post.[5]

Unfortunately, such intrinsic moderation by the Italian authorities was all too often interpreted as a sign of weakness and ultimately fostered an increase in the aggressive action of a small group of pan—Germans. These were instigated from beyond the border and occasionally also were inspired by personal advantage; many of them had held posts in the Austro-Hungarian administration that they now feared they would lose. They proposed to "create" an Alto Adige problem at the international level rather than one on an emotional or individual basis. To a certain extent, they "created" the will to resist of the German-speaking population at a time when the first tenuous signs of an inclination to collaborate had already appeared.

On July 20, 1919, that is to say before the signing of the Saint Germain peace treaty on September 10,[6] the administration of Venetia Tridentina, which included the Alto Adige, was entrusted to a special civil commissioner, assisted by the existing local adminstrative bodies. This was done along the pattern of similar arrangements made for the Venetia Julia. In Trent, the post of commissioner was entrusted to Luigi Credaro, who had been for many years a member of Parliament and who was a professor at the University of Rome. Known as a man of enlightened liberal views and as a keen scholar well versed in Germanic culture and way of life, he symbolized a very positive assurance for the German-speaking inhabitants. Shortly after his appointment Credaro set forth the general ideas of the program he proposed to carry out in the Alto Adige in a long letter to the prime minister, Francesco Nitti. One passage in particular is worth quoting:

> I will now express my personal conviction. Italy has always declared, through her statesmen and the press, that she intended to reach and secure her natural frontier, the Brenner Pass, not because she was moved by a desire to conquer lands inhabited by foreign populations, but rather for strategic reasons, that is to say, in order to safeguard access to the peninsula against aggression from the numerous and aggressive Germans. If this be so, and if we want to give our new Germanic fellow-citizens and the world at large proof of our justice, equity, sincerity and moderation, we must take all the wishes of the people of the Alto Adige into careful consideration, so long as they do not intend to lessen our rights and dignity, or weaken the defense and sovereignty of our State.[7]

The first consequence of Credaro's appointment was the resignation of Tolomei who, aware that a total "disparity of views" existed between himself and Credaro, preferred to relinquish his post as commissioner for language and culture in the Alto Adige. In effect, Credaro's tenure proved to be characterized by great moderation and, even if it did not satisfy all the aspirations of the German-speaking inhabitants of the Alto Adige—a thing which would objectively have been difficult indeed within the framework of the Kingdom of Italy—it nonetheless fulfilled many of their expectations. Certainly the population, accustomed to Austro-Hungarian civil servants, was somewhat confused by the frequently different methods of the Italian officials. At the same time, the complaints of the local inhabitants, in the main referring to the system of taxation, were substantially identical to those of the Italians in the Trentino and in Trieste, who found themselves facing similar problems stemming from the differences between the old and the new administrations.

With the creation of the Commissioner General's Office, the Italian government had temporarily given up the idea of enforcing any particular pattern of administration in the Alto Adige. This appears to point to the government's determination to carefully consider the studies initiated some time before on such problems as the feasibility of establishing two provinces for Trent and Bolzano versus the plan for a single one for the whole of Venetia Tridentina, or the possibility of granting a special administration to the Alto Adige so as to favor as far as possible the German-speaking group, thus giving practical application of the aforementioned assurances of Nitti, Tittoni, and Victor Emmanuel III, as well as the September 2, 1919 communication of the President of the Peace Conference.

On November 18, 1919, Prime Minister Nitti received in Rome representatives from the Alto Adige, who submitted to him their political and economic program.[8] This contained demands for such a broad measure of autonomy that it forebode far-reaching consequences. The Italian government, however, did not hesitate to take this request into consideration and shortly afterward initiated a study of the matter.

In March 1920 the Alto Adige delegates submitted considerably increased demands. The concept underlying this new project of autonomy[9] was one that gave birth to a state within the state. Only foreign policy, finance, justice, communications, and defense were reserved for the Rome government, as might exist between a confederation of states, but with one difference—to the Alto Adige's advantage—of exemption from military service for its inhabitants. Even in a confederation between states, participation in the common defense of the country becomes an accepted and normal obligation. It should also be noted that Austrian laws would have remained practically unchanged in the South Tyrol and that not only would all civil servants retain their posts (transferable only with their consent) but Austrians would also be entitled to compete for vacant posts. Tax revenue would have been reserved for local needs, while the Rome government would have been accorded only the privilege to obligate itself to provide the necessary funds for the needs of the province. The draft contained no provisions regarding the protection of the Italian minority in the Alto

Adige, justified by the absence of any specific requests on this point. The entire matter was postponed and the only reference on the subject was of a general nature regarding the autonomy project itself. This attitude reflects something of the same spirit that had earlier led the Diet of Innsbruck to reject the Trentino inhabitants' requests for their own autonomous administration, alleging at that time (though denying it after the war) that a common bond existed between the Trentino and the Alto Adige.

The presentation of this proposal led to a break in talks with the Rome government. These were resumed after some weeks, but again adjourned when certain declarations by the president of the German Reichstag, Loebe, at the time that the Austrian Chancellor Renner was visiting Rome April 8–12, 1920,[10] conveyed the impression that the Berlin government might well be planning to raise the problem at the international level.

Both this impression and the increasing demands made by the Alto Adige population regarding autonomy undoubtedly influenced the attitude of the new government formed by Giolitti in June 1920. The measures that had been adopted by Senator Credaro and that had been fully acceptable to the Italian state so long as the Alto Adige problem remained within the domestic sphere, led to some confusion now that *pan-German* groups began to apply themselves with renewed vigor to the question.

On the other hand, as a result of the intransigent attitude demonstrated on several occasions by the alto Adige leaders and the action pursued by irredentist associations such as the Andreas Hofer Bund, a wave of reaction was developing in Italy that could not but influence the actions of the government. Despite this, it is interesting that at that precise time, the question of electoral constituencies was settled in accordance with the wishes of the Alto Adige population. The entire mixed language zone was thus assigned to the constituency of Bolzano, which received four seats, one for every 11,000 electors, whereas, with clear disproportion, the Trent constituency was only apportioned one for every 16,000 constituents, that is to say, seven seats. As a result, at the April 1921 elections, the four candidates elected at Bolzano were all German-speaking, leaving the Italian element in the entire mixed language zone without a representative.

The problem of autonomy was mentioned once again in the King's speech at the opening of the new Parliament on June 11, 1921. Almost two years of debate and, even more important, the difficulty that the new Parliament had in reaching a majority on the question because of the diverse views among the principal groups in Parliament, led the government to prepare a speech for the Sovereign which, though not denying the principle of autonomy, was couched in more cautious terms than before.[11]

Among the remarks by other speakers on this occasion, those of Mussolini and De Gasperi are worth noting because of the influence their statements would have on subsequent developments on this question in the years that followed.

After strongly criticzing the existent administration in the Alto Adige and taking a clear position against the attitude of the Alto Adige people and their organizations, Mussolini stated:

We demand the following measures be adopted forthwith:
—The suppression of every evidence, even esoteric, reminiscent of the Austro-Hungarian monarchy.
—The breaking up of the *Deutscher Verband*.
—Immediate dismissal of Credaro and Salata.
—One single "Tridentine" province with the seat at Trent, and a strict adherence to bilingualism in all public and administrative acts.

I do not know what measures the government will adopt, but I hereby declare, without striking any exaggerated attitudes, and I so declare to the four German deputies, that they must say and make it known beyond the Brenner that on the Brenner we stand and there we shall remain at all costs.[12]

As for De Gasperi, he outlined a program that he would continue to expound until 1945. He said:

Confronted by this problem (a frontier line on the Brenner), I feel that our centralized state, with its tradition of liberalism and unity, does not have the experience to draw on, the solutions to offer, or the political instruments to operate with. For this reason, I believe that the problem, though the aim is to reinforce the framework and ensure the solidarity of the country, must have a regional or, if you prefer, a "local" solution. This is not only because of the experience which can be brought to bear here by those politicians who have learned, studied and applied compromise solutions necessary to the coexistence of different nations and languages, such as in the Austro-Hungarian monarchy, but also, and above all, because in the institution of local autonomies in the new provinces there exists an amount of freedom and an amount of security guarantee for the right to national existence, which we must and can grant to citizens of different languages without impairing the central structure of the state.

Accordingly, we ask for the reconstitution of the local autonomies in the new provinces. We do so not only because this is in keeping with our conception of the state, or because of the necessity now confronting us of initiating changes from one set of laws and regulations to another, but we do so because it is our duty to ensure a possible coexistence among different nationalities on the northern border and because we believe that the political activity of those of other languages can find expression in these local autonomies, like cells at the service of, and not at odds with, the state.[13]

If the plan for autonomy in the Alto Adige was not immediately carried out in its entirety, it was in part due to the difficult situation that all of Italy was experiencing at that time and also, to a greater extent, to the uncompromising stand of the local leaders, who mistook the fundamentally moderate and responsible attitude of the Italian government for weakness. Indeed, the German-speaking minority received wide-ranging concessions during this period in the fields of education, the press, local administration, and parliamentary representation. These were the pillars of an effective autonomy granted by a liberal state to the mixed language zones, and certainly not, as later alleged, a policy that could be deemed oppressive. Besides, the measures adopted could have represented a point of departure and not one of arrival, a determination that would also depend upon the degree of allegiance and loyalty demonstrated by the German-speaking group and its leaders.

[2]

In October 1922, when the first Mussolini government was formed, the Alto Adige problem was to a certain degree already compromised by the not completely successful beginnings of democratic Italy's liberal policy. Public opinion on the peninsula had been deeply shocked to see that the most conciliatory measures had been received locally with hostility and that in Austria and Germany there were tendencies to shift the question to an international level, a clear-cut interference in the state's internal affairs. All this made it easier for the Fascist government to alter the liberal course and to adopt a rigid policy that Mussolini could present as justifiable, based on previous failures and the necessity to wrestle with pan-German activities. The result was that two political ideologies, fascism and pan-Germanism, both based on violence and inspired by the most narrow-minded nationalism, clashed in the Alto Adige.

The guiding principles of the policy which the new government proposed to follow were announced on July 15, 1923, in a speech delivered in Bolzano by Ettore Tolomei, who had shortly before been appointed a senator. He announced a program that was primarily concerned with the eventual creation of a single province comprising the Trentino and the Alto Adige with its seat in Trent.[14] As was foreseeable, such measures triggered strong reactions in the Alto Adige, in Austria, and in Germany. This, however, only served to speed the implementation of a program that may well have been initially conceived more as a threat than with a firm intention of complete execution.

Tolomei's program was vigorously implemented. Some of its aspects actually only constituted a projection of the general political line that fascism was enforcing throughout Italy, such as the control of the press and government appointment of local officials. Nevertheless, undoubtedly the sum total of those measures aimed at depriving the Alto Adige minority of all autonomous life was realized and pursued by oppressive methods. Within the space of a few years, the Alto Adige was incorporated in the province of Trent; the Italian language was declared obligatory in official acts and in the schools; private teaching, to which German-speaking families had initially resorted, was suppressed—though it still continued; geographical, and to some extent also family, names were Italianized; German newspapers were suppressed, with the exception of one naturally controlled by the government; and plans were envisaged, though only later and only partially implemented, for settlement of Italians in the Alto Adige.

[3]

At the international level, the Alto Adige problem again assumed considerable importance early in 1925, when agitation increased in Austrian and Bavarian circles in support of the German-speaking people in the Alto Adige. There was a revival in Germany and Austria of trends favoring an Anschluss.[15] Such a revival was basically dependent on two factors: the recovery of Germany's economy and international status on the one hand and the worsening of the Austrian economic crisis on the other. A majority of Austrian public opinion believed that it would be possible to overcome this crisis only through "annexation to the great German fatherland," a view voiced publicly by Vice-Chancellor Waber himself in April 1925[16] and widely repeated by the Social-Demoncrats during this period.

For this reason the Tyrolese press reacted strongly when foreign press reports circulated information according to which, in the opinion of the British foreign secretary, Sir Austen Chamberlain, the Rhine security pact then under discussion should also guarantee the Italian frontiers. The *Tiroler Anzeiger*, in an article published under the heading "Betrayal of the South Tyrol," asked in horror whether Germany could ever allow or, indeed, guarantee "the eternal slavery of the Germans beyond the Brenner in order to hasten liberation of the Rhine-land," and the *Innsbrucker Nachrichten* suggested that "confirmation of the injustice perpetrated at Saint Germain" was the price demanded by Britain for giving her assent to the "inevitable" Austro-German Anschluss.[17]

The latter assumption was, in fact, very close to Sir Austen Chamberlain's opinion on the Austrian problem at the time that the negotiations for the Rhineland security pact were begun.[18] However, the Italian government was not immediately aware of this fact. From the very beginning, Mussolini's attitude had been favorable to the proposals of the German foreign minister, Stresemann. Moreover, he did not attach particular weight to early advice from the Italian ambassador in Paris, Baron Romano Avezzana, who tried to warn him as to British intentions, since he considered that France (as she had announced) was certain to accept the Rhine pact only on the condition that the existing peace treaties be respected in their entirety.[19] In any event, he communicated his opinion to the Ambassador in London: "With particular regard to our frontiers with Austria, we intend to abide by what has been solemnly and clearly established and recognized under the peace treaties. We should be concerned only if subsequent special agreements, even though indirectly and by the mere fact of their existence, were to detract from, rather than strengthen, the effects of the treaties themselves."[20]

Meanwhile, agitation against the policy of Italianizing the Alto Adige continued to be intense both in Austria and Germany, to the extent that on May 8, 1925, the Italian ambassador to Berlin, Count de Bosdari, called Stresemann's attention to a whole series of events that were threatening Italo-German relations. Stresemann gave appropriate reassurances, but took advantage of the occasion to note "with considerable regret" the unfavorable attitude adopted by Italy toward the Anschluss, at the same time permitting it to be understood that such an attitude was not shared by all the other concerned powers. This declaration and, even more, the acquiescent assertion of the Ambassador [21] evoked a strong reaction from Mussolini. He cabled de Bosdari in Berlin that adversities might often be avoided by speaking "clearly and in time." He, moreover, added that he would consider "the war lost and victory totally annulled, on the day that Germany was able to realize her annexation program."[22] Mussolini, on the other hand, harbored no doubts that Stresemann expressed himself in those terms only because of previous assurances received from London.

In any event, the statement by the German Foreign Minister and his speech delivered on May 18, 1925 to the Reichstag (hinting at an action aimed toward establishing more intimate Austro-German relations "within the limit of the treaties"), as well as the fact that the draft for the Rhine pact submitted by France on May 18 contained no mention of the adherence to the peace treaties that also guaranteed the Brenner, induced Mussolini in his speech before the Senate on May 20, 1925,[23] to emphasize Italy's firm opposition to the idea of the Anschluss.

Mussolini's speech attracted considerable attention. In Germany it was realized that the threat of Anschluss could endanger Italian support of the Rhine Security Pact, and Stresemann hastened to assure Italy that "the Germans did not intend to raise the question of the *Anschluss* in connection with the pact of guarantee."[24]

The French government's concern was even greater, particularly from the moment it was informed that Britain intended to assume no further obligations outside the strict limits of the Rhine guarantee, thus rendering possible an Italian refusal to subscribe to the proposed pact. Consequently, on June 3, 1925, Briand offered in behalf of France, a separate guarantee to cover the Brenner frontier, but this received a negative response from Mussolini. He justified his stand by reasoning that a unilateral French guarantee could not be of much value unless it was also accompanied, as was the Rhine guarantee, by an open acceptance of the pact on the part of Germany. On the very same day, Mussolini learned through a confidential remark (probably well calculated, by the secretary-general of the Quai d'Orsay, Berthelot, to the Italian ambassador in Paris, Baron Romano Avezzana) that: "Lord d'Abernon [the British ambassador] in Berlin [had] lately been encouraging the German government to proceed with the annexation of Austria, assuring it that this would not encounter opposition."[25]

This communication clarified for Mussolini the role played by Britain in the question and how, perhaps, due to such action, Stresemann had felt encouraged to sound out de Bosdari on the matter on May 8. Mussolini now established the new line he proposed to follow. First, he made it clear that an eventual Austro-German Anschluss would so strengthen Germany that it would be logical to foresee within a short time a German attempt to seek revenge and that this would trigger a new war. As for the Alto Adige problem, this was regarded as very different from the more questionable one of Alsace-Lorraine because there were geographical realities that could not be ignored. Consequently, Italy undoubtedly had a great interest in preserving Austrian independence, but an equal and perhaps even greater interest should be shared by other European countries, France above all others. As a last resort, concluded Mussolini, one could also envisage the possibility of Italy's obtaining specific guarantees for the Brenner and then ceasing to be actively concerned about the Austro-German union, thereby focusing its effect exclusively on the western frontier and its guarantors.[26]

This attitude, brought to Sir Austen Chamberlain's attention by Senator Vittorio Scialoja, Italian delegate to the League of Nations, led the British Foreign Secretary to review his own position with regard to the problem of the Anschluss. Chamberlain did not alter his own point of view of limiting Britain's commitments to the Rhine, but he assured Scialoja that: "for a generation at least, not only should no discussion be entertained on the annexation of Austria to Germany as a working hypothesis, but that even any conversation on this subject should be avoided. Should Germany attempt to raise the question subsequent to her admission to the League of Nations, she would find herself confronted by the most decided opposition from Britain."[27] Sir Austen Chamberlain also made it clear that, in his opinion, although the agreement on the Rhine frontier was in the form of a territorial guarantee, it was substantially a political instrument "in which the collaboration of the four European powers was essential," thereby rendering Italy's sharing in it mandatory.[28]

France, as has been noted, had endeavored to secure Italian consent by offering a separate guarantee for the Brenner. This offer was renewed on June 17, 1925, but again with negative results.[29] Mussolini, confronted with the prospect of seeing protection of the Austro-Italian frontier weakened, decided on a wait-and-see policy. In this he was also motivated by the hope that the proposed Rhine Security Pact would eventually come to nothing due to the opposition it met within Germany itself.[30]

Meanwhile, the situation in the Alto Adige was still tense, and agitation within Germany and Austria in favor of Anschluss continued vigorous. At the end of June, the Austrian chancellor, Monsignor Seipel, affirmed his conviction that if a plebiscite were held immediately "90% of the Austrian votes would be in favor of the *Anschluss,* and this not because of a real leaning toward annexation, but because of the belief now prevalent throughout the entire population that annexation to Germany is the only solution that presents any hope for a better future, especially in the economic field."[31] This declaration was actually identical to the one made by Austrian Vice-Chancellor Waber in April of the same year.

As for Germany, if on the one hand her unwillingness to raise the question of the Anschluss for the moment was confirmed, on the other, it was also stated there that "in no case would any declaration to this effect be made nor would any obligation that ran counter to the *Anschluss* be entered into, considering it natural that one day unification of all Germans in a single state should come about."[32] At the same time the Tyrolese leaders in Innsbruck were endeavoring to raise the Alto Adige question at the international level by calling the attention of the accredited diplomatic representatives in Vienna to the treatment of the German-speaking inhabitants of the Alto Adige, with particular reference to the educational problem.[33]

The first change in the wait-and-see policy previously adopted by Mussolini occurred toward the middle of August 1925, when news came via London that Briand and Stresemann had reached a definite agreement over the Rhine guarantee and that, as they considered the stage of diplomatic consultations to be concluded, the two parties intended to call a meeting of legal experts to put the understanding into the form of a draft treaty.[34] Mussolini, even before receiving communication of the details of the understanding, asked that Italy also attend the meeting of experts "so as to render Italian support for the security pact easier."[35] The reason for this change is fairly easy to identify: evidently Mussolini, once it was established that contrary to his expectations the negotiations were coming to a conclusion, did not want to be excluded from the European alignment taking shape.

This change of attitude was met with differing reactions in London and in Paris. The British government, although it would have preferred receiving a prompt and explicit consent to the treaty,[36] extended an invitation to the meeting of experts. The French government, though the British guarantee for the Rhine was already assured, also showed interest in securing Italian participation. The French, however, on this occasion for the third time repeated the offer of a guarantee to cover "the Brenner frontier and the frontier of Austria" in return for explicit and speedy Italian support.[37]

This afforded Mussolini an opportunity to emphasize more forcefully a view he had already expressed: that France was making no concession by her offer inasmuch as she also was interested, in equal if not greater measure, in a guarantee of Austrian frontiers and independence.[38] Toward the end of September, spurred by the unanimous opinion of his advisors, who had alerted him to the drawbacks of assuming an isolationist stance,[39] Mussolini decided to support the proposed Locarno treaties.

In effect, the consequences of the real success achieved by Stresemann, and in its wake by the Austrian pan-Germans soon became evident. Agitation in favor of the Anschluss increased considerably, provoking two vigorous Italian protests to Vienna[40] and a deterioration in Italo-German relations.[41]

On February 5, 1926, in an already very tense situation,[42] Bavarian Prime Minister Held, delivered a speech in which, after criticizing the methods employed by the fascist administration in the Alto Adige, dedicated himself to doing everything possible to bring freedom to the "German brothers" in that area.[43] Mussolini, who had for some time been awaiting the opportunity to intervene strongly in the affair,[44] replied the following day with an angry speech before the Chamber, ending with the oft-quoted sentence: "Fascist Italy can, if necessary, raise its flag higher, but never lower."[45]

In turn, Stresemann reaffirmed, though in very moderate terms, his solidarity with the German population under Italian rule. He also added that in the course of the negotiations for the Locarno Pact, the Italian government had put forward a request for a guarantee of the Brenner frontier, but that this had been rejected by the German Chancellor "for reasons that were self-evident."[46]

The last statement was in point of actual fact completely false and provoked a rebuttal from Mussolini. However, in the absence of French documents, we do not know whether or to what extent the making of such statements was perhaps facilitated by a belated and not wholly precise report made to him by Briand of the Brenner guarantee that he had spontaneously offered to Italy. In any event, Mussolini, besides denying that the Italian government had ever sought a guarantee for the Brenner, also explicitly reiterated, though in less aggressive tones, the spirit and the contents of his previous speech.[47]

The incident was closed, thanks to an understanding between Rome and Vienna, after which Austria gave up the idea of appealing to the League of Nations.[48] The episode had shown how interested public opinion was in the fate of the minority in the Alto Adige both in Austria and Germany. At the same time, it brought about a certain abatement in the impetus of the pan-German movement, at least in its official expressions, thereby also easing the state of Italian relations with both Germany and Austria.

With the latter, in fact, after the head of the department for commercial agreements at the Austrian Foreign Ministry. Dr. Schüller, had arrived in Rome and met with Mussolini on March 23, 1926,[49] negotiations were opened which led to the drafting of a customs union project between the two countries. Subsequently, however, this was to be abandoned because of the opposition it met within the League of Nations.[50]

In December of the same year, in an atmosphere of generally relaxed tension, the province of Bolzano was created, with a provision indicating some concession to the wishes of the Alto Adige population,[51] even though the new province did not include, as did the present one, all the mixed language muncipalities and was within the administrative framework of the Kingdom of Italy. Many observers abroad interpreted this measure as a first step toward abandoning the policy of de-Germanization until then pursued by fascism. But when it was realized that no substantial change in the situation had taken place[52] and, furthermore, that Italian workmen and farmers were beginning to be sent to the Alto Adige, public opinion in Austria again became alarmed. The critical attitude adopted toward Italian actions in the Alto Adige by the German press and, somewhat more cautiously, by the Berlin government,[53] once again influenced Austrian public opinion and the attitude of the Austrian government itself.

In the meantime, the matter was again brought up in the Vienna Parliament, where Chancellor Seipel stated on February 23, 1928, that a policy of friendship between Italy and Austria would be impossible until the Alto Adige problem was solved, and he reaffirmed Austria's right to concern herself with the fate of the German-speaking group in the Alto Adige "in the name of International morality."[54] Mussolini reacted very sharply. The Italian minister to Vienna, Giacinto

Auriti, was promptly called to Rome for consultations and not returned to his post. Mussolini then replied publicly, making it clear that it was the last time he would speak on the subject and that next time "events would speak." He then announced that the decrees on Italianization would be applied even more strictly should the pressure from beyond the Brenner become stronger.[55]

The incident opened a period of increased tension between Rome and Vienna. A personal message from Chancellor Seipel to Mussolini early in May [56] met with no positive results: the Italian Prime Minister replied to the request for concessions favoring the German-speaking inhabitants of the Alto Adige by restating that the question was and would remain a matter of domestic concern, and that relations between the two countries would not improve as long as those responsible in Vienna and Innsbruck continued to deal with the problem and lend support to the anti-Italian and anti-Fascist campaign.[57] Even the return of Minister Auriti to his post in Vienna early in July 1928 did not help to improve the situation. Auriti made repeated protests against the anti-Italian episodes that took place in Austria, and his talks with Monsignor Seipel took on a strongly controversial tone that pointed to the impossibility of reconciling their respective basic positions.[58]

In fact, the atmosphere was again to become at least temporarily calmer only when the need to secure Italian support for certain vital German problems, such as reparations and disarmament, induced the Berlin government to modify its policy in support of Austria over the Alto Adige question.

[4]

With Hitler's advent to power in January 1933, the entire question, if not formulated in completely new terms, at least came to be looked upon from a substantially new angle. It would have been logical to expect that the National Socialists, who made the in-gathering of all Germans one of the basic tenets of their foreign policy, would make the Alto Adige an international issue. On the other hand, Hitler, both in a pamphlet on the Alto Adige question published in 1926,[59] and in his major work *Mein Kampf,* had expressed ideas which appeared rather unorthodox in terms of the general lines of his party's programs. His opinion was based on the assumption that the Alto Adige problem could not be solved by mere verbal expressions of opinion, such as those made in Germany at the time, but only by having recourse to arms. From this he proceeded to argue that to entertain the idea of a conflict with Italy over the Alto Adige was unthinkable. The German people, he wrote, had the task of again bringing into the fatherland seven million Germans who had been torn away by the Treaty of Versailles, and to accomplish this task Germany needed to enter into an alliance with Britain and Italy. Since friendship with Italy would not be possible until the problem of the South Tyrol was solved, a preliminary decision had to be made: the two hundred thousand Germans in the South Tyrol would have to be abandoned in order to create conditions that were conducive to reuniting the German people.[60]

These ideas were not received without opposition. For some time, they had already provided other German parties—the Social Democrats and especially the Catholics—with opportunities to attack Hitler and charge him with betraying the cause of Germany's brothers in the South Tyrol. At the same time it was also clear that such a policy toward the Alto Adige met strong resistance within the National Socialist party. In a public speech in July 1931, Franck himself had spoken of a "strong Germany from Salorno to the North Sea." Intense dissatisfaction over a line which offended feelings that were deeply rooted in the southern regions of Germany was expressed particularly in the fringe organizations of the party.[61]

Even before coming to power, Hitler had been approached by the Alto Adige leaders who tried to persuade him to change his attitude on the subject. Such attempts apparently met with no success. After he became chancellor, Hitler, in speaking to an Italian diplomat, again repeated, in February 1933, that he understood perfectly the reasons that led Italy to defend the Brenner frontier. He added however, that, much as this grieved his heart as a German, he was convinced that the fate of a few thousand former Austrian citizens should not affect relations between the two countries, especially since, within the framework of a reinforced Italo-German friendship based on the affinity of the two systems of government, it was to be hoped that the dispute over the Alto Adige could be mitigated and the problem rendered less acute.[62]

Hitler's position appeared to be clear enough. He did not intend to raise the Alto Adige question so as not to endanger the rapprochement he sought with Italy. At the same time, and in a long-term perspective, he did not wish to render more difficult Italy's acquiescence to the Anschluss. On the other hand, he could not completely ignore the movement in favor of the Alto Adige German-speaking group that was active within and without the party,[63] and for this reason he hoped to obtain some concessions from the fascist government so as to attenuate criticism of his program.

The Berlin government refrained from taking any initiative with regard to the Alto Adige. Even the German press, or at least the important newspapers that were more effectively controlled, ceased to deal with the problem. However, there was no cessation of the Nazi fringe organizations' activities to keep the irredentist movement alive. During 1933 the Italian authorities noted with growing concern that Nazi propaganda was meeting with increased success among the German-speaking group in the Alto Adige. Previously, the latter had not shown particular sympathy for the Nazi movement due to Hitler's "program of renunciation," to the ideological links between nazism and fascism, and to the fairly widely held conviction that nazism was a transitory episode.

After Hitler's rise to power this attitude had quickly changed and the hope spread that, in spite of all contrary declarations, the Nazi movement would be led to support irredentism in the Alto Adige by the very principles of racialism that lay at the base of its doctrine. This hope was also stimulated by the apparent ever-increasing antagonism dividing Germany and Italy in Austria, where the Italian government supported the anti-Hitler and anti-annexation political movements of the Christian-Socialists headed by Dollfuss and Prince Starhemberg's *Heimwehren.* This caused people in the Alto Adige to hope for a crisis in Rome–Berlin relations that would persuade Hitler to alter his ideas on the regional question.

[5]

In Austrian politics the importance of the Alto Adige question was further enhanced by the vigorous campaign that the Nazis conducted against the Christian–Socialists and the *Heimwehren,* who were accused of being so anxious to secure Italian support as to "betray their brothers in the South Tyrol." [64] This propaganda theme was widely echoed by the Austrian public and also found reverberations in the Catholic sphere, where Tyrolese associations advanced a request that the principle of freedom to teach religion in the "mother tongue" be respected in the Alto Adige. [65]

Confronted by these events, the Austrian government decided to discreetly and confidentially sound out Rome about obtaining some concessions in favor of the Alto Adige population that could be presented to the Austrian public as the fruit of the policy of friendship being pursued toward Italy. The move was not without some risk, in view of the manner in which Mussolini had previously reacted to similar initiatives, which he had characterized as interferences in Italian internal affairs. But in Vienna it was considered vitally important to be in a position to demonstrate that the policy adopted toward Italy, far from marking the abandonment of the region's German-speaking group, constituted the most effective means of obtaining an improved treatment in its favor. The question was brought up for the first time by the Minister Plenipotentiary Richard Schüller, during a talk with Mussolini on February 7, 1933. The Austrian diplomat approached the question with much caution. [66]

Schüller's move was more a discreet probe than a direct request, aimed at ascertaining in advance whether the subject of the Alto Adige could be touched upon in conversations with Mussolini. The latter made no reply, but then neither had his reaction been negative as Vienna had feared. This encouraged Chancellor Dollfuss to broach the subject directly with Mussolini during their first meeting in Rome on April 12 of the same year.

Lastly, Dollfuss, though stressing that on no account does he wish to interfere in our home affairs, but prompted also by his memories of Bolzano, where he claims to have spent his military service, urges me to meet Austrian wishes on the question of *Privatunterricht* in the province of Bolzano. I confine myself to replying that I shall bear his words in mind and that when I follow a policy of friendship toward a state I am also prepared to give proof of this. [67]

This time Mussolini had not merely listened but had offered an overall expression of good will. This first step could, therefore, be looked upon as important. Following this, the minister of justice, Schuschnigg, a few days later in a conversation with the under-secretary in the Italian Foreign Ministry,

Suvich, took the initiative and asked whether, in the interest of good relations between the two countries, it would be possible to concede the freedom of private schools in the Alto Adige.[68] After some months had passed without further developments, Dollfuss again touched on the question, first during his meeting with Mussolini at Riccione in August 1933[69] and then during Suvich's visit to Vienna in January 1934. On the last occasion, the Austrian Chancellor also presented an interesting explanation of the reasons behind his insistence on bringing up the point:

> He remarks that today the National Socialists have monopolized *Deutschtum* abroad, and to them it acquires an irredentist character. He also would like to intervene, but following a very different line, in the defense of those Germans abroad who are at present attacked under the excuse of fighting Nazism, especially in some countries such as Czechoslavakia. Naturally, no one could attribute any idea of aggrandisement and imperialism to him; instead, this would heighten Austria's prestige and accordingly weaken the monopoly held by the Nazi party in the matter. Naturally, he is not thinking of the Alto Adige, about which he has already made definitve declarations. We should recognize that he has succeeded in eliminating pro-Alto Adige propaganda in Austria, where it had assumed considerable proportions and reflected emotions deeply rooted in the population. However, once again he asks the Italian Prime Minister to settle the matter of private schools. This would, of course, take the form of an act of generosity on the part of the head of the government, but for him, Dollfuss, it would greatly facilitate the very difficult task he is carrying out.[70]

The Austrian Chancellor's line of argument was undoubtedly interesting, even if one can assume that he was concerned primarily with internal affairs. The latter aspect was later emphasized by Schüller, who on two occasions, April 10, and May 14, 1934, again insisted to Suvich that some provisions should be made favoring the Alto Adige population. Schüller stressed that there was much unrest among the Nazis, who charged Dollfuss with being a traitor over the South Tyrol, and he called attention to the fact that in this situation the concession of German language teaching in the Alto Adige would be "of the greatest help" to the Austrian Chancellor in effectively replying to the attacks made on him.[71]

These pressures were the bases of the measures adopted on May 30, 1934, by the Ministry of Education, Department for Trent, which authorized the institution of private German schools and language courses in the province of Bolzano. This provision, however, does not appear to have met with the widespread and favorable response that the Austrian government had anticipated. The pan-German and National Socialist newspapers—even though they had previously emphasized the importance of the question—now found that, all things considered, all that had been accomplished was a return to legality, since the rules governing education in Italy contained no provisions prohibiting the teaching of the German language and because, in any case, judgment should be withheld until one could gauge the extent to which the new provision would be given practical application.[72]

In fact, in actual practice the resistance of the local Fascist authorities rendered it difficult to adequately apply the provisions: the courses were limited to the major towns in the zone and, in any case, it was a question of schools set up by private initiative which the authorities merely tolerated, and not of courses officially established and financed. The political value of the provision was thus reduced.

After the assassination of Dollfuss on July 25, 1934,[73] and Schuschnigg's accession to the chancellorship, the Austrian government's activity on behalf of the Alto Adige German-speaking group increased in intensity. When the new Chancellor met Mussolini in Rome on November 19, 1934, he presented a memorandum on the question of private teaching of German in the Alto Adige, "earnestly" beseeching the head of the Italian government to issue instructions ensuring that the provision would be applied according to the spirit of its framing. The Chancellor added: "This is also necessary in order to counter the propaganda conducted by national socialism in the Alto Adige, which affirms that the question can only be solved through the rise of Hitlerism to power in Austria."[74]

Later, on March 7, 1935, Schuschnigg addressed a letter to Mussolini in which, after referring to the persistent and violent Nazi campaign against his government, accused of passively looking on while the German population in the Alto Adige was being denationalized, he suggested that the wishes of the Germans in the Alto Adige should be met in order to prevent their embracing Nazi ideology. The Chancellor added that, if care were taken to explain that such measures were motivated by the friendly relations existing between Italy and Austria, this would weaken national socialist propaganda on both sides of the Alps, and at the same time contribute markedly toward improving the internal situation in Austria.[75]

Schuschnigg, therefore, while repeating some of the points which, according to the Austrian records he had already raised during the Rome talks of November 1934, had notably increased the Austrian requests. This appeared to confirm the impression that in Vienna it was no longer considered sufficient to secure a few concessions that could be exploited to counteract Nazi propaganda, but that the Austrian government proposed to initiate a new course for Fascist policy in the Alto Adige. This attitude, however, led to difficulties that were stressed later during a conversation between Mussolini and Prince Starhemberg. The latter remarked that the situation in the Alto Adige made it difficult for the Austrian government to maintain its present policy. Mussolini replied that in order to help Austria he was prepared to grant concessions to these people, but that the latter had by now "all become Nazis, especially the young who no longer want to hear Austria mentioned and look forward to receiving everything from National Socialist Germany." In such a situation, Mussolini concluded, "any concession made to the Alto Adige today would be interpreted as weakness in the face of National Socialism."[76]

Nevertheless, two ordinances meeting the requests of the Austrian government were enacted in 1935. It was announced in May that beginning in the fall

German language courses would be instituted *in all the communes* of the province of Bolzano, and in September fairly extensive provisions of clemency were adopted toward those who had had difficulties with the police. However, the favorable effects of these provisions were canceled by the commotion caused by the conscription of Alto Adige inhabitants for the Ethiopian war.

Schuschnigg again broached the problem at the meeting of April 22–23, 1937, in Venice. Mussolini declared he was disposed to grant concessions to the German-language group regarding the use of the German language, German newspapers, and private schools. He also gave his assurance that, in any case, the German-speaking population in the Alto Adige would be accorded concessions not inferior to those granted to the other minorities existing in Italy.[77]

The Austro-German Anschluss of March 11, 1938, interrupted the patient work pursued by the Austrian government in behalf of the region's minority. On the whole, the concessions that had been obtained were modest and certainly far from laying the groundwork for the change in Fascist policy that the Vienna government had perhaps hoped to bring about. The efficacy of the measures adopted as a result of the pressures exerted by Dollfuss and Schuschnigg was negligible, perhaps more because of the obstacles created at the implementation level by the local Fascist authorities than because of any ill will on the part of the government in Rome. It should be noted, however, that Mussolini, who had always opposed vigorously any foreign attempt at interference in the Alto Adige problem, had agreed to discuss the question with Vienna in the framework of Austro-Italian friendship, and the subject of the Alto Adige subsequently came up for discussion routinely at all the meetings between Italy and Austria.

[6]

No conversation of a similar nature had taken place during this period between Rome and Berlin. The Alto Adige question was apparently not mentioned even during Hitler's visit to Italy in 1934 or Mussolini's to Germany in September 1937. The problem was touched upon in some detail only during the talks between Goering and Mussolini in Rome in January 1937. At that time Goering stated:

Regarding the Südtirol, the National Socialist party has made its own stand quite clear ever since 1923, when it recognized Fascist Italy. It is precisely over the question of South Tyrol that the party has been attacked in an indescribable manner. The party has been charged with having been bought by Italy and with having for this reason forsaken the South Tyrol. Suits about this matter have often been brought before the courts, and the accounts of the proceedings could be shown to the Duce. Today, no such thing as a problem of South Tyrol exists. There is only an Italian frontier that will be respected at all costs. It is understood even in Germany that a national state such as Italy is particularly sensitive in its borderland, and it is recalled that the Duce once said that the problem of the German inhabitants of the South Tyrol would be resolved much more easily if they lived in Apulia. In Germany, it is natural that people want all Germans to be well treated wherever they live, but this does not mean that Germany has designs on the territories of other states. Nevertheless, binding treaties could be solemnly concluded by Germany, in which the present Brenner frontier would be guaranteed over and beyond all doubt. On the other hand, other Germans live to the north of the Brenner, and Germany wants the territory extending down to the Brenner boundary for herself. At this point it is relevant to mention that Austria has also lost a part of her territory to Yugoslavia. But here again, Germany has not the least intention of becoming involved in a conflict with Yugoslavia over these territories. If Italy continues to insist on a buffer state between herself and Germany, it means that she does not have full confidence in Germany.[78]

Summarily, Goering's intention had been to emphasize that while it was impossible for national socialist Germany to renounce her program regarding Austria, an eventual Austro-German Anschluss would not call the Brenner frontier into question. This was in keeping with Hitler's well-known position, which considered the Brenner as the definitive frontier between the Italian and German peoples. Toward this end, the possibility of negotiating a special and solemn treaty guaranteeing the permanent character of the Alto Adige frontier was not ruled out in Berlin. In fact, this was the first time that the South Tyrol problem had been discussed at such a level and with such frankness. At the same time, however, with Goering's announcement of Nazi readiness to work out a solemn guarantee, the establishment of a connection between the frontier guarantee and Italy's acceptance of the Anschluss began to appear implicit. Subsequent events were to confirm the connection barely implied by Goering, between the Anschluss and the guarantee of the Brenner frontier. It was actually only in conjunction with the historical event of such a union that the entire problem of the Alto Adige was to enter a new and apparently conclusive phase.

However interesting and noteworthy Goering's statement had been, it only partially reflected his own ideas, for he was personally inclined to far more radical solutions where the Alto Adige was concerned. In a talk with the ambassador to Rome, von Hassell, shortly before going to the Palazzo Venezia for his meeting with Mussolini, Goering had in fact made the point that

he would be prepared to give the Italians any possible guarantee covering frontiers if a firm Italo-German friendship were established, being prepared to go as far as to sacrifice the Germans in the South Tyrol; these could not be helped indefinitely and under all circumstances; no alteration of the policy of Italianization was actually possible and, if the Germans in South Tyrol wanted to preserve their national character, the only course open to them, in the last resort, would be to settle in the Reich. In all events, the highly important relationship between Italy and Germany could not constantly depend on the small German minority in the South Tyrol.

At this point in the conversation, Ambassador von Hassell, who had already shown that he did not wholly share Hitler's line of "relinquishment" with respect to the German-speaking inhabitants of the Alto Adige, raised some objections:

I remarked that at the present stage he would probably not be willing simply to give the Italians a boundary guarantee, which I felt would be premature and only to be considered in connection with a basic and comprehensive understanding. As far as the German element in South Tyrol was concerned, it was not only a question of this minority itself but also of a very important moral factor in our policy, because the total abandonment of any German elements abroad would have a crushing effect on all other Germans in foreign countries. I would, therefore, in case of such an understanding, deem it necessary at least to express the definite expectation that the Germans of the South Tyrol would now receive better treatment in economic and cultural fields.[79]

Von Hassel's remarks may be looked upon as confirmation that, in spite of improved Italo-German relations, the prospect of abandoning the Alto Adige populaiton met with strong resistance in Germany. Von Hassell's words partly achieved their desired effect, because though Goering in his subsequent talk with Mussolini mentioned the possibility of concluding "solemnly binding treaties" with regard to the Brenner frontier, he refrained from making any reference to a possible transfer of Germans from the Alto Adige to Germany. At this time, therefore, the Italian government was not made aware of Goering's ideas, and, at the same time, what Goering had said to von Hassell may be looked upon as being of vital importance for a precise understanding of the true origins of the agreements of 1939 on the transfer of the German-speaking group from Italy to Germany. The fact that as early as January 1937 Goering was convinced of the necessity of solving the problem by a transfer of population seems to really remove any doubt as to who first envisaged such a solution. At the same time, this episode also enables one to prove the accuracy of the statement made by Goering himself on April 21, 1938 to the Italian counselor in Berlin, Magistrati, that the idea of transferring the German-speaking inhabitants of the Alto Adige to Germany had been *exclusively his and a personal one.*[80]

Chapter III

From the Anschluss
to the End of World War II

[1] German reassurances of the Brenner frontier: Hitler's letter to Mussolini of March 11, 1938. Increasing restlessness in the Alto Adige. Hitler's speech of March 18. Hitler's instructions on the Alto Adige question. Goering's first suggestion of a possible transfer to Germany of all the German-speaking inhabitants of the area. Goering's explicit proposal, of April 21, 1938, to transfer this group. Unfavorable reception of this proposal by Mussolini and Ciano. Hitler's visit to Rome and his toast on May 7, 1938, at Palazzo Venezia.   [2] Resumption of negotiations in January 1939. Diverse positions of Rome and Berlin on the problem. The Magistrati—Heinburg talks of April 5, 27, 1939. The Alto Adige problem at the Milan meeting of May 6, 1939, between Ciano and Ribbentrop.   [3] The negotiations for the transfer; the Berlin meeting and the conclusion of the agreement of June 23, 1939. The Bocchini—Himmler meeting at Tremezzo. The agreement of October 21, 1939: its contents. Tension between Rome and Berlin due to Nazi activities in the Alto Adige. The results of the options. [4] Critical examination of the 1939 agreement and historical evaluation.   [5] Limited application of the 1939 agreement regarding transfer of those opting for Germany. First signs of change in the German attitude toward the question.   [6] Repercussions to events in the Alto Adige after the armistice of September 8, 1943. Berlin's intentions concerning the adjustment to be made to Italo-German borders: the views of Goebbels, Moellhausen, and Dollmann.   [7] Action taken by the Nazi government aimed at annexing Italian territories to the Reich. Creation of two "operational areas." Action of the two "high commissioners," Hofer and Rainer. Mazzolini's letter to Anfuso of August 8, 1944.   [8] Local situation in the Alto Adige after September 8, 1943. The report presented to the Comitato Liberazione Nazionale Alt 'Italia (CLNAI) in June 1944. Attitude of the German-speaking inhabitants in the Alto Adige. Flow of this group into the Nazi forces. Historical importance of these events.

[1]

The Alto Adige problem entered a particularly difficult phase after Germany's annexation of Austria on March 11, 1938. Even though the German government had acted on the assumption that unfavorable reactions from the Italian government were unlikely, Hitler deemed it necessary to explicitly mention the Brenner question in a letter to Mussolini on March 11, 1938, informing him of his final decision to carry out the Anschluss forthwith. In this communication he again alluded to the idea, already outlined by Goering at the Palazzo Venezia meeting of January 1937, of a link between the Anschluss and the Brenner frontier. Hitler declared that the Brenner constituted the clear-cut demarcation line between Italy and Germany, and that this frontier would never be either questioned or altered.[1] Mussolini's acceptance of the Anschluss was welcomed in Berlin with great satisfaction, for it confirmed that the advance on Vienna would meet no obstacles. At least 80 percent of the Austrian population was in favor of unification with Germany, and the fact that this union was accomplished by Nazi Germany instigated opposition only from supporters of the democratic parties and from the Jews.

In Rome that portion of Hitler's message concerning the Brenner was immediately deemed to be of the greatest importance. Mussolini saw in it a guarantee of security for Italy's northern frontier, a sort of compensation for his having failed to defend Austria's independence and, at the same time, a justification of his policy in the eyes of the Italian public.[2] Nevertheless, secrecy diminished the value of the declaration and this—together with the desire to bring this knowledge to the Italian people—explains the prompt request to Berlin for permission to make the text of the letter known.[3] Permission was granted at once, together with a subsequent request, made a few days later, that the Chancellor's speech to the Reichstag on March 18, 1938, include a new public confirmation of the Brenner frontier.[4] Italy's request that Hitler's letter be published in Germany, however, was rejected.[5]

Meanwhile, the Anschluss was greeted in Italy with a hostility that in character and intensity went far beyond the worst expectations of the Italian government. On March 14, 1938, under precise instructions from Rome, Magistrati, informed von Weiszäcker that disturbing incidents had occurred in Austria after the entry of German troops, and he drew the Foreign Ministry's attention to these so that appropriate measures could be taken.[6]

Magistrati, speaking unofficially to von Weiszäcker, stressed the fact that since the Anschluss was carried out in full agreement between Mussolini and Hitler and with the Brenner frontier recognized as the definitive border between the two countries, it was becoming a matter of necessity to find, sooner or later, a "basic and friendly" solution for the Alto Adige, a final and clear solution relating to the German-speaking group.[7]

This démarche has been interpreted by some authors, in the light of subsequent events, and specifically of the Italo-German agreement on options in the Alto Adige, as a proposal to resolve the Alto Adige problem by transferring the German-speaking population to Germany, and as the origin of the negotiations that were to lead to the 1939 agreement.[8] Apart from the fact that the idea of their transfer had been expressed by Goering to von Hassell in January 1937, this interpretation is difficult to accept for various reasons. In the first place, the documents in the Italian archives do not contain the slightest indication that instructions to such an effect had been sent to the Italian Embassy in Berlin by

Palazzo Venezia or Palazzo Chigi, nor that Attolico or Magistrati had subsequently reported on the subject to the Ministry. In the second place, it is worth mentioning that when talking to Magistrati on the following April 21, Goering was to refer to the possibility of such a transfer as an idea of his own, adding that he did not know what the Italian views on the matter were. He certainly would not have done this if the move made by Magistrati on March 14, 1938 had carried the significance now attributed to it.

Most probably, in alluding to a definitive solution, Magistrati simply meant to refer to some move that might once and for all put an end to the irredentism of the German-speaking citizens. In fact, the German minority was openly showing that it hoped to be united to the Reich.

On February 20, 1938, Hitler had declared that he planned to return to the fatherland the ten million Germans still abroad.[9] The Austrians were only six and a half million, and the German-speaking group in the Alto Adige considered that they were included in the remaining three and a half million, along with the German minority in Czechoslovakia, who totaled a little over three million. Basically, they took Hitler's declaration to be a tactical move toward Italy and with this conviction adopted a challenging position, resulting in numerous incidents, some of which were serious. At the same time, rumors that the Alto Adige would shortly be united to the Reich were also circulating in Germany, and when Hitler's visit to Rome was announced, it was even suggested that Mussolini intended to make a gift of the area to Germany at that time.

The headquarters of the Nazi party intervened with considerable energy against this type of rumormonger.[10] The Anschluss did not, in fact, represent the final goal in Hitler's policy. Rather, it was the point of departure for a new drive the objective of which was the revision of Germany's eastern frontiers. In this light, an alliance with Italy assumed particular importance, and the German government did not intend to let the activities of irresponsible groups compromise its success.

The increasing importance that Italy's position was assuming in the eyes of the German leaders was underlined shortly afterward by the appointment of von Mackensen as ambassador to Rome. He replaced von Hassell, whose attitude had not always pleased the Italian government. Before leaving for Rome on April 2, 1938, he was received by Hitler, who emphasized the importance of his mission and reminded him that the Alto Adige had been "written off" and would so remain. Therefore, no propaganda in favor of a reunion of the South Tyrol and Germany must be permitted.[11]

Meanwhile, Italian public opinion's critical attitude toward the Anschluss disturbed Mussolini noticeably. He construed it to be an increase in the strength of the opposition groups, especially the Catholics. In this atmosphere, the Fascist leader learned with dismay of the disturbances in the Alto Adige. These culminated in the demonstrations at Lasa on April 16, when shots were fired.

Accordingly, the Alto Adige question became one upon which the Rome government concentrated its attention. On April 3, 1938, Ciano suggested to

Mussolini that he speak directly of the matter to Hitler during his imminent visit to Italy, proposing a transfer of the Alto Adige inhabitants to Germany so as to make the ethnic and geographical frontiers coincide.[12] The origin of this idea, which was here considered for the first time by Italy, is unknown. However, it is interesting to note that not only was it not made known to the Germans at the time, but that later a similar proposal by Goering in Rome was coldly received.

During a conversation with the Italian consul general in Berlin, Renzetti, on April 8, 1938, Goering, in fact, declared that now that the obstacle of the Anschluss had been removed it would be possible to think of an alliance between the two Axis countries in concrete terms. He once again stressed the unalterability of the Brenner frontier, which, he said, divided both the rivers and the two countries, the Mediterranean Power and the Central European Power, but at the same time united them in that it afforded each complete freedom of movement in the event of war. The conversation touched lastly on the Alto Adige, and Goering said "that he had given very strict orders to eliminate the known instances of propaganda." He continued: "A few days ago, I had the Gauleiter of Innsbruck come to Berlin and gave him most clear and precise instructions. On the other hand, the Germans in the Alto Adige, let us say 200,000, represent a mere nothing beside the 75 million in Germany. Those of them who do not wish to become loyal Italian citizens can leave the Alto Adige. We want no more trouble-makers."[13]

Goering's remarks were of special importance. It was the first time that one of the parties concerned had brought into the open the idea of settling the problem through a voluntary transfer of population. We have no record as to whether such an idea had been previously discussed by Goering with Hitler. It was certainly a question of a well-conceived plan; he had already spoken in similar terms to von Hassell in January 1937.

In the meantime, in spite of the reassurances of Goering and those given by von Mackensen during his first talk with Mussolini,[14] the unrest in the Alto Adige did not diminish. After the incidents at Lasa, Ciano instructed Magistrati in Berlin to again discuss the matter with Goering to stress the necessity of Germany taking vigorous steps to restrain the officials at Innsbruck, who, to all appearances, were to be held responsible for the recent incidents.[15]

Magistrati conferred with Goering on April 21, 1938, and submitted to him the text of the letter he had received from Ciano. Goering replied that from the official point of view the German government's position had already been clearly indicated. Thus, the only problem outstanding was one of local propaganda. At the same time, if Germany could choose to take firm action against elements residing in the Austrian Tyrol, it certainly could not take action against propaganda centers in the Alto Adige because Italy would obviously not tolerate such a clear interference in her internal affairs. Magistrati recognized the validity of these remarks, but stated that in the region of Innsbruck there were two or three thousand persons who came originally from the Alto Adige, to which they were bound by family ties, interests, and common memories. These people were to be considered as the real motivating force behind the disturbances, and it was against them that the German government should take decisive action. Then Goering summarized the situation as follows:

Two great nations that today form a block of 120 million people, in the center of Europe and the Mediterranean, governed by strong and totalitarian regimes, cannot allow their friendship to be compromised by 200,000 people in the Alto Adige. A large portion of these 200,000 certainly have no political ideas, especially if they find—as I hope and believe—that good economic conditions for their livelihood and a favorable moral atmosphere within the Italian borders are to their advantage.

Ciano's letter informs us that there are unfortunately some who are discontented and restive. The majority of these are certainly acting in good faith. For example, there may well be some of Germanic race and language who feel it would be their duty to do their military service in the ranks of the German rather than the Italian army. In this case, it is necessary to deal with the problem at its roots. We are prepared to accept these malcontents in our country permanently. In other words, the Alto Adige German-speaking group should be presented with an alternative choice, namely: either to move to Germany, naturally after fair disposal of all of their property in the Alto Adige, or else to forever denounce being considered Germans.

After exercising this option, every link of a German nature between the German fatherland and the inhabitants of the Alto Adige would cease and the problem be automatically eliminated at its roots.

I do not know your ideas on the subject and what I tell you here is entirely my own personal idea. It would, in fact, be wise not to make such a solution publicly known. But I should be grateful to you if, still acting in a strictly personal capacity, you could as soon as possible let me know what would be the Italian reactions to this idea that the Reich absorb the forementioned group. . . . The transfer of a group of Alto Adige inhabitants to Germany would provide, at the same time, should such a thing still be needed, a new and clear demonstration of our strong and unwavering determination to destroy at its roots any German problem with respect to the Alto Adige. Indeed, it is obvious that if we had the remotest idea of reopening the problem again in the future, it would be in our interests to encourage and increase, rather than disband, the German nucleus living there.[16]

Judging from what Goering said, it was clear that the problem was taking definite shape in his mind, and this was further demonstrated by his request to be informed of the Italian reactions. This was basically a real and proper proposal, to which Magistrati did not react immediately, since he had no instructions on the matter. The possibility was now offered of opening negotiations, should Goering's solution be accepted. Moreover, the tenor of Goering's remarks again clearly pointed to there having been no such thing as a previous hint from the Italian side of a possible population transfer. In fact, Goering had not only said that the suggestion was his own personal idea, but even added that he did not know what Italy's view on the subject would be.

Magistrati's letter did not reach Rome until April 24, 1938.

Goering's proposal was not well received either by Mussolini or by Ciano. Mussolini later telephoned Ciano, commenting that "if the Germans behave well and are dutiful Italian subjects, I can countenance their language and their culture. If they propose to edge the frontier line even one meter further to the south, we know that this could not happen without direst conflict."[17]

This was the situation in Rome that on April 30, 1938, gave birth to the idea of settling the problems arising out of the Anschluss through a "pact of mutual respect," to be presented to Hitler on his forthcoming visit to Italy.[18]

The first two articles of this draft instrument[19] clearly indicated that the previous German declarations concerning respect for the Brenner frontier had not been sufficient to dissipate the apprehensions of the Italian government. The latter had, on the one hand, to consider the reactions of public opinion and, on the other, found new cause for anxiety in the increasing disturbances in the Alto Adige. Certainly, the unrest there and the irredentist demonstrations that took place beyond the Alps could be due to the activities of fringe organizations, but the fact that the central authorities in Berlin had not intervened effectively to put an end to them was in itself a disturbing sign. Consequently, before entertaining the idea of strengthening the links between the two countries, the Italian government sought to obtain clear and public guarantees for the Brenner frontier and the entire Alto Adige question.

Contemporarily, preparations were being made in Germany to negotiate a treaty of alliance with Italy. This plan—even if it had been envisaged earlier—had taken more definite shape only after the friendly attitude shown by Mussolini at the time of the Anschluss had provided evidence of the solidarity of the Axis, and strengthened Hitler's conviction that it was necessary once and for all to sacrifice the fate of the people of the Alto Adige on the altar of Italian friendship. The German Chancellor must also have been moved in this direction by the need to obtain Italy's support in view of the imminent crisis over Czechoslovakia.[20]

Preparations for the negotiations led to the drawing up of various drafts,[21] from which Ribbentrop chose the version to be presented to the Italians during Hitler's visit. This version provided for reciprocal military aid in the event of unprovoked aggression by either France or Great Britain, and, in Article 1 established: "The High Contracting Parties restate their full agreement that the present frontiers of Germany and Italy are recognized as final and inviolable."[22]

This formula could be considered satisfactory from the Italian point of view, even if it was so broad as to cover all the frontiers of the two countries, which made it less forceful with respect to the frontier that most concerned Italy, the Brenner.

On May 5, 1938, this draft was presented to Ciano by Ribbentrop. Its reception was decidedly cold: Ciano in turn replied by presenting the draft pact of mutual respect drawn up by Palazzo Chigi. This appeared not so much as a counterproposal but as a rejection, and was immediately considered as such by the Germans.[23]

It was almost certainly an awareness of this coldness that led Hitler on May 7, 1938, to pronounce his well-known words at the Palazzo Venezia toast: "It is my unshakeable will and also my political legacy to the German people that they should consider the Alpine frontier erected between us by Nature as permanent and unalterable. I am certain that a glorious and prosperous future for Rome and Germany will result from this."

These words served to clear the atmosphere of the tensions that had until then undoubtedly existed in the Fascist government, and it exercised a lasting positive influence on Nazi–Fascist relations. But it came too late to permit immediate development of the negotiations for an alliance.

However, the Alto Adige question was discussed during Hitler's visit to Italy. Ribbentrop spoke of the problem to Mussolini during the naval review at Naples. Mussolini affirmed that the problem ought to be considered as finally resolved in so far as the territorial aspect was concerned, and declared that he was ready to insure "cultural autonomy" to the German-speaking inhabitants of that region, including education and the press. He added that he did not intend to proceed with any efforts toward Italianization. Ribbentrop also spoke of the matter later with Ciano; the latter urged his colleague to move effectively toward persuading the Alto Adige people to abandon their irredentist ideas and to collaborate loyally with the Italian government.[24]

These statements are of considerable interest. Those of Mussolini confirm the fact that he was at that time very far from seriously considering Goering's views on a possible transfer of people. Those of Ciano had the effect of inducing Berlin to act promptly and energetically to halt the disturbances in the area. This is demonstrated not only by the orders Ribbentrop gave on his return, but by a plan to have Hitler receive a delegation of the German language group for the precise purpose of making it clear to them that the South Tyrol question no longer existed.[25]

[2]

After Hitler's visit to Italy and the solemn pledge he made at the Palazzo Venezia toast, the Alto Adige was not discussed between Rome and Berlin for some time.

Should the Germans, however, again mention an agreement between the two Axis countries, Ambassador Attolico received instructions that touched generally on three points, the first of which referred to the "frontiers."[26] It was in line with these instructions that on June 19, 1938, when Ribbentrop again brough up the idea of an alliance, Attolico designated the question of the common frontier as the prime factor in an agreement. The German Foreign Minister accepted the idea without difficulty, but wanted the common frontier to be mentioned in the preamble.[27] The worsening of the Sudeten crisis interrupted these negotiations, and they were resumed in a more concrete form late in the autumn.

It was not until early January 1939 that the Italian government gave its support, in principle, to the idea of an Italo-Japanese alliance.[28] In instructing Attolico on how to advise Berlin, Ciano said that it would be judicious to initiate the plan for evacuating from the Alto Adige "those Germans who wish to leave this region,"[29] and Mussolini advanced the idea that "the Fuhrer should make a public statement guaranteeing the obligations assumed in 1938, and announce their execution according to a graduated detailed plan."[30] Neither of them made it clear whether the planned transfer should concern only those German citizens (i.e., the former Austrians who had become German citizens with the Anschluss who were residents in the Alto Adige (about 10,000), or all the German-speaking inhabitants of the Alto Adige who preferred to adopt German citizenship. But it seems clear, even from the concise but brief notes in Ciano's diary, that an eventual transfer was to be based on the free choice of those concerned. The German Foreign Minister's reactions, however, were basically unfavorable: he categorically ruled out Hitler's making a public statement in compliance with the wishes of the Italian government.[31] Faced by this attitude, Ciano informed Magistrati that the Alto Adige problem could be solved "calmy, without useless and excessive publicity, [it would be sufficient] that the Germans, who at this moment need men badly, take those natives that do not desire to remain in Italian territory south of the Alpine range."[32]

Ribbentrop gave some assurance on his government's intention of bringing back a considerable number of German citizens within the country's borders, possibly during the current year, but expressed the opinion that the problem could only be solved completely "over a number of decades" or else when the Reich should be in a position to more easily settle the German-speaking inhabitants of the Alto Adige in its territory, this depending on future developments in the European situation.[33]

Circumstances prevented the two Axis governments from further discussing the question for about three months. After the occupation of Czechoslovakia, tension in the Alto Adige mounted, causing concern in Rome.[34]

Attolico was instructed again to raise the question in Berlin. He did so on March 31 and April 1, 1939, in two successive meetings with von Weizsäcker. After mentioning the activities of Nazi emissaries in the Alto Adige, he asked that the plans for transferring the German citizens to Germany be renewed.[35] Immediately afterward an official from the Department of Political Affairs at the Wilhelmstrasse, Dr. Heinburg, was instructed to make an initial contact with Magistrati and start discussing the question in concrete terms with him. During the conversation, the Italian diplomat attacked the problem at its roots and suggested an overall solution which, in the interests of the Axis Powers and in order to avoid future incidents, consisted of the transfer of the German-speaking peoples to Germany. Such an operation would be facilitated by the existence in Germany of a large fund of lire that had been frozen after the Anschluss, and which would render it possible to compensate the emigrants for the property they left behind.[36]

With this démarche by Magistrati, Italy for the first time requested a solution through the transfer of the entire German minority to Germany. This seemed to indicate a new attitude, but the unexpected change of position was really the result of a momentary reaction by Mussolini to the information that continued to reach Rome about the Alto Adige situation, and it was to again change almost immediately. In fact, when the conversations were resumed on April 27, 1939, Magistrati, who had in the meantime received instructions on the matter directly from Mussolini,[37] again asked merely for the transfer of the 10,000 former Austrians. The new meeting with Heinburg lead to nothing definite.[38]

Contacts reached a more advanced stage during the meeting between Ciano and Ribbentrop in Milan on May 6, 7, 1939, to discuss the conclusion of the Italo-German alliance. Ciano wrote in his notes:

I discussed this problem with Ribbentrop with great frankness and gave him a number of particulars with which he was not familiar. I formed the conviction that until today the problem had never been presented to him in its entirety and full seriousness.

Ribbentrop, after restating the Reich Government's lack of interest, now and in the future, in the Alto Adige, informed me that he intends to begin work with Attolico immediately in order to solve as soon as possible that problem, at least, which concerns the evacuation of the 10,000 ex-Austrian Germans. Today Attolico will confer with Mastromattei and immediately on his return to Berlin will make contact with Ribbentrop in order to find a concrete solution to the problem.[39]

The Italian requests were thus again clearly confined to the "ten thousand" former Austrians,[40] even if Ciano, for tactical reasons, had advanced this solution as the minimum necessary to put an end to the difficult situation.

In the meantime, and as a consequence of the meeting in Milan, the problem of the frontier also assumed a more concrete form in the draft of a treaty of alliance that the Wilhelmstrasse handed to Attolico on May 12, 1939.[41]

In this draft there was no mention of a guarantee of the Brenner frontier, although two days before, Attolico had suggested that such a guarantee be written into the preamble when speaking unofficially to von Weizsäcker.[42] When he received the German draft, Attolico again pointed out to the legal advisor at the Wilhelmstrasse, Gaus, that the Brenner should be mentioned in the preamble, but the latter replied that "surely a strange impression would be created if, after the Führer's historic declaration in Rome, the question of the Brenner frontier were still to receive mention in a German–Italian document."[43]

The comments sent by Attolico to Rome, together with the text of the German draft,[44] resulted in a request to change the preamble, the second paragraph of which was amended to read as follows: "Now that a safe bridge for mutual aid and assistance has been established by the common frontier between Germany and Italy [having been] fixed for all time, both Governments reaffirm the policy, the principles and objectives of which have already been agreed upon by them, and which has proved successful, both for promoting the interests of the two countries and also for safeguarding peace in Europe."[45]

After much discussion, a new wording was thus adopted. The inviolability of the Brenner was construed to be premise of the alliance, and reaffirmation of the common frontier was invested with a military significance, being described as "a safe bridge for mutual aid and assistance." Accordingly, on May 22, 1939, the Pact of Steel closed the long negotiations on the subject of the frontier guarantee.

[3]

Shortly after this, the negotiation for the transfer to Germany of the German-speaking population of the Alto Adige was also concluded. In accordance with the pledge already made in Milan on May 13, 1939, von Ribbentrop had informed Attolico that he was ready to discuss the most suitable means for solving the "problem of the ten thousand." He had obtained Hitler's consent to this proposal and was prepared to consider the setting up of an Italo-German commission on repatriations from the Alto Adige.[46]

On June 17, Hitler personally instructed the chief of the German police, Himmler, to start negotiations,[47] and a meeting of the two delegations took place on June 23, with Himmler, Attolico, and the prefect of Bolzano, Mastromattei, taking part. The following exerpt is from the minutes of the meeting:

Himmler greets the Italian representatives and announces immediately that Hitler has delegated him personally to solve the problem of the German inhabitants of Alto Adige at its root once and for all; Hitler wishes to eliminate forever all motives for dispute in the Alto Adige, the inviolability of the Brenner frontier remaining firmly established. Attolico replies with a short greeting and the discussion begins. Mastromattei describes the situation fully, forcefully upholding the Italian point of view: repatriation of German citizens and, possibly, free option only for the 1,000 to 2,000 German-speaking Alto Adige inhabitants who refuse Italian citizenship. The entire Italian delegation reacts strongly against Himmler's insistence on a radical solution. The Italians oppose Hitler's proposal on grounds of humanity and justice and also in defense of the ethnic principle itself, for not all the German-speaking people of the Alto Adige are of true German origin. Finally, a compromise is reached.[48]

It was decided that the transfer should take place in three stages:

1) Resettlement of the "politically undesirable" Reich Germans, in particular the former Austrians (i.e., the "ten thousand") was to be carried out in the course of that year, if necessary, by the most forceful measures.

2) Resettlement of the *Volksdeutsche* (Italian citizens of German mother tongue) attached to the land as laborers. It was proposed to resettle some tens of thousands of these in the course of next year.

3) Resettlement of the *Volksdeutsche* attached to the land as landowners.

Appropriate Italian and German offices were to be established in the five chief towns of the region, with the task of carrying out practical measures for the repatriation of the ten thousand and facilitating, through a special setup in Munich, the attainment of German citizenship by those Alto Adige inhabitants who requested it. At the same time, Italy would take all appropriate measures to assist the operation, including financial measures. These last, however, were to be defined more clearly in subsequent negotiations made through the Italian Embassy in Berlin.[49]

With this decision, the Alto Adige problem seemed to be finally on the road to solution. But, in spite of having successfully persuaded Himmler to accept the principle of free individual option instead of a total transfer imposed from above, the prospect of a mass exodus of the population caused misgivings in Rome. For years, the Fascist government had been trying to assimilate the German minority, and the fact that a large number of *Volksdeutsche* should now be preparing to opt for the Reich was the clearest demonstration of the failure of this policy. The simple fact was that those directing Italian foreign policy, although they wished to be rid of those Alto Adige Germans who were behind the frequent disturbances in the region, had not foreseen such a radical solution. They were against it both for serious economic reasons and for reasons of prestige.

The Germans, on the other hand, once the problem had been squarely faced, were prepared to solve it once and for all, though well aware of the doubts on the part of the Italians.[50] In line with this policy, the efforts of the German offices in the region were focused on inducing the greatest possible number of German-speaking people to move to Germany. This was achieved by exerting pressure of various sorts, often based on a deliberately distorted interpretation of the terms of the agreement, the actual text of which had not been made public.[51] Moreover, the respective financial positions of the two countries took on considerable importance. Italy preferred not to shoulder too heavy a financial burden; Germany, in the full upsurge of her economic and industrial effort in preparation for the war, was greatly in need of foreign currency.

Italy tried to counteract this massive intervention, reaffirming that transfer was completely voluntary and that those who opted for Italy would remain undisturbed on their own land. The prefect of Bolzano, Mastromattei, supported this with an article reprinted in all Italian newspapers and distributed abroad by the "Stefani" agency.[52]

The situation worsened after September 1, 1939, following Italy's declaration of nonbelligerence, which provoked a considerable crisis in Italo-German relations. The Italian authorities in the Alto Adige found themselves confronted with the discontent of those who saw themselves forced to leave their country, and with the provocative attitude of those who having applied for German citizenship no longer felt themselves bound by Italian laws, though not yet subject to those of Germany. The Italian consulates in Germany reported resumption of intense irredentist activities in former Austrian territories and in Bavaria, where a number of meetings were held in favor of annexation of the Alto Adige to the Reich without the German authorities taking steps to intervene.[53]

This was the first but not the last time that the differing military and diplomatic stands assumed by Rome and Berlin in regard to World War II interfered with the Alto Adige problem. The above circumstances induced the Italian government to take a series of steps designed to speed up execution of the agreements of June 23. Even at this stage, however, Italy took no action to bring about compulsory and overall exodus of the minority. On the contrary, it again stressed that a decision to leave the country was entirely the free choice of each individual.[54]

Germany, on the other hand, began to reveal a tendency to raise difficulties, especially over the financial aspects that had become particularly important to the German economy since the outbreak of war between the Reich and the Western Powers. Since at that very moment Germany was preparing to remove the German minority in the Baltic countries with exceptional speed and under unsatisfactory economic conditions,[55] the Nazi government's attitude gave rise to legitimate suspicions that they were attempting to exploit the Alto Adige situation in order to exert pressure on Italy.

On September 17, 1939, Ciano instructed Ambassador Attolico to make it known that a solution to the problem must be found within the established time limits, "given, among other things, the chaotic and dangerous situation which has been created among the German-speaking population."[56] But even this request had no effect: Attolico received many promises, but the entire month of September lapsed without results, and it was only on October 4, 1939, that negotiations were resumed.[57]

October 11–13, 1939, the two chiefs of police, Bocchini and Himmler, met at Tremezzo, and agreed on several points that were essential for a final understanding. These included:

a) that the purpose of the original agreement had been "a lasting and fundamental ethnic solution";

b) that under simplified procedures the closing date for option would be December 31, 1939;

c) that the Italians would desist from proceeding with arrests in the area for political motives;

d) that no propaganda for or against resettlement would be allowed;

e) that both sides would in the future "really cooperate in a cordial, open and comradely manner."[58]

On October 21, after Italy had accepted some changes in the financial clauses, the agreement on the *Rules for the repatriation of German citizens and for the emigration of German-speaking inhabitants of the Alto Adige to Germany* was finally signed. This established (1) that repatriation of German citizens was obligatory and was to take place in general within three months; (2) that by December 31, 1939, German-speaking inhabitants would have to make a definite choice between Italian or German citizenship. Those who opted for German citizenship would have to move to Germany before December 31, 1942.

The section of the agreement dealing with economic matters was of particular importance. In the first place, the request—on which the Germans had strongly insisted—that the rate of exchange for the mark, officially fixed at 7.63 lire, should in this case be calculated at 4.50, was accepted. This gave the inhabitants who emigrated a bonus of about 45 percent. The latter were also authorized to transfer all their belongings, namely—as specified in the agreement—bank deposits; the market value of stocks; credits of all kinds, even including those covered by mortgages; the value of industrial, commercial, handicraft, and agricultural undertakings; interests in business enterprises and professional partnerships; real estate; capitalization value of annuities and pensions and credits accrued from private or social insurance. Furthermore, those opting for Germany would be able to take with them, exempt from customs dues and rail transport costs, all movables in their possession as of June 23, 1939. The cost of packing and transport to the station was also to be refunded; further, the Italian government was to provide the money for those lacking the necessary means. The agreement specified that movables included not only household goods and provisions but also "objects forming part of interior furnishings, even if fixtures, which have artistic or sentimental value (for example, wall cupboards, antique wall coverings, tiled stoves, etc.)," personal vehicles, 50 percent of livestock, private collections and archives concerning German culture, and tombstones.[59]

The actual operation of the mechanism of the option caused more friction between Rome and Berlin. This was largely due to the activities of the German commissions, who quite clearly were trying to obtain overwhelming pro-German support by the German population of the Alto Adige and to this end used heavy and indiscriminate means of pressure. On November 9, 1939, Ciano instructed Ambassador Attolico to present a strong protest in Berlin against a state of affairs that was becoming intolerable.[60]

A new agreement between the Prefect of Bolzano and the German consul general in Milan, Bene, was signed on November 17, 1939. It again affirmed *inter alia* that the option was to be made freely and without the exertion of any undue pressures. Above all, it solemnly stressed—in contrast to insistent German propaganda—that those who opted for Italy would remain in their country of birth or residence and enjoy full rights of Italian citizenship. Furthermore, severe sanctions were threatened against those exercising moral or economic pressure to influence or affect the decision, whether yet to be taken or already made, to emigrate to Germany or to retain Italian citizenship.[61] Other provisions were made in an agreement signed by Giannini and Clodius on December 22, covering financial obligations in connection with retirement pensions of those who opted for Germany.[62]

The date limit for exercising the option expired, as planned, on December 31, 1939, and an official communiqué gave the results on January 10, 1940; of 266,985 eligible persons, 185,085 had opted for Germany. To these were added the German subjects who were automatically transferred to the Reich.

[4]

Some aspects of the agreement entered into on June 23, 1939, and their execution are worth further consideration, if only to correct certain errors still being repeated today. Based on documentation that leaves no reasonable room for doubt, it appears quite clear that the idea of solving the Alto Adige problem by population transfer was first explicitly advanced by the Nazi leaders. This is emphasized because, even recently, it has been again asserted by a writer[63] that the proposal to evacuate the German minority from the Alto Adige was tenaciously insisted upon by Italy until the time that the Fascist government was offered the possibility of formally executing it as a compensation for acquiescence to the Austro-German Anschluss. The writer supports this theory by recalling that immediately after World War I there were some people in Italy, such as Tolomei and Colocci-Vespucci, who promoted a similar solution.

This thesis has little historical validity. After the annexation of the Alto Adige, there were undoubtedly some people in Italy who wanted the transfer of the German minority. But this seems of minimal importance, since it was never translated into a plan of action, nor, indeed, did it ever have a consistent following in leading Italian government circles then or during the Fascist period. As a matter of fact, during the Fascist era, a completely different policy was followed: the government wanted to carry out a policy of Italianization and this assumed that the German-speaking minority would continue to remain where it was. It was publicly proclaimed that the great majority of the Alto Adige inhabitants were not German, but people of Italian stock who had been "Germanized." Possibility of a transfer was not only not contemplated but also not desired, if only because it would have been tantamount to an admission that the policy of assimilation had failed. The Italian authorities were also perfectly aware of the serious repercussions that an exodus of the Alto Adige population would have had on the economic situation in the area, especially on agriculture, as there was no possibility of adequately replacing the farmers who would have left.

Apart from all this, the German documents themselves, in a manner difficult to challenge, prove that the plan for transferring the persons was first conceived in Berlin. It was Goering, a fact that seems to have escaped the aforementioned author's attention, who in January 1937, first expressed a conviction that it was necessary to solve the problem by transferring the minority to the Reich. Again, it was Goering who, in April of the following year, first brought up this plan for practical discussion, informing the Italians of it in talks with Renzetti and Magistrati. The lack of interest that this prospect aroused in Rome is illustrated by the fact that, in spite of these definite and authoritative overtures, the Fascist government did not develop the idea and not until the beginning of 1939 did it resume talks on the subject.

Another point worth emphasizing relates to the differing roles played by Rome and Berlin in working on the agreement. Here again, the record appears to leave no room for doubt. At the beginning, the Italian government sought to transfer only those former Austrian citizens who had remained in the Alto Adige after opting for Austrian citizenship on the basis of the peace treaty of Saint Germain. It probably also hoped to take advantage of the opportunity to eliminate the most active irredentist and pro-Nazi groups, i.e., those few thousand persons to whom was attributed the chief responsibility for disturbances in the area. Briefly, at the beginning of April 1939, there was a moment in which, confronted by increasing tension in the Alto Adige, the Italian government put forward the idea of extending the possible transfer to all the German-speaking inhabitants. But a few days later, when the unrest in the region abated, the plan was promptly abandoned and the Italian government again asked only that the German citizens be removed. On the other hand, it was the Germans who, once the decision to effect the transfer had been taken, adopted a root and branch solution. Such a solution, possibly suggested by Himmler, was undoubtedly desired by Hitler. He may have harbored a certain resentment toward these frontier people, who risked compromising good relations between Italy and Germany by their irredentist stand, and he decided to give Chief of the S.S.S. Himmler, the task of putting this solution into practice.

Most noteworthy about the provisions of the agreement is the fact that it was the Italians who proposed and obtained the voluntary character of the transfer. Thus, the nature of the agreement changed completely; instead of providing a forced mass exodus, it led to voluntary individual migration. The view has also been recently reiterated by an Austrian writer[64] that the decision to propose an agreement on this basis was due to the expectation that a majority of the German-speaking inhabitants would opt for Italy. In effect, it is probable that the Rome government underestimated not only the strong appeal of Nazi Germany at that time but also the resentment of the residents of the area toward Italy. This further confirms that Italy in no way ever planned or sought the transfer of the entire German minority in the Alto Adige.

A third aspect that needs clarifying concerns the application of the agreement of June 23, 1939. In Austria, it has often been stated, even in official documents, that the majority of the Alto Adige inhabitants were influenced to move to Germany because of Fascist and Nazi pressures. That there was Nazi pressure and that it was forceful is indisputable: the German government wanted to give the entire operation the character of a mass exodus on an epic scale, having the overtones of a popular vote of loyalty to the Reich on the part of all Germans living abroad. Contrarily, there is no evidence that either the central or local Italian authorities exerted similar pressure to induce the people to leave the country. The Italian government and the authorities in the province of Bolzano emphasized repeatedly that the decision was completely voluntary. They also took every opportunity to deny rumors circulated by Nazi officials concerning the difficult future awaiting those who decided to remain. If any blame is to be laid on the Italian authorities, it lies in their failure to intervene effectively against the German and the Alto Adige Nazi officials who were responsible for these excesses. At the same time, no judgment of the situation can disregard the delicate nature of the relations betwen Rome and Berlin during the first stage of Italian nonbelligerency.

Another facet that should be considered is the attitude of the German minority at the time the option was exercised. The figure of 185,085 opting for Germany out of 266,985 eligible voters is certainly striking: it must be concluded that these people were very susceptible to Nazi propaganda and dazzled by the power of Germany as the German army gave its first proof of exceptional strength in its lightning victory over Poland. Moreover, Nazi propaganda knew how to skillfully play on vital issues: the National Socialist ideology toward which a goodly number of the German-speaking inhabitants of the Alto Adige had for some time shown their sympathy, the pan-German ideal, resentment toward Italy, and, finally, the prospect of material advantages. Certainly, even taking into account the effect of the general mood of excitement under those circumstances and the marked efficiency and unscrupulous methods of the Nazi propaganda machine, certain ideas would never have taken root if the terrain had not already been prepared and if the Nazis of the Alto Adige had not collaborated. The latter were the only people in a position to reach out everywhere, especially in the country areas where there was an extremely high percentage of people opting for Germany, in spite of any religious scruples they might have had over emigrating to a country openly opposed to the Catholic church.[65]

As far as an historical evaluation of the agreement is concerned, it must again be noted that even today it is still the object of extremely violent attacks seeking to present it as a *pactum sceleris,* a shameful deal between the two dictators. This picture, which bears the stamp of a negative moral judgment rather than a political evaluation, might be acceptable if the agreement itself had involved a forced exodus of the German-speaking residents. The thesis is not tenable if one considers that, apart from the former Austrian citizens, the German-speaking people of the Alto Adige had the right to option. Moreover, it need only be recalled, without going back to more remote precedents, that at the end of World War I all the peace treaties and many of the other agreements contemplated a system of options as a means of protecting minorities without evincing any moral and political criticism.[66]

The criticisms leveled at the agreement of June 23, 1939, really stem from a political consideration not from a moral one which would, in this particular instance, be groundless. The agreement, in fact, presupposed a desire to consider the Brenner frontier as the definitive Italian frontier: this was the only time when the people living on the other side of the Alps gave up their hope of reclaiming the Alto Adige territory, and the question was considered closed.

[5]

On the basis of the agreements signed at the end of 1939, all Alto Adige inhabitants who chose to emigrate to Germany should have moved to the areas assigned to them by December 31, 1942. Only about 70,000 of them had left Italy by the end of World War II.

Various factors influenced this very limited application of the 1939 agreements. A first great obstacle to migration, especially for landowners, was that it was impossible to determine for certain where the emigrants would be resettled. Clearly, the decision depended on the outcome of the war and on the territories that the Reich would have at that time. Initially, a rumor circulated that the Alto Adige emigrants would be transferred to Burgundy. This solution would appear to have pleased those involved, but it could hardly be confirmed officially until a peace treaty had been concluded with France. Other rumors followed which only increased the uncertainty and lessened the people's enthusiasm for a transfer. The local Italian authorities took advantage of these circumstances to carry out a campaign to obtain the greatest possible number of conversions in Italy's favor, without paying much attention to the fact that the terms of the agreement did not provide for the annulment of any decision taken before December 31, 1939.

This campaign was conducted chiefly, if not exclusively, with respect to the small landowners. Not only would their transfer have increased the already heavy financial burden on the Italian state, influencing the Italo-German balance of payments in favor of the latter, but also it appeared very difficult to replace the Alto Adige farmer with farm workers from other parts of Italy.[67]

Toward the middle of 1941, the phlegmatic tempo of the transfers and the rumors circulating about German ambitions in the Alto Adige caused increasing concern in Rome.[68] It was said that Berlin did not really want to apply the 1939 agreements and that at the end of the war it would ask for this territory in compensation for aid given to Italy during the war.[69]

Undoubtedly, these rumors were made even more credible by the unsuccessful campaigns of the Italian army (and here again the events of the war interfered with the normal evolution of the question) and by the consequent progressive strengthening of German predominance in the Axis. In any case, it should be noted that, according to reports from the Italian Consul at Innsbruck, whenever a situation developed that presented a more or less remote possibility of imposing a revision of Italy's Alpine frontier, Austrian irredentism was promptly resurrected.[70] The situation was far from reassuring and suggested that, in spite of the agreements and the repeated declarations of the Germans that they wanted to solve the problem,[71] a complete reversal of Berlin's policy toward the Alto Adige was not entirely inconceivable.[72]

As the war dragged on and Italy grew steadily weaker the recurrence of irredentist activities, accompanied by alarming signs of a shift in the German position, became increasingly clear. The announcement of the Italian armistice on September 8, 1943, was to bring this situation to a head and to initiate a tragic phase in the history of the Alto Adige question.[73]

[6]

The events that took place in the Alto Adige during the period between the announcement of the Italian armistice and Germany's capitulation on May 8, 1945, deserve particular study. They are fundamental to a proper understanding of certain psychological aspects of the present relationship between the Italian and German ethnic groups. During those terrible twenty months, the Berlin government carried out its annexation policy with regard to not only the Alto Adige but other Italian territories as well. The German-speaking inhabitants of the zone gave free rein to their resentment of the Italians, taking ample revenge for the administrative policies of the Fascist period.

What happened then has left deep and permanent scars. First, the break in the continuity of government by Rome established a precedent that inspired hopes and yearnings for a new reversal of the existent situation. Second, in addition to definitely arresting the application of the 1939 agreement on the options, it began to encourage the return of many of those who had emigrated to Germany. This repatriation option was formally presented by Austria during the negotiations with Italy in Paris in the summer of 1946 and was inserted in the text of the De Gasperi—Gruber agreement, becoming a recognized right upon the latter's signature on September 5, 1946. Third, among the Italian ethnic group there has grown a conviction that an excessive German autonomy for Bolzano might well lead to retracing the footsteps of the Nazi regime. Fourth, favored by special circumstances and in compliance with precise orders from Nazi leaders, the majority of the German ethnic group had during these twenty months cast aside any restraint in their dealings with Italians. Fifth, events during this period of Nazi government indicated the existence of precise plans for annexation, not only with regard to the Alto Adige but also with other Italian territories (including the provinces of Trento and Belluno). Lastly, the identification of ex-officials of the former Hapsburg monarchy as those chiefly responsible for Hitler's directives for annexation and the effective destruction of any vestige of Italian life clearly revealed the origins of an entire political concept.

With reference to the German government's moves to annex Italian territories, it should be noted that plans had already been prepared in the summer of 1943, that is to say, before the Italian armistice. In July a political division under the direction of the Gauleiter of the Tyrol, Hofer, was at work in Innsbruck, and a similar body had been set up at Klagenfurt under direct control of the Gauleiter of Carinthia, Rainer. Both Hofer and Rainer were ex-Austrian officials and considered the reconquest of the territories lost by Austria after World War I an "historical mission": they had probably been preparing this action for some time, for immediately after Mussolini's downfall Rainer was able to submit to Himmler a proposal for military occupation of the ancient Austrian territories of Istria and the Venetian provinces.[74]

Hofer repeated this proposal at a meeting with Rommel and General Feuerstein, to whom he outlined the urgent necessity of occupying the Brenner Pass in order to prevent the Italians from blocking it by explosives or defending it by utilizing the fortifications of the "Vallo alpino del Littorio."[75] It can also be noted that even before the September 8 armistice the Wehrmacht high command had foreseen the advisability of securing the collaboration of loyal persons in the Alto Adige. In August, General Witthoft visited Hofer for this purpose and the latter had promised him the support of the network of trustworthy Germans in the region and of the local *Volksdeutsche* movement.[76] The need to avoid an untimely break with the new Italian government, presided over by Badoglio, for the moment, made it impossible to translate these plans into action.

The armistice of September 8, 1943, permitted the Germans to define the problem on a much more precise basis. Various German sources reveal their intentions and the steps to be taken to realize them. Among these sources, Goebbels's *Diary* is particularly important not only because of the author's position and the authenticity of the text, but above all because the Nazi Minister of Propaganda was in a position to learn first hand of Hitler's proposed settlement of the Italo-German borders. These pages are of exceptional interest and they merit being quoted verbatim where they touch specifically on this problem.

September 10, 1943
... We must now do everything possible to pacify the Italian regions which we are taking over. Naturally, we do not have sufficient police to set up a regime based on force there. For the same reason, we must defer political changes in the Italian area for a while. For instance, we cannot seize the southern Tyrol now, because we would absolutely irritate the Italian people and would politically paralyze any new Fascist government. Similarly, Hofer cannot be sent to the southern Tyrol as civilian governor. His appearance there would be like waving a red flag in front of a bull.
... We also heard from Gauleiter Rainer. Our Austrian Gauleiters certainly excel at making territorial claims. There can naturally be no talk of that at present. But one can understand why the Austrian Gauleiters are now feeling their oats. As in everything else in life, eating stimulates the appetite. . . .
... An animated conversation ensued on the kind of regime that should be set up in the occupied regions of Italy. The Führer is right in believing that we cannot afford to install immediately the sort of regime that we would prefer. . . .

September 11, 1943
... In so far as the Duce is concerned, I believe that, from a sentimental point of view, it would naturally be most regrettable if we could not liberate him. From the political standpoint, however, it would not be particularly pleasing to me. We must assess all of these things with an unemotional opportunism. If the Duce were to lead a new Fascist Italy, we should undoubtedly have to consider him in many matters on which we can now act without restraint. Even though he denies it, I do not believe that the Führer would have the courage to take, for example, the South Tyrol away from a Fascist Italy led by the Duce, and which conducted itself well for the rest of the war. However, we must not only get back the South Tryol but, as I envisage it, draw the boundary line south of the two Venetias. We must recover whatever was once an Austrian possession. The Italians, by their infidelity and treachery, have lost every claim to be treated as a modern national state. They must be punished most severely, as the laws of history demand. . . .

September 13, 1943
... It seemed to me that, besides the South Tyrol, our boundary ought to include the Venetias. That will be very difficult if the Duce reenters politics. It will be very difficult for us to put in our claim for the South Tyrol. Under the leadership of the Duce, assuming he becomes active again, Italy will attempt to organize a national rump state toward which, in many respects, we shall have obligations. . . .

September 14, 1943
... The Führer is very happy at being able to meet the Duce again soon. *Talking to Gauleiters Hofer and Rainer he said, however, that our policies regarding Italy are not to be changed. I welcome this. I had already feared that*

the Duce's reappearance might change things. It looks, however, as though the Führer were determined to remain firm. . . .

September 15, 1943
. . . The Duce will no doubt have to renounce certain things that he has hitherto been taking for granted, for in the final analysis we must receive some sort of compensation for Italy's terrible treachery against the Axis. . . .

September 23, 1943
. . . Even the Führer is convinced that mere territorial guarantees can give us no security vis-à-vis Italy. . . .
. . . I then posed the very serious and important question to the Führer, as to how far he intends to extend the Reich. His idea is that we ought to advance as far as the Venetian border, and that Venetia should be included in the Reich in a sort of loose federation. Venetia would be all the more willing to accept this, since the Reich, after a victorious war, would be able to enhance it's tourist industry, to which Venice attaches the greatest importance. I regard such a boundary line as the only practical and right one. I only hope that the Führer will remain firm and not let anything, especially his reawakening friendship for the Duce, modify this decision.[77]

Three observations of major interest emerge from these entries. First and foremost, they reveal the extent of the German "claims." These went far beyond the Alto Adige to embrace not only the lands lost by the Hapsburg monarchy after World War I, but even Venetia, whose annexation to the Reich could apparently be justified by puerile considerations relating to tourism.

Second, the arguments put forward by Hitler to justify the need for such territorial expansion: besides the wish to "punish betrayal" he added security needs, based on the very same strategic arguments that Sonnino and Orlando used both at the drawing up of the Treaty of London and at the Peace Conference of 1919. But there was a difference: the Italian requests aimed at bringing the border between the two countries back to the line of the natural frontier, while the Germans went far beyond this.

The role played by local Austrian officials in applying and formulating the annexation program should also be emphasized. The efforts of Gauleiters Hofer and Rainer, whom Goebbels himself defined as "true masters at formulating territorial claims" (this presumably did not express a merely personal opinion), seemed aimed at carrying out a program that was most unlikely to lead to the one objective of incorporating in the Reich the German minority in Italy. On the contrary, they did not merely act as the instruments but as the active promotors of a policy of conquest that squared perfectly with Nazi precepts.

Finally, it is clear from these notes that Hitler and his lieutenants intended right from the beginning to deceive the Italians and Mussolini himself over the fate of a large portion of Italy's northern territories. This fact has been confirmed recently by another German source, the *Memoirs* of the ex-counselor of the Germany Embassy in Rome and at Salò, Moellhausen, who adds certain important details:

Over the question, Hitler coolly deceived his partner; for after September 8, he declared to his close associates: "At least this betrayal will have served to recover two fine German provinces." . . .

Hitler had given full powers and a free hand to the two Gauleiters, Hofer and Rainer, on the single condition that they make some attempt to maintain appearances.

It is difficult to say exactly who was the most fanatical of the two. From the moment they received the impression that their only restraint was that of acting out a role and that Hitler's wishes were clear that the two provinces must become part of Germany, they concentrated on bringing this about as soon as possible and were imperturbable and insentitive to any other consideration.

They were inspired neither by a love of truth nor scorn by pretense, but by a frantic desire to enlarge their personal domains, to exercise their power as soon as possible, to excel in the noble race of forging ahead without awaiting orders to see who would cross the finishing line first and present the Führer with a new jewel for his crown. Starting with this premise, they launched an attack on the Italian administrative system, dismissing the Prefects appointed by the Salò Ministry for Home Affairs and replacing them with men of their own. They reduced leading Fascist officials to a passive role, forcing them either to remain at home or leave, replaced the mayors and all other officials, changed the teachers in the schools, took over the administrative system and all important business firms in the area, created an all-German local police force and so on.

In February 1945, Hofer even emptied the *Risorgimento* Museum in Trent, not because he wanted to abscond with some valuable item, but in order to continue the frenzied work of removing all and every trace of the Italian character and history of the country.[78]

What Moellhausen wrote confirms the entries in Goebbels's *Diary* regarding the deliberate misleading of the Salò government by the Germans; it also adds important details on the role played by the two Austrian Gauleiters in the whole question. These, far from being mere executors, appear to have been the leading figures in the annexation policy, so active as to have braved a whole series of disagreements with other German authorities so as to carry out their plans completely in the shortest possible time.[79]

Particularly relevant is the fact that in 1945, when Germany had already clearly lost the war, Hofer still made every effort to erase all Italian traces from the territories he administered: his action could no longer be to Germany's advantage, but maybe the Tyrolese Gauleiter looked further ahead and counted on creating a situation that would permit fresh discussion of the existing frontiers in favor of his Austrian fatherland. This seems to be confirmed by Hofer's behavior during the negotiations for the surrender of the German troops in Italy in April–May 1945.

Then the German generals who were secretly negotiating with the Allies deemed it necessary to be assured of the collaboration of the Tyrolese Gauleiter, foreseeing that the final actions of the war would take place in territory under his control. Hofer gave his support at a meeting of the conspirators on April 22, 1945, at the Recoaro headquarters, but requested that clauses recognizing the "political autonomy" of the whole Tyrol, including the Alto Adige, be inserted in the agreements for surrender. Four days later, during a second meeting at

Bolzano, Hofer repeated his request, completely refusing to support an uncondi-tional surrender. He had already been in contact with the chief of the Gestapo, Kaltenbrunner (whom he seems to have tried to convert to the idea of a "separate surrender for Austria") and, when confronted with the prospect of an agreement with the Allies that did not take Tyrolese aspirations into account, not only withdrew his support from the conspirators, but did not hesitate to inform Marshal Kesselring of the entire affair. It was only by a lucky sequence of events that Hofer's action, with which the sudden dismissal of two of the chief negotiators, Generals Vietinghoff and Roettinger is connected, did not cause the negotiations to fail altogether.[80]

[7]

Hitler's annexation policy began to take concrete shape immediately after the announcement of the Italian armistice. A decree issued on September 10, 1943, created two "operational zones" in northern Italy under direct German control: one, the "Adriatic seaboard operational zone" (*Operationszone adriatisches Kustenland*), was to include the provinces of Udine, Gorizia, Trieste, Pola, Fiume, and Lublijana, which had been annexed to Italy after the invasion of Yugoslavia; the other, "the pre-Alpine zone" (*Voralpenland*) covered the prov-inces of Bolzano, Trento, and Belluno. Two "high commissioners" directly responsible to Hitler would administer them: the Gauleiter of the Tyrol and Vorarlberg, Franz Hofer, for the pre-Alpine zone, and the Gauleiter of Carinthia, Friedrich Rainer, for the Adriatic seaboard zone. The choice was significant not only because of the new positions to which these two officials would be appointed and which created a sort of personal link in the administrative field between German and Italian territories, but primarily because of the programs that they had always planned for the ex-Austrian territories.

In fact, the two high commissioners acted in unison, in accordance with a single order, to Germanize the areas under their adminstration as quickly as possible. They did this by a series of measures that ranged from promulgating a special law that prohibited enlistment in the Italian army, created local armed forces, and introduced German newspapers.[81] Not surprisingly, Hofer's activities in the pre-Alpine zone were more effective. Here the local German population was eager to enthusiastically cooperate with their high commissioner.

For motives of political expediency, all this was masked under the guise of military necessity and was presented as a temporary measure. In reality, there is no doubt at all (as the German documents themselves overwhelmingly confirm) that the ground was being prepared for the annexation of those territories to the Reich.

This fact did not escape even the new Fascist government. At the Rastenburg talks in September 1943, Hitler avoided giving any assurances to Mussolini regarding the fate of the Italian provinces under German administration.[82] Mussolini added this to the news that was beginning to come through from those areas and moved to take a first step toward blocking the activities of the

Austrian irredentists. On September 23, he requested that his government be established at Bolzano or Merano, but the request was rejected by the Germans.[83] Writing to Hitler on the following October 3, Mussolini emphasized the "painful impression" caused in Italy by the appointment of a commissioner at Innsbruck for the provinces of Bolzano, Trento, and Belluno.[84]

Almost at the same time, the Allies broadcast the news that Germany was preparing to annex those territories. The new ambassador of the Italian Social Republic at Berlin, Filippo Anfuso, was immediately instructed to ask that an official communiqué deny the enemy's "insinuations," but he had to report that he met with much resistence. The communiqué was actually published in the form of a short announcement.[85]

For some time yet, however, German ·bad faith succeeded in deceiving the leaders of the Salò republic, who appeared not to fully understand the threat that hung over their country. This is evinced in a report by Anfuso of December 10, 1943, which, although laying stress on "the violent campaign conducted against Italy by the Austrians, now Germans, who are happy to have found an opportunity to take vengeance for the 1915 war," went on to state that "the group that is most enlightened and closest to the Führer is anxiously awaiting a resumption of activities by Italy." It concluded that what was happening in the two occupied areas "ought not to be considered as an actual political program whose implementation has already been decided on, but simply as a consequence of the appalling situation in which the local inhabitants have found themselves after disbandment of the Italian army."

So Anfuso took Ribbentrop's statements in good faith. The latter assured him that he knew nothing of the excesses in the occupied areas and placed responsibility for them on "Austrian or irredentist groups" who had "imposed themselves on the occupation authorities in order to exaggerate or affirm a principle that has nothing to do with the plans of the military authorities."[86]

It was clear that the Nazi Foreign Minister wished to continue deceiving the leaders of the Salò regime, relegating purely peripheral importance to events that were in reality the consequence of a general situation that the German government approved of and which was fully known to him.[87] On the other hand, Ribbentrop spoke the truth when he put responsibility for the large number of excesses in the two areas on "Austrian or irredentist" factions, and when he attributed to them actions that went beyond instructions received from the central political authorities. This point has been repeatedly emphasized by many Italian and German witnesses[88] and while it did not lessen the seriousness of the decisions taken in Berlin over the future of the Italian territories, it confirmed the importance of the Austrian contribution to such a policy.[89]

The Salò Republic apparently intended to bring up the question of the two operational zones at the meeting between Hitler and Mussolini scheduled for the end of April 1944. At least this was anticipated by Rahn, who did not conceal his anxiety over Mussolini's attitude on the subject.[90] But at the Klessheim talks on April 22–23, 1944, Mussolini, evidently wishing to avoid disagreements with

Hitler, confined himself to commenting on the difficulties caused by the German authorities' measures, only to recognize later that they were necessary.[91]

Still, the question was becoming more and more disturbing. On August 8, 1944, Mazzolini, under-secretary at the Foreign Ministry in the Salò government, wrote a letter to Anfuso dealing precisely with this subject and requesting the Ambassador to take definite action in Berlin to see that the situation, which had by now become intolerable, be changed:

You know how delicate the situation is in the "pre-Alpine zone" and in that of the "Adriatic seaboard": Italian provinces in which our sovereignty has been practically suspended, where the entire administration and other powers completely depend on the German Gauleiters, who issue decrees with the force of law, often in contradiction to the laws and regulations in force in the Italian state.

All this is distressing, but it would be easy to be patient if we knew the reason for such a *temporary* and exceptional regime was the unavoidable need to enforce order in areas where there are groups of inhabitants speaking other languages, so as to avoid situations that could jeopardize military security, especially on the eastern borders.

However, in these provinces, and especially in the pre-Alpine zone, the local German authorities are clearly acting in a manner that suggests a precise plan, not only to cancel all that fascism had done to adapt the provinces themselves to the other provinces of Italy but also to destroy every Italian trace there.

These activities have, moreover, a clearly "Austrian" character, rather than a German one, almost as if the possibility of reestablishing an administration similar to that of the old Hapsburg regime was foreseen, should things not go well for the Axis.

All Italian officials, whether forming part of the central administration or holding local offices, have been in practice transferred or dismissed, Italian organizations closed or forced to close, instructions and signs in Italian replaced or forbidden, outward signs of things Italian abolished.

Paralleling these *practical* steps, continuous activity has been exercised that may be described as "doctrinal": on all sorts of occasions local authorities, or German people of note passing through the country, have touched directly or indirectly, in writing and in speech, on the question of the "South Tyrol" belonging to the great German nation.

All this not only runs counter to the premises of the Italo-German alliance but also to the Führer's solemn declaration concerning the "final and conclusive" character of the northern borders of Italy.

Steps have been taken to interest Ambassador Rahn here in the matter, but they have had no result at all. . . .

I send you here enclosed No. 152 of the "Borner Tageblatt," dated July 3, to supply you with an opportunity to initiate your talks. It quotes a speech made by the Gauleiter and Reichsstatthalter, Franz Hofer (the governor of Bolzano), at the opening of the 7th national shooting range competition held at Innsbruck.

As you will see, this speech is full of references to the matter I have put to you. But it is merely one case among very many.

I should be grateful if you would keep me informed on your consequent action.[92]

Mazzolini's letter clearly pinpointed the spirit behind the measures taken by the German administration, the Austrian origin of some of the activities involved, and the far from temporary character of the measures taken. The mention of the "doctrinal" activity of the local authorities appears especially important, an aspect that must be considered in trying to understand the reasons underlying the difficulty that the different ethnic groups in the Alto Adige experienced in living together. The twenty months of Nazi regime there undoubtedly touched off a whole series of psychological reactions that have left deep imprints; among the German groups, the concept of racial superiority, which the lesson of war did not succeed in completely eliminating, took even stronger hold, while the Italian residents acquired a clear idea of the sort of life they would have to lead in the event of a German majority in control.

Anfuso's subsequent move did not, however, attain any satisfactory result. The secretary of state, Steengracht, recognized the validity of some of the observations made to him, but he pointed out the difficulty of eliminating them "more on technical, than on political grounds."[93] This was the exact opposite of the truth, because the difficulties were precisely political in character, and to illustrate this it would have been sufficient only to point out that Hofer and Rainer were directly dependent upon Hitler.

This state of affairs was not to change until the collapse of the Salò government and the final defeat of Germany. Writing to Mussolini on November 18, 1944, Anfuso remarked that as far as the situation in the German-occupied provinces was concerned there was now "no possibility of persuading the *Reichsführung* to renounce the policy followed so far" and suggested that the only means of safeguarding Italian interests, at least in some measure, was to make direct contact with the two Gauleiters. As for the basic problem of affirming Italian sovereignty in those zones, some attempt was made to obtain a reassuring statement, but without effect.

When questioned on the subject, Ambassador Rahn said that "naturally" there was no difficulty, but that this would again be talked about "at an appropriate time and place."[94] Ribbentrop, with whom Anfuso had a long talk on December 1, 1944, gave a reply that was even more disquieting. He answered that the system adopted for those regions responded solely to the requirements of war and that, therefore, there could be no talk of either occupation or violation of Italian sovereignty, But, he added: "If Germany loses the war, the fate of the Italian frontiers will certainly be endangered for who knows how many years; if Germany wins the war, the question of the border provinces will certainly be examined by the Führer and the Duce in the same spirit of understanding and friendship that has always characterized relations between the two leaders. Thus there is no need for anxiety on any account."[95]

The reply was meant to be reticent, but its meaning was perfectly clear, even if Anfuso did not draw attention to it in his report. The statement that the regime installed in the Italian provinces responded entirely to military considerations was completely contradicted by the fact that Ribbentrop recognized the existence of a "border provinces question" that Hitler and Mussolini would have to discuss at the end of the war. In other words, the question would be discussed when military considerations were no longer a factor, the entire statement assuming a positively threatening tone when taken together with the subsequent long tirade launched by the Nazi Foreign Minister against the "betrayal" of September 8.

Therefore, it is clear that the Germans wished to deceive their fascist allies to the very last and, what is even more serious, to the end they remained unshaken in their decision to take those territories away from Italy. This fact should not be overlooked. To a certain degree, it was understandable that Berlin decided in September 1943 to annex the Italian provinces as a reaction to the Cassibile armistice and the uncertainty of future military events. But it is highly significant that at no time, not even when on the brink of defeat, did the German government alter its decision.

[8]

If the annexation of Italian provinces by the Nazi government after September 8, 1943, and Berlin's show of bad faith toward the neo-Fascist government are from various points of view important at the highest government levels, they are no less significant locally. Within a few days after the entry of Nazi troops into the Alto Adige, all trace of Italian administration was eliminated and an intense process of Germanization initiated. This included the provinces of Trent and Belluno, where obviously the political aim was to pave the way for annexation of the territory to the Reich at the end of the war.

Interesting testimony on this state of affairs is found in a report given by the president of the Committee for the National Liberation of Northern Italy, Alfredo Pizzoni, to his fellow partisans in June 1944:

Details of the situation that has developed in the Alto Adige since September 8 and become more clear-cut in the last six months are already known. Our intention here is simply to summarize its precise and fundamental features.

(1) The institution by Germany of the so-called "Pre-Alpine Operational Zone," which was approved by Mussolini for purely military purposes, has become a case of fraud; it was directed toward and fulfilled a political end, that of the detachment of the province of Bolzano from the Italian state. It has not been merely a question of military occupation, but a complete and absolute seizure of political, administrative, and economic power throughout the province, thereby ousting and replacing all the legitimate Italian authorities.

(2) This seizure of power has taken place under the protection of the German military authorities, who, on the night of September 8, disarmed the local military forces, leaving not a single *carabiniere* or policeman in the province, and consigned all to internment in Germany.

The Gauleiter of Innsbruck, Franz Hofer, whom Berlin had appointed as supreme commissioner with exceptional powers in the area, permitted and went out of his way to encourage this seizure of power, which now amounts to an annexation preparatory to its becoming final.

In this way the Reich government played the double game of encouraging the process of annexation while officially refuting and denying this annexation aspired to and demanded by the local Nazi representatives.

(3) In this manner, a situation has been created that is illegal and arbitrary in the extreme, chaotic in both law and administration, enabling the new authorities to indulge in despotic acts and tyrannize Italian citizens on Italian soil; many were forced to leave, and harassment and threats rendered life difficult for those who remained.

The region of Ampezzo in the province of Belluno and the one to the north of the Salorno Pass in the province of Trent have been incorporated in the province of Bolzano by the Supreme Commissioner. No military requirement demanded such a move. It was aimed, in fact, at preparing the province, already a self-contained unit, for annexation to greater Germany or to a reconstituted Austria. The two provinces of Trent and Belluno were included in the "Pre-Alpine defense zone" solely in order to disguise this political end more effectively and to prepare the institution of the new German-speaking province of Bolzano.

(4) This take-over of the province, amounting to virtual annexation, was carried through with all the ease that the protection by bayonets affords, and later became total. It could not, however, have deceived any of those who achieved it into thinking that it would lead to a direct annexation, except in the event of a German victory. But the local supporters, while acting in the name of the German movement and as Nazis, bore in mind the possibility of a German defeat in order to present to the winning side the right to loyal Tyrolese autonomy or annexation by Austria.

All the various processes of Germanizing the administrative and economic institutions of the province are directed toward this end.

A German veneer is created by imposing the language in official acts, advertisements, the names of streets and squares, newspapers, cinemas, and theaters. With these activities, the Gauleiters think they will surprise and deceive the conquerors, presenting them with a land that is German in every appearance. It is said that they are preparing the people's right to self-determination.[96]

The picture given by this document, although sketchy and limited to the province of Bolzano alone, is of much interest chiefly because it focuses attention on the aims and methods of the local Tyrolese authorities, who were traditionally bound to the pan-German ideal. Most significant is the behavior of the German-speaking inhabitants of the Alto Adige during this period. They were quick to give an enthusiastic welcome to the Nazi troops entering the Alto Adige after the armistice in September 1943. The local Nazis, who had already made contact with the Wehrmacht high command through Gauleiter Hofer,[97] effectively collaborated in facilitating the progress of the German army. While the local authorities eagerly went about their task of dismantling the Italian administration, a ruthless persecution of Italians was initiated. This was conducted, both on the personal level and, in a more organized way, through the SOD (Südtiroler Ordnung Dienst), the local volunteer police force. During these events, the German group clearly revealed their racial intolerance and sympathies toward Nazi ideals.

Since there is a tendency to pass over these events in silence or even to ignore them, it seems appropriate to quote the chief passage in the memorandum on this subject presented by the Italian delegation at the Paris Peace Conference in 1946. This contains a detailed, even if necessarily incomplete, list of the atrocities committed against Italians in the Alto Adige and in the provinces of Belluno and Trent:

I. Province of Bolzano

As soon as Italy had signed the armistice with the Allies, the Alto Adige was immediately invaded by German troops which had been kept ready for this purpose. All they had to do, therefore, was to march through the region on their way south and occupy a few of the principal towns. All over the Alto Adige, the local Nazis had some time before prepared carefully detailed plans for taking power and, in particular, had already organized the local volunteer police, called S.O.D., which was to persecute ferociously Italian patriots. Below are the main episodes of violence for which the Alto Adige Nazis were responsible.

(a) On September 8 and 9, 1943, the Italian troops stationed at Bolzano, several thousand in number, were concentrated in the empty gravel-bed of the river Talvera, where they were left for several days without food or shelter. The South Tyrol Nazi police repeatedly shot at the Italian prisoners as they attempted to get some food for themselves, killing eight of them and wounding many others. Italian women who tried to throw pieces of bread to the prisoners were also fired upon. The worst elements of the Bolzano German-speaking population jibed and scoffed at Italian prisoners, tormenting them in every way.

(b) Near Brunico, six Italian soldiers who had lost their unit, were denounced to the South Tyrolean police by local women on September 12, 1943; when they were found, they were immediately shot by the local police.

(c) The S.S., recruited almost exclusively among the South Tyroleans, lost no time in erecting the Bolzano concentration camp, which was to become so sadly notorious for the murders and tortures committed there. Nineteen Jews were strangled by the camp police and several other prisoners were tortured. It was here that two of Italy's finest patriots were tortured to death: Manlio Longon and Antonio Manci. The criminals who were responsible for the carnage were all members of the South Tyrolean S.S. They have since been identified and are now up for trial; among the most ill-famed may be mentioned Joseph Mittermaier, Philip Lanz, Peter Mietterstieler, Franz Meraner.

(d) On October 4, 1943, near the railway station of Bolzano, South Tyrolean militiamen of the S.O.D. shot three British prisoners of war who had strayed from the train they were traveling on, during an air raid. On the same day, two other British prisoners succeeded in escaping and reaching Switzerland with the assistance of Italian patriots from Bolzano. These two episodes clearly show the difference in the feelings entertained toward the Allies by the German and the Italian populations in the Alto Adige.

(e) At a later date, during an air raid over Bolzano, members of the South Tyrolean S.S. killed some British officers who were held there as prisoners of war. For this murder the ill-famed S.S. Major Schiefer and the three noncommissioned officers who were his accomplices were sentenced to death a short time ago by the Allied Military Court of Caserta. Two more British officers, Lt. Bradourne and Lt. Vivian, were killed by the S.S. near the station of Bronzolo, after having been captured as the result of information given by the German-speaking population of that village.

(f) Several isolated Italian soldiers were killed by the local South Tyrolean police in September and October 1944: an *Alpino* at Avalengo on September 9, a soldier at San Genesio, whose corpse was abused even by the women of the village. The Italian Courts are already trying the authors of the above-mentioned murders, who have been identified.

(g) Also ordinary Italian civilians were arrested in large numbers by the South Tyrolean police and many of them were tortured or deported to Germany, and most never returned. A compulsory labor service of the cruelest kind was organized for all Italians, male and female, between the ages of 18 and 60.

(h) Immediately after September 8, 1943, the South Tyrolean police arrested all the members of the Jewish community in Merano, numbering 35. The Jews were reported and found in their hiding places, thanks to the offices of well-known South Tyrolean Nazis (Schöner, Gutweniger, Hölzl, etc.), and after being subjected to the usual mistreatment, were sent to concentration camps in Germany. Only one of these 35 is known to have come back alive.

(i) In January 1944, at Brunico, the Italians Giacomo Monti and Giuseppe Grepaz were seriously wounded by a South Tyrolean dealer, Johann Habicher, who suspected them of being anti-Nazis. Habicher was not punished.

[no j, k]

(l) Between September 1943 and February 1944, the South Tyrolean police arrested many Italians in Merano, who were deprived of their belongings and sent to concentration camps, Two of them, Giovanni Piacentini and Adolfo Zadra, were so seriously manhandled in prison that they are maimed for life.

(m) During the whole period of the German occupation, tortures and abuses of all kinds were carried out in the provincial labor office of Bolzano, run by the Austrian, Hans Röchlich, and the South Tyroleans, Hans Tirler and Maria Fossinger. Very often the Italians who were sent out for compulsory labor along the railway lines were not even allowed to take refuge in the shelters during air raids. The raping of Italian girls was an every-day occurrence; if the girls refused to submit, they were generally sent to concentration camps in Germany.

(n) At the beginning of 1944, at San Giacomo near Bolzano, a Polish soldier who attempted to escape was tracked and killed by the South Tyrolean, Joseph Lungher.

(o) On September 10, 1944, at Brunico, the Italian Carlo Mario and Adelino Belliguli were wounded by the local South Tyrolean police and imprisoned for a long time as anti-Nazis.

(p) Also, Alto Adige natives whose sympathies were for Italy were arrested and beaten by the South Tyrolean police. One of them, the innkeeper, Spechtenhaus, was sent to the Dachau concentration camp, where he died from mistreatment. Two women, Caterina Schopf of Collalbo and Caterina Scherter of Sarentino, were kept in prison for some time by their own fellow countrymen, the reason being that they were against Nazism.

(q) In February 1944, the Italian *Alpino,* Alberto Rocci, was killed by the well-known South Tyrolean S.S. officer, Teo Krahe, and his corpse abused. It should be noted that Krahe was one of the S.S. officers from Merano who were responsible for the mass murder of 320 Italians at the Fosse Ardeatine in Rome in March 1944.

(r) In 1944 the special German Court established in the *Alpenvorland* sentenced to death five Italian patriots who were members of the Peruzzo band; the men were hanged. The members of this Court were for the most part from the Alto Adige (Richard Staffer, Hans Kiene, Heinrich Hölzl, Carl Neubauer). At these trials, as well as all the others of the same kind, the South Tyrolean judges refused to forward the appeal for reprieve made by the condemned men.

(s) Even after the liberation, the Nazis of the Alto Adige continued to vent their fury on the local Italian population. At Merano, on April 30, 1945, the Italians were celebrating their liberation when groups of Tyrolese soldiers fired on the unarmed crowd, killing fifteen persons, among them several school children. Part of the German population looked on at this slaughter and applauded.

(t) On the night of May 2, 1945, at Lasa, men of the Tyrolese police, assisted by German soldiers, for no apparent reason, killed the village doctor and 9 Italian workmen a few hours before the arrival of the first Allied troops.

(u) Also at Bolzano soldiers of the Wehrmacht and Tyrolese policemen attacked Italian workmen who were celebrating their liberation on May 3, 1945. For many hours there was fighting on the bridges across the Talvera and in the center of the town. By the end of the day about fifteen Italian patriots had been massacred by the still undaunted Tyrolese Nazis, in the name of the Hitler ideals.[98]

II. Province of Trento

(a) At Riva sul Garda and at Arco, during January and February 1944, eleven patriots were killed in a few days by the South Tyrolean S.S., commanded by Hölzl from Merano, who set up a real reign of terror in the lower Trentino.

(b) In December 1943, at Rovereto, an Italian patriot and lawyer named Bettini was murdered in his office by members of the S.S. of Merano, among whom was the notorious Captain Friederich Amort.

(c) At Trambileno, on September 14, 1944, the farmer, Albino Lorenzi was murdered in the countryside, without any apparent motive, by members of the South Tyrolean police.

(d) At Novaledo, on February 16, 1944, the farmer Domenico Scalzer was killed in his home by members of the Bolzano S.S. Regiment.

(e) At Ala, on April 25, 1945, the Italians Marco De Micheli and Vito Franchetti were killed by an officer of the Tyrolese S.S., Albert Nagel, while trying to escape from compulsory labor.

(f) At Brentonico, on May 2, 1945, the Italians Orazio Mignani and Romolo Mezzetti, who had escaped from the concentration camp at Bolzano, were caught by the South Tyrolean S.S. and, after barbarous mistreatment, killed in open country.

(g) At Castel Tesino, during the winter of 1944–1945, seven young partisans and a woman were killed at various times by the local unit of the Tyrolean police.

(h) At Telve Valsugana, the Tyrolean police killed a woman, Bianca Dalle Baste, and a farmer, Riccardo Trentini.

(i) At Strigno, on April 27, 1945, the Tyrolean S.S., commanded by Captain Eggenberger, killed the Italian patriots Antonio Bordato, Giuseppe Vesco, Luigi Betegan, Marino Betegan, Emilio Clari, Remo Ferrari, and others whom it has not been possible to identify.

[no j, k[

(l) At Borgo Valsugana, in April 1945, the farmer Vittorio Andriolo was killed for no reason by Tyrolese militiamen.

(m) On June 28, 1944, the South Tyrolean police started to carry out large-scale raids on the Italian patriot movement for liberation in the Trentino. About eight patriots were arrested, among whom was Count Gianantonio Manci, the leader of the movement, who shortly afterward committed suicide in the Bolzano concentration camp to escape the tortures inflicted upon him. For over a week, Count Manci and his comrades were tortured with the most refined cruelty by the Gestapo; some of them lost their minds and others will be maimed for the rest of their lives. The perpetrators of these actions were Rodolfo Thyrolf, major of the Tyrolean S.S.; August Schiffer, who has already been sentenced to death by the Allies; Heinrich Andergassen, Hugo Tribus,

Joseph Egger, Ferdinand Pasquali, Wilhelm Weiss, and others; they were all natives of South Tyrol and members of the S.S. The list of Tyrolean Nazi criminals in the hands of the Italian authorities contains several hundred names and is at the disposal of the Allied authorities.

III. Province of Belluno

During Nazi occupation, the province of Belluno came under the German administration of the *Alpenvorland* and was completely withdrawn from Italian jurisdiction. This patriotic province, where the partisans contributed valiantly to the Allied victory, suffered terrible Nazi reprisals and paid for its faith in the cause of liberty with hundreds of lives and the destruction of scores of villages. The S.S. troops in the province of Belluno were composed almost exclusively of German-speaking Alto Adige units, which were sometimes incorporated in Austrian regiments. In no other region did the South Tyrolean Nazi terror take on such violent forms; the units that stained their names with the most terrible crimes were the S.S. Police Regiment *Bozen*, the S.S. Police Regiment *Schlanders*, and the S.S. Police Regiment *Alpenvorland*.

On April 3, 1945, the Bishop of Belluno wrote a letter to Gauleiter Franz Hofer, proclaiming that "for several months the population has been living in a nightmare, the most terrorizing and blood-curdling systems of reprisal and repression having been adopted against them."

Following is a list of the worst atrocities committed by the Tyrolean Nazis in the province of Belluno, complete with photographic evidence:

(a) In the province of Belluno the following villages were completely burned and razed to the ground:

Aune	Federt	Campon d'Alpago	Fonzaso
Croce D'Aune	Taibone	Cesio	Trichiana
Valle di Seren	Gares	Bolzano di Belluno	Fortigna
Borgata di Seren	Fregona	Forno di Canale	Cadola
Valle di Canzoir	Valesina	Falcade	Schievenin
Caviola	Pieve del Pago	Lamon	Gela Alta

(b) In the same province more than twenty Italian priests, among whom were Monsignore Giulio Gaio, Monsignore Candido Fent, and Don Giuseppe Mosoch, were arrested, beaten, and mistreated in many ways.

(c) The seminary at Feltre was destroyed with hand grenades thrown by the Tyrolean S.S.

(d) At Lamon a poor old woman was burned alive in her house and the population, headed by the Bishop of Belluno himself, was obliged to stand by and look on.

(e) When the village of Caviola was set afire, 20 innocent victims were killed by Tyrolean police.

(f) At Bosco delle Castagne, 8 patriots were killed.

(g) At Piazza Campitello, 4 patriots were killed.

(h) At Bassano del Grappa, 15 patriots were hanged in the principal avenues of the town and left there on display for some time.

(i) At Avasinis in the Friuli, a battalion of the S.S. Regiment *Bozen* murdered over 60 partisans after destroying the village. The Committee of Liberation of Gemona possesses a detailed documentation concerning this episode.

[no j, k]

(l) The following members of the South Tyrolean S.S. were charged with the repression of the patriot movement at Belluno and Feltre and were operating the torture chambers. (A list of names follows).

IV. In other regions of Italy

All over Italy, many German-speaking natives of the Alto Adige enlisted in the S.S. or in the German police forces persecuted patriots and were responsible for countless murders and for employing systems of torture, clearly branded of the German type, in the prison of the Gestapo. Some S.S. units in the principal Italian towns were made up for the most part of natives of the Alto Adige: because they knew the Italian language, they were considered particularly suited for this kind of work.

The S.S. unit which in March 1944, conducted the mass murder at the Fosse Ardeatine in Rome was largely made up of South Tyroleans who have since been identified.

The Gestapo headquarters in Milan, at the notorious Hotel Regina, consisted largely of natives of the Alto Adige. Scores of Italian patriots were tortured by them in 1943, 1944, and 1945, many of whom died as a result of these tortures or in the concentration camps to which they were sent.

The Gestapo of Verona was also composed almost exclusively of natives of the Alto Adige.

(There follows a list of the natives of the Alto Adige who held important positions in the S.S. or Gestapo).[99]

Such a list of facts requires no comment. It should be considered, however, along with other significant aspects of the support that the German-speaking inhabitants of the Alto Adige gave to Nazi Germany.

Particularly notable in this connection is the fact that after September 8, 1943, the German authorities decided to form separate units of the S.S., composed almost entirely of Alto Adige inhabitants, precisely because of the pro-Nazi feelings so prevalent among them. The task of these units was largely to combat the Italian partisan formations. Another memorandum presented by the Italian delegation to the Paris Peace Conference in 1946 gives the following list of such formations:

First S.S.–Police Regiment "Bozen." This was in order of time, the first unit of its kind to be constituted, thanks to the initiative of the Commissioner for the pre-Alpine operational area, Hofer, and to the leading pro-Nazi elements of the Alto Adige. The enlistments began as early as October 1943. The regiment was employed up to the very last days of the war against the Italian partisans operating in the Belluno region. Units of this regiment were also used in Rome in the infamous round-ups which took place during the winter of 1943–1944. It was a unit of the *"Bozen"* regiment which caused the wanton retaliation against 320 civilian hostages murdered at the Fosse Ardeatine, near Rome, on March 23, 1944.

S.S.–Police Regiment "Ersatz Bozen." Formed on February 23, 1945. Also sent to Silesia. At the time of the German collapse, a number of the men of this regiment were still in Germany for training.

S.S.–Police Regiment "Schlanders." Formed in September 1944, with men of all ages who were unfit for front-line service. This unit was also employed in the operations against the Italian partisans, thereby distinguishing itself for its fierceness.

S.S.–Police Regiment "Alpenvorland." Formed in May 1944, with recruits of the 1926 draft call. This regiment was also employed against Italian partisans in the Belluno area. Losses were so high that shortly afterward it was found necessary to reassemble it completely.

S.S.—Police Battalion "Ersatz Alpenvorland." Composed of over-aged re-cruits, including men unfit for active service. This unit was also employed against the partisans.

S.S.—Police Regiment "Brixen." Organized on November 15, 1944. Em-ployed on the Russian front, in the Silesian sector.

Waffen—S.S. Battalion "Nederland." Organized on January 10, 1944, with men of the 1922 to 1926 draft calls. Was employed as occupational force in the Netherlands.

Waffen—S.S. Battalion "Ersatz Kommando Hallein Salzburg." At various stages, composed of over-aged recruits or men on punishment list. Was employed as occupational force in various countries.

Local Police S.O.D. units (Südtiroler Ordnung Dienst) after June 1944, called *"Landwacht."* Formed of men not liable for military duty (disabled, farmers, and employees rated as indispensable to local agriculture and administration, etc.). The men belonging to these units served intermittently, an average of 24 hours a week. The training was given at Bressanone, Bolzano, and Silandro.[100]

The above evidence reveals the conduct of some of the German-speaking inhabitants of the Alto Adige during the twenty months that followed Italy's armistice with the Allies. Two factors, their respective influence not always easy to assess, operated at the time: sympathy with Nazi ideology and resentment against the Italians. They determined a whole series of tragic events that had no parallel in either the Austrian or the Fascist administration. This is another instance where the events of the war interfered with the Alto Adige problem.

Chapter IV

The Peace Conference
and the De Gasperi–Gruber
Agreement of
September 5, 1946

[1] Moscow's statement on Austria, November 1, 1943. The State Department's position on the Alto Adige problem in 1944. The August 1945 memorandum on the northern Italian border and the letter sent at the same time by De Gasperi to Byrnes. The Austrian memorandum of September 12, 1945. The London Conference: the decision of September 14, 1945, regarding the Brenner.   [2] The Austrian memorandum of November 5, 1945, brings up the Alto Adige question again. The Italian request for a statement on the Brenner frontier. Gruber's proposal for a meeting is rejected by De Gasperi. The Coppini–Gruber talks in January 1946. Austria's note to the Allied Powers, January 21, 1946.   [3] The Italian memorandum of February 4, 1946: Vienna's reactions to the Italian documents. Shift in the Soviet position on the Brenner problem. The Council of Deputy Foreign Ministers proposes to reject the Austrian note of January 21, 1946.   [4] The first session of the Council of Foreign Ministers in Paris endorses the Deputies' proposal. Austria's new request of May 10, for minor adjustments considered by the council on May 14. May 30, 1946: the speeches of Gruber and Carandini in the Council of Deputies. Gruber's visit to London early in June: the choice of tactics. The Carandini–Schmid and Carandini–Gruber conversations on June 4 and 5. The second Paris session of the Council of Foreign Ministers and the June 24, 1946, decision to leave the Brenner frontier unaltered, rejecting Austria's request for minor rectifications.   [5] Gruber's speech to Parliament July 3. Gruber's new proposal for a meeting with De Gasperi. The Commons debate on July 25. Carandini's renewed apprehension. De Gasperi's reply and the British suggestion to invite Austria to attend the plenary conference at Paris.   [6] De Gasperi's speech at the Palais de Luxembourg on August 10: his concern over the future Italian minority in Yugoslavia. Gruber invited to address the conference. Soviet opposition to this, and Vishinsky's statement of August 17. De Gasperi's decision to initiate direct negotiations with Austria.   [7] The Italian memorandum of August 21 on Art. 10 of the Peace Treaty. The negotiations opened by the Carandini–Gruber meeting of August 22. The initial Austrian requests presented on August 24 as a draft agreement. The Carandini–Gruber conversations on August 26.   [8] De Gasperi clarifies his instructions and formulates Italy's counterproposal for the agreement, based on a clear distinction between the various matters and under-

takings involved. August 31: Gruber agrees to continue negotiations on the basis of the Italian counterproposal, accepting its basic principles. Discussion of individual clauses. Final clarification between De Gasperi and Gruber.   [9] The signing of the agreement and the exchange of letters on September 5. The question of submitting a copy of the agreement to the Secretary General of the Conference.   [10] De Gasperi's press conference on September 7. Protest from the inhabitants of the Alto Adige. The Carandini–Gruber talks on September 16 and confirmation of the meaning of the agreement. On September 19, Carandini receives the Alto Adige representatives, who promise to collaborate in carrying out the agreement. The real weakness besetting the agreement: opinion in Austria. The resolution voted on by the Commission for Foreign Affairs of the Vienna Parliament on October 1.   [11] Conclusions.

[1]

The restoration of Austrian independence at the end of World War II was first taken into consideration by members of the prospective victorious coalition during talks between the British foreign minister, Sir Anthony Eden (later Lord Avon) and the Soviet leaders in Moscow, December 16, 22, 1941. When Soviet Prime Minister Stalin touched on the problems of the postwar settlement of Europe, he told Eden that as far as he was concerned "Austria should be restored as an independent state."[1]

The question was taken up again by the Foreign Office in the summer of 1943, during consultations with the State Department on the agenda for the imminent Moscow conference between the foreign ministers of Great Britain, the United States, and the Soviet Union. In the British view, the conference should consider issuing a declaration on Austria; this would proclaim the principle that the United Nations would reestablish the independence of Austria—"the first country to fall victim to Nazi aggression"—and then form part of a confederation with neighboring states. This declaration, however, was to contain a pro-memoria that the Austrian people could not escape their own responsibilities, and that the final settlement would inevitably take into consideration the part they had played in helping to expel the German invaders.[2] The British proposal was based on a desire to create a stable basis for a central-European confederation in order to reestablish the postwar balance in Europe, as well as on the fact that the war had taken a favorable turn for the Allies, which improved the chances of creating difficulties for Germany by encouraging resistance and sabotage in Austria. In London, it was believed that there existed in Austria some signs of anti-German sentiment and that it was advisable to encourage them by providing assurances on the future of the country.[3]

The State Department's reply was favorable to the idea of a declaration, but raised some questions on the wording proposed because, in the first place, it was pointed out that the United States had not yet taken a position on the future postwar settlement of Europe, and, further, that it should be very clear that the United Nations was not undertaking the obligation to liberate Austria against the wishes of the Austrian people or without waiting for them to make some contribution to their own liberation.[4] Accordingly, the State Department drew up a new outline for a declaration on Austria[5] that was adopted by Great Britain and submitted by Eden at the Moscow Conference; in the meantime, the Soviet government had concurred that the matter should be included on the agenda.[6]

Once the point regarding Austria's participation in a Central European Confederation—the only one on which the Soviet Union might have raised objections—was eliminated, the discussion of the British proposal during the conference's session on October 25, 1943, was extremely brief, and the proposed outline was immediately passed on to the drafting committee.[7] Here, however, the Soviet representative successfully requested that the final paragraph should be formulated with greater precision and incisiveness, insofar as it related to Austria's responsibility for taking part in Hitler's war.[8] The declaration on Austria, which was announced on November 1, 1943, ran as follows:

> The Governments of the United Kingdom, the Soviet Union and the United States of America are agreed that Austria, the first free country to fall victim to Hitlerite aggression, shall be liberated from German domination.
>
> They regard the annexation imposed upon Austria by Germany on March 15, 1938, as null and void. They consider themselves as in no way bound by any changes effected in Austria since that date. They declare that they wish to see re-established a free and independent Austria, and thereby to open the way for the Austrian people themselves, as well as those neighbouring states which will be faced with similar problems, to find that political and economic security which is the only basis for lasting peace.
>
> Austria is reminded, however, that she has a responsibility which she cannot evade for participation in the war on the side of Hitlerite Germany, and that in the final settlement account will inevitably be taken of her own contribution to her liberation.[9]

The contradiction between the statement in the first paragraph, that Austria had been Hitler's first victim, and the statement in the final paragraph, already included in the British proposal, that Austria was held responsible for participation in Hitler's war, is so obvious that it needs no further emphasis. This, however, was the formula used to reconcile the demands of war propaganda with historical reality. The fact was that during the first period of Nazi domination, there had been no serious sign of opposition; nor, once war had broken out, had there been any positive acts of resistance against German "domination." The ensuing years, 1944 and especially 1945, were to thwart completely all hopes of Austria's contribution to her own liberation and to reveal, on the contrary, Austria's total solidarity with Germany. This went as far as her allowing the destruction of portions of her towns and territory in order to slow down the advance of the Allies and thus prolong the resistance of the German army.

In spite of the entirely negative outcome of the appeal contained in the Moscow declaration, the State Department Committee on postwar programs recommended, among other proposals for the future settlement with Austria, that the Italo-Austrian frontier should be altered by ceding the province of Bolzano to Austria, according to a demarcation that would be determined by taking into account the distribution of language groups. This proposal was advanced because the committee maintained that: (a) it recognized this area as Austrian in its history, culture, and tradition and as an area that would probably be predominantly Austrian in population at the end of the war; (b) the retrocession of this region to Austria would aid both in the political and economic reconstruction of an Austrian state; (c) the loss to Italy through this cession would be slight in comparison with the advantage of Austria.[10]

During 1944, however, no inkling of these State Department proposals reached the Italian government. It was not until late in the spring of 1945 that news that the Brenner frontier was also very likely under discussion reached Italy. At first it was mainly a question of rumors reported in the press,[11] and these found little credence in Rome because they were considered improbable. As rumors increased, however, and especially when the behavior of the French occupation authorities in the northern Tyrol[12] was seen openly to favor the semiclandestine repatriation into the Alto Adige of optants for Germany, anxiety at the capitol began to increase. Therefore, it was decided to include a reference to the problem in a note on Italy's position with regard to the imminent discussions on the peace treaty. This memorandum was sent by the Italian ambassador to Washington, Tarchiani, to President Truman on July 6, 1945, as he was leaving for the Potsdam Conference.[13]

Meanwhile, a memorandum on the northern Italian border was prepared in Rome, explaining the reasons that justified maintaining the Brenner frontier. Attention was drawn chiefly to the historical precedents of the question, from the Treaty of London on. This section underlined the reasons presented by Italy in support of her request for the Brenner at the 1919 Peace Conference and the favorable reception they had found with the Allied and Associated Powers. There followed a section explaining how, from a geographical point of view, there was a perfect correlation between the natural border and the existing political one, except for three minor areas: the Resia (Reschen) Pass, the Sesto valley and the Tarvisio basin. The reasons for these exceptions were given. The third section examined the problem from the point of view of security and noted what the effect of moving back the frontier might be on Italy's defense possibilities: the Brenner and the upper valley of the Adige had always constituted the traditional routes of invasions from the Germanic world. If it were sought to draw a distinction between Germany and Austria, the trend that had existed in the latter in favor of the Anschluss long before Hitler actually carried it out should not be forgotten, nor the possibility that such a tendency could reappear, even if in new forms and with different long-term solutions as its aim. The fourth section of the note dwelled on the economic aspect of the problem by emphasizing first, that the Alto Adige markets were oriented toward the Po valley, as had been illustrated by the recession that had taken place after 1860 and, second, how this natural gravitation had, after World War I, made possible considerable industrial development in the province of Bolzano. This had been achieved through substantial investments, which had transformed the economic picture of the province when compared to the pre-1918 years. The fifth and final section dealt with the ethnic situation and the changes it had undergone as a result of the population movement that took place after the options in 1939. The Italian-speaking inhabitants and those Germans who had not opted for Germany now formed 64 percent of the population as against 25 percent German who, though they had decided to become German citizens had either not yet taken the necessary steps or had not, in fact, moved because of the events of 1943.[14]

The foreign minister, De Gasperi, transmitted the note to the principal Italian embassies, giving instructions, however, not to present it, since no one had yet raised the question either officially or informally. This was done in order to circumvent the possibility that retention of the Brenner frontier would be held out as compensation for possible Italian territorial losses in other areas. De Gasperi was, in fact, confident that no one would deny the Italians the natural defense against the Germans that they already possessed, at a time when all European countries were taking precautions against the possibility, however remote, of a revival of German aggression.

Early in August 1945, rumors became more insistent that a movement in favor of transferring the Alto Adige to Austria was forming in the United States and France. The Italian government became convinced that the question would be raised officially, in the guise of the German-speaking minority question, at the conference scheduled to open in September in London. At the same time, the Italian government began to formulate those principles forming the basis of the new democratic state that would also insure a peaceful and civilized coexistence to the minority within the country's borders.

In view of the impending convening of the conference, De Gasperi, in a long letter dated August 22, 1945, to the American secretary of state, Byrnes, explained the Italian point of view on the various questions involved. As to the Brenner frontier, the Italian Foreign Minister emphasized particularly the importance which the Alto Adige had assumed in the economy and in the industrial structure of Italy; the Nazi sentiments shown by the German-speaking group both over the 1939 options and in their conduct after September 1943; the inconsequential contribution that this area could make toward the reconstruction of a strong Austria; and, lastly, the policy that would guide Italy on its resumption of the administration of the region. De Gasperi wrote: "Between 1919 and 1922, democratic Italy assured the German-speaking inhabitants cultural equality and representation in Parliament. Negotiations were also in progress with a view to establishing local autonomies in the whole of the Tridentine Venetia. The Fascist dictatorship upset the local situation; but now the Italian democratic government, in agreement with the Allied Military Government has already taken proper measures with regard to German schools and a plan for local autonomies is being completed."[15]

Toward the end of August, De Gasperi finally arranged for the dispatch of the general memorandum on the northern frontier to the four major powers. Byrnes's reply was not very encouraging. Although no precise position was taken on any of the points touched upon by De Gasperi concerning frontiers, the sentence stating that Italy should show "full comprehension for the legitimate interests of her neighbors"[16] carried the suggestion of a warning. However, as Ambassador Tarchiani was able to ascertain at the beginning of September, the American position was undergoing a substantial change in favor of maintaining the Brenner frontier. The idea of the complete cession of the Alto Adige, suggested by the committee on postwar problems and endorsed by the previous secretary of state, Stettinius, was not immediately accepted by Byrnes, and its supporters judged it more profitable to put forward a proposal for a plebiscite. However, not even this proposal met with Byrnes's immediate approval, giving the Italian supporters in the State Department the opportunity to exert all their influence.

Rome could entertain no assurance on what the American delegation's attitude might be, and the possibility of a plebiscite appeared to remain open. Consequently, before the London Conference began, the Foreign Minister once again clarified the situation to Washington, drawing attention to the following points:

1) The 186,000 optants for Germany had at the time declared "that they were irrevocably committed to choosing German citizenship and moving to the Reich".

2) On the basis of the 1939 agreements, which were still valid, Italy could request the actual removal of all those who had remained.

3) These optants, in the event of a plebiscite, should not in any case have the right to vote.

4) The Italian democratic government, however, moved by basic humanitarian ideals, had already shown that it intended to permit a review of the options. Therefore, a possible plebiscite would work against the liberal measures that Italy proposed to apply.

Lastly, De Gasperi stressed that the options had taken place when Germany had already begun her war of aggression and while Italy was still neutral. He concluded by stating that he did not see from what point of view a sacrifice in Austria's favor could be justified. She had never been attacked by Italy and had fully participated in Hitler's war without there ever having been the slightest trace of effective anti-Nazi resistance: it was inconceivable that she should advance territorial claims against Italy, who had fought on the side of the Allies for twenty months.[17]

Yet, the claims were presented. Karl Gruber, in his capacity as governor of the Tyrol, first asked President Truman for the right of self-determination for the South Tyrolese on August 23, 1945. On September 5, Renner's provisional government in Vienna issued a statement in which he claimed the restitution of the South Tyrol to Austria.[18] This statement was followed on September 12, by the presentation of a note to the four Great Powers of occupation. Repeating almost exactly the same arguments as those used in 1919, this document asked officially for the Alto Adige question to be definitively resolved by a plebiscite.

This request was essentially ignored in London, where it was not even considered by the Foreign Office, since it came from an unrecognized govern-ment.[19] In Paris, on the other hand, it served to strengthen the pro-Austrian bias that had already been noted in the conduct of the French occupation authorities in the Tyrol. Saragat, the Italian ambassador in Paris, had already reacted vigorously toward such a possibility in August. He had noted that support for a plebiscite was incompatible with the explicit statement previously made by the Quai d'Orsay to the effect that Italy would be satisfied with France's attitude at the conference in London. When he had learned of the demonstrations at Innsbruck in support of the Renner government's request, Ambassador Saragat had expressed his surprise to French Foreign Minister Bidault over the fact that France was playing Austrian Nazism against Italian anti-fascism.

Shortly before the conference of the four Great Powers opened at Lancaster House in London, the Italian ambassador in Moscow, Quaroni, Carandini in London, and Saragat in Paris called the attention of the governments of the countries to which they were accredited to the arguments that Tarchiani had advanced to the State Department. At the same time, according to information in possession of the Italian government, the form that the Alto Adige problem would take during the discussions scheduled to begin in London on September 11, 1945, in preparation for the Italian peace treaty, would depend principally on the attitude of the American delegation. Great Britain seemed to have no interest in the problem, the Soviet Union had not made its view clear but did not appear likely to support a claim based on ethnic reasons, and France, although showing pro-Austrian inclinations, would not have been in a position to influ-ence a decision without the support of the United States. Consequently, such influence, in reality very limited, as Italy could exert scarcely four months after her liberation was focused on Washington.

The effect of the Italian action was generally positive, though the strong appeal made by the provisional government in Vienna was also weighed by the American delegation. In fact, the U.S. delegation proposed that Austria should be included among the countries invited to present their points of view on the Italian peace treaty, even though Austria's position was entirely different from that of countries attacked by Italy, including Ethiopia, Yugoslavia, and Greece.[20] At the same time, the United States included the Brenner frontier on the list of principal issues relating to the Italian peace treaty that the four foreign ministers would have to discuss and decide upon. These did not appear in the draft presented by Great Britain.[21] The American paper proposed that "the frontier with Austria would be unchanged, subject to hearing any case Austria may present for minor rectifications in her favor."[22]

On September 14, 1945, the problem of the Brenner was examined by the four statesmen and, as was divulged some days later, the American proposal was unanimously adopted.[23] When, at the end of the month, it was finally possible to obtain more details from the State Department on the meaning of the decision, it was made clear that the United States now intended that the Brenner frontier should remain in principle guaranteed to Italy without a plebiscite and that only a few minor rectifications could be considered in favor of Austria. This decision was to have considerable influence on the subsequent developments on the question at the Peace Conference, an influence that, at the time, was perhaps underestimated by both the Italian and Austrian governments. In Rome, where the danger of losing the Brenner frontier had been at first barely considered and then suddenly understood, the decision was greeted with much relief and no further concern was manifested for some time. The fact that the London decision was definitive apparently was not completely understood in Vienna, where it was still considered somehow possible to obtain a territorial revision: it was a matter of creating the right conditions.

[2]

On November 5, 1945, the Austrian government presented a memorandum to the representatives of the Allied Powers in Vienna, repeating its formal request for the restitution of the Südtirol and suggesting that the Allies should hold a referendum, supervised by them. Its results would unquestionably confirm that the people of the region desired reunion with Austria. The request was supported by other arguments, such as the historical unity of the Tyrol, the serious obstruction by the partition to traffic between the northern and eastern Tyrol, and the brutality of the policy of denationalization carried out by fascism. The memorandum reviewed the continuous friction between Italy and Austria provoked by this unresolved territorial question and ended with a warning that there was a danger of Südtirol becoming a perpetual source of unrest for the Italian state.[24]

This memorandum marked the beginning of an Austrian course of action that, favored by circumstances, was to assume unforeseen importance until the four occupying powers recognized the provisional government in Vienna at the end of October 1945.

Even before this, however, the Italian government had noted ominous signs of a resurgence of the unrest in the Alto Adige that had occurred during the summer, coincidentally with official and unofficial demands by the Austrian government to the Allied Powers and to the Peace Conference. To prevent this situation from continuing, which apart from everything else was rendering it difficult for Rome to finalize the preparation and application of the liberal plans benefiting the German-speaking population,[25] the Italian government sent a note to the head of the Allied Control Commission on November 6, 1945, asking for an official statement covering the retention of the Brenner frontier and at the same time confirming its intention of carrying out its declared policy.

The opportunity for such a statement could be presented by the announcement, which the Rome government believed imminent, that the northern provinces were to be restored to Italian administration. To demonstrate further its determination to put behind it, even in its relations with the Austrian republic, the sad memories of Italy's sufferings during the German occupation at the hands of units from the Austrian provinces of the Reich, the Italian government informed the Allied authorities in Vienna that it was ready to reestablish diplomatic relations between the two countries and accepted the invitation of the Allied Control Commission for Austria to resume commercial dealings with Vienna.

The Allied Control Commission not only refused to make the requested declaration regarding the Brenner frontier but instead declared that the announcement of the transfer of the northern provinces to the Italian administration on January 1, 1946, would contain an explicit reservation that this transfer would not prejudicate "any adjustment of frontiers." In spite of repeated Italian protests, it was impossible to obtain any but the mildest softening of this formula, since the Allies were anxious not to create the slightest impediment to the settlement of French and Yugoslav claims. On the same day that this announcement was made, December 19, 1945, at the first session of the new Austrian Parliament attended by the four commanders of the occupying armies, retiring Chancellor Renner, explicitly repeated his demand that the Alto Adige should immediately be restored to Austria. His justification was the pressing appeals reaching Vienna from the South Tyrol.[26]

Meanwhile, Italy had undergone a change of government also. De Gasperi had become prime minister, retaining the Foreign Ministry. Concentrating the heaviest responsibilities of government on his own shoulders, De Gasperi took a firm stand and on December 21, replied to Renner's words with a statement made at a cabinet meeting and released to the public, in which he explicitly declared that: "we cannot allow that the frontier of a state of 45 million inhabitants should be determined by a small fraction living in the boundary province; even less so if a major portion of this minority group distinguished itself before and during the war by the cordial welcome it gave to Nazism and by its participation in the war on Hitler's side up to the very end."[27]

A few days later, a letter reached De Gasperi from Austrian Foreign Minister Gruber. After congratulating him on becoming prime minister, he expressed a desire for a personal meeting for the purpose of exchanging views on the problems concerning their two countries. Considering the intransigent attitude of the Austrian government at the moment—even the new chancellor, Figl, had made pronouncements on December 21, 1945, promising the country a more dynamic policy for the southern Tyrol[28] —De Gasperi did not reply to the invitation, since it would have led to a discussion of the territorial problem and it was his policy to consider this matter not merely closed, but never opened. However, he thought it opportune to observe first-hand the situation in Vienna and so at the same time that he sent the commercial delegation he also sent Counselor Coppini, heading a small team of political observers.

Counselor Coppini's unofficial mission to Vienna began early in January. Coppini informed Foreign Minister Gruber, that President De Gasperi, for various reasons, found it impossible to agree to his proposal of an Austro-Italian meeting. However, he repeated Italy's desire to establish direct contacts, as indeed had already been done through the recent commercial agreement, in which provision had been made for setting up an Italian office in Vienna and a corresponding Austrian office in Rome.

Gruber showed no sign of displeasure at the rejection of his proposal. In fact, he was relieved because it was determined in Vienna that since the time the invitation had been tendered, the situation in Austria had improved to the point where direct rapprochement with Italy was no longer a necessity. A few days later, Gruber took advantage of another meeting with Coppini to list a number of considerations that would also arouse doubts in the Italian government over the advisability of continuing the policy it was endeavoring to pursue on the Alto Adige question.

Starting with the assumption that the problem would in any case be settled by the Great Powers, and that consequently his words now certainly were not directed toward convincing the Italians of the necessity for renouncing their claim to the Alto Adige, Gruber explained in these terms the reason why his government supported the proposition that the Alto Adige should be returned to Austria. Austria's demand was justified by many reasons: administrative, economic, geographic, and ethnic. But all of these, he said, were of only relative importance. The crux of the matter was Italy's declared intention, which he was certain would be carried out, to accord to the people of the Alto Adige everything necessary to preserve and insure the free and autonomous progress of their ethnic group. He, continued Gruber, was well acquainted with his fellow countrymen. They were the most determined and tenacious people on earth. The more freedom they were granted the more they would use, or abuse, to strengthen their insistence on being reunited to Austria. Every concession of autonomy, accorded them with the most worthy intention of creating a common bond, would only be turned into a weapon against Italy. Bit by bit, within the limits of the new freedom granted them, Italy's situation in the Alto Adige would become untenable. Then what would happen? The real problem, he added, lay precisely in this dilemma: if the Italian government set the machinery of autonomy in motion, this would then continue to move on its own, ever faster and faster, and by centrifugal motion slip out of Italy's hands, until annexation to Austria would practically be demanded in the name of freedom and autonomy. If, on the other hand, the Italians reacted by once again resorting to the restriction of local autonomy, the latter would become more and more circumscribed, to the point of creating a new oppression, as in the Fascist era. And, basically, the Foreign Minister continued, from the point of view of Italian interests, the policy that met the situation best had been that of Mussolini. Gruber said that he was not sure whether Mussolini had been aware of this. For his part, he had never believed that Mussolini seriously considered Italianizing the Germans of the Alto Adige. He thought, rather, that Mussolini had always been clearly aware that only by forcibly holding the population of the area in line would it be possible to retain the region as a part of Italy, at least administratively.

Given Italy's new policy, it was now inevitable that when the inhabitants were able to take advantage of the freedom granted them, they would use it to demand unity with Austria. This would have profound repercussions on the politics in Austria, and would endanger her friendship with Italy. If the Great Powers decided in favor of Austria, all difficulties would be removed and a real, firm friendship between the two countries would develop. It would be well, Gruber added, if Italy too realized that the policy of Dollfuss and Schuschnigg had never had the approval and understanding of the Austrian people.

This, Gruber concluded, was what he had wanted to say to De Gasperi at their meeting, to make him understand that the claims put forward by Vienna did not spring from nationalist sentiments in the Austrian people, nor from feelings of nostalgia, or even from significant ethnic, social or administrative considerations connected with the country's reconstitution, but were largely imposed by the temperament, will, and pertinacity of the inhabitants of the Alto Adige, who would stop at nothing to return to Austria.

Gruber's statement, attempting to show that the liberal policy that Italy started to develop as soon as the war was over would have failed to solve either the problem of peaceful coexistence in the Alto Adige or that of the Brenner frontier, is singularly interesting from three points of view. First, it contains an exposition of the Austrian government's real attitude on the problem, expressed as a personal opinion, but with a frankness and precision never again to be encountered in later Austro-Italian exchanges. Second, even today it offers valuable guidance in evaluating the implicit dangers in conceding an excessive level of autonomy to the province of Bolzano alone. Gruber, in fact, showed very clearly that this solution, later to be promulgated by the Vienna government as the only one consistent with a solution, would only have served to prepare the way for the entire Alto Adige region to secede from the Italian state. Third, from the historical point of view, attention should be called to the statement that the policy of active support of Austrian independence from Germany openly adopted by Italy, particularly during the years 1932 to 1935, was in no way understood or approved of by the Austrian people.

The resurgence of Vienna's faith that she could attain her objective and annex the Alto Adige, revealed in Gruber's statement, was less the result of the theory of necessity that he expounded than the consequence of assurances given by certain of the Allied Powers that the problem of the Alto Adige would be examined during the discussions of the Italian peace treaty. Such assurances led Gruber to reconsider his intention to seek a direct settlement with Italy, as they gave him reason to hope that the Great Powers would favor, if not total secession, at least a plebiscite.

Great Britain, in particular, had strengthened the hopes of the Viennese government, following the Austrian elections of November 25, 1945.[29] The result, the crushing victory of the two democratic parties, the Catholics and the Socialists, was registered in London as a factor of particular importance in the delicate political situation of central Europe. The Austrian people had shown that they were definitely anti-communist, and consequently deserved every encouragement to rebuild their country into a healthy, vigorous entity. The acquisition of the Alto Adige would help equally toward this end.

On the other hand, the decision of the London government to give a measure of support to Austria's claims was welcomed by certain sectors of British public opinion, either from a vague sympathy for the Austrian people or as a result of resentment and enmity still widely held toward the former enemy, Italy.

The British attitude was at this time shared by the government in Paris. French public opinion was influenced by the memory of historical bonds that greatly strengthened the sentiments of good will toward the Austro-Hungarian state, even during World War I, but above all it presented the opportunity to bring pressure to bear on Italy to cede Briga and Tenda and to make other adjustments of the Franco-Italian frontier. These were scheduled for consideration in the course of the meetings of the Council of Deputy Foreign Ministers at Lancaster House in January 1946.

Following the unfavorable decision of the London Conference, the Austrian government was given assurances that its claims would be considered again. On January 21, 1946, the Austrian government sent a note to the Allied Council in Vienna which called attention to the statement issued by Vienna on November 5, 1945, and demanded that the whole of the Alto Adige be annexed to Austria. The note continued that as soon as such a request was granted, Austria was disposed to accord the Italian-speaking inhabitants the right of option, with the choice of remaining on Austrian territory under a special status. The note also raised the question of the hydroelectric power stations, for which the Austrian government proposed to make special arrangements to insure their production for the benefit of the Italians, as well as to arrange for supplies of spare parts and materials from Italy. Finally, the note contemplated the possibility of placing the region under United Nations control.[30]

The Austrian government thus felt it had justified all ethnic, economic and strategic objections that could be offered by Italy against the cession of the Alto Adige.

[3]

Even before being informed that this note had been presented, the Italian government was aware that Austria, now that she had been recognized and had the support of Britain, was in a position to put forward official claims and even to obtain a hearing at the Peace Conference. It was, therefore, again deemed necessary to express the Italian point of view to the Great Powers and to refute the arguments that had caused London and Paris to favor Austria's case, if only temporarily and superficially.

On February 4, 1946, the representatives of the Great Powers received from Italy an *aide-mémoire* that consisted, first, of a résumé of the principal geographic, historical, strategic, and economic arguments set out in the general memorandum on the northern frontier presented to the victorious powers in August 1945. Next, the paper detailed certain factual matters that seemed to have been overlooked or misinterpreted by London and Paris. In the first place, the options revealed that of the 230,000 German-speaking inhabitants in the province of Bolzano, 167,000 were already pledged in December 1939, "in an absolutely final way to adopt German citizenship and settle in the Reich." Of these people, 70,000 had, in fact, left before the armistice with Italy, while another 50,000 who had already become German citizens had not yet departed but were nonetheless foreigners in every respect. In spite of this, however, the government, for humanitarian reasons, had already declared and subsequently confirmed by act of Parliament, on November 21, 1945, its intention to allow a broad and generous revision of the options taken. To now invoke on behalf of these people the right to self-determination, especially when in the name of a safer Europe the Potsdam Conference had elected to oust millions of Germans from their own lands,[31] would mean to apply against Italy the very humanitarian instincts that had restrained her from demanding at least the departure of all the German citizens from within her borders.

Second, the *aide-mémoire* stressed that the options had taken place in December 1939, "namely full four months after the ruthless and tragic war of aggression had been unleashed by Germany, and at a time when Italy was a neutral country." Whatever argument one used to counter this, even conceding that in some cases pressure was used, the fact remained that the 167,000 voters explicitly chose "Nazi Germany at the time of her most brutal and crushing victories." This was more than confirmed by the "marked pro-Nazi attitude" evident in the behavior of a large number of the German-speaking population of the Alto Adige both before and after September 8, 1943, distinguished by demonstrations of solidarity with the Hitler regime and above all by its contribution of many thousands of recruits to German police and S.S. units under German administration. Their comportment toward the Italian people had been identical to that of the most fanatical Nazis in the Reich.

Third, the Italian *aide-mémoire* stated that in 1938 the large majority of the Austrian population welcomed the arrival of the Nazi troops with great enthusiasm and took full part in the war, started by the Germans, up to the final day. Not even a modest attempt at anti-Nazi resistance had taken place, even after the three Great Powers had promised, at the Moscow Conference in October 1943, that Austrian independence would be reestablished and, at the same time, had stated that in the final settlement for Austria, account would be taken of the contribution she made to her own liberation. Yet Austria had done nothing for her liberation. She had stood unalterably united and faithful to Germany, in contrast to Italy, who for twenty months of loyal cooperation had fought side by side with the Allies.

The *aide-mémoire* also noted that in striking contrast to the treatment meted out to Italian minorities elsewhere, the German-speaking language group of the Alto Adige had every opportunity to live and thrive in full freedom of speech, language, and press. The measures already taken in this connection and those planned for the future and relating to autonomy were also mentioned here.[32]

Attached to the *aide-mémoire* were a copy of the general memorandum on the northern frontier; a detailed study of the hydroelectrical power plants in Venetia Tridentina, with the relevant data and documentation; and a note to illustrate the part played by Austrians and the Alto Adige citizens, as members of German units, in the war against Italy after September 8, 1943.

The quick reaction of the Austrian press when news of the *aide-mémoire* reached Vienna is a measure of the effect it had on the representatives of those governments who seemed to have lost sight of these and other matters. The press went out of its way to deny that there had ever been units of the German army recruited exclusively from Austria and the Alto Adige, or that such men had ever been used in the ranks of police directly employed in crushing Italian resistance in the provinces administered by the Reich.[33]   That both these facts are hard to deny, although the attempt is still being made,[34] is clear in the light of a single basic consideration: after the Anschluss the Austrians had become the German citizens of Ostmark, and were therefore subject to compulsory military service. They were, consequently, members of the German army, and men from Upper Austria were to be found in particularly large numbers in specialist units, such as the Alpine divisions. As it is also an established fact that there were no deserters or men who avoided conscription, it is clear that they must have fought among Hitler's troops up to the end of the war. Insofar as the units from the Alto Adige are concerned, existing evidence of their activities has already been presented.

However, the most violent reaction in Vienna was caused not so much by these specific charges as by the fact that all the circumstances recorded in the *aide-mémoire,* from Austrian enthusiasm for the Anschluss to the faithful obedience to Hitler on the part of Austrians in and out of uniform, confirmed that during at least seven years, no distinction at all had ever been made in Austria between Austrians and Germans or in the goals they were seeking. This completely undermined the theory of an historical, cultural, and behavioral difference bettween the two, on which the Vienna government was placing great emphasis at that time in its flight from the consequences of defeat. The theory had already been weakened by the large number of Austrians who had been purged because of their Nazi past and by the revelation that out of a population of six million, almost half a million Austrians had been members of the Nazi party.

Apart from the soundness of the Italian argument, a factor that unexpectedly worked in favor of Rome was the Soviet policy for Austria after the elections of November 25, 1945. The result of this vote, in which the Communists succeeded in winning only four seats in spite of the message of friendship addressed by Stalin to President Renner and other Moscow expressions of good will, including promises to support Austria's claims against Italy, led Moscow to an abrupt change of policy. The Kremlin accepted the outcome of the election, but the obvious inference was that nothing could be expected of Austria and that from that moment on she must be regarded as "a defeated Fascist country."[35]

The first confirmation of the new attitude, which the following pages will demonstrate to have been instrumental in blocking Austria's maneuver, reached Rome early in February. Carandini, the ambassador to London, reported a conversation that he had with the Soviet representative to the Council of Deputy Foreign Ministers, Vishinsky, aimed at clarifying for him the Italian view on the various problems under discussion. Carandini stated that on the subject of the Brenner frontier, Vishinsky replied in the following words: "Italy owes Austria nothing."[36] As a positive response to the Italian *aide-mémoire,* it could not have been more precise and to the point.

At this stage, however, it would have been dangerous to rely on Soviet support, especially when the first commitment of the U.S.S.R. was to uphold the rights of Yugoslavia in the matter of the eastern frontier. For this reason, Italy concentrated its pressure principally on Washington. At the beginning of February, Byrnes pledged his government's support for all the proposals passed in September at the London Conference. He drew attention, however, to the necessity of taking the opinions of the other powers into account. More reassuring news came from the U.S. delegate to the Council of Deputy Foreign Ministers, Dunn, who confirmed that his government was of the opinion that geographically, the border between Italy and the German states was the best possible one. Elaborating on this, he said that the "minor adjustments" that the U.S. delegation had allowed to pass at the London Conference referred to the San Candido and Tarvisio regions, which lie across the Alpine watershed.[37]

About March 10, 1946, word began to circulate that the Council of Deputy Foreign Ministers had decided to retain the Alto Adige as a part of Italy. Only four days later, confirmation came through from Washington that the Lancaster House Conference had decided not to uphold the Austrian claim for "the entire" Alto Adige. However, the problem of "minor adjustments" was left unsolved, since the points of view of the four delegations were not yet finalized. Discussion on this subject was to continue.

Subsequent information made it clear that the next point of focus in the controversy was to be Britain's disposition to pass off as "minor adjustments" the annexation of the Pusteria valley, though this would give Austria control of the Brenner–San Candido railway and so secure for her a more convenient link between the northern and eastern Tyrol. At the same time, Paris informed Rome that she now favored the recognition of the entire status quo in favor of Italy. The French ambassador, Maurice Couve de Murville, explained to Carandini that France would not even have supported an adjustment of frontiers limited to the San Candido area.[38]

However, the deputy foreign ministers' decision had to be ratified by the Council of Foreign Ministers, which also had to examine the problem of the minor adjustments. But the end of March brought further reassurance: the British government was also being induced to abandon its attitude. In conversation with Carandini, the Foreign Minister Bevin, told him that he was now in favor of preserving the Brenner frontier. Austria should receive some sort of economic compensation, and he hoped that eventually, if not immediately, there would be an Austro-Italian customs union.[39] Bevin's statement is of much interest in that it confirmed what Carandini had already pointed out, that the detailed analysis presented in the Italian *aide-mémoire* had begun to have its effect on the British government.

In searching for reasons why Austria's claims were refused, Gruber wrote in his memoirs[40] that after Italy had lost all her colonies, opinion in the West was generally that she should not also sacrifice territory on her northern frontier. He implied that Great Britain, faced with a choice between Libya and the Alto Adige, had decided to choose the former. Gruber's statement, however, appears hardly substantiated.

In fact, there was no dilemma: the colonial question had no influence in the matter because at that time it was still not entirely resolved, and, in any case, the two problems were entirely distinct. There were two factors that finally determined Great Britain's attitude: the isolated position in which she found herself when France, with the matter of Briga and Tenda satisfactorily settled, had no longer any reason to support her, and the realization that at the end of this war, whatever technical reasons might be advanced in Austria's favor, it was inadmissible that she be permitted to gain extra territory.

[4]

The situation remained unchanged during April 1946. The only notable occurrence was a large demonstration in Innsbruck on April 22, in support of annexing the Alto Adige; Chancellor Figl was present. The Council of Foreign Ministers considered the question of the northern Italian frontier on May 1, 1946. It adopted the proposal drawn up by the deputy foreign ministers. Austria's claims in her note of January 21, 1946, were rejected because they did not come under the heading of "minor adjustments" that the council had agreed to eventually consider. The council was no longer empowered to discuss any changes other than these.[41] This decision was officially communicated to Vienna on May 3, and after a few days, on May 10, the Austrian government sent a new note to the foreign ministers, in which its claims were confined to those coming under the formula. The council was about to adjourn its proceedings until the middle of June, and upon receipt of the new Austrian claims it was decided (May 14, 1946) to pass the evidence on to the deputy foreign ministers. These were still in session and were assigned the task of hearing both sides plead their case on the problem of the minor adjustments.

This decision of the four foreign ministers marked a notable departure from the earlier attitude of the council, since it permitted Austria, a defeated country, to take a place, with no justification at all, among the chorus of victors claiming what was due to them from the vanquished. The pressure exerted by Vienna and its consequent reverberations in Britain among those groups who were in favor of the Tyrolean cause, lay at the root of the questionable decision taken by the council to invite Austria to present her case in Paris.

On May 30, 1946, when Gruber was given the floor before the Council of

Deputy Foreign Ministers, it was inevitable that he should exceed the terms of his brief. Even the demands contained in the Austrian note of May 10, 1946 (the whole of the Pusteria valley, Bressanone, and the upper Isarco valley, that is to say 43 percent of the province of Bolzano, with a population of 74,000) hardly came under the heading of minor adjustments. Further, in presenting them, Gruber explained that they by no means constituted a definitive solution to the Alto Adige problem, but were only a "partial palliative," which might help to resolve certain disadvantages implicit in the present line of the frontier, in particular the difficulty of communication between the northern and eastern Tyrol. Gruber concluded by saying that his government reserved the right to refer the question of a plebiscite in the Alto Adige to an appropriate international assembly at a later date.[42]

The task of presenting the Italian reply was entrusted to Carandini. President De Gasperi had wanted to reply personally, but he was obliged to remain in Rome because of the imminent elections, the first since the war, and the constitutional referendum that were scheduled for June 2. Carandini's reply was forthright. He reaffirmed Italy's rights, but welcomed the possibility that future friendship and cooperation with Austria were real possibilities to be sanctioned in agreements once the territorial question had been settled.

Italy, he said, was ready to be invited to discuss claims advanced by those who had suffered under Fascist aggression, but she could not admit obligations that exceeded the bounds of this specific responsibility. It was a fact that Austria had fought with Hitler until the very end of the war, and Italy had found herself in direct conflict with her, fighting for her own liberation after September 1943. Italy was ready to forget the motives that led the Austrian people to share the responsibility for Nazism, but she could not tolerate that after a war of liberation fought against the Austro-German armies, Austria should present demands that would imply a serious diminution of her national integrity.

This declaration did not mean that the Italian government proposed to avoid the discussion, said Carandini. He went on to show that the Austrian demands were without foundation. They could not in any way be called "minor adjustments," implying as they did the annexation of two-fifths of the Alto Adige, with a population totaling 74,000; a third of them, moreover, were a part of the Italian or Latin language groups. In contradiction to Austria's assertion, the loss of this territory would cause serious economic damage, extending to the hydro-electric stations in the area, as was shown by the statistics and data that he had submitted. Further, the guarantees that Austria stated she was prepared to give Italy for the use of these stations could not solve the problem, since a real granting of such guarantees would, in fact, amount to the exercise of Italian sovereignty over the area. Finally, as to the Austrian argument that such a solution would provide more direct communications between the northern and eastern Tyrol, Carandini remarked that the two areas were not economically interdependent and that if the real problem were communications between

Innsbruck and Klagenfurt, the most direct line already ran within Austrian territory.

Carandini's final point was that none of his remarks were motivated by any elements of ill will or resentment toward Austria. Italy wanted to achieve an enduring and sincere collaboration with her and hoped that in the future the customs barrier would no longer keep them apart, but would simply become the political demarcation line. Meanwhile, Italy was ready to facilitate the movement of traffic along the Pusteria valley. Moreover, as evidence of her intentions, Carandini mentioned the measures already enacted by Italy for the benefit of the German-speaking group of the Alto Adige, the draft plans for an autonomy that would safeguard its traditions and interests, and for the projected revision of the 1939 options.

In his summation, Carandini drew attention to Gruber's statement that his government proposed to keep the question open. He asserted that Italy's conciliatory action would be helped only if the state of uncertainty in this area was eliminated. It was causing unrest among the inhabitants and was promoting an artificial opposition between ethnic groups whose proper role was fraternal collaboration, the only means by which general prosperity could be assured.[43]

The three Powers were placed in an embarassing situation by the Italian government's suggestion that the question should be settled speedily and definitively, since after the decision to allow Austria to present her own point of view, they ended by finding the entire Alto Adige question again open before them. The United States, France, and Great Britain were once again reduced to doubt and uncertainty by Gruber's speech, with its clear indication of the rigid line Austria was taking.

In Washington the attitude that seemed to emerge was in favor of making some concessions to Austria for the purpose of definitively settling the problem. For a variety of reasons, the decision to leave the Alto Adige to Italy was to remain firm, but discussion might be possible on the minor adjustments, so long as Austria's claim was restricted and the Bressanone area excluded. Thinking along similar lines also appeared to be developing in Paris. Washington and Paris, however, even according to Austrian sources,[44] found themselves up against unexpected opposition to such a solution from the unofficial representatives of the Alto Adige group and were also confronted with the refusal of the Austrian government explicitly to renounce any further claims.

It was in London that the explanation of this apparent contradiction became clear, and it was Gruber himself who pointed it out during his visit to that city early in June 1946.[45] In essence, he said that the Vienna government had no interest in the minor adjustments: he had responded to the invitation of the Great Powers to formulate Austrian claims only to keep the question open and to be able to again raise it for the purpose of trying to annul the decision taken in London on September 14, 1945. At the same time, the people of the Alto Adige were utterly opposed to the idea of Vienna's annexing only the "minor" area that she had been in a position to claim, as this would have destroyed the unity and structure of their ethnic group, and would have isolated and exposed the inhabitants of the upper Adige and lower Isarco valleys to a speedy Italianization.[46] In these circumstances, the only acceptable solution for Austria, apart from changing the views of the Great Powers, was to withdraw from the discussions and try to force Italy to agree to broach the question bilaterally at a later date. The British government, through its spokesmen, did not support this proposal. Nonetheless, the attempt to bring about this solution was developed in two directions: in the Commons, where prominent members of the opposition became active in seeking to impart fresh vigor to the campaign in support of the annexation of the Alto Adige by Austria, and by Gruber himself, who at once began to sound out the level of effective Italian resistance.

The first move was entrusted to Austria's representative in the British capital, Ambassador Schmid. In a conversation with Carandini on June 4, 1946, Schmid said that he was in no way interested in the minor adjustments; any solution would inevitably injure one of the two parties and relations between the two countries would be compromised. In Austria's case, if decisions were made against her interests, the least she could do was to keep the question open. Speaking personally, said Schmid, he wondered whether in this situation the most expedient solution would not be an immediate acknowledgment of the status quo, with proper guarantees from Italy to the inhabitants of the Alto Adige. The search for a solution acceptable to both peoples should be left for better days.

The following day, Gruber invited Carandini to call, wishing to give official sanction to the proposal put forward by his ambassador and to define its implications. The Austrian Foreign Minister spoke frankly. He said that he understood Italy's motives, he realized that it was impossible for the Italian government to accept substantial territorial sacrifices, and he appreciated Italy's determination to work toward a close relationship between the two countries in the future. He felt, however, that he should make a case for Austria, for hers was equally valid, and even if its basis was different, it sprang from national aspirations that were no less imperative.[47] This insoluble conflict of interests troubled him in particular because of its repercussions on future Italo-Austrian relations. To put the conversation on a more solid level, Carandini remarked that the proposal made to him by Schmid had the great disadvantage of exacerbating the hostility between the two ethnic groups as a result of the ceaseless stream of propaganda that would in such a case continue to flow from Vienna. If, however, Gruber had anything to suggest, he was sure that the Italian government would be happy to discuss it. Gruber said that he did have something to suggest, but that he needed to think it over a little longer before proposing it. By implication, however, he gave the impression that he was thinking in terms of a plebiscite at some future date.

Austria's sounding out of the Italian position can be summed up in a two-stage proposal: Austria was to withdraw her demand for the minor adjustments in exchange for an immediate undertaking by Italy to grant autonomy to the German-speaking minority, and to accept the plebiscite, in principle, as the means of reaching a final solution to the problem at a later date. A proposal such as this might appear to be naive were it not for the fact that Austria's offer to withdraw her demands was not a matter of indifference to Gruber at the time. It is important, in fact, to remember that the Austrian Foreign Minister put forward his proposal in London, the capital from which he could most easily convey the impression that Vienna's cause was just, and the acceptance of the minor adjustments a possibility, if not a certainty. It is true that he had received no explicit assurances at government level, but it would appear not unlikely that Foreign Secretary Bevin pointed to direct negotiations as the solution most likely to turn to Austria's advantage an eventual renunciation of the minor adjustments that neither Vienna, Innsbruck, nor Bolzano was interested in securing. In such a case this could only mean one thing: the intention of putting enough pressure on the Italian government to induce it to accept the proposal. This was, in fact, the purpose behind the mission of an influential Labor M.P. to Rome. As for giving Italy the impresssion that the minor adjustments demanded by Austria, which involved the amputation of a sizable section of Italy's northern frontier, stood a real chance of being accepted, evidence was provided by the debate that took place in the House of Commons on June 5, 1946, and by a proposal outlined to the Council of Deputy Foreign Ministers by the British representative.

On June 8, 1946, news reached Rome of the proposal advanced by Jebb, the British representative before the Council of Deputy Foreign Ministers, to the effect that his colleagues should nominate a technical committee to study the conditions and the possibility of insuring Italy's use of the hydroelectric stations of the upper Isarco valley in the event the region were annexed to Austria. The proposal was accepted and within a few days the committee was at work.

All the arguments that could present a direct agreement with Austria as the lesser evil for Italy had been put forward by the British government, but far from accepting Gruber's proposal, De Gasperi decided that every effort must be made to "set one of Italy's gates back on its hinges." In view of the fact that the Council of Foreign Ministers was about to resume work (June 15), the Italian Ambassador in Washington was instructed to press the State Department to seek to secure the maintenance of the Brenner frontier. The Italian Ambassador in Moscow was at the same time instructed by De Gasperi to warn the Soviet government against Britain's pro-Austrian campaign, in hopes that the Soviet Union would continue to support Italy's position.

The replies of the two ambassadors differed both in tone and content. Quaroni communicated from Moscow that there was no danger of a change of attitude in the Soviet Union: it was not sympathy for Italy that prompted Moscow (all the more so since the recent Italian elections had not fulfilled the expectations of the Left), but a reaction to the excessively pro-Western policies of Vienna. From Washington, Tarchiani could only report that the situation had deteriorated and that whereas no explicit undertaking to support Austria existed, the United States would probably vote in favor of the British proposals. However, in the event of Soviet opposition, the United States would not look upon the cession of the Pusteria valley as a question of principle and would suggest a compromise solution on the lines of direct negotiations between Austria and Italy.

A remarkable change had taken place in the attitude first expressed in March to Rome by the Powers. The reason for the change was the hasty decision to allow Austria, a defeated country and actually a portion of Hitler's Reich, to appear on the conquerors' tribune. Whereas it once had been considered a certainty that the Brenner frontier would remain untouched, not only did this no longer appear true, but there was a distinct possibility that the concept of minor adjustments might be applied on a clearly unjustifiable scale. The only feature that remained unchanged was the attitude of the Soviet Union.

This was the situation on June 24, 1946, when the question of the claims advanced by Austria on May 10 came up on the agenda at the Council of Foreign Ministers. Instead of opening the discussion, Molotov, whose turn it was to chair the meeting, tabled the following resolution:

"After examination of the report of the committee of experts on the question of hydro-electric power, in relation to Austria's requests for minor adjustments to the Austro-Italian frontier and her claims to the north-east sector of Alto Adige (Südtirol), the Council of Foreign Ministers cannot regard Austria's claims as minor adjustments, as they are described in the note of the Austrian federal government."

Molotov followed his reading of this resolution with a proposal that Austria's claims should be rejected *in toto*. Several minutes of embarrassed silence followed, while Byrnes, Bidault, and Bevin consulted with their respective delegations. According to the Russian transcript of the session, they expressed themselves each in the following terms: Byrnes declared that "the United States delegation was able to adhere to the Soviet proposal." Bidault said that "they could not consider the Austrian claims as minor. The Council of Ministers had no reason to deprive Italy of the important electric power existing in the southern Tyrol." Bevin gave "the approval of the British delegation to the Soviet proposal, at the same time expressing the hope that Italy and Austria would reach a reasonable agreement with regard to the use of the railway that joins the eastern and northern regions of the Austrian Tyrol."[48]

The decision of the Council of Foreign Ministers marked a moment of vital importance to the Alto Adige question. The maintenance of the Brenner frontier assumed a definitive character, the Great Powers having agreed on the principle of refusing to modify the territorial settlement reached by the Council of Foreign Ministers, for fear of destroying the delicate balance achieved.

In considering the decision of June 24, 1946, it should be acknowledged that it was not only a consequence of Soviet action but also of the way in which Molotov caused his own point of view to prevail. His handling of the situation was successful also because he realized that when the other three Powers were unexpectedly faced with the responsibility of a final decision, their judgment would be inspired by overall policy rather than by a discussion on matters not connected with the essence of the problems facing the Peace Conference. The task at hand was the definition of the frontiers of a defeated country, Italy, and so could hardly permit consideration at the same time of territorial claims put forward by a country no less defeated, and against which Italy had fought during the two years of her struggle for liberation.

During those decisive minutes this truth prevailed over the statement made at the Moscow Conference in 1943 that Austria had been Hitler's first victim. But, other considerations also carried weight. Granted that an Alto Adige group existed within the Italian borders, and that the conference presented an opportunity for this problem to be considered, any concern for their plight had become superfluous after the assurances given by the Italian government. Not only had the government voiced its promise of a revision of the options in favor of Hitler's Germany taken in December 1939 by the majority in the Alto Adige (thereby indicating that it was disposed to ignore the implications of support for the Nazi regime which the options had revealed) and to allow the people to return to their native land, but the government was also ready to give the minority group in the zone generous safeguard for its language, its way of life, and its development. All this, it should be noted, at a time when the Western Powers, by virtue of the peculiar logic of war and of the common victory with the Soviet Union over Hitler's Germany, had witnessed large portions of the German peoples relinquishing land, homes, and possessions in places where they had been established over many centuries, to become refugees in a land brought to the brink of economic and social disintegration by the violence and destruction of war.

Two other elements made their contribution in these decisive moments: the recollection of Italy's sacrifices in World War I, side by side with France, Britain, and the United States, to insure strategic security to the North by securing the natural geographical frontier with the German world; and the weight of the economic argument against depriving Italy of an area that was inextricably involved with her productive capacity, especially at a time when she had to cope with reorganizing herself after the war.

Finally, an element of expediency in the Western Powers' decision must not be overlooked. By rejecting the Soviet proposal, they would have placed themselves in a less favorable position than Moscow toward Italy on this delicate problem. This was at odds with their oft repeated declarations of friendship, and with the fact that a sympathetic attitude entailed no sacrifice of their direct interests.

[5]

The news of the decision taken by the Council of Foreign Ministers took Vienna completely by surprise. The Austrian government no longer expected to be able to carry out its program without delays: Gruber had been made aware of this during his journey to Paris and his visit to London. But his conversations in the British capitol had led him to conclude that there were solid grounds for hoping that the minor adjustments would be accepted by the four Powers. This would represent a foundation on which direct conversations with Italy in the search for a future definitive solution to the problem might be based.

The feeling that the defeat was now irreversible spread quickly, not only to Vienna but to Innsbruck and Bolzano. There were no reactions, protests or demonstrations comparable to those that followed the decision of the Council of Foreign Ministers in May 1946 to reject Austria's earlier demands. Now both avenues, that of the peace conference and that of direct negotiations with Italy were suddenly blocked.

Gruber's statement to Parliament on July 3 reflected this feeling of profound pessimism. He referred to the government's actions and to his own activities in Paris and London. He pointed out that he had been given positive assurances by France and equally encouraging promises by Great Britain. Even the Soviet Ambassador in Paris had given him the impression that his country was at least uncommitted on this question. From all this, he said, he had felt justified in inferring that the four Powers were favorably disposed toward accepting the frontier adjustments requested by Austria. Instead, he was forced to the bitter realization that the attitude of the Great Powers had changed. He was unmistakably resentful toward both the United States and Great Britain. With reference to the Soviet Union, he said that its opposition to Austria's case would have ceased if Vienna's foreign policy had been Moscow oriented.

After this defense of his personal position, Gruber stated that the failure to get the requested frontier adjustments also ruled out the possibility of Vienna's discussing the entire question with Rome in an effort to find a solution that was mutually acceptable and that might form the basis for a sincere political friendship between the two countries. He concluded by declaring that the Austrian government would be uncompromising in its demands for a plebiscite, and that such demands would be advanced on every possible occasion, both to the peace conference and before any other international body.

The position adopted by Chancellor Figl toward Italy was less trenchant. After expressing the government's support for the action taken by the Foreign Minister, Figl added that he had confidence that the democratic feeling of the new Italy would lead her to a just solution of the controversial problem.

This was the attitude which prevailed in the Austrian capitol after sober reflection and perhaps, also, as a result of advice received from London and Washington. The decision taken on June 24 had definitely removed any possibility that the Alto Adige might become a part of Austria. Consequently, further consideration of the problem had to start from this new fact. If Italy had won the territorial battle at no personal cost, there was no doubt that she had benefited in her case before the Western Powers from her declared intention not only to pursue a liberal policy toward the German-speaking population in the

Alto Adige but also to resume a policy of friendship and economic collaboration with Austria.

Now that Austria had lost the opportunity provided by the Peace Conference and the frontiers of Europe had crystalized, for her to continue obstinately to demand a plebiscite would have meant walking down a blind alley. If, on the other hand, she agreed to the dialogue proposed by Italy, she might gain positive benefits for the German-language group in the Alto Adige and at the same time be able to nourish some sort of hope for the future.

On July 13, 1946, having reached this decision, the Austrian Foreign Minister informed the Italian consul, Gaja, temporarily in charge of the Italian mission to Vienna, that he very much desired an opportunity to reach an agreement with Italy that would permit the growth of a stable relationship and friendly coopera-tion. Gruber said that toward this end he intended to make personal contact with De Gasperi, seeking a broad exchange of views on the problems facing the two countries. If it were preferable, the meeting could take place in Italy before the end of the month. According to Gaja, Gruber had no concrete proposals to offer and had left Italy the initiative, but in replying to a question concerning rumors of economic adjustments and of an eventual future customs union between the two countries, Gruber had replied that such a possibility was not to be ruled out.

De Gasperi welcomed Gruber's move for two reasons: because his own past references to Italy's intentions had not been made for tactical reasons, but in the sincere hope of friendship and because, after the decision of June 24, Washing-ton and London had been quick to emphasize their expectation that the Brenner frontier would become the catalyst for friendship and cooperation between the two countries. In response to Gruber's overture, De Gasperi promptly ordered that the plans for an Italo-Austrian customs union drawn up in 1926 should be examined for the purpose of resubmitting them. As soon as he received a favorable report on this he instructed Gaja on July 20, 1946 to inform Gruber that it would give him pleasure to meet him, but that since he had to hold himself in readiness to attend the Paris Peace Conference, early September would be the first possible opportunity for such a meeting. In order to lay due and proper stress on the lasting character of the Austro-Italian cooperative agreements that both men earnestly desired, De Gasperi continued, he felt obliged to inform Gruber that he felt it was necessary to agree beforehand that there would be no discussion of territorial questions.

On July 24, 1946, when Gruber received this communication, he requested Gaja to thank Prime Minister De Gasperi for the positive reception he had given his proposal and agreed to a meeting the beginning of September, adding that a few weeks' pause would be a good thing in view of a further clarification of the international situation during the interval. With regard to the condition made by De Gasperi that territorial questions should not be included among the possible subjects of discussion, Gruber at once replied that he certainly did not expect

Italy to be disposed to make concessions of this sort. Austria, at the same time, had ceased to harbor any illusions. However, Gruber continued, the Italians must realize that the Austrian government could not do less than again submit its claims, however hopeless, to the Conference of Twenty-One Allied Nations.

These overtures from Gruber to De Gasperi are of great interest, as they reveal with the utmost clarity the starting-point of the negotiations that followed in Paris between the end of August and the beginning of September. This was not Austria's first invitation to start negotiations, but the earlier one had not been accepted by De Gasperi because, with the territorial question still unresolved, he might have exposed Italy to the risk of having to submit to unacceptable compromises. Now that the Brenner frontier was intact, he welcomed Gruber's proposal, since it gave him the opportunity to demonstrate friendly intentions toward Austria in concrete terms. For his part, Gruber agreed that negotiations with Italy should be conducted on the strict understanding that the territorial question would not be raised; that is, that the settlement reached would not again be the subject for discussion. Thus, the decision of the Council of Foreign Ministers of the Four Great Powers on June 24, 1946, leaving the Alto Adige within Italy's borders, was declared by both parties to be, by common agreement, the fundamental premise on which subsequent negotiations were to be based.

A group of M.P.s at Westminister showed less sense of reality and no desire to see relations between Italy and Austria prosper. Ever since the end of June they had been putting their signatures, as individuals, to a motion stating that the proposal to leave the South Tyrol in Italian hands, without consulting the inhabitants, was a violation of the Atlantic Charter. The motion, tabled by the Conservatives, subsequently gained the support of an equal number of Labor members, and in the end totaled 190 signatures.[49]

In this connection, the Italian Prime Minister sent Carandini, in London, the draft project of the Tridentine region, which gave the minority group ample guarantees and safeguards. He also informed the Ambassador that the Prefect of Bolzano had just passed on to him the proposals put forward, at the government's invitation, by a committee whose majority was composed of experts from the German ethnic group, aimed at solving the problem of the revision of the 1939 options. Moreover, in the case of the *Volkspartei*, its leaders had issued a written declaration to the Prefect of Bolzano stating that following the decision confirming beyond question that the Alto Adige belonged to Italy, the party had struck the demand for the right of self-determination from its program. The *Volkspartei* offered its full cooperation, as had the other parties, toward the solution of local problems, as it was already doing in connection with the plan for autonomy. Finally, the *Volkspartei* issued a written statement assuming the obligation to work for an easing of tension among the population of the Alto Adige.

On July 25, 1946, the motion was discussed in the House of Commons. The principal speaker was Boothby, a Conservative. Supporting speeches were made by two Conservatives, three Labor members, and two Independents. The arguments made by all the speakers can be summarized in the following points: the clear ethnic link between the Alto Adige and Austria; the policy of oppression carried out under fascism; the use of intimidation in 1939 to force the German-speaking inhabitants to take up options in favor of the Reich; the influx of 70,000 Italians into the Alto Adige, which had distorted the regional characteristics; failure to consult the people, which was an abandonment of the Atlantic Charter; and, finally, the irrelevance of the strategic arguments in Italy's favor.

Foreign Minister Bevin closed the debate with a speech in which he stated that despite the Atlantic Charter, Britain had been forced by the exigencies of war to accept the new Polish frontiers and the resettlement of no fewer than millions of Germans; that the Italian armistice contained no word of any mutilation of territory and that a more appropriate aim than the concept of independence would be that of interdependence between nations. In his view, the best solution to the Alto Adige question would be a customs union between Italy and Austria. An Anschluss to the south instead of one to the north would be the most desirable way of safeguarding Austria from the dangers that had threatened her and of settling the controversy.[50] Bevin's statement was warmly received by a majority of the House, the number of the supporters of the Austrian cause being restricted to the subscribers to the motion, numbering a third of the House.

About a week after the debate took place, Ambassador Carandini reported his concern that Austrian propaganda in London might spread to other countries represented at the impending Conference of Twenty-One. The possibility was consequently not to be ruled out, as Bevin had stated in reply to a question from Boothby,[51] that the smaller states at the Paris Conference might claim the right to alter the decision adopted by the four Powers by making a move toward assigning the Alto Adige to Austria. De Gasperi wrote Carandini to bring it to the notice of the British government that whereas a third of the House of Commons had rallied to the support of those Germans of the Alto Adige who had themselves fought to the bitter end on Germany's side, not a voice had been raised in support of a similar number of Italians who were under the threat of being handed over to Yugoslavia. No one bothered to insure that they were given the guarantees that were being so insistently demanded on behalf of the Germans; guarantees, what is more, that Italy was perfectly ready to give and give generously.

However, Carandini did not see these instructions immediately, having been called to Paris as a member of the Italian delegation attending the Conference of the Twenty-One. As soon as he arrived in Paris he was requested to seek an explanation of Bevin's remark from the British delegation, and to make it clear that to invite a delegation from the Tyrol to the conference would be an unfortunate step. Carandini complied and in his report on the meeting stated that the British delegation had told him that Bevin was speaking extemporaneously and that the Foreign Office understood him to be referring to the possibility that the Austrian government might be given another invitation to the conference, not that there was any possibility that representatives of the Tyrol would be given a hearing.

[6]

This was the situation when De Gasperi reached Paris to address the Peace Conference. He decided the Brenner frontier should not be mentioned. There were two basic reasons for this. First, in conformity with the decision taken by the four Powers on June 24 in the draft treaty, the reference to Austria in Article 10, which stated that Italy undertook to grant or confirm facilities for transit between the northern and eastern Tyrol, was formulated in such a way as to conform entirely and precisely with the wording of Article 1, which confirmed the frontier to the north of the said transit-line as it stood on January 1, 1938, i.e., the Alpine watershed. Second, what was generally understood in Italy was expressed by the British under-secretary of state for foreign affairs, McNeil, to Saragat, president of the Constituent Assembly, on August 9, 1946. He said that the draft treaty was the product of a compromise, one which the Great Powers had undertaken not to change. It had many negative aspects for the Italians, but one was positive. This, McNeil explained, was the retention of the Alto Adige, however much of a problem the decision had been for the British government.

When De Gasperi spoke at Luxembourg Palace on August 10, however, he decided to mention briefly the provisions for the German-speaking group in the Alto Adige that were in the process of being implemented, both as official affirmation of the Italian government's proposals and to stress the difference between this attitude and the lack of guarantees offered by the draft treaty to the Italians who would find themselves a minority group through the separation of their homelands from Italy. He pointed out that under the proposed revision of the eastern frontier no less than 180,000 Italians would become Yugoslav subjects. He continued, "you have made not the least provision for this group, whereas we are preparing a generous revision of the options for the Alto Adige, and agreement has already been reached on a broad measure of local autonomy, for submission to the Constituent Assembly."[52]

The problem of the Italians destined to become a minority group within the Yugoslav state meant a great deal to De Gasperi because of his own experience as a member of a minority within the territories of the Hapsburg monarchy in Trent. The United States made itself the spokesman for the Italians on this point, and proposed that a clause on the subject should be writeen into the peace treaty for the purpose of securing at least cultural and other basic freedoms for these Italians.[53] Molotov, however, pointed out that it was unnecessary to guarantee rights already contained in the Yugoslav constitution, and the American proposal was defeated.

On August 12, 1946, the British delegation raised the matter of an invitation to Austria to present her point of view before the Conference of the Twenty-

One, taking advantage of the discussion then taking place about inviting Albania and three other countries. It seemed natural to the British delegation, according to the delegate, for all the other countries to be in agreement about the desirability of hearing Austria on the Alto Adige question. When Vishinsky replied that unless the proposal was withdrawn he would ask for the floor, Alexander announced that he withdrew it for the time being.[54]

On August 17, McNeil, who had informed Carandini of his intention, rose to sponsor Austria's request that a delegation from Vienna be allowed to present her point of view "on the question of the line of the Austro-Italian frontier." He based his argument chiefly on the fact that the "future of the southern Tyrol, inhabited largely by German-speaking elements,"[55] was under discussion. In the face of such insistence, Vishinsky intervened with a long circumstantial speech explaining the reasons why the Soviet Union opposed Austria's claim. After making the point that Austria had not justified her claim, Vishinsky continued:

I have to say that McNeil's reasoning has failed to convince us in any way. I do not think it could convince anyone. He says that Austria has a common frontier with Italy. Very good! Austria has indeed a common frontier with Italy. But in the first place, the draft peace treaty presented to the Conference for its inspection contains no modifications to this frontier, or to the *status quo*. As we all know, the draft peace treaty specifically provides for the confirmation of the Austro-Italian frontier as it stood on January 1, 1938. The draft peace treaty, therefore, offers no threat to Austria's interests. Certainly, Austria has claims to put before Italy. But the Soviet delegation considers that to submit these claims to the study of the Peace Conference is inadmissible, since the purpose of the present meeting of the Peace Conference in Paris is to examine the draft peace treaties with the five former enemies, and the Conference is not qualified to consider the claims of any one state against any other state. How could it be otherwise, especially if we do not lose sight of Austria's special situation? It is precisely this that we must continue to bear in mind.

The declaration of October, 1943, issued by the Soviet, American, and British governments ruled that Austria could not evade the responsibility she had incurred through her participation in the War on Germany's side. It added, however, that when the time came to make a final settlement in matters concerning Austria, account would have to be taken of the extent of her contribution to the Liberation. What did this statement imply? First, it raised the question of Austria's responsibility for the fact that she had taken part in the war against the United Nations on the side of Hitler's Germany. In the view of the Soviet delegation, this responsibility is all the greater as a result of the fact that Austria remained on the side of Hitler's Germany up to the end. It is known that Vienna was taken by the Red Army on April 13, 1945, after fierce fighting which caused the Soviet troops heavy losses because of the bitter resistance put up by the Austrian troops, fighting side by side with the Germans and under German commanders. It is also known that the fall of Vienna preceded that of Berlin by only three weeks. This is why we have the right to state that Austria remained by Hitler's side up to the end of the War. And this despite the fact that in their declaration on the subject of Austria, the Soviet, British, and American governments had called upon Austria to break with Germany and come over to the Allied side. They also warned her that she would be held responsible for continuing the fight against the Allies and on Hitler's side. Moreover, despite the

assurances given in three ministers' declaration, that in making the final settlement account would necessarily be taken of the particular contribution made by
Austria to her own liberation, this country made no effective contribution
whatsoever to her liberation, nor did she participate with the Allies in the
struggle for the liberation of all, that is, in the struggle against Hitler's Germany
and its accomplices.

The Soviet delegation is firmly convinced that the Conference should not and
cannot undertake to consider questions outside the framework of the tasks it has
set itself; questions, that is, that have nothing to do with the drawing up of the
peace treaties with the five Powers mentioned above. It is perfectly evident that
the consideration of claims made by Powers not at war with the former enemy
states mentioned does not fall within the jurisdiction of the Conference. Up to
the end Austria remained the ally of Hitler, of the man chiefly responsible for
the War. Austria and Italy were not engaged in fighting on opposing sides. There
is, therefore, no reason why the Conference should now consider the claims
made on one another by these states. According to the British delegation's
interpretation of the question, the Paris Conference has a duty to consider the
claims made on each other by states which were in the enemy camp and in
conflict with the Allies.

Was it for this that this Conference was called? One has only to ask this
question for it to become perfectly clear that it is no business of the Paris
Conference to consider the territorial claims with which the Austrian government intends to take up our time. The Austrian government may—indeed,
clearly does—have claims against Italy, but these have nothing to do with this
Conference. Austria may submit her claims elsewhere, but not here in this
Conference, for which this type of problem lies outside its terms of reference. . . . For, indeed, what right has the Conference to waste its own time
examining the claims that the Austrian government intends to make against Italy
in the southern Tyrol, thus presuming to make use of the Paris Conference in
order to bring about a revision of the 1919 Treaty of Saint Germain? Austria is
scheming to acquire new territories. But my question is, by what rights? As a
reward for her great efforts on the side of democratic countries against Hitler's
Germany? But there were no efforts actually made in this sense, and so the claim
cannot even be raised. This was precisely how the Council of Foreign Ministers
saw the situation when they rejected Austria's claim.

At this point, "to avoid making unsubstantiated statements," Vishinsky
recalled the proceedings of the session of the Council of Foreign Ministers held
on June 24, 1946, and read the extracts from the Soviet minutes that were
mentioned earlier. He then continued:

[Thus] the four delegations unanimously recognized: first, that the substance
of Austria's claims against Italy was non-receivable; second, that they bore no
relation to the minor adjustments that the Council of Ministers was prepared to
allow; and third, that in view of all this, Austria's request must be rejected.
These are the facts of the matter. In the light of all that has been said, I ask the
Conference: on the strength of what reasons, legal, political, and I might even
say political from a moral point of view, should Austria be invited to this
Conference?[56]

Not a single delegate could find a pertinent reply to this question. Cohen, the
American, was the only person to make a fundamental contribution when he
said that if Austria were given the right to be heard, then the decision of June

24, 1946, would be strengthened, not weakened.[57]   A vote was then taken and the result was 15 to 6 in favor of inviting Austria.[58]   This result may at first sight have appeared to have serious implications, in that the majority of the Twenty-One states, despite their inability to make any reply to Vishinsky's arguments, decided to support Austria's request to be allowed to present her own case. This might conceivably give the Austrian government the impression it had scored a success that might in theory enable it to concentrate on obtaining the larger goal it had in view: autonomy for the Bolzano province alone, internationally guaranteed, with a clause to such effect written into the Italian peace treaty.[59]   As a matter of fact, something of considerable importance did take place on that occasion, and this was not in favor of Austria's cause. By agreeing to give Gruber a hearing, the conference was depriving Austria of the opportunity to maintain that the peace treaty was a *Diktat*. The maintenance of the Brenner frontier was to be confirmed by the Peace Conference after all the Austrian arguments had been weighed.

However, this vote made it quite clear to De Gasperi that the Alto Adige was a matter that would continue to demand his attention. It was no longer a question of defending the Brenner frontier, but of facing up to a new Austrian line of approach the possible inherent threats and future developments of which he was fully aware. Consequently, at a meeting held at the Italian Embassy in Paris on August 19, 1946, with his collaborators, he raised the matter by saying that in the face of the hearing granted to Austria, it was necessary to clarify the state of Austro-Italian relations. He instructed Carandini to draw up a memorandum on the subject, to be presented to the conference together with other observations by Italy on the draft peace treaty. He also gave the Ambassador detailed instructions on the next steps to be taken directly with the Austrian delegation.

For the Austrians, too, the way was far from easy. The invitation had been won, but the cost had been heavy. The Austrian Foreign Minister was forced to devote a large part of his speech to an attempt to destroy the negative impression that Vishinksy's words had created on the Austrian question generally. He tried to refute as best he could the accurate records of his country's regrettable past, to which the Soviet delegate had directed the attention of the conference and of international public opinion.[60]

[7]

On the same day as Gruber's speech, August 21, the Italian delegation presented to the Secretary of the conference the memorandum on Article 10 of the draft peace treaty that Carandini had been commissioned to prepare. This paper was to form the documentary basis for Italy's part in the direct negotiations with Austria that were to begin on the following day. The memorandum first considered the problem of facilitating road and rail traffic between the northern and eastern Tyrol. It stated that Italy unreservedly agreed to act in conformity with the provisions of Article 10, as, indeed, she had already declared her willingness to do. The document continued:

In that same statement of May 30, 1946, the Italian government declared that it was firmly resolved that the Upper Adige should become the best possible example of the way in which peaceful and useful collaboration could be brought about between two racially distinct groups, by giving an equitable and liberal solution for a whole series of problems of long standing and by guaranteeing to the German-speaking populations that their traditions and special interests would be safeguarded. Accordingly, the Italian government has already provided for a bilingual system of education, the use of both languages in government offices and documents and the names of localities, and the re-introduction of the German form of recently Italianized names. Pending the forthcoming free municipal elections, the Italian government has appointed German-speaking mayors and town counselors in all communes with a German majority. The Italian government has also decided to admit German-speaking employees in the governmental offices and has instituted special preparatory courses for their benefit.

Following this list of measures which had been adopted, the third point raised by the memorandum was the problem of the options. It recalled that the Italian government "had agreed in principle to revision of the 1939 options, including those who have in the interval formally acquired German nationality." It added that the text of the legislation on the subject, which had already been prepared, was undergoing final revision by a group that included members of the German-speaking community. The aim was to insure that the restoration of Italian nationality was carried out with the utmost tolerance.

In its fourth section, the memorandum referred to the promise of far-reaching administrative autonomy. The Italian government, in collaboration with the *Südtiroler Volkspartei,* representing the German-speaking people's interests, was preparing a bill which it would present to the Constituent Assembly for approval. The memorandum went on to emphasize that

All these arrangements, already in effect or in the process of being put into effect, not only represent a political undertaking entered into by the Italian government in order to solve the special problem of the Alto Adige but also reflect the broader aspirations and views of the Italian people on the general problem of the protection of racial minorities which the territorial *status quo* in the Alto Adige and the cessions suggested for other areas would leave on one side or other of the Italian frontiers. In other words, they correspond to the ideal of protection of human rights which is entirely in the tradition of our Risorgimento. This principle, forgotten by Fascism, has now been revived by the new Italian democracy in a spirit of reciprocity and will be faithfully observed by the Government of the Republic for the defense both of the minorities under its own protection, and the Italian minorities which may be left outside its frontiers.

Finally, the memorandum declared that in its relations with the Austrian people, the Italian government would act in conformity with this principle, safeguarding the minorities. The government would also act "in a broader spirit of solidarity calculated to clear the way for more comprehensive economic agreements," and in spite of the still valid vivid recollection of the struggle that Italy also had had to sustain throughout the war of liberation against Austrian troops actually enlisted in the Nazi army.[61]

On August 22, following instructions received from De Gasperi, Carandini requested an interview with Gruber. There was nothing unusual in this, in that it was Carandini's normal assignment to begin to prepare the ground for Gruber's meeting with De Gasperi. This had been requested by the Austrian Foreign Minister in July and had been arranged by common agreement for September, following a preliminary examination through the ordinary diplomatic channels of the subjects to be discussed.

When the meeting took place, Carandini said that the two main problems to be considered concerned the Alto Adige in particular, and the more general question of future Austro-Italian relations. The two problems were, of course, closely connected and their solutions were interdependent. Carandini then expounded the Italian government's view on these two points on the basis of the memorandum referred to above. In the case of the German-speaking minority in Italy, the adoption of a series of further measures that would insure the greatest degree of security for its ethnic characteristics and the granting to it of a statute of autonomy. As regarded broader Austro-Italian relations, Italy was ready to show her friendship by offering a customs union on the lines suggested in 1926. The establishment of this economic bond would stabilize closer relationship between the two countries, and the Brenner frontier would thus simply become a political demarcation line. Finally, Carandini touched on the problems of the options and of transit through the Pusteria valley, remarking that one could even look upon the latter as a step in the direction of closer economic cooperation.

Gruber thanked him for his exposition and reaffirmed his wish to meet Signor De Gasperi. He, too, he said, was motivated by a firm intention to build a solid friendship with Italy. With regard to the proposed customs union, however, the plan could not be considered for the time being, as it would not be approved by the Allied Control Commission. But the idea could be born in mind for the future. Meanwhile, one could deal with the other matter at hand, the problem of the minority group. Although he was forced for obvious reasons to press for a territorial solution that favored Austria's aspirations, he had little confidence in his ability to alter the decisions already taken by the four Great Powers. The alternative was the maintenance of the territorial status quo, and moving from this base it was gratifying to ascertain that both Austria and Italy were equally sincere in their desire to reach agreements that would guarantee that the arrangements to be made came within the framework of the preservation of minority interests. This matter was of no less concern to Austria in the Alto Adige than it was to Italy in Venetia Julia. Gruber ended by inviting Carandini to call on him again in two days' time to further examine the matter.[62]

On August 24, Gruber sent Ambassador Schmid to the appointment with Carandini. Schmid said that the Minister had charged him to state that the Austrian delegation was about to submit an *aide-mémoire*[63] to the Secretary of the conference, and handed him a copy. This was the text:

The Austrian government still considers that the natural solution of the question of the South Tyrol lies in the consultation of the population of that region on the nationality they desire to have and on the regime they wish to see established in their territory. If the Conference were to find it impossible to adopt this solution which is based on the United Nations Charter, there should at least be some guarantees insuring freedom of economic life and the free exercise of language and cultural traditions for the peoples of the South Tyrol were they to be attached to Italy.

Detailed arrangements should be made between Italy and Austria and these arrangements should form the subject of Italian legislation.

In order that their application shall not wholly depend on the good will of the Italian government in power at any given moment, these arrangements should be guaranteed by the inclusion of a general clause in the Peace Treaty. This clause should embody the following points:

(1) An autonomous administration similar to that granted by Italy to the population of the Val d'Aosta. This administrative unit would include the province of Bozen (Bolzano) and a number of neighboring communes, i.e., the German and Ladin-speaking districts, and not the whole of the territory formerly belonging to Austria, namely the province of Bozen and the Trentino. This would insure that the German-speaking element does not become a minority as compared with the Italian population. At the same time, measures should be taken to annul the effects of the population transfers which resulted from the Hitler–Mussolini agreements.

(2) Up to the present the economic life of the South Tyrol population has been particularly endangered by the systematic immigration, sponsored by the Fascist government in Italy, of Italians from Italy, who enjoyed preferential treatment over the Tyrolese both in the public services and private business. It would obviously be necessary to protect the Tyrolese population against the continuation of this policy, by making any further influx of Italian elements into this region subject to the approval of the autonomous regional administration.

(3) The autonomous region should be put under a special customs regime, whereby both Italian and Austrian imports would be free of customs duties and other dues while the export of South Tyrol produce to Italy and Austria would be likewise exempted from having to present certificates of origin.

(4) An agreement should be concluded between Italy and Austria on the basis of the principles outlined in (1) and (3) above, and this agreement should be filed with the United Nations and its enforcement guaranteed by an international body.

A time limit should be imposed on the Italian government for the drafting of proposals for the enforcement of these guarantees, and such proposals should be so drafted as to meet with the approval of the Austrian government.

In the absence of agreement, the Austrian government should be entitled to appeal to the United Nations, who would decide any outstanding differences of opinion.

Moved by the above considerations, the Austrian government proposes, if the Conference is unable to agree to the plebiscite proposed at the outset, that Article 10 governing the frontier arrangements between Austria and Italy should be amended as follows:

Article 10

Within a period of one year, Italy shall conclude agreements with Austria so as to guarantee, irrespective of the Hitler–Mussolini agreement of 1939, freedom of economic and cultural development by the grant of an autonomous regional administration for the native population of the province of Bolzano and the communes listed in the attached annex, and to insure the free movement of passenger and freight traffic between the said region and Austria so far as concerns produce originating from that region and its normal import requirements.[64]

Besides this modification, the Austrian government requested that Article 14, referring to the safeguard of human rights, should include the following addition: "Italy in particular guarantees to the native population of the Südtirol living north of the Salorno Pass, complete freedom in every aspect of life, and especially cultural freedom without any discrimination, including the right to provide, by means of native elected officials, for all the cultural needs springing from its particular ethnic status."[65]

After reading these proposed amendments, Schmid conveyed Gruber's desire that Italy and Austria should agree on their inclusion in the Italian peace treaty, so that they could present the conference with the *fait accompli* of a voluntary Austro-Italian agreement.

Some of the points raised in this Austrian *aide-mémoire* were also contained in Carandini's memorandum, but the solutions to them were almost all reversed.

Carandini noted the breadth of Austria's claims and their marked divergence from the Italian position. He asked Schmid what weight he should give to the Austrian proposal to draw up a voluntary agreement to jointly present the stipulated amendments, since this agreement might have real meaning and positive results if Austria dropped her principle demand, which concerned territorial claims.[66] Schmid replied that Austria's attitude was a realistic one: Austria wanted to reach a solution that would provide an international guarantee of the autonomy of the German-speaking population of the Alto Adige, and planned, at the same time, to use this as a sound basis for the establishment of future good relations with Italy. An open undertaking to renounce any territorial claims, Schmid continued, *although the prospect of an agreement carried this implication,* would have placed Gruber in an extremely difficult situation as far as public opinion in Austria was concerned; Austria was not yet sufficiently prepared to accept any such solution. Schmid concluded by remarking that although the Austrian *aide-mémoire* could not avoid mentioning the possibility of a plebiscite, it actually went no further than the proposal of international guarantees for the minority group, with no mention of the territorial demands that Gruber had so energetically made when speaking before the deputy foreign ministers on May 30.

Carandini took note of this explanation and then said that in his view there could be no possibility of an agreement on the suggested amendment to Article 14. Italy was opposed to such an article, which sounded offensive to her as a democracy. He felt, however, an agreement on the various questions raised by the amendment to Article 10 might constitute a basis for negotiation. Nonetheless, even here, he considered that no commitment could be given involving limitations in territorial administrative boundaries, since there were many practical reasons that justified the regional union of Trento and Bolzano. In response to this, Schmid was quick to insist on the necessity of confining autonomy to the Bolzano province, to prevent the disappearance of the German-speaking minority into an Italian majority.

On the same day, August 24, Carandini sent De Gasperi an account of his contacts with the Austrian delegation. He remined him that he was due to see Gruber again on the 26th and that a decision must be taken immediately if there were to be time to influence the conference's decision.

De Gasperi considered the situation and agreed to initiate negotiations. In one sense, he did not have total freedom of choice, since Austria had the alternative of putting her claims to the Peace Conference and having them taken into account, whereas Italy was more likely to be called on to express her opinion than to enter into negotiations on the proposed amendments. There was the possibility of her having a treaty with Austria imposed on her with terms and conditions already fixed. At the same time, the idea of direct negotiations with Austria had already been taking shape in De Gasperi's mind. Such a course would give a concrete demonstration of democratic Italy's will to establish sound, friendly relations with her northern neighbor once the territorial dispute was settled. The pursuance of such a policy had been one of the major reasons influencing Britain and the United States to change their attitude on the Brenner problem in Italy's favor. Such a policy also implied, on Austria's side, a spontaneous and voluntary confirmation of the status quo on the frontier. It could also create a useful precedent in Italy's endeavor to secure some sort of guarantee for the Italian minority group that would soon come into being beyond the eastern frontier.

This last consideration further prompted De Gasperi to accept considerable amplification and change in the scope of the direct negotiations in relation to what he had proposed in July. Instead of the Customs Union, the question of legislation for the minority groups was now the main topic for discussion. But quite apart from the force of political expediency, De Gasperi was unwilling to withdraw from negotiations which, provided they were kept within strict bounds, would show the non-Italian-speaking community that the Italian government firmly intended to create for them the conditions that would best enable them to live peaceably within the Italian community.

On August 26, an hour before the appointment for his meeting with Gruber, De Gasperi gave Carandini his instructions: the negotiations proposed by Austria were accepted, since he was not opposed to the principle that protection of the minority group be written into the peace treaty, but on condition that such protection only be outlined in succinct and general terms. The formula might even be fairly similar to that proposed by Austria, but without listing the townships.

On the first point, the Italian Prime Minister felt one could reach an agreement without serious difficulties, since it was a question of general principle and affected Italy actively in the Alto Adige and passively in the Venetia Julia. De Gasperi's position was more reserved when it came to putting the provisions for autonomy into effect; this was quite a separate problem from the first, and could be deferred for discussion at a later date. This difference clearly revealed the precise distinction he made between the part of the Austrian proposals that was acceptable as a basis for negotiation and the part that was not. If it were possible to keep within this limit, then agreement might be reached.

De Gasperi's reply, conveyed by Carandini, was acceptable to Gruber. On the subject of the firm request made by Carandini during his conversation with his colleague, Schmid, that there be no discussion of the amendment to Article 14, Gruber explained that this had been prepared as a last defense in the event the amendment to Article 10 was rejected, and he consequently had no difficulty in accepting the Italian request. With regard to the kind of agreement envisaged by De Gasperi, Gruber said that if Italy agreed in principle to the inclusion of a general protective formula in the peace treaty, on the line of the one outlined in the suggested amendment to Article 10, he was ready to omit the list of townships to be included in the Bolzano province, accepting on this point, too, a general statement deferring the description of the "special area" to later agreement and clarification.

The Austrian Foreign Minister was convinced that he had secured De Gasperi's overall support for his plan to bind Italy to establishing, in agreement with Austria, all necessary measures to safeguard the minority group in the Alto Adige through an international undertaking. He made it clear that he intended to promptly conclude the agreement on the joint presentation by both countries of the amendment to Article 10.[67]

Accordingly, Gruber and Carandini spent their meeting the next day in a close examination of the text of the proposed Austrian amendment to Article 10 of the Italian Peace Treaty. First, Carandini made the point that the expression "without reference to the Hitler–Mussolini agreement" represented an altogether too hasty and unconditional solution to the problem of the options. Italy was prepared to grant her own citizenship once again to those who had opted for Germany but remained inhabitants of the Alto Adige, but those who had emigrated were another matter. Gruber replied that he hoped for a general act of indemnity for those who had opted for Germany but still resided in Italy, and for setting up a racially mixed committee to examine the position of those who had migrated and who now wanted to return, i.e., about half the total number. Naturally, one would have to make sure that the more violent Nazis did not return or again acquire Italian citizenship, and even in the case of the others, their return must be dependent on the practical possibility of their being resettled.

Carandini had asked that the communes covered by the phrase "and the communes listed in the attached annex" should not be referred to by name. Gruber proposed a more general wording, such as "and other ethnically German communes as specified in subsequent agreements." As to the character of regional autonomy mentioned in the suggested amendment, Gruber pointed out that this was a question to be dealt with by him and De Gasperi personally at a future meeting. At Carandini's request, he explained that he would, of course, undertake to ensure that once agreement on the text of the amendment was reached, the *Volkspartei* would willingly collaborate in the preparatory work, although for internal political reasons he had to insist that the proposed agreement over autonomy should be reached between the two governments and not between the Italian government and the *Volkspartei*. Later in the discussion, however, Gruber returned to the subject of autonomy, observing that, in general, he accepted the plan drawn up by the Prefect Innocenti, which the Italian government was studying, on condition that a number of modifications were introduced. These could be summarized under five headings:

1) the autonomous region should be limited to the province of Bolzano and the agreed upon communes to be included within it;

2) the entry of additional Italian elements into the province should be limited;

3) the number of German-speaking officials appointed to the regional administration should be proportional to the German-speaking population;

4) the Region should determine its own taxes, an agreed fixed percentage of which were to go to the state, and be responsible for the local police;

5) the inviolability of the Regional Statute should be guaranteed.[68]

Carandini pointed out that the proposal to include a minorities guarantee clause in the treaty, since it was under discussion, should be general and nonspecific. De Gasperi had made this quite clear to him in his instructions of August 26, and, therefore, the plan could not now be made conditional on specific practical solutions that were still under study with the *Volkspartei,* prior to submission to the Italian Constituent Assembly for final examination and adoption. Gruber did not press the point, repeating that he was satisfied with the commitment in principle contained in the proposed amendment to Article 10: there was no objection to deferring to a later date discussion on implementation of the agreement. Carandini took advantage of the opportunity to stress the practical reasons in favor of the administrative union of the provinces of Bolzano and Trent, but Gruber said that he did not share his conviction.[69]

Apart from the clear statement of Austria's view on the autonomy question, one which was to be very useful to De Gasperi in reaching his own decisions, another important question that came up in the course of this conversation was the problem of options. At the moment this was of almost greater importance to the Viennese government than the problem of autonomy, since it would determine how large and how closely knit the German-speaking minority in the Alto Adige was to be. Here too, even though Gruber had shown his willingness to abandon the formula of unconditional cancellation of the 1939 options, the two sides were still a long way from agreement. Whereas Austria wished to hand over to an ad hoc committee only those cases involving persons who had already moved abroad, the Italian proposal also provided for submission of the claims of those who had acquired German citizenship but had not expatriated, and sought to limit cancellation to the cases of those who had opted for German citizenship but had not definitely acquired it. The Italian proposal, however, also contemplated the possibility of a return to the Alto Adige even for those who had implemented their option and left Italy.

[8]

This would have been the problem attracting most attention during the rest of the negotiations had not Carandini given De Gasperi an accurate, detailed account on August 28 of his meetings with Gruber and the Austrian delegation. From this report De Gasperi realized immediately that the negotiations had strayed considerably from the path he had intended them to follow. It is quite clear from his earlier instructions, that he firmly believed that only a strictly generic provision on the protection of minorities could be included in the peace treaty. The possibility of Italy having to accept a proposal to come to an agreement with Austria in terms that would injure her own national sovereignty was, in fact, an important motive behind the Italian Prime Minister's initiative in responding positively to Gruber's suggestion for direct talks, made in July. Now, however, he had to consider that the approval he had in broad terms voiced in favor of the general international principle of protection of minorities had been taken for specific support of Austria's proposed amendment to Article 10, sanctioning the very situation that he had sought to avoid.

When Carandini had finished his report, the Italian Prime Minister offered his interpretation of the agreement in the following terms:

It is out of the question that the peace treaty should lay upon us an obligation to settle the question of autonomy directly with Austria, since we are dealing with concessions that we can make in the free exercise of our sovereign rights. Therefore, it is preferable to state outright in the treaty the concessions that we have already decreed and approved. We can negotiate with Austria only matters of an international nature, that is to say, the improvement of rail and road traffic facilities across the frontier and the revision of the options for citizenship.[70]

On this general basis, De Gasperi prepared an outline of the proposed agreement, which divided the subject matter into three distinct sections: (1) list of the minority protection provisions adopted; (2) stipulation to grant autonomy; (3) international problems to be agreed upon with Austria.

Carandini worked with Innocenti all the next day on the drafting of Italy's counterproposal. After a final review by De Gasperi, this read as follows:

(1) The Italian government shall adopt provisions in favor of the Province of Bolzano and the multilingual communes of the Province of Trento to safeguard the ethnic character and guarantee the social and economic development of their German-speaking inhabitants.

In particular, German-speaking Italian citizens will be guaranteed:

(a) German-language primary and secondary schools;

(b) equality of Italian and German in public offices and documents, as well as bilingual place names in communes and areas where German is the main language;

(c) the right to revert to the original German form, names recently Italianized;

(d) equal rights for Italian and German-speaking citizens, particularly with respect to nomination to public offices and posts in public administration.

(2) Autonomous exercise of regional legislative and executive powers will be guaranteed to the inhabitants of the Province of Bolzano and the multi-lingual communes in the Province of Trento, even if later included in a wider administrative area. Local German-speaking elements will be consulted on the legislation required for this purpose.

(3) The Italian government is ready to proceed with the revision of the Hitler–Mussolini agreement in 1939, in order to restore Italian citizenship to those who opted for Germany. To this end it will consult with the Austrian government and declares its desire to re-examine the problem in an honorable spirit.

(4) The Italian government will seek Austrian agreement to a convention to facilitate the movement of persons and goods between the Province of Bolzano and Austria, and between northern and eastern Tyrol.

(5) The Italian government is ready to give close attention to any eventual suggestion that might reach it from the Austrian government concerning the subject matter of the present agreement, so that the most satisfactory solution may be reached.

In the preparation of this counterproposal, De Gasperi's aim was to force a decisive change in direction of the negotiations. The importance of this move can be fully appreciated by comparing this text with the Austrian proposals that Carandini had brought to Rome. There were six basic requirements in the Austrian document: to bind Italy to an international obligation to protect minority groups, to be entered into with the signatories to the peace treaty and with Austria; to give Austria the right to a role in determining the text of the autonomy legislation that the Italian government had declared itself ready to concede; to impose straightaway a pro-Austrian solution on what was likely to become the most controversial problem—definition of the territorial boundaries of the autonomous region; to dispose of the problem of the options, or, if not, to establish at once the criteria that Italy would be required to follow in solving the problem in accordance with the concessions that Gruber had indicated he was ready to make; to set up a special international guarantee system; to provide for a political organization such as the United Nations to settle any future "substantial divergence of opinion."

Apart from the last two requirements, which were clearly an attempt to perpetuate the whole Alto Adige question and to bring it up once again before the United Nations at any suitable moment, it is important to note that if these were the subjects concerning which the Italian government was to assume a specific obligation, the documents accompanying the proposal in question divulged at least three other points that revealed the line Austria intended to officially adopt. Her intention was to make perfectly clear the stipulations on which the next round of negotiations were to be based. These assumptions were:

Italian citizens would not be allowed to move freely into the future autonomous region; the autonomous administration was to employ German-speaking officials in a number proportionate to the German-speaking population; the autonomous administration was to have exclusive control of local taxation and the local police force.

Italy's counterproposal rejected much of this plan. The only part of the Austrian draft to remain was an Italian obligation to guarantee the protection of the German-speaking minority. This had been pledged by De Gasperi from the beginning and represented the basic common interest on which the Austro-Italian agreement rested. Apart from this, the Italian counterproposals gave no support to any suggestion of an international guarantee of the measures foreseen by the proposed Austro-Italian agreement.

They declined to accept that the territorial boundary of the autonomous area be restricted to the province of Bolzano, making explicit reference to the possibility of incorporating it in a wider administrative area; they also refrained from establishing in advance the exact lines along which the option problem would be settled. Austria's formula tended to perpetuate the Alto Adige problem on an international basis and to provide means for it to be reviewed on a political level, based on the acceptance of her right to treat with Italy on all question relating to the German-speaking minority. In contrast, the Italian counterproposals presented the principle of a rigid distinction between matters that were the sole concern of the Italian government and those whose international aspect allowed them to be discussed with Austria. The category of strictly domestic matters obviously included all questions concerning autonomy. This not only implied rejection of the points submitted in the Austrian draft but also meant that Italy was making it clear that she was not taking into consideration Austria's other points regarding autonomy, and reserved the right to frame her own independent judgment. She was, however, ready to hear the views of the interested parties within the borders of Italy, namely, the local German-speaking elements, concerning the type of legislation that was required.

The firmness with which De Gasperi distinguished between exclusively domestic matters and those admitting international consultation was further demonstrated by his initial reluctance to accept the inclusion of Carandini's proposal for Article 5, although this article merely referred to the Italian government's readiness to consider any suggestions that might be forthcoming from the Austrian government about the matters that the agreement dealt with. The sole purpose of this article was to demonstrate Italy's desire for friendship with Austria, but De Gasperi later deleted it for fear that it might pave the way for misunderstandings to develop.

On August 31, 1946, Carandini returned to Paris and handed the text of the Italian counterproposals to Schmid.[71] Meanwhile, on August 30, without waiting for Carandini to return with the Italian reply to the suggestion for a joint amendment to Article 10 along the lines described earlier in this chapter, Gruber had sent the Secretary of the Peace Conference an *aide-mémoire* containing the request for the amendment to Article 10 that he had prepared, together with a number of attached statements and documents, pointing to the need for the amendment, should a preliminary request for a plebiscite to resolve the Alto Adige question be refused.[72] By this action the Austrian Foreign Minister protected himself against a possible refusal by Italy to come to an agreement and, at the same time, brought to bear on the negotiations the alternative that Austria had been in a position to take advantage of from the outset.

Nevertheless, Gruber was forced to make a difficult decision, for the Italian counterproposal confronted him with a more delicate choice than he had envisaged. If he rejected the counterproposal, he would be forced to fight hard to have the conference successfully concede the guarantees for the German-speaking minority sought by his government or, in any case, to obtain more than Italy was offering. If he accepted it, he would have to completely abandon the approach the negotiations had followed until then, one that came very close to achieving Austrian aspirations in full, since it was incompatible with the principle of a strict division of the subject matter into two categories, which was fundamental in the Italian proposals and which made itself felt in the lexicon of every phrase. The first alternative carried the greater risk, both because Austria's supporters favored a compromise[73] and because it would lead to a marked deterioration in Austro-Italian relations. Theoretically, it could bring greater dividends, for while the fruits of the second course of action were more certain, they were modest. Gruber's choice of the latter course was supported by his advisors;[74] he intended to avoid the serious risk of failing to obtain anything from the conference and to reciprocate Italy's demonstrated willingness to establish friendly relations between the two countries.

Gruber's abandonment of Austria's principal demands, implicit in his decision to continue negotiations on the basis of the Italian counterproposals took place gradually, word by word, as the talks developed, even when it became clear to him that it would be absolutely impossible to induce Carandini, and even more so, De Gasperi, to accept amendments that would erode the logical basis of the Italian thesis.

On September 1 and 2, 1946, the first discussions on the English translation of the Italian counterproposals[75] took place between Carandini and Schmid. Not surprisingly, the first part of Article 2 was the most debated. Carandini recorded in his minutes:

> Gruber requested that all reference to the possibility of widening the administrative boundaries of the autonomous area be removed from Article 2. I pointed out to him that his preoccupation with the prospect of the German-speaking minority submerged in the vastness of the Trentino-Alto Adige region correspond to ours at the prospect of the submerging of the Italian-speaking minorities (about one-third of the population) confined within the province of Bolzano and the neighboring multilingual communes. The need was, therefore, for a compromise formula which, I pointed out, was happily provided in the Innocenti proposal. This proposed the administrative union of the two provinces into a single region, but at the same time retains their separate legislative and

executive identity. This would give the German-speaking zone all the safeguards it needed to proceed autonomously in matters of particular interest to their ethnic group. The Committee on Minorities holding legislative power, coupled with the division of the *Giunta* into two sections for executive matters created a system offering the German element sufficient freedom from any possible negative effects stemming from the unified administration charged with other matters of a general nature. Gruber had seen the Innocenti plan, but it was my impression that he did not have a very clear idea of the practical value of this duplication within the unified administration of the two provinces. *He now understood my argument and told me he was taking no final decision on the subject.* I added that if he sought a formula that his Parliament would accept, we, too, had to find one that our Constituent Assembly would accept, for the latter was hardly ready to make such a wide range of concessions. *Gruber concluded by saying that he wanted in all honesty not to prejudge the question.* He did not request any formula to be included that implicitly limited the autonomous territory to the province of Bolzano, and asked us to do the same, by making no direct allusion to the unification of the two provinces.[76]

Gruber was clearly beginning to show his basic acceptance of the principle of separation of issues on which the Italian counterproposals were based. This also applied to the problem of the boundaries of the autonomous area. In this case, a matter falling entirely within the Italian government's jurisdiction, the greatest concession that could be made in order to meet Austrian internal political demands and Gruber's own need to show some trace of the resistance he had opposed, was to suppress any reference to a possible broadening of the administrative area involved, leaving the question open. This was how the text of the final Italian counterproposal was designed and this was what Gruber asked for. Further confirmation of Gruber's attitude may be found in that portion of Carandini's minutes referring to the Austrian request for an amendment to the second part of Article 2: "On the subject of consent by the local inhabitants, I pointed out to him that, as this concession was a result of the free exercise of our national sovereignty, we could not go beyond the principle of consultation with local representatives. The formula that he proposed was unacceptable to us because it was too binding. Gruber told me that he was prepared to revise the formula."[77]

On September 3, 1946, De Gasperi arrived in Paris and he reviewed the text drawn up as a result of Carandini's discussions with Gruber.[78] At the end of this detailed revision, De Gasperi found that the only point that might cast some shadow of misunderstanding on the basic principles underlying the agreement was Article 5. He, therefore, decided to purge it and substitute a statement addressed separately to Gruber. For the same reason, he condensed the agreement into three articles, the third of which contained all the points for future negotiation with Austria. Finally, a new version of Article 2 was drawn up along the lines suggested by Gruber, in these words: "The population of the above-named territories shall be guaranteed the exercise of autonomous legislative and executive powers. The nature and extent of these provisions on autonomy shall be settled also in consultation with the German-speaking inhabitants."[79]

The final text, translated back into English with all the agreed modifications and additions and once again discussed at length with Schmid, was presented by Carandini to Gruber on the afternoon of September 4. In accordance with De Gasperi's instructions, Carandini made it clear that there could be no further negotiation. He also said that if Austria were not entirely satisfied with this text, Italy also had reason for dissatisfaction in the absence of an article in which the original Austrian territorial claims were explicitly renounced. Gruber replied that once the question of autonomy had been settled, the German-speaking minority's satisfaction within the Alto Adige would be fully shared by Austria. At this stage, he went on, it was politically impossible for him to refer explicitly to the fact that the territorial claim had been given up, *but he would exert all his authority to insure that this renunciation, implicit if not actually expressed in the agreement, be a historical fact.*

He would give unmistakable proof of his intentions, in a gesture that left no room for misunderstanding: he would present the agreement to the Peace Conference and would refrain from renewing his earlier demand to annex the Südtirol following a plebiscite, which had still been retained in the note to the conference on August 30. All this would be included in the conference records, and would give a clear indication of the Austrian government's attitude toward the territorial problem. He was ready to do all within his power, under the circumstances: he would provide a written statement to De Gasperi, declaring that he considered the agreement as the starting point for improved Austro-Italian relations.[80]

Carandini accepted this offer. Gruber next turned to the subject of autonomy, not in order to contest the substance of the agreement that had been reached, but to once again emphasize the drawbacks he saw in the formulation of Article 2. According to Carandini's minutes, he said:

Gruber asked that the phrase "The structure and circumscription . . ." be modified, since it was too precise and such as to spell serious difficulties for him. He was willing to leave the question of the geographical boundaries open, but he would prefer a more general phrase. He finally accepted my suggestion of the wording: "The frame within which the said provisions of autonomy will apply, will be drafted in consultation also with local representative German-speaking elements." With reference to the consultation with local German-speaking elements, Gruber wanted to remove the word "also." I pointed out that we could not allow this, as it was clearly evident that the Constituent Assembly would first have to be consulted and then, together with the Italian-speaking groups, "also" German-speaking representatives. This was accepted by Gruber. On the English translation of the word "esponenti," we agreed on the formula "will be drafted in consultation also with local *representative* (as an adjective) German-speaking elements.[81]

Now that they reached complete agreement on even this last detail on the form of the text, Carandini, on De Gasperi's instructions, informed Gruber that if the Austrian government saw any advantage in including the agreement in the Italian Peace Treaty (Article 10) (Italy had no particular reason to urge its inclusion), Gruber was free to ask the Peace Conference either to take note of the agreement or to include it in the treaty. Italy would confine herself to communicating the text of the actual agreement to the four Great Powers and to the secretary-general of the Peace Conference.[82]

This conversation ended the final stage of the discussions. The three representatives of the Alto Adige in Paris had been kept informed.[83] They were the ones putting the most pressure on the Austrian delegation, but in the end, faced with the alternative of persisting in an attempt to introduce further amendments to matters already discussed—an attempt which De Gasperi's stand had shown to be quite fruitless—or of accepting the agreement, they were unwilling to run the risk of obtaining nothing.[84]

At the end of the negotiations, De Gasperi received the Austrian Foreign Minister at the Italian Embassy for a full and exhaustive discussion of the various solutions embodied in the agreement and on its general significance. De Gasperi repeated the reasons that had prevented his taking Austria's view on the subject of the geographical boundaries of the autonomous area into consideration and restated his conviction that the formula adopted went as far as possible to meet Austria's requirements. Gruber then repeated the remarks that he had earlier made to Carandini about his need to find a formula to which the Austrian Parliament would agree; confirming that the question of the boundaries of the autonomous area remained open, and that a solution satisfying the German-speaking minority would be fully acceptable to the Austrian government. The conversation next touched on the more general theme of Austro-Italian relations. De Gasperi and Gruber expressed their faith that the agreement they had reached would form the basis for a fruitful and good-neighborly relationship between the two states, capable of expansion within the wider framework of the peaceful development of a Europe freed from the nationalisms of the past.[85]

[9]

At five o'clock on the evening of September 5, 1946, De Gasperi and Gruber signed the agreement. This is the final text constituting the official version:

(1) German-speaking inhabitants of the Bolzano province and of the neighboring bilingual townships of the Trento province will be assured a complete equality of rights with the Italian-speaking inhabitants, within the framework of special provisions to safeguard the ethnical character and the cultural and economic development of the German-speaking element.

In accordance with legislation already enacted or awaiting enactment the said German-speaking citizens will be granted in particular:

(a) elementary and secondary teaching in the mother tongue;

(b) equalization of the German and Italian languages in public offices and official documents, as well as in bilingual topographical naming;

(c) the right to re-establish German family names which were Italianized in recent years.

(d) equality of rights as regards the entering upon public offices, with a view to reaching a more appropriate proportion of employment between the two ethnical groups.

(2) The populations of the above-mentioned zones will be granted the exercise of autonomous legislative and executive regional power. The frame within which the said provisions of autonomy will apply, will be drafted in consultation also with local representative German-speaking elements.

(3) The Italian Government, with the aim of establishing good neighbourhood relations between Austria and Italy, pledges itself, in consultation with the Austrian Government and within one year from the signing of the present Treaty:

(a) to revise in a spirit of equity and broadmindedness the question of the options for citizenship resulting from the 1939 Hitler–Mussolini agreements;

(b) to find an agreement for the mutual recognition of the validity of certain degrees and university diplomas;

(c) to draw up a convention for the free passengers and goods transit between Northern and Eastern Tyrol both by rail and, to the greatest possible extent, by road;

(d) to reach special agreements aimed at facilitating enlarged frontier traffic and local exchanges of certain quantities of characteristic products and goods between Austria and Italy.

De Gasperi then sent Gruber his letter embodying the content of Article 5 of the earlier Italian counterproposals. Gruber sent him the following reply:

Dear Prime Minister,

You have been kind enough to send me today the following letter dated September 5, 1946:

"Following our verbal understanding, I wish to confirm that the Italian Government will be prepared to give careful attention to any suggestions which the Austrian Government may wish to set forth concerning the best solution to be given to the matters covered by Article 10, as in the wording we agreed upon."

In acknowledging receipt of the above letter I wish to add that the fact the Italian and Austrian Governments have been able to submit to the Conference a joint proposal to amend Article 10 is viewed by us with real satisfaction.

I hope very much that our agreement will be the starting point for a fruitful development of Austro-Italian relations in the spirit of friendly neighbourhood and of international cooperation.

I have been deeply impressed by the spirit of impartiality and frankness which you have shown in dealing with these matters and which, I trust, is a good omen for future relations of confidence between the Austrian and the Italian Governments.

I beg you, dear Prime Minister, to accept the expression of my highest consideration.

GRUBER[86]

Once the agreement had been signed, it was only a matter of transmitting it to the Peace Conference so that it could sanction the settlement of the Alto Adige question as agreed to by Italy and Austria. De Gasperi and Gruber then had to draft a letter to Fouques Duparc, the secretary-general of the conference, with copies to the foreign ministers of the four Great Powers. They attempted to include in a single document the simple transmission of the agreement, as proposed by Italy, and the request that the agreement be included in the peace treaty with Italy, which Austria wished to support.[87]

They discussed the preparation of this document all day, but could not agree on the text. The Belgian and Dutch delegations intervened and proposed, at Britain's suggestion, a solution that both Italy and Austria found acceptable since it took the requirements of both into account. Belgium and Holland would support the Italo-Austrian agreement and would request the conference to include in the Peace Treaty with Italy a new article which would state simply that the Allied Powers "noted" the agreement reached by the Italian and Austrian governments on September 5, 1946, the text of which would be appended to the treaty.[88]

On September 20, the delegates of Belgium and Holland on the political and territorial committee for Italy, presented the amendment that was discussed the next day.[89] The amendment was debated at length, for the Soviet Union continued its announced opposition to it, but in the end the proposed additional Article (10 a) was adopted by the necessary two-thirds majority (13 in favor, 6 against, 1 abstention).[90]

The question of including the De Gasperi–Gruber agreement in the Peace Treaty was not raised again by its opponents during the general debate on the treaty with Italy that took place at a plenary session of the Assembly of the Peace Conference on October 7–9, 1946. The only speakers to refer to the Alto Adige problem were those in favor of including the agreement in the treaty, to emphasize their satisfaction that the subject had been dealth with through an agreement between the two parties.[91]

Article 10a was put to the vote at the afternoon session of October 9, 1946, and obtained the 14 votes needed for its adoption as a recommendation from the Peace Conference to the four Great Powers. Norway added her vote; 6 remained opposed, as in the committee stage, and Ethiopia continued to abstain.[92]

The recommendation voted by the Peace Conference was considered by the four Great Powers at the final session of the Council of Foreign Ministers' meetings, held in New York during November and December 1946. Renewed Soviet opposition had no effect. However, some modifications were introduced, which brought the form of the article more into line with the spirit of compromise underlying the original amendment.[93] This was the final disposition of the written proposal submitted to Carandini by Schmid on August 24, and to the Secretariat of the Peace Conference on August 30.

[10]

Before drawing any conclusions, it might be pertinent to consider the many discussions that accompanied the birth of the De Gasperi–Gruber agreement. The public and, still more, the private statements made at the time are of considerable importance in assessing the results of the work done during the negotiations and the depth of the understanding that the Italian Prime Minister and the Austrian Foreign Minister achieved.

De Gasperi was the first to make a public statement. He held a press conference on September 7, 1946, at the Italian Embassy in Paris. His objective was to clarify the causes, content, and implication of the agreement. The two salient points of De Gasperi's statement concerned the interpretation of Article 2, and the significance of the agreement as a whole. On the first point, he spoke as follows:

The Article is naturally couched in generic terms. It refers to autonomous legislative and executive powers, but it does not define which matters will be the concern of the regional assembly or executive branch and which will be those of the State. The Innocenti proposal is very far-reaching, and attributes ruling powers to the regional assembly in matters concerning agriculture, public water-ways, farm credit and mortgages, welfare services, charitable institutions, second-ary roads and railways, tourism, sports, and in particular, elementary and vocational education, supervision over the communes, etc. But the limits of broader or more restrictive regional powers will be set in accordance with the criteria adopted by the Constituent Assembly in establishing the institution of the "region" in Italy generally and the particular demands of the area concerned. The Austrians have a precedent for this in their Diets (Landtage). It is important to realize that the question of whether the region will include only the Alto Adige or the whole of Tridentine Venetia has not been decided. The Govern-ment has undertaken simply to also consult the representatives of the German-speaking population on the matter and to insure at any rate that the German peoples enjoy autonomous legislative and executive powers.

In conclusion, De Gasperi had this to say about the implications of the agreement:

(1) *The effect of the agreement, and its significance are that it provides a definitive solution to the problem of our northern frontier, a solution obtained by agreement between the two parties concerned and including the strongest possible guarantees for the German minority.* The Alto Adige must become a bridge instead of a barrier. Italian democracy will offer its German-speaking citizens the finest opportunity for progress. Italians and Germans in the area must work together on fully equal terms for the improvement of the economy and tourist industry of this fine region.

(2) We have set an example of political good will and uprightness. *May this example serve to provide strength in support of our inviolable claims for national protection for the Italian minority groups which may remain in Yugoslavia.* The experiment of a free, protected minority will demand certain sacrifices of us, but we have done it for the sake of fraternity among peoples: it is an act of faith in a new international way of life.[94]

The political and territorial committee for Italy was scheduled to go into the problem of the Italian minorities in Yugoslavia at the time that discussions were being held on the American proposal to add a fourth paragraph to Article 13 of the peace treaty with Italy, which had now just been put forward as an amendment by the Australian delegation. Its object, it will be recalled, was simply to have Yugoslavia undertake to guarantee the Italians within her new frontiers the enjoyment of fundmental rights and liberties. But this result was not attained.[95]

Despite the moderating action which Gruber and the Austrian delegation endeavored to exercise on them, the two leaders from the Alto Adige, Dr. Otto von Guggenberg and Dr. Friedl Volgger, who described themselves as "plenipotentiary representatives of the Südtirol," sent De Gasperi the following letter: "We are obliged to express our absolute amazement at the statement made by you at the press conference held on September 7, that the question of the territorial boundaries of the autonomous area of the Südtirol laid down in the Austro-Italian agreement of September 5, was not yet resolved. Such a statement, if it were confirmed, could not fail to rouse an official protest and very strong reactions in the Southern Tyrol."

When De Gasperi was informed of this letter, he reacted immediately. In a letter to Carandini, he reminded him that he had not wished to make any precise definition whatever in the agreement as to the territorial boundaries of the autonomous area, and that he had only accepted the final text on the clearly stated condition that it left undecided whether autonomous power was to be guaranteed to an area with a German majority or to one of broader compass. Whatever Austria might have said to Messrs. von Guggenberg and Volgger, Gruber could bear witness to this. He ended by stating that any attempt to distort the sense of the understanding endangered the agreement itself. Carandini met Gruber on September 16, 1946, to inform him of De Gasperi's warning. Gruber replied in the clearest of terms that there was no doubt that the question of the territorial extension of the area had been left open for solution as the Italian government thought best, after consultation with local representatives, in a spirit of harmony that he personally pledged himself to further loyally in every way at his command. He regretted the letter sent by von Gruggenberg and Volgger, and begged Carandini not to pay undue attention to it.

A few days later, on September 20, in an interview in a Parisian newspaper, Gruber stated publicly that there would be no discussions with Italy about the limits of the territorial extension of the area that would be granted autonomy: "It has been agreed with De Gasperi that the statute of autonomy is to be drawn up in consultation with the people involved. Conversations are to be held with persons considered to be representative of the Tyrolese people. We have no doubt that these people will succeed in coming to an agreement with the Italian Government on the boundaries of South Tyrol and on the other matters involved."[96]

Apart from certain ambiguities in the terms used, Gruber's statement is a public recognition of the fundamental principle governing the agreement, namely, that the matters contained in the first two articles—among which is that of the territorial extension of the autonomous area—lay within the exclusive jurisdiction of the Italian government.

The Alto Adige representatives in Paris did not react on this occasion. The previous day, Carandini had followed Gruber's advice to invite von Guggenberg and Volgger to the Embassy, talking to them at length on every aspect of the agreement, so as to resolve any possible doubts. When they had had the matter explained to them, von Guggenberg and Volgger agreed that the territorial boundaries should remain an open question, since it was an aspect of the autonomy that the Italian government proposed to extend in the free exercise of its national sovereignty. In conclusion, they stated that they were prompted by the desire to cooperate and they were able to consider the possibility of an administrative union of Bolzano and Trento on condition that effective safe-guards were created within it for the rights of the German-speaking minority. Carandini then gave them a detailed description of the main features of Inno-centi's proposals. He pointed out that the plan made specific provision for exceptions to the administrative unity of the *Regione Tridentina* (Bolzano and Trento) where legislative and executive matters were concerned, so that the German-speaking minority was guaranteed an effective and broad autonomy in all matters that concerned their particular requirements. Von Guggenberg and Volgger replied that the Innocenti plan could in general terms be accepted, apart from certain modifications that they would like to see; in particular, they mentioned the matter of fiscal autonomy, the designation of Trent as the only capital, and the inclusion in the general autonomous area of the three Ladin communes in the province of Belluno. In any case, they declared themselves willing to discuss even these subjects sympathetically, and took their leave, promising that they would go back to Italy determined to cooperate in finding a fair solution and confident that their good will would be appreciated and reciprocated.[97]

It is interesting to set the outcome of this conversation in context to the later polemics about the extent to which the representatives of the German-speaking minority freely accepted the statute of autonomy, when the question was raised in a letter written by Ammon and von Guggenberg on January 28, 1948. It is evident from the conversation that this was no extemporaneous agreement extorted after a succession of refusals and protests, as it was subsequently interpreted to be.[98] It was expressed after full consideration of the situation. They reached an understanding when Carandini explained matters to them in their conversation on September 19. At that time, von Guggenberg and Volgger affirmed that they accepted the principle of the Trentino–Alto Adige region put forward in the Innocenti proposals and promised their cooperation in finding a fair colution.

A final meeting between Gruber and Carandini took place on September 24 at a dinner given by the Austrian delegation in Carandini's honor, marking the renewal of friendship between the two countries with the signing of the agree-ment to their mutual satisfaction. Here the spirit and meaning of the agreement were referred to frankly and freely. Carandini reminded Gruber, in general terms, that the agreement that had been signed was unilateral only in its outward form. Italy had undertaken to grant autonomy without claiming from Austria an explicit renunciation of her territorial demands, because of her conviction that this renunciation was clear from the fact that Austria had abandoned all her earlier claims made to the Peace Conference, and that the attachment of the agreement to the peace treaty set an international seal on the Austro-Italian question. The item had been raised at the Peace Conference in the form of a territorial claim, and was closed, in the same setting, by the granting of autonomy to the minority group involved. The reason for this was to circumvent the creation of any difficulties for the Austrian government in the face of a nationalist public opinion. Carandini then asked what Austria's response would be.

In his reply, Gruber recalled a statement of his made during the negotiations, that once the question of autonomy was settled and the aspirations of the German-speaking minority were thus satisfied, Austria would then consider the matter closed.

On the subject of the territorial limits of the autonomous area, Carandini asked Gruber to confirm his statement that there was no shadow of doubt that the question was understood to remain open, and that it was left to Italy to solve it in the free exercise of her national sovereignty, subject to her under-taking to carry out the consultations specified in the agreement. Carandini did this in order to be able to make a last exact statement of the position to De Gasperi at the end of his mission. Gruber reassured him in every way on these points. He repeated that all decisions lay with Italy, and that he would do all in his power to help things. He only asked that for a time at least, he should be allowed to avoid the embarrassment of having openly to acknowledge, in the face of his own nationalist public opinion of various persuasions, an obligation which, though clear from the formula used ("the frame within which"), he had accepted for this very reason, at the same time relying on the discretion of the Italian government.

These remarks fully confirm the interpretation of the wording of Article 2 of the agreement, which was later claimed to be controversial but the significance and implications of which Gruber and the Austrian delegation found perfectly clear at the time, as well as during the entire course of the negotiations. More important still, they pinpoint the real element of weakness inherent in the agreement: the failure of Austrian public opinion, not just the nationalists as Gruber declared, to appreciate the great achievement that the agreement consti-tuted for the German-speaking minority in the Alto Adige. In a Europe con-vulsed by the horrors of war, where new boundaries were being imposed with almost uniform inhumanity, these people alone were assured a peaceful exis-tence in the land to which they had come centuries ago, free from any threat to their ethnic and cultural traditions. This failure to understand is comprehensible in view of Austria's recent past history of dictatorship and nationalism, know-ingly entered into and ended only as a result of the military defeat of Hitler's Reich. Austria had not suffered the travail of a war of liberation that would, as in Italy's case, have made her recognize her past errors and seek to redress them. It would necessarily be some time before the majority could understand the new spirit of democratic international coexistence on which the agreement was founded.

The accuracy of Gruber's remarks was proved during the debate in the

Foreign Affairs Committee of the Austrian Parliament on October 1, 1946. The Foreign Minister was forced to appear almost as a defendant, and though his action was approved, a resolution was passed that included the following statement:

The Committee . . . expressed its regret that no way had been found of affirming before the Peace Conference the rights of the people of South Tyrol to freedom. . . . There is no evidence that the agreement with Italy will have the approval of all the people of South Tyrol, and there are many points to be clarified before it can be considered as a provisional solution. . . . Austria's attitude by no means implies that she renounces the Austrian State's inalienable rights over the South Tyrol. The Committee expresses the hope that improvement in the world situation will give the peoples of South Tyrol the opportunity to express their own view of the national ties that bind them. The Committee is of the opinion that the principle of self-determination is the only form of lasting solution to the problem of the South Tyrol that Austria could accept as just and adequate.[99]

All these statements, accompanied by the acceptance of the agreement, show how greatly the actions of the Austrian government were hampered by its own public opinion, and how the members of the two majority parties were forced to bow to it, adopting an equivocal stand. On the one hand, they approved the agreement and on the other, they gave the country the impression that they were rejecting its contents.

Disturbed over what effect this resolution might have on the Italian government after so many assurances, Gruber summoned the acting head of the Italian mission in Vienna, Gaja, on October 2. He asked him to make it clear to De Gasperi that the wording of the resolution was the result of an understandable preoccupation by the majority parties with the electorate, but that the Austrian government intended to remain faithful to the spirit of the agreement that it had reached with Italy.

[11]

The controversy surrounding the early stages of the De Gasperi—Gruber agreement caused its practical application to pass the test of time, from which it emerged with the clarity of its meaning substantially reaffirmed. At the same time, however, these discussions made it clear that the agreement could only be applied constructively to the extent that both parties committed themselves honestly and sincerely to the democratic principles of international coexistence that had inspired its framing.

Public opinion in Austria and in the Tyrol made it immediately clear that it was not yet ready to make its contribution to putting such principles into effect. But if this constituted the negative aspects of the problem, perhaps even the cause of it, the positive side was of considerable importance. In the first place, neither Gruber nor his supporters ever wavered, even at the height of the dispute, in their desire to prove to the Italian government their firm intention to stand by the agreement subscribed to. Second, the statements made and the assurances given with this purpose in mind provided a clear point of reference to confirm unequivocally the nature and meaning of the obligation undertaken. This is a point to which due weight should be given in order to assess the inconsistency of subsequent alleged differences of interpretation of the meaning of certain clauses among the signatories. If there was a moment in which it would have been possible to bring up reservations that could be exploited when the agreement was put into effect, that moment coincided with the weeks following the initialing of the agreement. Gruber and the Austrian government were then fully aware of the difficulties that might in the future hinder an implementation of the agreement in accordance with the content and meaning given to each clause, jointly agreed upon, during the negotiations in Paris. One need only recall Gruber's unambiguous words in his letter to De Gasperi on September 5: "I have been deeply impressed by the spirit of impartiality and frankness which you have shown in dealing with these matters."

The reconstruction of these negotiations abundantly reveals the points on which Italy and Austria were clearly and unmistakably in agreement. A brief summary need only identify the most important ones. Italy pledged herself to ensure that the German-speaking minority enjoy equality of rights with all other Italian citizens, together with a special protection that would allow it to retain its particular cultural and traditional characteristics. On her part, Austria at the same time pledged that she had an obligation to recognize that it was reserved exclusively to Italy, in the free exercise of her sovereign rights, to formulate and pass the required legislation to bring this about. This obligation applied to all matters contained in the first two articles of the agreement and, therefore, included the matter of the territorial boundaries for the autonomous area.

A revealing aspect of the reconstruction of these negotiations has been that the origin of the expression "the frame within which," lay not in Gruber's failure to accept the principle that the autonomous region could include the whole of *Tridentine Venetia,* but in the Austrian government's need for a formula that would reveal to the extremist movements within its own country the territorial limits that the Italian government intended setting. This, too, developed at the very time that Austria completely renounced her claim to take part in defining this autonomy and, in abandoning such claim, recognized that the problem would be handled by the Italian authorities in keeping with the broader scope of Italy's interests as a whole.

This was not all that Austria renounced. She also accepted the withdrawal of all the claims she had advanced, directly and indirectly, in her note presented to the Secretary of the Peace Conference on August 30, and which found no place in the Paris Agreement of September 5. However, she officially abandoned the chief claim on which all the others depended: the demand for a plebiscite. Reference has repeatedly been made to the fact that direct negotiations between Rome and Vienna began after the decision adopted at the meeting of the Foreign Ministers of the Four Powers on June 24. These made clear that the Alto Adige would remain within Italy's frontiers, and followed Gruber's explicit acceptance of this decision as a preliminary condition to starting Austro-Italian negotiations. The bilateral nature of the obligations contained in the Paris Agreement of September 5, 1946, depended upon Austria's abandoning her claim. This meant that if at some future time Austria were to seek to bring up the problem of revising the Brenner frontier, on the basis of international legal principles, the whole agreement would collapse because one of the parties, i.e., Austria, had violated her pledge.[100] By depositing the De Gasperi—Gruber agreement with the Secretary of the Peace Conference, the renunciation by Austria of any territorial claim on the Alto Adige received its formal sanction.

In this way, the Paris Agreement represented Austria's freely expressed recognition of the Brenner frontier. The absence of any such free recognition before this time makes it noteworthy. In 1939 the German government had expressed it on behalf of the people of the *Ostmark*. But on this occasion it was the Austrian government itself that had freely acknowledged it. At the same time, confirmation of the Treaty of Saint Germain came from the Peace Conference, after Austria's claim had been fully discussed both by the foreign ministers and the plenary Assembly.

Attention has already been drawn to the fact that in order to continue the bilateral negotiations, Gruber had to give up the two Austrian proposals that had been designed to keep the Alto Adige problem open, or else to reopen it when the time seemed appropriate, at the international level. These were: the special international guarantee and the agreement to refer differences of opinion to an international political body such as the United Nations. Assuming that Gruber undoubtedly made the two unusual proposals at least with the full knowledge of his two advisers from the Tyrol and the Alto Adige, the decision taken on September 4, 1946, also as a result of advice from the Alto Adige, not to insist on these dubious devices but to accept De Gasperi's plan *in toto,* assumes an obvious importance.

The Paris Agreement of September 5, 1946, is evidence of the determination of the democratic Italian government to make every effort to follow a liberal policy—originally promised after the Brenner frontier was acquired, but later abandoned—in order to ensure the inhabitants of the Alto Adige a peaceful existence.

After the policy of denationalization pursued following the March on Rome and after the options policy initiated in 1939, this was the third solution possible: a solution consistent with democracy and international coexistence. It was also the most difficult to achieve. But perhaps it was worth the effort to make it part of Italy's program because it proved to her and to others that Italy's intentions were above suspicion, and because it was a touchstone to the sincerity of others.

Chapter V

Diplomatic Aspects
of the Application of
the De Gasperi–Gruber
Agreement

[1] Italo-Austrian conversations on the option revision problem. The Austrian point of view set out by Schoner in January 1947. The Austrian note of March 31, 1947; Italy's reply of May 28. The Austrian note of June 26, 1947; the Italian reply of September 9 and the end of the first phase of the discussions: the Austrian note of September 19, 1947. The discussions of November 13–22, 1947, and those foreseen by the Paris Agreement. Gruber's statement of January 31, 1948. [2] The Austrian stand as to the territorial extension of the autonomous area. Gruber's letter to De Gasperi of June 25, 1947, and the Italian Prime Minister's reply on July 14. De Gasperi's speech of July 20, 1947, confirms Italy's obligations to the Alto Adige minority. Reactions of the *Südtiroler Volkspartei* to the draft statute of autonomy. Gruber's letter of January 10, 1948, and the last consultations with Alto Adige representatives. The Alto Adige and the Austrian governments agree to the setting up of the *Trentino-Alto Adige* Region. [3] Pressure exercised by the Austrian government to induce the Alto Adige optants to reopt for Italy. Decisions taken by the Austrian government in November 1948 and on May 14, 1949. Italo-Austrian clarifications on March 28, 1950, concerning the law on the revision of options.

[1]

The Paris Agreement of September 5, 1946, was put into effect, in so far as concerned matters requiring consultation or agreement with Austria, with discussions on the problem of the options. The subject was raised by the Austrian foreign minister, Gruber, on January 18, 1947, even before the Italian peace treaty had been signed, in the course of a conversation with Coppini, the Italian political representative in Vienna. Gruber did not go into the matter in detail, but simply drew Coppini's attention to the problem of those who had opted for German citizenship, and suggested that the Italian representative might contact the Ballhaus for a preliminary exchange of views on the subject.

Schöner, who was in charge of the special foreign ministry branch dealing with the Alto Adige question, personally renewed the invitation to Coppini to discuss this particular problem a fortnight later, while Gruber was away. He

121

hoped that a friendly, unofficial discussion would lay a firm basis for the subsequent official conversations that the Minister himself could hold upon his return, with the possibility of an eventual visit to Italy to conclude them. Schöner said that Austria was willing to acknowledge that the revision of the options for the inhabitants of Southern Tyrol who had taken German citizenship but had not emigrated should be considered as a purely internal Italian affair. However, his government was interested in the earliest possible repatriation to Italy of those who had taken German citizenship and moved into Austrian territory. A majority of these now wished to return. As to procedure, Schöner expressed the opinion that the options should not be reviewed on an individual basis, but that the right to return to South Tyrol should be granted to whole categories of people, and that Italy should simply confine herself to examining certain special cases individually. Schöner justified this procedure on the grounds that these emigrants must be considered as displaced persons, who should be given every assistance to return to their country of origin.

This exposition by the Austrian diplomat made it clear that the Vienna government had returned to reaffirming its original claim for a general act of amnesty for those opting for German citizenship. Such a claim had already been advanced in the draft of the Austrian amendment to Article 10 of the Italian peace treaty and rejected by Carandini. It had subsequently been modified on August 27 by Gruber to mean that the amnesty applied only to those who had not emigrated, and that an examination of the reoptions was to apply only in the case of those who had emigrated to the Reich. In fact, the declaration now being made that the question of the nonemigrant group was the sole concern of the Italian government was of little value indeed, since Rome had already decided that in all but special cases Italian citizenship would be granted for the second time to all who found themselves in this situation. The request for the emigrants to return to Italy en masse was a request for a general amnesty for the only category of persons to whom the Italian government was not disposed to make an indiscriminate concession of the right to change its original option. The most striking feature of Schöner's suggestion was the fact that the Austrian government's approach to the problem was singularly reminiscent of Himmler's approach to the same problem in 1939, when the head of the S.S. had proposed a mass transfer of the German-speaking group without the least concern for individual wishes.

Even setting aside the question of respect for the freedom of the individual, this procedure would lead to the compulsory acquisition of a condition as personal as citizenship. This was clearly unacceptable on two counts: Italian law made no provision for granting citizenship collectively, and this method would allow undesirable foreigners to enter Italy without any controls. A final important point was Schöner's comparison of the emigrant group to displaced persons. This corresponded neither to the legal nor the factual aspects of the matter, besides engendering suspicion that the Austrian government might be proposing to exert great pressure on the former emigrants to persuade them to again opt for Italy, and to threaten recalcitrants with the loss of citizenship.

However, as Italy reflected on Vienna's singular approach, its chief concern was the realization that the Austrian Foreign Ministry appeared more interested in creating a situation for real negotiations leading to a new agreement between the two countries rather than in initiating a simple consultative procedure on the lines clearly stated in the Paris Agreement of September 5, 1946. Accordingly, Coppini was sent instructions to point out to the Foreign Minister that the conversations being planned were to start from the assumption that the De Gasperi—Gruber agreement did not envisage reaching further agreement on the subject of the revision of the options but only a consultation between the Italian and Austrian governments, and that the final settling of the matter should, of course, rest with Italy. Gruber agreed that this was entirely the case and, consequently, said he was prepared to have the conversations follow the line indicated by the Rome government. The following procedure was agreed upon: the Austrian government would identify the points upon which it wished to draw the attention of the Rome government for possible eventual modifications; the Italians would then communicate their relevant observations. In this manner, consultation would be particularly comprehensive throughout and go considerably beyond merely taking note of the Austrian point of view.

Once the conversations were aligned to the terms provided by the Paris Agreement, the procedure was put into effect with the presentation on March 31, 1947, of a memorandum in which the Austrian government made a detailed examination of the Italian plan for the revision of the options. There were two points which the memorandum was particularly interested in modifying: the first concerned the demand, which Schöner had already made, for equalization of status for former South Tyrol inhabitants who had opted for and emigrated to Germany with the naturalized Germans who had continued to live in South Tyrol. Members of both categories should automatically be granted a renewal of Italian citizenship along the lines laid down by the Italian plan for the second category only. The second reservation concerned the wording of Article 5 of the draft of the Italian bill, which listed the grounds for refusing the renewal of Italian citizenship. According to the Austrian government's memorandum, such cases should be restricted to those in which the applicant had previous criminal convictions, and should not include those in which the applicant had held "important" posts in German institutions, organizations, or departments—along the lines of the laws in force in Germany and Austria for denazification of the state—especially during the period of the German occupation.

The communication also demanded that provision should be made in the Italian draft to allow the return of the Austrian citizens, the so-called "ten thousand," who had been prevented from living in South Tyrol in 1939 and obliged to move into the Reich. Attached to this memorandum, which was presented with the explicit reservation that the Austrian government would subsequently add further points, was a note requesting that the Italian government should allow the immediate repatriation of a first group of 10,000 optants to be chosen from lists drawn up by the Innsbruck regional government or by the federal government. Coppini quickly rejected this request because it was tantamount to once again demanding the mass return, even if only for a portion of the optants, on the principle of collective reoptions that the Italian government had already rejected. The Austrian Foreign Ministry then implied that Gruber would probably allow the suggestion to drop, as long as Italy gave special assurance in favor of the optants who had returned to Italy secretly up to that time.

On the whole, the Austrian government's reservations and requests were aimed at securing repatriation into Italy and renewal of Italian citizenship for all those who had opted for the Reich, with no exceptions. The full numerical complement of the German-speaking group in the Alto Adige would be restored and would also include, as far as residence in the area was concerned, those 10,000 Austrian citizens who had, in truth, indeed poorly repaid the liberal concession granted them in 1919 of the right to live in Italy. The same intent of promoting the return to the Alto Adige of those elements who would have contributed least to the peaceful living in mutual tolerance within the Italian frontier lay in the Austrian government's demand that no objections be raised to the return of those who through their personal behavior had most obviously demonstrated their Nazi loyalties and their aversion toward the Italians living in the community.

In weighing the reservations and demands contained in this Austrian memorandum, the Italian government was guided by two main considerations: faithfulness to the principle underlying the draft, which in turn was based on the Italian legislation on citizenship, according to which all optants must make an individual statement of their desire to renew their Italian citizenship; and determination that the small group of naturalized Germans, whose behavior in the 1939–45 period had been such that it would be foolhardy to believe that they would fit peacefully back into community life in the Alto Adige, should neither remain nor return there.

In May 1947 Italy informed the Austrian Foreign Ministry that whereas it was not possible to introduce into the plan for the parity of reoptions of emigrant and nonemigrant naturalized German optants, since in the case of the first group Italy had to insist on investigating their conduct during their residence outside the country, the situation of those who had returned to Italy secretly would be given benevolent consideration. They would not be given parity with naturalized Germans who had remained in Italy, as Austria had demanded, for this would constitute an unjustified amnesty for perpetrators of an illegal act, but their applications for reoption would be considered, in the order of the submission, before those of reoptants resident abroad. No consideration could be given, however, to the proposal to limit the cases of those excluded from renewal of citizenship with respect to those already listed in

Article 5 of the draft. On the subject of the request that the 10,000 Austrians repatriated in 1939 be allowed to choose to return to Italy, the Italian reply stated that this question was separate and distinct from the matter under discussion and could only be settled elsewhere.

The Austrian government was not satisfied with the Italian reply, presented on May 28, 1947, and did not conceal its displeasure that the draft plan for the reoptions had not been modified at every point to bring it into line with Austria's requirements. Coppini pointed out that the memorandum dated March 31, and the discussions that followed it, had revealed both a feeling of distrust toward Italy and a definite desire on Austria's part to return all the optants to the Alto Adige, with the single exception of war criminals and convicts, ignoring the fact that many of the optants, both before and after the options, had shown a deep-seated anti-Italianism, implying an innate desire, once they returned to Italy through the generosity of Rome, to pursue policies aimed at separating the Alto Adige from Italy, or, at least, of fomenting conditions that would favor this separation, in anticipation of more favorable circumstances. Coppini also pointed out that despite so many demands, not only had the Austrian government never uttered a word assuring Italy of the loyalty of the groups scheduled to reenter the Alto Adige, but in the meantime there had already been statements reaffirming Austria's right to the Alto Adige.

On June 26, 1947, the Vienna government voiced its dissatisfaction in a new memorandum, presented in reply to the observations of the Italian government. The solution previously suggested in the memorandum of March 31 was proposed once again. However, notice had been taken of Coppini's firm words and, in tendering him the Austrian document, Minister Leitmeier said that Gruber had authorized him to state that if the question of the options was settled to the satisfaction of the Vienna government, the latter would in turn assure the Italian government of its conviction that those opting for Italian citizenship would return to the South Tyrol as loyal citizens. Though the formula proposed by Gruber was not entirely suitable, the fact that he had accepted the idea of issuing a statement at the close of the consultation could be taken as a step forward. At the same time, one element prompting this gesture was naturally the prospect of putting pressure on the Italian government to secure the modifications to the draft text on the revision of options that Austria sought.

Italy's reply to the June 26 memorandum, drawn up in August, was presented by Coppini on September 9, 1947. It consisted of a long note that once again explained why certain points and demands advanced by Austria could not be taken into account further. It clarified all the aspects of the draft revision of options and underlined their absolute conformity with the undertaking assumed by Italy to settle the question in a spirit of justice and understanding.

Vienna, however, had a different point of view. In a note dated September 19, 1947, the Austrian Foreign Ministry informed Italy that, despite the results already achieved, the notes exchanged up to now had left certain problems unresolved, problems on which no further progress could be made in writing, beyond the present situation in which two divergent points of view had been clearly stated. It was consequently opportune, the note concluded, to try by means of personal contact to achieve that level of understanding to which both parties aspired. When transmitting this note, the counselor at the Ballhaus, Kripp, allowed it to be clearly understood that in the event of a failure to reach agreement over the options, the Austrian government proposed "to resume its freedom of action." This implied raising the entire question of the Alto Adige once again, as was confirmed promptly afterward in a speech, irredentist in tone, delivered by Renner, the federal president, in Innsbruck on September 21, 1947.[1]

The note of September 19, and the acts that accompanied it, betrayed a new Austrian attempt to exceed the terms of the agreement of September 5, 1946, similar to the one which had already been made early in January 1947. At this time, however, and more seriously, it took the form of a threat, actually as inadmissable as it was impracticable, to claim that Austria would no longer consider herself bound by the De Gasperi–Gruber agreement. It was inadmissible because an international agreement can only be rescinded if the other party to the contract breaks or fails to carry out its obligations; impracticable because the Vienna government was well aware that such a justification would not bear examination, inasmuch as it was inspired only by a conscious bad faith in its interpretation of the agreement and by the lure of extremist nationalism, to whose tenets a part of public opinion and some of its leaders had fallen prey.

The reappearance of these disquieting signs presaged unavoidable obstacles in the path of Austro-Italian relations, especially if the same negotiating tactics should be resorted to in further meetings between the two countries, a forecast that was unfortunately from time to time to reveal itself justified in the years that followed. Nonetheless, Italy faced up to this situation with notable calm, but with no less firmness. The new Italian foreign minister, Carlo Sforza, informed the governments in London and Washington of Austria's improper behavior. He then once again spelled out for Vienna Italy's obligations regarding options under the De Gasperi–Gruber agreement, to the effect that the Italian government, in reviewing the question of options, was only to consult with the Austrian government, not under an obligation to reach agreement with it. The contemplated revision was, in fact, not the implementation of an international agreement between Italy and Austria, but a law enacted by the Italian state in the exercise of its sovereignty. Should this be clear to the Vienna government, Sforza continued, the Italian government would not have refused the further exchange of views by means of personal contact, as proposed in Austria's note of September 19. However, confronted with this new evidence of Italy's good will and desire for the broadest possible consultations on the problem of options, Vienna had not only failed to respond with an equal display of good will, but had even gone so far as to issue official statements such as the one now made by President Renner. *The Austrian federal government should, consequently, always bear well in mind that the basic premise of the De Gasperi–Gruber agreement was Austria's renunciation of territorial claims in the Alto Adige. This renunciation was attested to by the transmission of the agreement to the secretary of the Peace Conference.* Further, it was essential for the Austrian federal government to confirm its intention of respecting the agreement by providing precise and explicit assurances that the former inhabitants of the Alto Adige who were readmitted into Italy would act as loyal citizens of the Italian republic, and that the Austrian government would discourage any irredentist activities on their part in the Alto Adige. The problem in this zone, Sforza's document concluded, could not arbitrarily and without justification be transferred from the sphere of race and culture to that of politics and territorial claims.

The attitude of the Italian Foreign Minstry brought about the desired clarification of the situation. The Vienna government stated that it accepted the conditions laid down for the continuation of consultations in the form of personal consultations. From November 13 to 22, 1947, an Austrian delegation was in Rome for this purpose.

A fairly favorable atmosphere pervaded the discussions. Austria refrained from making the most sweeping of the claims she had previously advanced and Italy further defined her intentions, particularly in connection with the controversial Article 5, listing the grounds for refusal to regrant citizenship.[2]

The efforts of the two delegations ended in an agreement that the text of the legislative provision as drawn up by the Italian government to deal with the revision of the options constituted "a satisfactory and just solution to the problem."[3] The Austrian delegation clarified all the aspects of the measures on which further information had been sought and subsequently declared itself satisfied and gave a formal assurance that, as soon as the draft had been approved at the appropriate levels, Gruber would issue the following public statement:

I am pleased to be able to inform you that the recent consultations between the Italian government and ours concerning the revision of the options, conducted with complete integrity and sincerity on both sides, have been crowned with success. Those who opted for naturalization will thus be able to choose their future freely under the aegis of just and liberal laws.

In this way one of the most important problems facing the South Tyrol is happily resolved, for its solution is the essential prerequisite to the definition of other serious political, economic and social problems. The understanding shown by the Italian government in these consultations justifies our confidence that the actions of the bodies responsible for putting these delicately balanced laws into effect will also be imbued with the same spirit of justice and equity. As a result, the Austrian government considers that one of the most important factors in a friendly and lasting relationship with Italy has been secured, *and recognizes the truth of Italy's contention that this relationship would be disrupted if the inhabitants of South Tyrol who renew their Italian citizenship were not to acquire and maintain an attitude of honorable loyalty toward Italy.* The Austrian government is ready to do everything in its power to this end, to influence the behavior of these people and to bring about this attitude toward Italy.

The Austrian government is convinced that the welfare and future development of the German-speaking group in the South Tyrol represents the aim and interest of Italy; it is also convinced that, with the implementation of the Paris Agreement, this group's fundamental requirements will be satisfied. On this basis, I feel justified in saying that any activity or attitude on the part of the people of South Tyrol *that lacks this spirit of loyalty and aims to alter the situation in the South Tyrol, on which the Paris Agreement is based, would gravely endanger the friendship between the two countries, and could only be censured by the Austrian government itself.*[4]

On January 31, 1948, immediately after the legislative decree for the revision of the options had been approved, Gruber released his statement. The extent to which the assurances freely given in this document were destined to be translated into actual fact will be evaluated later. These assurances, however, remain, and no thoughtful evaluation of the facts bearing on the Alto Adige question as a whole, and of the subsequent behavior of the political leaders in Vienna, Innsbruck, and Bolzano can ignore them.

[2]

Article 2 of the De Gasperi–Gruber agreement related to matters reserved solely to the decision of the Italian state. Putting it into effect did, however, have certain repercussions internationally, and these should be considered in formulating an opinion on the Vienna government's subsequent attitude on the subject.

The Austrian government's determination to seek to circumvent the terms of the Paris Agreement on the subject of the revision of options reached the level of threats to "resume its own freedom of action" should its claims not be met. On the subject of autonomy, on the other hand, Vienna scrupulously respected the attitude assumed by Gruber on September 5, 1946, to accept this as a matter that came exclusively within Italy's jurisdiction. Austria, therefore, recognized that autonomy should not be limited to the Bolzano province and the bilingual communes in the Trent province, as Vienna's draft had demanded, but allowed that the territorial extent should be subsequently defined by Italy in the exercise of her sovereignty. Equally faithful to the letter and spirit of the Paris Agreement was the significance attached by the Austrian government to the contemplated consultations, to include local representative German-speaking elements as part of the process through which the Italian authorities would define this area.

While such consultations were being held on every aspect of the draft scheme for autonomy—that is to say, on the lines suggested in the plan drafted by De Gasperi on August 28, 1946, instead of being limited to the territorial limits specified by the Paris Agreement—on June 25, 1947, Gruber took advantage of the opportunity to send De Gasperi a letter to express the "satisfaction" of the federal government and the people of Austria upon learning that the Italian Prime Minister had invited representatives of the S.V.P. to Rome, in their role as members of the strongest local party, to discuss the autonomy of the Südtirol, as envisaged in Article 2 of the Paris Agreement and for according these representatives the opportunity to express their own point of view.[5]

In the second part of the document, Gruber did not refer to the exchange of letters with De Gasperi of September 5, 1946, which gave Austria the opportunity of explaining, on a friendly basis, her point of view on the questions considered by the agreement. Gruber only referred to the willingness shown by the Italian government officials to listen to Austria's opinion on the problems concerning the South Tyrol and emphasized the important contribution to friendship between the two nations to be derived from the forging of an autonomy that fulfilled the fundamental desires of the people of this territory.

This discrete suggestion, referring neither to the letter nor the interpretation of Article 2 of the Paris Agreement but to the friendship between the two countries, was actually not necessary because the Italian government had already for some time been well on the way to creating an autonomy in line with the terms laid down by the agreement, as indeed acknowledged by Gruber in his letter.

In fact, as soon as Carandini had explained the details of the Innocenti project to von Guggenberg and Volgger in Paris on September 19, 1946,[6] and had obtained the agreement of both leaders of the German-speaking population of the Alto Adige to the general scheme of the plan, the Italian Prime Minister's office circulated the same plan to the mayors of the towns and to the political groupings in the province of Bolzano.[7] On November 6, 1946, the chairman of the S.V.P., Amonn, sent his reply in the form of a memorandum containing the views of his party.[8] At the end of June 1947, after the personal meeting which De Gasperi had arranged with representatives of the Alto Adige on April 7, 1947 (the meeting over which Gruber had expressed his government's appreciation), Amonn sent to the counselor of state, Innocenti, further observations of the S.V.P. on the plan under consideration.[9]

On June 27, 1947, the Italian Constituent Assembly gave provisional approval to Article 116 of the Constitution which specified which regions, under the new constitutional settlement, would be granted a special Statute of Autonomy. Among those was listed the Trentino—Alto Adige region. The assembly's decisions was the cue for critics in Bolzano, Innsbruck, and Vienna to insist that further consultations with representatives of the German-speaking group in the Alto Adige were now meaningless.[10]

In fact, the worries about autonomy that the German-speaking group in the Alto Adige expressed at this time, and the discreet invitation to give the problem close attention contained in Gruber's letter, sprang less from the causes propounded by latter-day critics than from the uneasy suspicion with which Italian public opinion, already divided on the subject of the regional settlements, clearly regarded the special statutes. Such statutes were in point of fact a genuine response to specific conditions existing in certain regions. But, at the same time, public opinion, deeply shocked by the loss of portions of the national territory imposed by the peace treaty, whose ratification was at that very moment under discussion, could not forget that certain of these regions had been the object either of separatist designs or of aims by other states to annex them, both before and during the peace conference. This cloud, which existed from the beginning and finally overshadowed all the regions subject to special statutes, was an important factor in influencing the attitude reflected by public opinion and the attendant misgiving that surrounded the debate on the subject in the Constituent Assembly.

It was not easy for the government to honor the obligation it had undertaken regarding the German-speaking population in the Alto Adige, and the anxiety nurtured in Vienna and Bolzano under these circumstances is understandable. De Gasperi, consequently, while unofficially communicating assurances to the Austrian government that he had not forgotten the pledges he had given in Paris and that he intended to fulfill them in every respect, at the same time sought to publicly reassure the people of the Alto Adige.

In replying to Gruber's letter on July 14, De Gasperi wrote that he welcomed the opportunity to affirm the Italian government's unwavering desire, a desire that he shared, to further strengthen the bonds of lasting friendship between the two countries that all of them had been so anxious to forge. He reminded Gruber that even before the Paris Agreement the Italian government had adopted a wide range of provisions in favor of the German-language citizens, and that currently it was endeavoring to define the delicate question of the revision of the options in the most liberal terms possible. De Gasperi next approached the problem of the establishment of autonomy. He pointed out that there too his government was moving toward a solution that conformed with the Paris Agreement, and at the same time accommodating those inviolable requirements recognized by the Constituent Assembly. He had appointed a special committee composed of members of Parliament and experts who would examine and consider the plan for autonomy, and the leaders of the S.V.P. would once again be asked for their opinions before it was presented to the Constituent Assembly. The objectivity, political experience, and acknowledged high qualifications of the members of this committee,[11] De Gasperi concluded, made it possible to hope for a satisfactory solution to the problem. He had no doubt that the government and the Constituent Assembly would concede that the Alto Adige, even within a broader territorial extension, should be entitled to an exclusive legislative and executive power of its own. This would apply particularly to matters of race and culture. These autonomous bodies offered the best guarantee for the protection of those distinctive characteristics of the German-speaking citizens to which the Paris Agreement made special reference.

It is worth noting that this precise confirmation by De Gasperi on matters referring to autonomy contained in the agreement of September 5, 1946, evoked no comment whatever on the part of Austria in the correspondence that followed nor through normal diplomatic channels.

De Gasperi's public reassurance to the people of the Alto Adige was given in a speech in Trent on July 20, 1947, at the local Christian Democrat convention. After referring to the problem of autonomy and to the objections which were being raised, he said:

The people of the Alto Adige can set their minds at rest. We shall honor the pledge we gave, within the limits established by us and shall enact all the measures possible in order to insure a fuller life and safeguard the fundamental rights of the ethnic groups. We shall not retrace our steps. We shall never give anyone the impression that we want to make Italians out of those who are Germans. We shall leave their liberties inviolate, we shall respect their way of life and system of education. This is the solemn obligation that we wanted observed when we were in that position and we shall honor it now that we are the governing majority. We ask our German brothers—brothers, in the real sense of the word—to be equally honorable toward us.[12]

In September 1947 the S.V.P., while awaiting the final draft announced by De Gasperi, sent a new memorandum restating their position to the office of the Prime Minister in Rome.[13] In mid-October, Chancellor Figl took advantage of Minister Pertner's trip to Rome to entrust him with a confidential mission. He was to talk to De Gasperi about the matter of the revision of the options, which was then at a delicate point in the negotiations, and about the problem of autonomy. He was to press for a prompt and friendly solution to both. In his reply to Figl, De Gasperi assured him of his concern and confirmed that the draft plan for autonomy then under discussion would be submitted to the political parties at the earliest opportunity. This was presented to them after mid-November 1947.

The leaders of the S.V.P. received the draft of the special committee neither completely negatively nor as unfavorably as has afterward been claimed. It was true that not all the requests made in the various memoranda were granted, for the special statute had to harmonize three diverse sets of requirements: the general demands of the state, the specific demands of the German-speaking and those of the Italian-speaking citizens, for an Italian-speaking element did exist in the province of Bolzano and was in a majority in the largest towns. The requests had been taken into account, and even the S.V.P. had to acknowledge the requirements that the statute had to accommodate. The greatest disappointment to its leaders actually lay in the fact that they, together with all the other local political groupings, were only asked for their observations in writing. In their opinion, this reduced the possibility that the amendments they proposed would be accepted. As a result, they assumed a rigid position, giving the impression of rejecting the entire draft unless they were verbally consulted.

On December 18, 1947, the ambassador in London, Carandini, reported that he had received a visit from the Austrian foreign minister, Gruber. The latter had said that "people" in the Alto Adige were dissatisfied with the plan for autonomy. They maintained that it refuted the Paris Agreement, and they advanced specific suggestions about the way in which the Austrian government should, in their opinion, intervene so as to promote a settlement of the question. Gruber immediately added that the Austrian government felt that its greatest contribution to a solution of the problem would be to consult amicably with the Italian government. This opinion was based on two things: the improvement in relations between the two countries resulting from the successful outcome of the consultations about the options, and the conviction held by the Vienna government that a solution to the problem of autonomy would be found if consultations with the German-speaking minority were again entered into. The reply came from the office of the prime minister in Rome, in the form of an invitation to the representatives of the local parties to express their views verbally before the special committee of the Constituent Assembly on the regional statutes.

On January 10, at the same time that these representatives arrived in Rome, a long letter from Gruber reached De Gasperi.[14] It expressed the Austrian government's "great satisfaction" at the solution found by the Italian draft bill to the question of the revision of the options. Gruber gave a résumé of the agreement as reached under Article 2 of the Paris Agreement, expressing himself in terms similar to those used in his letter to von Guggenberg in September 1947. Regarding the scheduled consultations, Gruber added that, in fact, conversations had taken place between individual members of the committee drafting the plan and persons from the South Tyrol, but that there had been no thorough oral exchange of views of the sort that the South Tyrol had hoped for. Then Gruber came to the main point of his letter. He had heard from Schwarzenberg, the Austrian representative in Rome, that the representatives of the South Tyrol would be given the opportunity to place before the special committee of the Constituent Assembly on the drafting of the plan for autonomy, the modifications that they would like to see made in the plan itself. Schwarzenberg had also understood that there was a possibility that these might be accepted. The Austrian federal government, Gruber stated, was anxious to play its part in doing everything possible to maintain the present good relations with Italy.

Accordingly, it had recommended that the people of the South Tyrol accept the Statute of Autonomy within the present framework, that is to say, as part of the common Trentino–South Tyrol region, provided certain minimal requests, which the South Tyrol representatives would present to the Special Committee of the Constituent Assembly[15] in the next few days, be granted. Gruber closed his letter by saying that he was sure that the Austrian government's efforts to influence "Tyrolese" public opinion, as far as this was within its power, in the direction of accepting the structure of autonomy that was so dear to De Gasperi, would be fully appreciated. He appealed to him to use his influence to see that the strictly limited requirements of the people of South Tyrol, listed earlier in the letter, would be satisfied.

One can easily understand the effort it cost Gruber to write this letter attempting to reconcile the demands of the peoples of the Alto Adige and of nationalist and Tyrolese public opinion with the pledges that he knew he had given De Gasperi on September 5, 1946. In fact, he was reflecting the substance of that covenant only in a very vague and distant way, now stating that the Austrian government would be satisfied with a territorial solution to the problem of autonomy that would meet with the approval of the German-speaking element in the Alto Adige. Article 2 of the Paris Agreement stated three things very distinctly: the non-Italian population would be granted an autonomous legislative and executive power; the territorial extent within which this power would be granted would be decided by the Italian state; in view of defining such extent, the local German-speaking representatives would be consulted.

It was more than clear, and Gruber was aware of this, that the decision-making authority in connection with this matter lay with the Italian state in the exercise of its sovereign power, and that the advisory opinion expressed by the non-Italian-language group was not binding. It was, therefore, very inappropriate to speak of the German-language group's "approval" of the solution of the territorial problem, as Gruber was impelled to do to protect his own position from the extremists.[16] It may further be mentioned that, from a legal point of view, both the agreement of the German-speaking group and the satisfaction of the Austrian government with the solution adopted were irrelevant to the application of Article 2. In any event, Gruber succeeded in avoiding all the pitfalls in his letter; his appeal to De Gasperi was couched in a form that honored the agreement and at the same time was both friendly and effective.

During the consultations held in Rome toward the end of January 1948, the claims for modifications to the special statute for the Trentino—Alto Adige region presented by representatives of the S.V.P. were discussed and examined with marked understanding by members of the special committee. The fact that the majority of these claims were accepted is due also to De Gasperi's active interest in the matter.[17] The president and the secretary-general of the S.V.P., Amonn and von Guggenberg, moved from the almost completely unsympathetic position toward the central power that they had held a month before, to that expressed in their letter to Perassi dated January 28, 1948:

As President of the *Südtiroler Volkspartei*, and in the name of the German-speaking group, I wish to thank you and the members of the Sub-Committee for the kindness with which you listened to our views on the draft statute for the autonomous structure of the Trentino—South Tyrol region.

I wish, in particular, to express my satisfaction, and that of the group I represent, at the understanding displayed in examining our remarks and the granting of many of our requests. Thus we note with pleasure *that the De Gasperi—Gruber Agreement of September, 1946, on the fundamental question of autonomy has now become an accomplished fact.*

We express our confidence that the application of the statute will create among the language groups of our province that atmosphere of trust and understanding so essential to fruitful collaboration in the development of the region and the general interests of the nation.[18]

Of even greater importance, especially for the evidence it provides to refute subsequent derogatory evaluations of the above document,[19] is the letter sent by Amonn to De Gasperi on January 31, 1948. This was the same day on which Gruber released his statement publicly expressing the satisfaction of the Austrian government with the solution to the problem of the revision of the options, and its condemnation of any who should opt to renew their Italian citizenship and then fail to act as loyal citizens of the country. In his letter, Amonn said:

Before leaving Rome I should like to express my personal gratitude, and that of the group I represent, for the personal interest you have shown in order that, prior to the closing of the Constituent Assembly, *a vote be cast on the Statute for our autonomy, including all the modifications introduced by the Sub-Committee for Regional Statutes which largely satisfy the hopes of our population, and particularly for your personal intervention in discussions held by the Constituent Assembly on the 29th and the warm words you had for autonomy.*

No one better than you, born in the Trentino, can understand that the desire for autonomous government, rooted in our people for centuries, is not a threat to national unity but the finest way of capturing the hearts of our population and speedily reaching a stage of fruitful and peaceful collaboration between groups with different languages and customs living in our province.

Our satisfaction is also expressed in a letter written on the 28th last to Signor Perassi as representative of the Constituent Assembly and which I consider necessary to bring to your attention as Prime Minister.

Please accept my profound respects and that of the group I have the honor to represent.[20]

The following letter addressed to De Gasperi on January 30 by Schwarzenberg, the Austrian minister in Rome, should also be added to the communications quoted above. It was a personal statement, but obviously reflected the authority of the government in Vienna:

Yesterday the Constituent Assembly approved the Statute of Autonomy for the Trentino—South Tyrol region. To mark this occasion you delivered noble words that related to ideals of wise and political foresight.

I must express to Your Excellency how deeply impressed I am by your words and my own personal satisfaction over the achievement of this peace-making, unifying task. I am also entirely in sympathy with your concept of an autonomy that must be dynamic, not static.

I shall always remember that you have enabled me to personally take part as an individual in an achievement that I trust may bring benefits during generations to come and constitutes the point of departure toward an ever-growing prosperity of one of Italy's fairest provinces, whose Tyrolese name you yourself have chosen to preserve.

An entire people, even beyond the frontier, will bear you lasting gratitude for this.

In expressing to you my heartfelt good wishes that your tenure of office may continue to be accompanied by similar peace-bringing successes, please accept, Sir, my highest regard.[21]

The Vienna government followed this testimony with a public expression of its appreciation. This took the form of a speech broadcast on the Austrian national radio network by Leitmaier, the director-general of the Political Department at the Ballhaus. In his speech, Leitmaier said:

The second act, which during these days was passed by the Italian Constituent Assembly and is of exceptional importance for the South Tyrol, is the Statute of Autonomy for the Trentino—South Tyrol region.

The Paris Agreement had envisaged consultation with representatives of the

South Tyrol as a background to the contemplated structure of autonomy in the region. Definitive discussions between representatives of the People's Party of the South Tyrol, the South Tyrol Socialist Democratic Party and interested Italian bodies took place in Rome during January. A generous measure of consideration was accorded to the wishes of the South Tyrol. The South Tyrol's own representatives, that is to say the delegates of the two parties, present in Rome, were thus in a position to express their satisfaction over the final formulation of the Statute of Autonomy. . . .

Although the Statute of Autonomy rests on the basis of a common region covering Trentino and the South Tyrol, the province has been assured of a life of its own. This finds its expression, in terms of the people involved, in the appointment to the province of its own President of the Provincial Council. *At the same time, union with Trentino in certain specific fields can even, from some points of view, be to the advantage of the German-speaking people.*

So public opinion in Austria can welcome the Statute of Autonomy. It can bear in mind that in the matter of the options, as well as in settling the question of autonomy, the Italian authorities have acted with generous receptiveness and understanding of the South Tyrol's special position. [22]

The representatives of the S.V.P. also gave public expression of their attitudes. Amonn, von Guggenberg, and Dr. Joseph Raffeiner granted an interview published by the *Dolomiten* on January 30, 1948, in which they listed the modifications obtained in the course of the final consultations. Also, at the party convention on February 25, 1948, the Chairman of the S.V.P. gave a more detailed account of the mission to Rome, adding the following comment:

So far we have been unable to win the formal structure of autonomy. Instead of the title of *Region* for each of the two areas, the designation of *Province* has been maintained, and instead of united Diets, we have the regional Diet. However, two autonomous units have, in fact, been created within the Region, with the result that in practice the two provinces of Trento and Bolzano have become two bodies on the same level.

On all matters pertaining to our national way of life we are completely independent of the Region. Our powers and our economic strength from all points of view are so promising that we would be indeed incompetent if in the days to come we failed to assume, not only in our own Province, but in the Region as well, the role and position we merit and for which we are striving. [23]

Confronted by so many declarations of evident approval, it was to be expected that the extremists would quickly propound a theory that would permit their denial of the value of such statements in the future. It appeared that the best method for doing this was to spread the rumor that these statements had been extorted. The fact that today there are still those who note this interpretation is proof of the effectiveness of the ruse. [24] However, the prompt propagation of these rumors had one unfortunate consequence that interestes the objective observer. In the same speech, delivered before the Convention of the S.V.P. on February 25, 1948, President Amonn said:

. . . and now there is another matter that I must raise because it touches on the honor and loyalty of the representatives of the South Tyrol who issued a statement in Rome. *It is a falsehood to wrongly construe the statement made*

before the committee of the Constituent Assembly, to whom we expressed our
thanks and satisfaction at the exhaustive consultations afforded us and the
resulting acceptance of a part of our major demands, and to whom we also
expressed the hope that the same spirit and atmosphere that pervaded the
workings of the committee would be carried into the execution of the bill, I
wish to state that it is a falsehood that any pressure, great or small, was exerted
to extort this statement from us. It is my duty to say that such a statement was
made by us in full awareness of our responsibility, and in a spirit of genuine
recognition for the understanding that was shown us in an atmosphere of trust.
Naturally the statement was discussed before being issued. It also doubtless did
enhance the possibility of gaining some important concessions. It is, however,
not true that it was extorted from us, as used to be the case in the days of
Fascism, and I declare before you and before all the entire people of the South
Tyrol that all of us who negotiated for autonomy in Rome will stand by this
statement, as well as by any other pledged word, as upright and loyal men of the
South Tyrol.[25]

These statements speak for themselves. The peaceful interlude in the Alto
Adige that followed the passing of the Statute of Autonomy is the best evidence
that as long as the Vienna government stood formally and intrinsically by the
contract it had reached through the De Gasperi–Gruber agreement—as it indeed
clearly did during this troubled period—the application of Article 2 was never a
problem. Some doubt on how long this general support would continue, however, was cast by subsequent developments in the matter of the revision of the
options.

[3]

The Act governing the system of reoptions was announced on February 2,
1948,[26] coinciding with the publication in the *Gazzetta Ufficiale della Repub-*
blica of the constitutional law instituting the Trentino–Alto Adige region.[27]
This is a very significant fact, for it shows that when the people of the Alto
Adige filed their applications to be allowed to resume Italian citizenship, they
were already acquainted with the provisions of the Paris Agreement and with
their application by the government in Rome, and also with the extent of the
protection guaranteed to the German-speaking ethnic group within the framework of the autonomous region.

With the publication of the act governing the system of options, there were
reasonable grounds for hope that one of the most difficult of the problems
raised in the application of the De Gasperi–Gruber agreement had been finally
set at rest. Instead, that very moment marked the beginning of a new period of
unrest in the story of the Alto Adige, revealing all too clearly what the Vienna
government's real aim was in championing the rights of the German-speaking
population.

Austria's eagerness to secure renewal of Italian citizenship for the largest
possible number of inhabitants of the Alto Adige has already been mentioned. In
practice, a first step in this direction was exhibited by an attempt to obstruct the
administration of the directives to be carried out by the Italian government
under Article 5. Methods for doing this were fully illustrated in a booklet

published in Innsbruck by the League for the South Tyrol and widely distributed.[28]

Despite this, the flow of requests remained very low. This was because, contrary to all expectations, many of those eligible, far from evincing a strong desire to return to their native land, were quite opposed to the idea and preferred to stay in Austria. To a large extent, this was probably also due to Austria's economic situation having very much changed as a result of the reform of December 20, 1947, which united the three zones and restored the stability of the schilling.

The previous uncertainty had been aggravated by the split into three zones of occupation, which frustrated initiative, the exchange of goods, and every activity without which a country almost destroyed by war was gravely hampered in its recovery. Now the situation had changed so dramatically that in the course of a single year Austria's economy began to show definite signs of improvement.

This chance of recovery obviously influenced the people who had left the Alto Adige for Austria some years before, and had begun to put down roots there. In the 1946–47 period, almost all of these had been inclined to escape from the serious economic crisis in Austria and once again begin a new life in the country they had abandoned and which was already showing signs of resurgence. With the change in the economic situation, they were attracted by the opportunities Austria offered. All of this upset what was all too clearly taking shape as the designs of the Austrian government, prompting it to resort to effective countermeasures.

In April 1948 the official press in Austria began to suggest that those who had come from the Alto Adige to Austria and who had been given provisional equality of rights with Austrian citizens in August 1945, might eventually be looked upon as stateless persons and would consequently lose both their jobs and even the right to remain on Austrian territory.

The Italian government protested vigorously against a maneuver aimed at restricting the freedom of choice of the former inhabitants of the Alto Adige. In spite of this, the Austrian government, through two successive resolutions adopted in November 1948, decided that these emigrants would lose their parity with Austrian-born citizens unless they submitted their applications for renewal of Italian citizenship before the established deadline, February 5, 1949. It was also stipulated that the possibility of a former inhabitant of the Alto Adige being granted Austrian citizenship would be dependent on his having exercised his right to opt for the renewal of his Italian citizenship (notice of this decision was given on November 27, 1948). A further measure adopted on May 14, 1949, added that all those seeking to obtain Austrian citizenship should also demonstrate that it was physically impossible for them to return to Italy.[29]

A situation was being created, at the Italian government's expense, analogous to that of 1939 when the Nazi authorities had strongly pressured the inhabitants of the Alto Adige to use their options for the Reich as an almost universal manifestation of German solidarity. It was now the Austrian government, who had always posed as a paladin of their well-being and interests, who applied coercion in an effort to reconstruct the German-speaking ethnic group beyond the Alps to an equal or even greater size than before. This represented the necessary premise upon which the Alto Adige question could continue to be kept open. At a later date, the Austrian foreign minister, Kreisky, in replying to the Italian minister, Pella, in the course of a debate at the XIV Assembly of the United Nations, actually claimed that the people of the Alto Adige had never really had a freedom of choice, because they had had to choose between two alternatives: to either return to Italy or become displaced persons. There were, consequently, no grounds either for inferring that there had been a choice in favor of Italy or that an obligation had been incurred to become loyal Italian citizens.[30] What Kreisky was forgetting, or professing to forget, was the fact that it had been Austria herself who had placed this alternative before the Germans of the Alto Adige.

As a result of the decisions taken by the Austrian cabinet, the Italian government found itself obliged to adopt an attitude encompassing the possibility that all applications for renewal of Italian citizenship submitted after November 27, 1948, would have to be weighed with particular care to insure that no encroachment had been made upon each applicant's freedom of choice. Austria's reaction to this was extremely sharp, and the lively exchange that followed lasted until early in 1950. A renewed effort by the Italian government to improve relations then led to a further personal exchange of views on the subject of the revision of the options, and the matter was conclusively settled on March 28. When the issues were finally resolved, the Vienna government agreed to grant citizenship to those who could demonstrate the necessity of remaining in Austria, up to a maximum of 25 percent of those who had emigrated under the 1939 options. In turn, Rome agreed to grant Italian citizenship, through an amendment to Article 5 of the law on reoptions, to those reoptants who had been expelled but should in the future evince themselves deserving of such citizenship. Further contacts between the two governments also enabled the financial problems connected with the renewal of citizenship to be subsequently solved.[31]

By 1952 the entire question of the options was finally settled. The figures given earlier, to the effect that 201,305 people[32] were granted Italian citizenship, with only 4,106 persons excluded,[33] testify that the Italian government faced and solved this problem not only with the same spirit of justice and understanding prescribed by the Paris Agreement but also with singular generosity. This fact is important because it led to the reestablishment of the German-speaking group in the Alto Adige that had been gravely impaired by the options. In fact, it was only the Italian state's extreme generosity that enabled this group to once again become the large majority in the province of Bolzano. This statistic alone provides unassailable evidence that, far from wanting to Italianize the area, the Rome government genuinely thought that the two main ethnic groups would arrive at a state of positive, harmonious coexistence and that it contemplated implementing the Paris Agreement in full sincerity.

Chapter VI

The Alto Adige Question
at the XV General Assembly
of the United Nations

[1] Austrian tendency to consider the Paris Agreement as sufficient to protect the Alto Adige minority. De Gasperi's speech at Bolzano, November 10, 1952, and the publication of Gruber's memoirs. Reactions in Austria, the Tyrol, and the Alto Adige to Pella's request on September 13, 1953 for a plebiscite on Trieste. Note sent to the Italian government by the deputies from the Alto Adige on February 15, 1954. Letter from Figl to Piccioni of July 31, 1954, and the latter's reply on September 18. Effect of the increased power of West Germany on the development of the Alto Adige question. The Austrian State Treaty and its consequences.   [2] The question of the territorial extension of the autonomous area. Raab's speech on July 4, 1956, and the Austrian note of October 8. Beginning of acts of terrorism in the Alto Adige and Gschnitzer's speech at Innsbruck, January 25, 1957. The Italian note of January 30, 1957. Statements made by Kreisky to the United Nations General Assembly in September 1959.

[3] New Italian efforts to reach a friendly solution of the autonomy problem: Segni's letter to Raab of January 10, 1960, and the latter's negative reply. Prime Minister Tambroni considers the possibility of referring the question to The Hague Court, May 18, 1960, while Raab indicates Austria's intention of bringing it before the United Nations. The Italian proposal of June 22, 1960, to have recourse to the Hague Court, and the Austrian application to the United Nations. Aims of the Austrian government in so doing.   [4] What Austria sought from the United Nations. The Italian government's decision as to the inclusion of the item on the agenda. The General Committee starts work September 22, 1960: speeches by Kreisky and Martino on item 68 of the agenda. Italian proposal to change the title of item 68. Canadian mediation and the agreement between the parties on new wording of item 68. Speeches to the General Assembly by Segni and Kreisky on September 28 and 29. The Italian memorandum of October 21. Unusual nature of the issue, the U.N. tendency often to lean toward compromise.   [5] Start of the debate in the Special Political Committee, October 18, 1960: Kreisky's speech sets out Austria's requests and the Austrian draft resolution of October 14. Segni's speech gives the Italian point of view. The morning session of October 20: Gschnitzer's speech and Martino's reply. Further intervention by Gschnitzer and Martino's new reply. The session of October 25: submission of the second draft resolution by Austria and that of the four River Plate countries. Kreisky's speech and

Martino's reply. The final phase of the debate, October 26, Kreisky explains
Austria's reasons for opposing recourse to The Hague; Segni rejects the Austrian
arguments and sets forth the Italian view.   [6] The afternoon session of
October 26: submission of the draft resolution of the Twelve. Martino intervenes
to reiterate the Italian position, declares the draft resolution of the Twelve
unacceptable. The search for a mutually acceptable solution. The joint draft
resolution of October 27. Its approval by the committee and the General
Assembly, October 31, 1960. Appraisal of the conclusions.

[1]

Although the essential terms of the September 1946 agreement had been put
into effect, it was during the same period that Austria initiated her allegations
that Italy had failed to fulfill her obligations. At the same time, the story was
circulated that the agreement did not constitute a sufficient safeguard for the
protection of the German-speaking group and that, in any case, it could not
represent a definitive solution to the problem. Immediately afterward, the
political parties in the Alto Adige also began to say that whereas the aim of the
agreement had been to protect the minority group, in practice it had not proved
to be sufficient to attain this end, and, therefore, action outside the limits set by
the instrument itself had become necessary.

These pronouncements inevitably aroused adverse reactions in Italy. The
regional elections in the Alto Adige were due to be held at the end of 1952, and
Prime Minister De Gasperi took this opportunity to make an important speech in
Bolzano on November 10, 1952. He reviewed the history of the Paris Agreement
and its application, and deplored the programmed disaffection of certain circles
in the Alto Adige and the attitude of a small group that seemed to look upon all
things only from its own parochial point of view, as if it had lost all its roots in
the nation's life.[1]

The Austrian reply to this took several forms. The first was the publication of
Gruber's memoirs, in installments, tracing his version of the course of the
negotiations leading to the agreement of September 5, 1946.[2] Gruber claimed
that it was he who had insured that the agreement should be attached to the
peace treaty with Italy so as to provide the German-speaking minority with an
international guarantee and that this had been achieved without an explicit
renunciation on Austria's part of her "rights" in the South Tyrol. Of notable
significance was the statement that the agreement had served to safeguard the
ethnic character of the German-speaking population until such time as developments in the European situation should warrant a revision of the existing
frontier.[3]

This was the situation on September 13, 1953, when the new Italian prime
minister, Giuseppe Pella, made his speech at the capitol. In it he requested a
plebiscite to solve the problem of the free territory of Trieste.

This plea had immediate repercussions in both Vienna and the Alto Adige.
Ebner and von Guggenberg, deputies from the Alto Adige, spoke in the debate

on foreign policy that took place in the Italian Parliament between September 30 and October 6. They maintained that the principle of self-determination invoked on behalf of Trieste must apply to all men equally and, therefore, to the population of the Alto Adige. In their case, the principle had been denied both in 1919 and at the end of World War II.[4]

Shortly afterward, the Austrian government supported this point of view officially in a note presented in Paris, London, and Washington on October 18, requesting a referendum in the Alto Adige. Nothing came of this move, as the governments involved confined themselves to advising the Austrian government not to raise the question in those terms. The fact remained, however, that Vienna was once again officially advancing the possibility of revising the frontier with Italy. This seemed to confirm that, notwithstanding the agreement of September 5, 1946, Austrian intended to keep the territorial question open.

On November 13, 1953, Gruber was replaced as Austrian foreign minister by the former chancellor, Figl. Two events followed which, although not directly implicating the position of the government in Vienna, were a clear manifestation of Austrian public opinion generally and that of the Tyrol in particular. On November 24, 1953, Alois Grauss, the governor of the Tyrol, made a speech at the Landtag in Innsbruck, in which he repeated the demand for a referendum for the Alto Adige. The tone of the speech was openly irredentist.[5] Such a speech, in itself serious, was accompanied by public demonstrations that took place in Innsbruck on the same day. These ended with the approval of a motion calling for a referendum by the representatives of the Tyrolese political parties, and bidding the Austrian government to spare no pains in putting an end to "the pitiless oppression endured by the population of the southern Tyrol."[6]

Further, in the course of a debate on foreign affairs held on December 8, 1953, in the Austrian Parliament, several members spoke on the Alto Adige question, demanding a popular referendum and charging Italy with violating the Paris Agreement and with seeking to de-Germanize the region.[7]

Clearly, these were reflections of a propaganda campaign designed to ultimately reopen discussion on the September 1946 agreement itself. Vienna had abstained from making any comments at the diplomatic level, but had at the same time refrained from dissociating herself from the position adopted by the extremist groups in the Tyrol.

The Italian Embassy in Vienna informed Rome toward the middle of February 1954 that as a result of some confidential discussions between Chancellor Raab and certain political leaders from the Alto Adige, the Austrian government intended to reopen conversations with Rome on the Alto Adige question. It envisaged the possibility of sending Foreign Minister Figl to Rome and, in the event such conversations failed to achieve the desired result, preparations would be made for bringing the matter before the United Nations.

There was probably a direct connection between Austria's resumption of hostilities and the long memorandum presented to the Rome government by the Alto Adige members of the Italian Parliament on February 15, 1954. In it, they lamented the incomplete fulfillment of the De Gasperi–Gruber agreement and indicated the need to revise the agreement itself, since it was inadequate for safeguarding the German ethnic group. Moreover, guarantees were sought, even at an international level, to ensure that such an agreement was put into effect.

In support of this memorandum, Figl wrote to the Italian foreign minister, Piccioni, on July 31, 1954, proposing discussions on the problems outlined in the document and the creation of an Austro-Italian committee.

The suggestion was not acceptable. In the first place, an eventual discussion between the Italian government and representatives of the Alto Adige was an internal affair, in which the Austrian government could not be invited to participate. In the second place, the memorandum made explicit reference to the need to modify the Paris Agreement, so that Figl's declared desire to support the claims made by the members of Parliament from the Alto Adige presupposed that the Austrian government intended to modify its obligation to observe the agreement itself.

Consequently, Piccioni limited himself in his reply to Figl on September 18, 1954, to assuring him that the Austrian government would be *informed* of any decisions and provisions that might be adopted, *within the framework of the Paris Agreement,* as a result of studies in progress and contacts established with those concerned. He also expressed his readiness to examine and to discuss with Vienna, always within the framework of the agreement, such suggestions as should be put forward by the Austrian government.

Figl replied that he was in agreement with these concepts, particularly endorsing the opinion that no widening of the scope of the Paris Agreement could come under discussion unless a European Union were to be created.

After this exchange, the Austrian government went no further with its proposals, for the moment. But the move revealed a tendency that was intensifying in certain circles in Vienna, the Tyrol, and the Alto Adige, giving new impetus to the entire question. The tendency grew stronger, largely as a consequence of the growing power of West Germany. The hardening of the cold war and the withdrawal of the Allied troops as an army of occupation, as well as the building up of the German army and Bonn's entry into NATO, all enabled West Germany to begin to recover her position among the European states. As in the past, as the fortunes of Germany rose, Vienna acquired an increased capacity for exerting pressure on Italy. This stimulated nationalist feelings among certain groups in Innsbruck and the Alto Adige itself, even more so because public opinion in southern Germany appeared more interested in the fate of the Alto Adige than public opinion in Austria itself.

The framing of the "State Treaty" in Vienna on May 15, 1955, should have introduced a new element to directly influence the Alto Adige problem. Under this treaty, Austria's definite frontier was explicitly stated to be that of January 1, 1938 (further evidence of the confirmation of the Brenner as the Austro-Italian frontier). It also imposed upon Austria the condition of a neutral state, forbidding its pursuing policies in any way aimed at obtaining additions to its territory. In spite of this, with the withdrawal of the occupying forces Austria was left in a position to more freely pursue its foreign policy. The Vienna government soon demonstrated that it would pay little attention to the obligations imposed by the special legal status that she had accepted.

[2]

Austria's new attitude was expressed both publicly and officially on July 4, 1956, when Chancellor Raab introduced his newly formed government to the National Assembly. His policy speech contained a statement charging Italy with having failed to fulfill the obligations assumed by her under the De Gasperi–Gruber agreement.[8]

Italy's reply pointed out that generic accusations unfortunately served only to provoke repercussions in public opinion in the two countries. Therefore, it would have been much more appropriate if the federal government had expressed its point of view in clear, concrete terms through normal diplomatic channels.[9]

Vienna's reply took the form of a memorandum, presented on October 8, 1956, in which four points were made: (1) the territorial extent of the autonomous region; (2) the effective equalization of the German and Italian languages; (3) equal rights of access to public office; (4) the need to restrict the number of Italian citizens from other regions entering the South Tyrol. However, it was on the first item that the document placed particular emphasis. It stated that the creation of the Trentino–Alto Adige region failed to satisfy either the spirit or the letter of the Paris Agreement, nor did it take into account the autonomous powers granted to the province of Bolzano under the regional statute, inasmuch as the German-speaking minority had no possibility of exercising sufficient influence over the administrative and legislative activities of the region. The memorandum ended with the proposal that a combined committee of experts be set up to examine all matters relating to the application of the Paris Agreement, and to submit to the two governments concrete proposals to resolve them.[10]

While Rome was preparing its reply to this document, the situation unexpectedly deteriorated as a result of the initiation of terroristic attacks in the Alto Adige. These were immediately followed, on January 25, 1957, by a speech made in Innsburck by Gschnitzer, the Austrian under-secretary for foreign affairs, sufficiently antagonistic to justify the impression that he was attempting to damage relations between Rome and Vienna in order to prevent their reaching any agreement on the entire question. Gschnitzer, in language strangely reminiscent of Nazi rhetoric, inferred that terrorist activites in the Alto Adige should be looked upon by every good Tyrolese as heroic acts of patriotism. He also discussed the problem of the German-speaking group in terms completely outside the scope of the Paris Agreement. The solutions he proposed would merely have made the Alto Adige a state within a state. He concluded by affirming that, failing this, a referendum was the only valid alternative that could again bring peace to the South Tyrol.[11]

The fact that the speaker was the under-secretary for foreign affairs obliged the Italian government to inquire of Vienna whether his statement reflected the letter and spirit of government thinking. If so, then Italy could justifiably assume that the Austrian government intended to question the very foundations on which the Paris Agreement rested.[12] The federal government replied by confirming that it intended to stand by the agreement it had previously reached,[13] and so on February 9, 1957, the Italian ambassador to Vienna, Corrias, presented Italy's reply to the Austrian memorandum of the previous October 8.

The Italian document answered, point by point, the Austrian charges of nonfulfillment. Further, it pointed out that the regulations governing the Trentino–Alto Adige statute had been issued after consultations with the leaders of the German-speaking population, who at that time had expressed their satisfaction with it and acknowledged that the regional statute introduced the autonomy they hoped for. This did not, however, exclude the possibility that within an atmosphere of mutual respect and trust, further provisions in favor of the minority might not be considered. The Italian government accordingly welcomed the proposal of an exchange of views on the application of the De Gasperi–Gruber agreement, so long as this exchange took place through normal diplomatic channels, and not by setting up a committee of experts, this being quite out of the question.[14] Rome's suggestion that it was disposed (even within the limits set by the reference to the climate of mutual respect and trust) to consider adopting "further provisions in favor of the minority" was significant for it became the point of departure for a political development with far-reaching implications.

For a number of reasons,[15] the conversations could not begin before February 1958. The new Italian foreign minister, Giuseppe Pella, intended to discuss the matter in the context of a comprehensive review of Austro-Italian relations. In this way he hoped that the negotiations might assume a broader base to stimulate the Vienna government's interest in a general agreement, extending especially to the economic sphere.[16] This attempt met with little success, for the preliminary conversations revolved almost exclusively around the Alto Adige question. The negotiations were pursued by the Italian Embassy in Vienna, and their protracted course was marked by increasing Austrian intransigence, especially on the subject of the territorial limits to the autonomous region.

In the meantime, the Italian government sought to give concrete proof of its desire to find a solution to the problem by unilaterally going beyond the position it had taken up in the memorandum of January 30, 1957. It adopted a whole series of provisions to further improve the conditions of the German-speaking group. Notice of such provisions was given on each occasion to the Austrian government,[17] though this failed to induce the Ballplatz to adopt a more conciliatory attitude.

In September 1959 Kreisky, the Austrian foreign minister, stated in a speech at the XIV Assembly of the United Nations that exchanges with Italy aimed at settling the South Tyrol question were not proceeding satisfactorily, because the September 1946 agreement had not yet been applied in full. According to the Austrian Foreign Minister, the only method for providing the necessary safe-guard for the minority group lay in granting autonomy to the province of Bolzano alone. Unless an agreement was reached to this effect, the Austrian government would submit the matter to the United Nations the following year.[18]

The impression that Austria no longer had any real intention of reaching an agreement acceptable to both sides, was confirmed through a note of October 29, 1959, from the Austrian Foreign Ministry,[19] and through another speech made by Gschnitzer on December 7. In a public address at Innsbruck he charged Italy with having "done everything she could to lessen, point by point, the concessions made, and to nullify them in practice through artful manipulation and roundabout interpretations." He concluded by again pointing to self-deter-mination as the only possible solution to the problem of the Alto Adige.[20]

In this context, Kreisky's announcement that in the event the two countries failed to reach an agreement by the following year Austria would appeal to the United Nations, assumed a clearer significance. On the one hand, such an agreement appeared clearly unattainable, Austria lacking the desire to achieve it; on the other hand, it was clear that Vienna was now looking for something more than what it considered would be the implementation of the De Gasperi–Gruber agreement–a solution, that is, exceeding the bounds set by this agreement. It was for this reason that instead of appealing to the international court at The Hague, whose function it was to deal with controversies of a legal nature arising between states over the interpretation of treaties, the Austrian government had decided to appeal to the United Nations, whose judgment would be largely political in character.

[3]

Notwithstanding the Austrian government's attitude, the Italian prime minis-ter, Antonio Segni, attempted to direct the conversation back to a constructive level. On January 10, 1960, he sent Raab a letter which included the following passage:

I do not believe that recent press campaigns and manifestations should be allowed to disturb relations between Austria and Italy which are so useful and indeed, I may say, so necessary for European understanding. . . . Hence I deem it advisable–and I hope you will agree–that the talks should be continued and even accelerated. I am personally following them from Rome; and also for this reason, and because you hold the highest position of responsibility for the politics of your country, I should like to propose, Mr. Chancellor, that from now on the talks be followed more particularly by you personally.[21]

In this way, Italy tried to mitigate the effects of the campaign by the extremist current of Tyrolean opinion conducted in the press and through the oratory of Professor Gschnitzer. Rome was prepared to resume negotiations, but without the Austrian Under-Secretary for Foreign Affairs taking part, since extreme intransigence appeared to be one of the main obstacles on the path to an acceptable agreement.

Raab's reply was, however, substantially negative. He did not mention Segni's invitation to assume personal direction of the negotiations. The conversations, he said, had until then led to "extremely unsatisfactory results." Returning to the idea proposed in the Austrian note of October 29, 1959, he repeated the belief that a solution to the South Tyrol problem would only be possible if the Italian government was ready to enter into concrete negotiations for granting autonomy to the province of Bolzano.[22]

The same opinion was expressed later in an Austrian memorandum dated May 4, 1960.[23] On May 18, the new Italian prime minister, Tambroni, wrote to Raab, pointing out that on such a basis it was most unlikely that an agreement would be reached. Such a difference of opinion, in fact, might well lead to the development of a legal controversy, and if the opposing claims should be irreconcilable, a solution could be found only by the qualified jurisdictional authority (a direct reference to the International Court of Justice at The Hague).[24] At the same time, the Italian ambassador to Vienna, Guidotti, was instructed to inform the Vienna government that Tambroni was ready to meet the Austrian Chancellor for a personal discussion of the question.[25]

Raab rejected the proposal. In reply to Tambroni's letter he wrote, on June 18, 1960, that it was now clear that Italy had no intention of concerning herself with "the question of regional autonomy for the province of Bolzano." The Austrian government, too, therefore, considered that "a fundamental divergence of opinion" existed between the two parties and that this could only be settled by the "qualified jurisdictional authority." The letter clearly implied that the "qualified" organization meant the United Nations and not The Hague Court.[26]

This attitude made any further attempt at reaching agreement by direct means impossible. The Italian cabinet accordingly decided to accept a suggestion by the Foreign Minister and, on June 22, 1960, Tambroni officially proposed to the Austrian government that the controversy over the execution of the Paris Agreement of September 5, 1946, be referred by common accord to the International Court of Justice.[27]

The proposal was brought to the attention of the Vienna government by Ambassador Guidotti on June 25, 1960,[28] and was officially rejected on the following July 14, in a letter from Kreisky. He gave his opinion that "the dispute concerning the existence and future of the Austrian minority" was first of all a political rather than a legal matter. The federal government had examined the question in depth "during its session of June 28" and had decided to submit it to the XV session of the United Nations Assembly. Kreisky added:

This decision was prompted, above all, by the fact that the dispute concerning the existence and the future of the Austrian minority in Italy is, in the first place, a political difference of opinion, arising from the denial of certain rights that are vital to the said minority.

For instance, the Austrian request to Italy for the granting of autonomy to the present province of Bolzano, does not arise solely from the Gruber–De Gasperi Agreement, but was advanced for the first time soon after the separation of the South Tyrol.[29]

This amounted to a clear declaration that the Austrian government had no intention of seeking a solution within the framework of the De Gasperi–Gruber agreement—as Vienna had on so many occasions stated—but sought a solution outside the scope of this document. As for Vienna's decision to appeal to the United Nations, notice of this had already reached Italy through Austria's request that the question be included on the agenda of the General Assembly of the United Nations. The document reached the Secretary-General of the United Nations early in July and was dated June 23, 1960, as Kreisky himself had rather ingenuously revealed in his letter of July 14. He had spoken of the decision by the federal cabinet on *June 28*; the document addressed to the United Nations had been back-dated for the obvious reason of showing that it was being presented before Italy's proposal to refer the matter to the International Court of Justice.

This decision by Austria marked the beginning of a new phase in the Alto Adige question and was the result of a deliberate action by the Vienna government. The latter was evidently convinced that the time to reopen the whole question, which Austria had been awaiting since 1946, was now ripe.

[4]

The subject of Austria's request to the United Nations was "the problem of the Austrian minority in Italy." It was accompanied, in accordance with the existing regulations, by an explanatory memorandum.[30] The details of the line of action that Austria intended to follow in New York were not yet fully known. However, the end which she pursued was clear: the setting up of the province of Bolzano as an autonomous entity, in such a way that the German-speaking inhabitants would be given control of the area. There was no ground for justifying this in the Paris Agreement, and, while such an autonomy might well be the prelude to a subsequent move in the direction of secession, it would in all cases have been a constant source of serious concern to the Italian-speaking minority, which made up a third of the population.

Two courses were now open to the Rome government at the diplomatic level: to agree or refuse to debate the matter before the United Nations. At the same time, the Italian ministerial crisis and the period of adjustment needed by the new Fanfani cabinet meant that a considered decision could not be reached before the beginning of September. The Rome government decided to follow a course representing a middle way between the two alternatives; namely, not to oppose the application to have the matter placed on the agenda, but to stipulate the condition that in the wording requested by the Vienna government, the expression relating to the problem of the "Austrian minority" be substantially altered to read as the problem concerning the "application of the De-Gasperi–

Gruber agreement." This would certainly have the effect of avoiding anything resembling a refusal to allow the subject to be put on the agenda and of setting the debate on a more appropriate track by confining it to a legal controversy. At the same time, however, this meant entering the controversy on difficult ground from the very beginning. In actual fact, debates before the General Committee are governed by Article 24 of the regulations, which states that in order to avoid repeated discussion on the same basic point, the General Committee must simply decide whether or not a subject shall be inscribed on the General Assembly agenda, making no provision for a change in the wording used by the submitter. There were very few precedents of attempts of this nature being successful.

On September 22, the XV Assembly of the United Nations opened and the General Committee, which is chaired by the president of the General Assembly and whose members consist solely of the vice president of the assembly and the chairmen of the seven commissions, broached the question of including Austria's request on the agenda, listed under point 68. Kreisky spoke first and was brief. He simply asked that his government's proposal be accepted. Martino, in his reply, indicated that strictly speaking there was no such thing as an "Austrian" minority under three classic headings of race, language, and religion. He went on to call the committee's attention to the Paris Agreement having used the term "German-speaking inhabitants," and pointed to the Vienna government's request omitting even the slightest reference to the De Gasperi–Gruber agreement, which, after all, constituted the sole legal ground upon which Austria could base a demand to have the question discussed in the United Nations. The dispute between the two governments was concerned exclusively with the application of the agreement, and while Italy was prepared not to opposed the inclusion of the subject in the agenda of the General Assembly, she could not accept that it be worded in the manner proposed.[31]

The debate that followed was not smooth. Some of the speeches were distinctly in Italy's favor, such as those of the representatives of Britain, France, Japan, and the United States and the merit of Martino's remarks received considerable recognition. They hoped for an understanding between the delegations of the two countries, enabling them to reach agreement on a better wording of the point to be included on the agenda. No representative voiced an opinion against including the subject, in the event the two countries failed to agree, while three delegates (Iraq, Panama, and Yugoslavia) stated that in such a case they would vote in favor of Austria.

The open expression of regret by the Anglo-Americans that the Vienna government had decided to apply to the United Nations, refusing Rome's offer to refer the matter to the International Court of Justice, as well as some of the specific points made by Martino, carried sufficient weight to convince even the Austrians. Kreisky's reply to Martino was somewhat weak, and he used an expression that revealed some inclination to take Italy's point of view into account. He said that the Italian delegate's proposed wording only covered one aspect of the substance of the matter and was, in his opinion, therefore inadequate. However, for the sake of agreement, he was willing to accept a different title, so long as it covered the substance of what his government wanted to discuss. Martino then asked whether the Austrian delegation could accept the title "The status of the German-speaking inhabitants of the province of Bolzano with reference to the Paris Agreement of September 5, 1946." As an alternative, Kreisky suggested "The status of the German-speaking inhabitants of the South Tyrol and the application of the Paris Agreement of September 5, 1946."

At this point, the chairman, Boland, suspended the discussion to enable the parties to come to an agreement on the exact wording of the title. Canada agreed to act as mediator between the two delegations. Agreement was finally reached on the following wording: "The Statute of the German-speaking element in the province of Bolzano (Bozen). Application of the Paris Agreement of September 5, 1946."

On September 23, the General Committee took note of and approved the Austro-Italian agreement, during a session which included another speech by the American delegate, resolutely supporting an appeal to The Hague Court. Statements were, of course, also made by Kreisky and Martino, foreshadowing the difficulties of the ensuing debate on the basic question under consideration.[32]

The result was distinctly favorable to Italy. The circumstances under which similar success was achieved were both difficult and unusual: once the decision had been taken, the Chairman deemed it necessary to remind the members of the General Committee of Article 24 of the Regulations. After the agenda had been approved and confirmed without further discussion by the General Assembly on this point, the General Committee unanimously agreed to entrust further examination of the question to the Special Political Committee, which normally handles specific problems not of major critical import.

Meanwhile, the General Assembly had continued to meet, open to general statements by the delegates and, in due course it was addressed by both Segni and Kreisky. Segni made his speech on September 28. The final sentences contained a single brief but firmly worded reference to the Alto Adige question, in which Segni redefined the problem in precise terms. He recalled the offer made to Austria to refer the matter by common consent to The Hague for a definitive judgment on a controversy the nature of which was legal. He also cautioned against attempts, to which Italy would be firmly opposed, to have the case debated before any but the appropriate gathering.[33]

Kreisky spoke on September 29. He clearly indicated that the Austrian delegation was now determined to embark on a very dangerous course, and tension increased as a result of his remarks. In spite of what had been decided in the General Committee, he made no reference at all to the De Gasperi–Gruber agreement, referred in deliberately ambiguous terms to the right of self-determination, and recalled Article 14 of the charter, relating to matters likely to endanger friendly relations between states. He gave a very personal and inaccurate account of the Austro-Italian conversations and concluded by stressing that the question could only be settled by granting the inhabitants of the province of Bolzano the type of autonomy he was demanding. In his words, it was not Austria that dramatized the problem, but the facts themselves.[34]

The three weeks that intervened between these speeches and the beginning of the debate before the Special Political Committee were a period of intense preparation by both of the delegations. It was, in fact, during this period that the Italian advisors prepared a long, printed statement in rebuttal of the Austrian arguments.

The document challenged the substance of Austria's contentions that the Paris Agreement of September 5, 1946 had not been adequately put into effect. As to equalization of the Italian and German languages in the autonomous region, it was pointed out that this clause had been interpreted by the Vienna government as meaning that both German and Italian should be recognized as an official language on equal terms. This interpretation, however, was not defensible, because the agreement contained no reference to this point. It merely provided that the German-speaking inhabitants should be guaranteed the right to use their own language in local government, public offices, and in public documents. In this connection, the Italian government could produce overwhelming evidence to prove that it had gone far beyond the limits of mere obligation in this matter.

An examination of Austria's demand for a fuller implementation of the agreement to the effect that German-speaking citizens be appointed to posts in local government led to a similar conclusion. The Austrian government had maintained that 90 percent of local government employees were Italian-speaking. This was not verified by the facts; and in any case the Italian memorandum provided indisputable evidence to illustrate that despite all the measures adopted to promote the entry of German-speaking citizens into local government employment, these people had shown a persistent lack of interest in activity of this kind.

The Italian document went on to question the defensibility of Austria's complaints that Italy was "failing to put autonomy fully into effect." On this subject, Vienna had presented two points: (1) that the statute of autonomy envisaged in the agreement had not been granted to the population concerned, because the province of Bolzano had been made a part of the Trentino–Alto Adige region and so had merely attained "a sort of provincial sub-autonomy"; (2) that, in framing its decision about the "context" of the autonomy to be granted, the Italian government had not consulted the local representatives of the German-speaking population.

On the first point, the Italian memorandum recalled how, during the negotiations leading up to the Paris Agreement, the Italian delegation and De Gasperi himself had never been mysterious about their intention to absorb the province of Bolzano as well. The aim was to preserve the administrative and economic unity that had been consolidated under the Hapsburgs. Thus the exact meaning of Article 2 of the agreement had been perfectly clear both to Gruber and to the political representatives of the Alto Adige at the time when the agreement was signed.

Equally unfounded was the charge of failure to consult with representatives of the German-speaking community. The Italian government's response to this was simply to delineate the numerous written and oral statements in which spokesmen of Austria and the Alto Adige had repeatedly and explicitly recognized Italy's integrity in the fulfillment of this obligation. Similarly, an objective view of the situation that developed in the Alto Adige after the agreement was signed rendered it convincingly evident that there was no foundation for Austria's contention that the statute granted to the German-speaking minority was insufficient to ensure their economic and cultural development.

Finally, the memorandum went into the exact nature of the controversy under discussion. It pointed out that the question brought up before the U.N. General Assembly concerned a matter that had been definitely settled by the two parties through the Paris Agreement. The Austrian government had itself based its demand on this agreement. The question was, therefore, strictly of a legal nature and could not be reopened on a political plane without prejudicing the rights conferred to the parties under the existing agreement. Both Italy and Austria were signatories to the European convention on the peaceful settlement of disputes (the Strasbourg Convention of April 29, 1957), according to which the two states had bound themselves to submit all controversies of a legal nature that might arise between them to the judgment of the International Court of Justice. This was, consequently, the only authority qualified to settle the question of the statute granted to the German-speaking population of Bolzano, a question that only Austria could raise inasmuch as the Paris Agreement existed.

The memorandum concluded that

in the presentation of her case to the General Assembly, Austria has, however, virtually ignored the agreement. *What are the real objectives pursued by Austria? Her conduct throws serious doubt on her intention to stand by the Paris Agreement. Italy's fears of Austrian schemes are made even more comprehensible and justifiable by the numerous signs emanating from Innsbruck and Vienna which indicate that beyond the claims put forward today, other goals are being pursued, and further actions planned.*
On this subject, repeated statements that other means will be restorted to if the United Nations show themselves unable to satisfy Austrian demands should be noted with deep concern. The same should be said of incitements to racial discrimination, which come not only from leaders of extremist groups, but also from members of the Austrian government. For example, statements have been made condemning mixed marriages, or calling upon German-speaking inhabitants to assume an uncooperative, unyielding attitude toward the Italian-speaking element. It should be clearly stated that while Italy is ready to make use of all legitimate ways and means to overcome any difficulty arising from the implementation of the Paris Agreement, she will firmly reject any demands that go beyond such agreement.[35]

In the meantime, Italy made diplomatic approaches to individual governments in their capitols and to their U.N. delegations in New York. The activity was considerable and laborious. Considerable, because there were ninety-six states and laborious, because it was difficult for countries who were often geographically distant and not always psychologically receptive to understanding even the fundamental significance of the issue. A number of delegations tended to base their decisions on day-to-day developments in the assembly.

Certain unique circumstances surrounded the entire subject. The Alto Adige question was not the type normally dealt with at the United Nations, in that the latter lacked precedent to guide the discussion and its conclusions. This left the outcome open to every possibility, for if some states, for reasons of their own, were sure to be reluctant to face any in-depth discussion of minority problems, it was equally true that for opposite reasons other states would be influenced in the opposite direction. Still other countries who had refused in the past to have certain cases referred to the International Court of Justice for a decision would certainly not be in a position to encourage submission of this case to The Hague. Furthermore, while the principle of the sanctity of treaties could rely on a broad consensus of support, not all the new states or those governments who leaned toward the dynamic political philosophies could be assumed to look upon the problem in the same way. Further, there was no way of anticipating the reaction to an appeal for self-determination by those countries that had achieved independence by such means.

At the same time, it was equally impossible to estimate beforehand the substance of the traditional drive toward compromise that often manifested itself in the workings of the United Nations. Austria was a small country, and neutral, and it was unlikely that the assembly would wish to humiliate her in front of a larger nation. In the final analysis, what attitude would the socialist states adopt? Could the silence they maintained throughout the discussions in the General Committee be interpreted as an expression of a clear-cut directive in a controversy which on the one hand led to a confrontation between a member of NATO and a neutral state, but on the other, aroused fears of a situation in which the marks of pan-Germansim were recognizable, even to the extent of questioning peace treaties and existing frontiers?

These were a few of the questions that only time could answer. Italy awaited confidently in a position that had been much strengthened by the fact that the Tambroni government had decided to suggest to Austria a joint application to the International Court of Justice. This could result in one of two things: either Italy had failed to fulfill her obligations as Austria claimed, in which case it was difficult to see why Austria should refuse a proposal that offered her the best assurance of complete success; or else Austria was making an entirely new claim, in which case she would have to display her cards and admit that what she was demanding was more or less a substantial revision of the Paris Agreement.

[5]

On October 18, the proceedings of the Special Political Committee opened with a long speech by Kreisky, which, on the whole, confused a considerable portion of his audience.

The Austrian Foreign Minister opened his presentation with a general survey of the historical antecedents to the question. He lingered over criticism of the Peace of Saint Germain in such a way as to give the distinct impression that he had in mind a revision of its territorial arrangements. He was critical of Italian policies between the two world wars, as if Austria, which had given birth to Hitler and fought by his side to the end, had been exempt from all blemish. Even his résumé of the events leading to the Peace of Paris in 1947 was made in such a way as to confirm the impression created by his earlier remarks on the Treaty of Saint Germain.

When he came to the De Gasperi–Gruber agreement, Kreisky stressed that Austria was an occupied territory at that time. He followed this with a violent criticism of the present Italian administration, and an explicit declaration that Austria rejected the idea of an appeal to the International Court of Justice because the question was not a mere matter of legal interpretation. The Vienna government demanded full autonomy for the province of Bolzano, and this, concluded Kreisky, was the only way of building a bridge not only between Italy and the South Tyrol but also between Italy and Austria across "a disputed frontier."[36]

The contention that Austria lacked the freedom to express her will at the time of the Paris Agreement of September 5, 1946, because of the Allied military occupation was one that could be dangerous for the Vienna government itself. The occupation ended only *after* the State Treaty of May 15, 1955 became effective, and its validity could consequently be questioned. Furthermore, it appeared hardly logical to call for the enforcement of the terms of an agreement which they held invalid, when such an agreement constituted the sole legal ground upon which Austria had any right to raise the subject of the Alto Adige with Italy. At the same time, such a stand underlined Vienna's being completely aware that the De Gasperi–Gruber agreement by no means entailed a separate autonomy for the province of Bolzano as a unit distinct from the Trentino region.

It seemed clear that the Austrian delegation had decided to start from an extreme position. In fact, on October 14, the Austrian delegation had also submitted a draft resolution asking the assembly to: (a) recognize as justifiable the demand of the South Tyrolese for a distinct and effective regional autonomy; (b) recommend to the parties concerned that they resume negotiations without delay aimed at creating an autonomous region of the province of Bolzano, with legislative and executive powers; (c) invite both parties to submit a report on the outcome of these negotiations to the XVI General Assembly.[37]

Whatever the long-term aims contemplated by the Austrian delegation, both the draft resolution of October 14 and Kreisky's speech on the 18th were to prove damaging to Austria's immediate objectives. The draft resolution totally ignored the Paris Agreement, although this was by now an essential part of the agenda under discussion. It also called on the assembly to make a decision on the substance of Austria's claims. This not only would show that such claims went beyond the existing agreement and, consequently, implied a revision of it, but, in so doing, threatened to create a precedent alien to the normal functions of the United Nations. The result was that *not* a single one of the many delegates who were later to address the Special Political Committee said that he would vote in favor of the Austrian draft resolution without its being amended.

Kreisky was followed at the rostrum by Segni, who presented a general outline of Italy's case. The Italian Foreign Minister began with a rebuttal of Austria's claims as being outside the subject on the agenda and, therefore, unacceptable. He followed this with an accurate restatement of the historical antecedents, which pointed to Vienna's design toward a revision of the existing treaties. Segni then expanded on the significance of the De Gasperi–Gruber agreement, quoting a number of remarks from statements by the Austrian Foreign Minister himself and by the leader of the *Südtiroler Volkspartei,* Silvius Magnago. He described in detail the measures adopted by Italy in fulfillment of the obligations assumed in Paris in 1946, and followed this with an account of the Austro-Italian negotiations and a refutation of Austria's charges that the obligations had not been fulfilled. The strategy underlying Austria's tendency to increase her demands was pointed to through a number of quotations testifying to the basic aims pursued by Vienna and Innsbruck. Another section of the speech was devoted to describing in plain and simple terms the real situation in the area, the reasons behind Italy's rejection of Austria's demands, and the dangers concealed behind such requests. Segni made it clear, however, that notwithstanding all this, the Rome government was presently ready to resume conversations on the application of the Paris Agreement and, in the event of failure to agree, to make a joint application to The Hague Court.[38]

The debate continued on the following day with remarks by the Argentinian and American delegates, Amadeo and Willis. Both were openly in favor of the Italian point of view.

At the morning session on October 20, Gschnitzer availed himself of his right to reply. His main object was to challenge Italy's statement that the Brenner was the natural frontier between the two countries. He also maintained that the question of the South Tyrol fell within the competence of the United Nations as an essentially political issue; he upheld the thesis that the only solution to the problem lay in the concession of autonomy to the province of Bolzano as a separate unit along the lines demanded by Austria. He sharply denied that the Vienna government had any intention of disregarding treaties or engagements it had entered into, especially, since, in his view, the De Gasperi–Gruber agreement imposed obligations on Italy alone.

When Gschnitzer ended, Martino asked for the floor. He replied point by point to the Austrian Secretary of State's remarks. Then he counterattacked by giving detailed and specific references to a whole series of Gschnitzer's writings and speeches that plainly revealed both his ambition to achieve territorial revision and the spirit of racial intolerance that moved him.[39]

Five other delegates spoke during the morning. All of them spoke out against the Austrian draft resolution. They supported Italy's contention that resorting to judgment by The Hague would be the appropriate solution to a controversy over the interpretation of the Paris Agreement and criticized Austria's approach which, in ignoring such an agreement, was tantamount to demanding the revision of a treaty.

Gschnitzer opened the afternoon session with a new speech. He denied that his writings and statements, quoted by Martino, had the meaning ascribed to them and only admitted his opposition to mixed marriages. Once again Martino's reply was prompt and pertinent. He stated that unquestionably the present situation had been created solely by the liberal interpretation that Italy had placed on the Paris Agreement. But, why did Austria refuse the suggested appeal to The Hague? Gschnitzer had admitted the statements quoted by Martino. He concluded by posing a question: whether, in a world bent on industrialization, Italy was gravely at fault for having set up industries in Bolzano; was it desired, rather, that the Alto Adige should be turned into a sort of national park of the type set aside for the preservation of bisons or wild bears.[40]

Six other delegates then spoke in succession. The following day, October 21, the Special Political Committee met in the morning only, and four delegates spoke.

So ended the first week of discussions, with the debate about to enter its final phase. At this point, a decision had to be taken. All the delegates until then had spoken against accepting the Austrian draft resolution and had to a large extent supported Italy's case. Austria had been impelled to submit a draft resolution of her own and this had met with general opposition. How could the debate be brought to a close, and would this be done in the form of a motion or otherwise?

There were, in fact, precedents for discussions to be closed without any decision being reached. The President had simply given a résumé of the proceedings and a verbal statement of the conclusion attained, in a text agreed to by the relevant parties. This solution was not fully compatible with Italy's somewhat strong position. So, after careful consideration, this course of action was not chosen. At the same time, the idea of submitting an Italian draft presented the drawback of its securing a simple but probably not a two-thirds majority vote. The most hopeful course, therefore, seemed to be to encourage other powers to put forward a draft resolution. Account also had to be taken of the fact that opposition had been voiced to *the specific* draft resolution submitted by Austria, and a new formula conforming more closely to the wording of the agenda and more moderate in its demands might reverse the situation.

The first speaker at the session of the Special Political Committee on the morning of October 24 was the head of the Indian delegation, Krishna Menon. He was followed by the delegates from Uruguay, Yugoslavia, the United Arab Republics, Yemen, Lebanon, and Mexico. However, a majority of the delegates had remained silent.

[6]

On the afternoon of October 25, the Special Political Committee was presented with two new draft resolutions, one of them a new Austrian effort and the other presented by Argentina, Brazil, Paraguay, and Uruguay.

The Austrian draft *invited* Austria and Italy to start without delay discussions on the application of the Paris Agreement of September 5, 1946. The aim would be to *find a just and democratic solution.* The resolution *requested* the Secretary-General to put himself at the disposal of the two parties to provide them, directly or indirectly, with any assistance that they might find it necessary to seek.[41]

Austria's objectives were clear enough. "A just and democratic solution" could only mean something different from the application of the existing De Gasperi—Gruber agreement. The intervention of the U.N. Secretary-General would simply have the effect of making the negotiations multilateral and of conferring permanent jurisdiction to the United Nations as a means of keeping the question open.

The draft proposed by the four South American states *urged* the two parties to reopen negotiations, with the intent of settling all differences over the application of the Paris Agreement. It *recommended* that in the event of a failure to reach a satisfactory conclusion within a reasonable period of time, the parties should give favorable consideration to the possibility of submitting the dispute to the appropriate judicial organs. It *invited* the two countries to refrain from taking any action that would prejudice the friendly relationship between them.[42]

In the framing of this latter draft, attention had been given not only to Italy's requirements but also to the various opinions within a majority of the committee. The chances of its being accepted by two-thirds majority had been carefully calculated. This was the reason for using the phrase "appropriate judicial organs" instead of mentioning The Hague Court explicitly.

The first speaker was Kreisky. He gave a brief account of the Austrian draft resolution and replied to certain earlier criticisms of the first draft. In his view, minorities "that had been deprived of fundamental democratic rights" were inevitably a cause of mounting distrust between the states concerned.

Martino then asked to reply. He began by listing a number of criticisms of the new Austrian draft resolution and went on to demonstrate once again the revisionist character of Vienna's real intent. If the negotiations were to be confined to the application of the 1946 Paris Agreement, Italy was ready to reopen discussions with Austria and, if these should fail, to refer the matter to

The Hague Court for judgment.[43] Martino was followed by the delegates of Pakistan, Jordan, Ireland, Turkey, Ecuador, Lybia, Cyprus, and Peru. The Chairman then called on Velasquez of Uruguay to speak, and the latter briefly outlined the draft resolution presented by Uruguay, Argentina, Brazil, and Paraguay. The session was then declared closed.

At the morning session of October 26, the first delegate scheduled to speak was Kreisky. His long speech was certainly the best he had made during the entire debate. Among other things, he omitted nothing in the way of arguments or appeals that might elicit sympathy from the majority of his audience. Typical of this were his opening remarks urging the committee not to betray the hopes of those who had put their faith in the United Nations. This was followed by an attempt to refute the charges of pan-Germanism. The next statement was probably the most important point made by him during the entire discussion. He was endeavoring to explain Austria's reasons for opposing an appeal to The Hague Court. *If the Court gave judgment for Italy, the Austrian government would see its ability to support the interests of the people of the South Tyrol severely compromised, but the problem would remain largely unsolved, since these people, as a minority group, felt themselves ill-treated and discriminated against.* If The Hague Court gave judgment for Austria, negotiations with Italy over autonomy must follow. It was, consequently, better to negotiate at once. In concluding, he suggested the wisdom of sending a commission of inquiry into the South Tyrol to decide whether he or Segni had given the more accurate account of the situation and expressed the hope that the new Austrian draft resolution would be approved.

Kreisky was a staunch advocate of this idea of the commission of inquiry and was to raise the matter on many other occasions under different circumstances. The purpose of this suggestion was really to make the application of domestic Italian legislation, including that touching on the Alto Adige, a matter of international concern. No one could deny that the De Gasperi–Gruber agreement had created an international diplomatic aspect to the question, but, nevertheless, the problem retained an important domestic character. The international commission of inquiry would simply have the effect of adding fuel to the illusions and troubles there and of prejudicing the domestic factor. For this reason, the Italian government rejected this proposal whenever it was submitted by Kreisky or his successor.

Segni spoke after Kreisky. He expressed his appreciation of the attitude adopted by a majority of the speakers in the discussion and summed up the arguments advanced by both sides. First, a general opposition to the first Austrian draft proposal had emerged; he listed all the grounds for this opposition. Second, it was clear that there was no case of Italy denying its German-speaking inhabitants their basic human rights. Third, it had been demonstrated that the dispute concerned the interpretation and application of an international treaty. It was true that at first Austria had given the impression of wishing to take a different line, but this had met with "opposition from all those who had the maintainance of peace in Europe at heart, and who know that the existing frontiers there cannot be altered without the use of force." Finally, Segni said, there was clearly a general desire that Austria and Italy should resume direct negotiations as soon as possible to resolve the difficulties that had arisen over the application of the Paris Agreement.

The last part of his speech contained a statement of the Italian position. Italy had always expressed itself in favor of resuming negotiations, but it was important at this stage to consider what would happen in the event negotiations broke down. Here, Segni listed the reasons for referring the case to The Hague Court and pointed out what Austria's opposition to this really meant. He ended with a warm appeal to Kreisky to set out with Italy on the high road of respect for treaties and for the principles of the United Nations Charter.[44]

At this point, the chairman, Auguste, brought the general debate to a close and invited the committee to rule on the two draft resolutions. The first speaker was Martinez of Chile, who said that he would vote for the draft resolution put forward by the Four. Similar statements were made by Berard (France), Ramirez Boettner (Paraguay), and Amadeo (Argentina). Massoud-Ansari (Iran) said that he was inclined to vote for the Austrian proposal, provided it was amended by the inclusion of a clause recommending that both parties consider the possibility of referring to The Hague Court for judgment all questions concerning the interpretation of the rights laid down in the 1946 agreement. Iran was likewise supporting the draft resolution of the Four, but would also favor any amendment that would reconcile the points of view of the two governments concerned.

Kreisky then stated that he opposed both the draft resolution of the Four and the request for a priority vote made by Amadeo. In his view, the Austrian proposal was constructive, whereas the South American proposal was based on the expectation that negotiations would break down. Kreisky spoke as though he saw no difference between the initially stated intentions of the two proposals with regard to the aims of the negotiations and asked why the Austrian formula was not accepted, without explaining why Austria opposed that of the Four.

Finally, O'Brien (Ireland) gave his opinion that the points of view of the two parties had drawn noticeably closer together, and called for the session to be adjourned for the preparation of a new text capable of securing a large majority, if not unanimous support. Mexico and India supported Ireland's request, which was thereupon approved.

At the opening of the afternoon session of October 26, the Irish delegate produced a draft resolution seconded by 10 countries, including: Cyprus, Denmark, Ecuador, India, Iraq, Jordan, Mexico, Ceylon, and Ghana (Bolivia and Cuba later supported it, too, which brough the number of its co-sponsors to 12).

The operative part of this draft *invited* Austria and Italy to press on with conducting negotiations to put into effect the Paris Agreement of September 5, 1946, to find a solution *which conformed with the principles of justice and of international law;* it *recommended* that if within a reasonable period time these negotiations failed to produce satisfactory results, both parties should consider favorably the possibility of seeking a solution to their differences that made use of other peaceful methods, chosen by them; and it *recommended* that the two countries refrain from any action that might compromise the friendly relations between them.[45]

O'Brien then gave a detailed account of the new proposal. Jung of India, El-Farra of Jordan, Seidenfaden of Denmark, and Rossides of Cyprus, all supported the draft of the twelve cosponsors. The Chairman then suspended the session for twenty minutes to give the various delegations time to consider the new documents that had just been distributed.

This was undoubtedly a difficult moment for the Italian delegation. When the meeting was resumed, Willis of the United States made an important statement in which he totally rejected the Twelve-Power draft and declared that he was only prepared to vote in favor of that of the Four. This was the first time that America had put all her weight behind a statement pro-Italy. But the situation was far from being clear-cut. Asante, the representative of Ghana, and Shaha from Nepal, spoke immediately after Willis in favor of the Twelve-Power draft.

Martino then joined the discussion. He clearly stated that Italy could not accept the proposal drafted by the Twelve. It was a compromise, but only pro-Austria. The first paragraph of the document gave the impression that none of the earlier negotiations had ever taken place, and that until that moment Italy had failed to fulfill the terms of the Paris Agreement, since a solution according to the principles of justice and international law still had to be found. As for the second point, O'Brien's explanation of recourse to "any other peaceful method" in the event of a breakdown in the bilateral negotiations, actually inferred the exclusion of recourse to The Hague Court. This was clearly absurd. So much was said about respecting the Charter, but why was no reference made to Article 36, according to which legal controversies were to be referred to The Hague Court? The dispute had arisen over a difference in interpretation of a treaty: was this not a legal controversy? In conclusion, Italy firmly rejected the draft put forward by the Twelve and would vote for that of the Four.[46]

After Martino's words, it was no longer possible to uphold the pretense that the Twelve's proposal respected the arguments of both parties, since one of them had explicitly demonstrated that this was not so and had declared that they were still a long way from a mutually acceptable proposal.

Amadeo of Argentina then said that in his opinion it was possible to take another step forward by finding a conciliatory formula that was really acceptable to everyone, and proposed that the session again be suspended. This proposal was accepted.

The negotiations to find a common draft resolution were neither quick nor easy. The final proposal, produced and signed by Argentina, Bolivia, Brazil, Canada, Ceylon, Cyprus, Denmark, Ecuador, Ghana, India, Iraq, Ireland, Jordan, Mexico, Norway, Paraguay, and Uruguay, stated that:

Whereas the status of the German-speaking inhabitants of Bolzano province was determined by the Paris Agreement of September 5, 1946;

since this agreement laid down a system to guarantee these German-speaking inhabitants "complete equality of rights with the Italian-speaking inhabitants," by means of special provisions to safe-guard the racial characteristics and the cultural and economic development of the German-speaking element (Article 1 of the Paris Agreement);

having regard to the fact that a dispute had arisen between Austria and Italy over the application of the Paris Agreement;

urged the two parties involved to reopen negotiations to reach a final settlement of the dispute over the application of the agreement;

recommended that if these negotiations failed to reach a satisfactory conclusion within a reasonable period of time, both parties should favorably consider the possibility of finding a solution to their problems through some other agency envisaged by the Charter, among them the International Court of Justice, or some other peaceful method chosen by them;

also recommended that the countries in question should refrain from any action that might compromise the friendly relations between them.[47]

This text included in their entirety points 1 and 3 of the text of the draft resolution of the Four. Point 2 in one respect went beyond that of the Four, since it mentioned reference to The Hague explicitly, but on the other hand it retained the wording of the Twelve, since it also mentioned other peaceful methods to be chosen by common consent in the event of a breakdown of the bilateral negotiations over the fundamental issue involved.

The text was submitted before the committee by Amadeo at the afternoon session of October 27. After a brief discussion, the draft resolution was unanimously approved, and the drafts prepared by the Four and the Twelve withdrawn. Austria did not request that a vote be taken on her proposal. On October 31[48] the committee's draft resolution was approved, also unanimously, by the General Assembly.

Although the U.N. decision was apparently only of procedural significance, the fact that the motion was passed after the Austrian government's request had been rejected is of some importance, since Austria thus found herself restricted to discussing only the application of the Paris Agreement.

Austria had failed in her efforts to obtain a decision on the substantive issue, and consequently had to fall back on the positions she had held before the U.N. debate. Even her attempt on the procedural side, to involve the U.N. Secretary-General in the negotiations, had failed. The question at stake had been confirmed as being the application of the Paris Agreement. The very fact that Austria had been induced to associate herself with the U.N. decision was also a point in Italy's favor, so that from this view Italy's position was stronger than before the debate.

At the same time, mention had been made of other peaceful procedures, apart from the reference to The Hague Court, to be chosen by common agreement in the event of a breakdown in the bilateral negotiations. In addition, the Alto Adige problem had been discussed at an international forum, and future negotiations would no longer be entirely a private matter between Austria and Italy. Finally, it must be recorded that Kreisky felt justified in claiming success by engaging Italy to *negotiate* over the application of the De Gasperi–Gruber agreement, an expression, he maintained, that Rome would never have accepted. A simple reading of the text of the U.N. resolution is sufficient to reveal the fallacy of this curious interpretation. The text says to "reopen," thus in itself disposing of the argument that such procedure had not been used before.[49]

Though the legal nature of the dispute emerged clearly from the introductory sentences of the resolution, it would have been preferable if the latter had contained a clearer reference to the International Court. But, if it appeared at the time that a straight majority could have been attained with comparative ease on the four-power draft which Italy preferred, it appeared nonetheless doubtful that the same could be said of the required two-thirds majority.

Chapter VII

The Italo-Austrian
Controversy, from the First Meeting
between Segni and Kreisky
to the Submission of the Report
of the Commission of 19

[1] The first Austro–Italian meeting at Milan. The second Segni–Kreisky meeting at Klagenfurt. The third Austro-Italian meeting at Zurich and the continuation of the violence in the Alto Adige. The Viennese government rejects the Italian proposals and in its note of July 4, 1961 declares the bilateral talks closed. Discussions on the eve of the XVI U.N. General Assembly. [2] Scelba sets up the Commission of 19: its composition and opening session. [3] The debate in the Special Political Committee of the XVI General Assembly. The U.N. Resolution of November 30, 1961 and its consequences. [4] Renewal of talks between Italy and Austria through a series of strongly worded notes during the first half of 1962. Developments leading to the meeting between Piccioni and Kreisky on July 31, 1962. The Venice meeting and its consequences. Statements made by the two ministers of foreign affairs before the XVII U.N. General Assembly on September 25 and 28, 1962. [5] Renewed tension between Italy and Austria early in 1963. The problem of the resumption of bilateral negotiations and the outbreak of terrorism in the Alto Adige. Further worsening of relations between Italy and Austria. Kreisky insists on a meeting at Salzburg and rejects Piccioni's offer of discussions at New York. Delays in the Commission of 19 and failure to agree on a date for a new meeting between the foreign ministers. Speeches by Piccioni and Kreisky at the XVIII U.N. General Assembly on September 26, 27, 1963. Kreisky's recourse to his right to reply and Piccioni's rejection of his charges. The Geneva meeting on October 23, 1963 and that at Paris the following December. [6] The Commission of 19 completes its work. The consequences.

[1]

The Italian government implemented the U.N. recommendation without delay and had already decided by November 16 to contact the Austrian government to propose the reopening of bilateral talks.[1] The Italian invitation was promptly accepted by the Austrians.[2] On December 14, Segni was able to meet his Austrian colleague, Kreisky, in the Italian Embassy in Paris and both were in broad agreement on the need to resume the proposed talks with a first meeting at the ministerial level, to be held in Milan on January 27 and 28, 1961.[3]

The meeting between the foreign ministers immediately highlighted the substantial difference in interpretation which the two sides gave to Article 2 of the Paris Agreement of September 5, 1946. From the Italian point of view, the Rome government had already carried out the international obligations it had undertaken in Paris regarding the German-speaking group, and, consequently, the special statute governing the region of the Trentino—Alto Adige satisfied in full the provisions of the article under discussion. According to the Austrian delegation, Italy was to be considered in arrears in fulfilling its obligations, since the De Gasperi—Gruber agreement could be carried out only by granting the province of Bolzano autonomous status along the lines foreseen by the Tinzl—Sand draft law (a draft submitted to the Italian Parliament by these two representatives of the German-language minority on February 27, 1959 and immediately viewed as so broad in its compass as to endanger the integrity of the state).

Minister Segni and the under-secretary for foreign affairs, Russo, at that time had stated that no change would be acceptable in the constitution of the Italian state nor in Italian provisions governing regional status, since this would go beyond the international agreement reached in Paris; only its application was in question, not its revision. Italy stated that it was willing to introduce further provisions, as a concession within present constitutional arrangements, in favor of the German-speaking population of the province of Bolzano, on the condition that Austria recognize that in so doing the international controversy involved should finally be considered as settled. Among the provisions anticipated, it was suggested in particular that a study of the following four points should be included:

1) granting the province of Bolzano administrative powers in conformity with Article 13 and 14 of the Statute of the Region;

2) further steps to encourage employment of officials of Italian nationality but German mother-tongue;

3) further extension of the laws and regulations on the use of both languages;

4) other possible provisions within the framework of the regional statute in favor of the German-speaking population of the province of Bolzano.

On the other hand, Kreisky and Gschnitzer promptly indicated that they considered these proposals unsatisfactory and maintained the stand they had previously propounded. It was impossible to reconcile the two positions, so the two ministers agreed to refer back to their governments and to pursue through diplomatic channels all further steps needed to carry out the U.N. resolution.[4]

This first bilateral meeting between Italy and Austria, in compliance with paragraph one of the U.N. resolution of October 1960, was of particular importance not only because it once again pointed to what plainly appeared to be the real objective of the Austrian government, but because the stand taken at that time by Segni was also adopted by his successors—Piccioni, Saragat, and

Fanfani. The Italian position was the result of a decision taken collectively by the entire government in Rome.

The choice reached there hinged on two points. First, recognition of the fact that there was an international dispute between Italy and Austria over application of the De Gasperi–Gruber agreement and a determination to find a solution to it. Second, Italy sought to resolve the dispute with Vienna "by further improving the application of the Paris Agreement." This meant, in practice, that the Rome government, although once again reaffirming its own position, whereby Italy had already implemented the agreement, was now willing to entertain a number of new provisions in favor of the German-speaking minority in the Alto Adige in order to reach a solution of the dispute with Vienna. The type of provisions foreseen has already been referred to. Among these, the first was particularly prominent: "granting the province of Bolzano administrative powers in conformity with Article 13 and 14 of the Statute of the Region," a phrase which simply meant broadening the autonomy of that province.

The result of the Milan meeting did not terminate the talks, as both sides testified in later statements.

On February 3, 1961, Segni once again pointed out, in a statement to the Chamber of Deputies, that the Alto Adige problem could in no way be considered one of frontier revision and dismissed the possibility of seeking a solution through granting regional autonomy to the province of Bolzano. After illustrating at length the problem at issue in its domestic and international aspects, Segni concluded by declaring himself at all times ready to resume direct contact with Vienna and, in case of failure, to have recourse to the International Court of Justice in The Hague as the most suitable means of resolving the controversy.[5]

In Austria, the Minister of Foreign Affairs at once reiterated his government's well-known thesis, but also confirmed its wish to see the talks reopened as soon as possible.[6] Approaches through diplomatic channels continued.

During the course of these approaches, Kreisky sent his Italian counterpart two memoranda dated February 1 and March 13, 1961.[7] Ignoring the Tinzl–Sand draft law, the memoranda set out the principles which in the Austrian view would make it possible to achieve that protection of the individual characteristics of the German-language minority, along with its economic and cultural development, which were foreseen by the De Gasperi–Gruber agreement. In reply, the Italian government sent a *note verbale* on April 5, 1961,[8] indicating that notwithstanding its belief that the measures already adopted satisfied its international obligations and providing that this ended for all time the entire controversy with the Austrian government it was prepared to consider the adoption of additional individual measures in order to overcome any remaining differences regarding: the delegation of powers by the state and the region to the province of Bolzano, the participation of the German-speaking citizens in public posts, the linguistic parity and related areas. The Italian Embassy in Vienna was at the same time instructed to propose that a second meeting take place in Klagenfurt between the two foreign ministers.

In its *note verbale* of April 23, 1961[9] the Austrian government accepted the Italian suggestion for the Klagenfurt meeting, withholding its reply on the Italian proposals until that meeting. It requested that Austria's proposals also be considered at the same conference and reaffirmed its opinion that the government in Rome had not yet fulfilled Article 2 of the De Gasperi—Gruber agreement.

Although the atmosphere at the Klagenfurt meeting, May 24—25, 1961, was undoubtedly the least tense in the first series of Italo-Austrian meetings, there was considerable strain as a consequence of the arrest on Italian territory of Dr. Stadlmayer (who had been a member of the Austrian delegation to the United Nations and at Milan and was, in addition, a member of the Tyrol regional government)[10] and of the resumption of terrorist activities in the Alto Adige.

The talks centered principally upon the Italian *note verbale* of April 5 and the two Austrian memoranda of February 1 and March 13, to which the Austrian delegation added a third, dated May 25,[11] detailing the nature of the legislative and administrative autonomy requested by the Viennese government for the province of Bolzano. Although no common consensus on the conflicting convictions was reached, the softer tone and the increased attention paid to the substance of the problem rather than to formal issues gave rise in some quarters to the hope that better things lay ahead. Unfortunately, this illusion was soon replaced by considerable pessimism. Because of the wide difference in the two points of view and the complexities of the latest Austrian proposals, it was agreed to adjourn the discussion to another meeting in Zurich on June 24.[12]

During the nights of June 11 and 12, on the eve of the Zurich meeting scheduled for June 13—17 to prepare the groundwork for the Kreisky—Segni talks, no less than forty-seven dynamite explosions occurred in the Alto Adige. On June 24, the Tyrol regional government made a solemn appeal to the United Nations and to Italy, circulated by the Austrian press agency APA, declaring that the government in Innsbruck had nothing to do with any acts of terrorism; the blame rested with Italy for having refused the request for a new and full autonomy.[13]

It is doubtful that this appeal to the United Nations at the very time that Austrian and Italy were holding talks in accordance with the resolution of the United Nations was proper. Moreover, several circumstances added further questions of a procedural nature. The Tyrol regional government confined itself to stating it was "deeply moved" by the acts of terrorism, instead of condemning them explicitly, and explained the "tragic developments of the situation in the South Tyrol" by placing the blame on Italy for not having "granted a true autonomy within the Italian State, as promised by the Paris Agreement." It did not overlook the opportunity to recall the "incredible patience" of the people of this zone in "setting aside (not, it will be noted, in renouncing) their "natural right of self-determination." The appeal called upon the United Nations "to face this special situation with special measures in order to re-establish calm and freedom in the South Tyrol and thus construct the groundwork for a just solution to the problem." The "special measures" they were advancing were divulged at the Zurich meeting by Kreisky, with whom the appeal must have been coordinated.

At the beginning of the talks between the two foreign ministers, Segni firmly reminded the Austrian government of its responsibilities, stressing the fact that the acts of terrorism were known to have been prepared beyond the Italian frontier and to have in many cases received encouragement from Austrian circles.[14] In his reply, Kreisky maintained that the Rome government had not indicated the source of its charges, and recalled that a member of the Austrian delegation (Dr. Stadlmayer) was still held in an Italian prison. He stated that the methods adopted by the Italian authorities had given rise to profound misgivings in Austria.[15]

The Zurich talks appeared to indicate that a marked increase in the influence of Austrian and Tyrolese extremist elements had forced the Viennese government's hand. Indeed, Austria decided to return to the position it had taken in Milan, insisting that only the project for autonomous status for the province of Bolzano, proposed by Tinzl–Sand on February 27, 1959, could provide a satisfactory solution to the problem. Confronted by the Italian delegation's opposition to this, Austria affirmed that the first part of the U.N. Resolution of October 21, 1960, (resumption of bilateral talks) should by now be considered as concluded and that the second part, the search for a peaceful solution of the controversy, would come up for immediate consideration. To this end, Kreisky formally proposed the appointment of an international commission of inquiry to study the facts and problems on the spot.

Segni declined to go along with Kreisky's view that the bilateral talks should be considered as completed and repeated the Italian thesis that the International Court of Justice could have provided in due course the most appropriate peaceful methods of solution.[16]

What Innsbruck's and Vienna's plans were at the time of the Zurich meeting now appeared clear. Relying on the acts of terrorism in the Alto Adige, it was hoped to awaken sufficient sympathy in the United Nations to force Italy—during a new debate at the forthcoming XVI Assembly—to accept some peaceful method of solution which, being other than the purely legal approach through the International Court of The Hague, could lead to an amendment or broadening of the Paris Agreement, an agreement by now deemed insufficient by the Tyrolese.

The statements made by Segni at his press conference in Zurich at the end of the talks on June 25, 1961,[17] and over the radio and television on his return to Rome the same day,[18] form two documents which even today, years after the event, provide a measure of the tension at that time. On the Austrian side, Kreisky held a press conference at the Hotel Dolder[19] at which he renewed the stand he had taken in the talks with Segni. Immediately upon his return to Vienna, Kreisky sent a note[20] to Italy, on July 4, 1961, formally stating that:

(a) Vienna considered the proposals made by Italy at the Zurich meeting to be unsatisfactory; (b) the federal government of Austria considered the phase of bilateral talks to be closed; and (c) with reference to point 2 of the U.N. resolution, Vienna formally renewed the proposal made at Zurich for the selection of an international commission of inquiry charged with ascertaining the facts and conditions prevalent in the Alto Adige and seeking a clarification of the controversy, thus to facilitate its solution.

The first Italian reaction to the Austrian diplomatic offensive and the continuation of the outrages was the decision to require visas for all Austrian citizens entering Italy, effective July 12, 1961. At the same time, the Italian Foreign Minister handed the Austrian Ambassador in Rome a note on the acts of terrorism carried out in the Alto Adige.[21] The note pointed out that the devices used in the explosions were unquestionably of Austrian origin and, further, that these outrages were preceded by a widespread campaign of agitation carried out on Austrian territory and aimed at creating the necessary atmosphere for them. It was also noted, regretfully, that no serious action appeared to have been taken by the Austrian government to curb these dangerous developments. Finally, the Italian government indicated its intention to promptly provide further details on the various points made in the note. Apart from Segni's statements at Zurich, the problem of Austria's responsibility was faced fully here for the first time, and this also represented an implicit reply to the appeal issued by the Tyrolese government in Innsbruck to the United Nations and to Italy.

The Italian position was further made clear by Prime Minister Fanfani, who, in a statement before the Chamber of Deputies on July 13, 1961, stressed that the continuation and extension of the violence, however, had induced the government to suspend its reply to the Austrian note of July 4.[22]

The exchange of notes on the outrages nevertheless increased. On July 21, the Austrian Ministry of Foreign Affairs handed a note to the Italian Embassy in Vienna[23] in which the Italian charges of coresponsibility were rejected.

On July 26, the Italian foreign office's reply took the form of a long note,[24] which, after recalling the principles of international law governing the obligations binding upon every state in preventing its territory from being used as a base for the commission or preparation of acts harmful to foreign states, gave details in 3 appendices and 36 documents of violations committed by Austria. The note concluded by requesting: first (a) painstaking search for and punishment of those responsible; (b) the adoption of effective preventive measures; second (a) public disavowal of the hostile activities of bodies such as the Berg Isel Bund; (b) the termination of any moral or material support to such bodies; and third, scrupulous avoidance on the part of members of the government and other public authorities of any form of approval or other encouragement of violence and acts prejudicial to the Italian internal order.

As early as July 18, 1961, the Austrian government, determined to continue a policy that it still felt could lead to the embarrassment of Italy abroad, provoking a possible revision of the De Gasperi–Gruber agreement, had requested inclusion on the agenda of the XVI U.N. Assembly the question of the German-speaking minority in the Alto Adige.[25]

Vienna's reply to the Italian charges on Austrian responsibility for the outrage took the form of a *note verbale*[26] handed to the Italian Embassy in Vienna on August 1, 1961. This note stressed that Austria had always recognized the basic principle of international law under which every state is bound to respect the sovereignty of other states and to avoid intervention or any other form of interference. Its interest in the South Tyrol did not, however, involve such interference, since it was based upon the Paris Agreement as confirmed by the United Nations. Moreover: (a) toleration of criticism of foreign states and their institutions did not give rise to the incurring of any international responsibility; (b) propaganda in favor of the right of self-determination could not be illegal, such a right being recognized by the U.N. Charter; and (c) dispatch of explosives, printed material, and money by private citizens did not imply any responsibility on the part of the state. However, being now faced with a repetition of the Italian charges, Austria reiterated her request for the selection of an international commission of inquiry.

In spite of these arguments, the substance of the points made earlier by the Italian Foreign Ministry, and above all the facts themselves, continued to remain unchanged. Moreover, the proposed institution of an international commission of inquiry did not appear to make very much sense, since *up till then* Kreisky had spoken of an inquiry to be held in the Alto Adige, while the accused were to be found in Austria.

In another *note verbale* on September 7, 1961[27] the Italian Ministry of Foreign Affairs replied by pointing out that, apart from the welcome recognition by Vienna of the principles of international law to which the government in Rome had referred, the Austrian defense was purely generic, the detailed points covered by the Italian documentation remained unanswered.

On the eve of the XVI U.N. General Assembly, September 18, 1961, the Italian government sent Austria a long note[28] through the Italian Embassy in Vienna, giving a detailed outline of its own stand. In this note, after criticizing Austria's hasty inclusion of the problem on the U.N. agenda, at a time when the negotiations authorized by the U.N. resolution had undergone no interruptions and no such thing as a deadline dictated its inclusion as a matter of urgency, the Italian government rejected the proposed setting up of an international commission of inquiry. It stated that the discussions between Vienna and Rome had confirmed that the controversy hinged upon an interpretation of the Paris Agreement and that the International Court of Justice would represent the most appropriate way for its settlement. Further, while underlining the importance of the proposals already made and the advisability of a more detailed study by the Austrian government, the note pointed out that Austria had insisted upon proposals in no way foreseen by the Paris Agreement of September 5, 1946 and had sought to prematurely close discussion on the first stipulation of the U.N. resolution.

Italy believed that Austria could well reconsider such measures as might bring, when combined with those already taken in carrying out the De Gasperi—Gruber agreement, new and substantial advantages to the Italian population speaking the German language. Notwithstanding the nonconstructive stand taken in the Austrian document, the Italian government added that it would not be diverted from its intention of protecting the heritage and free development of the German-speaking minority. For this purpose, it had recently taken the initiative, with the support of the leaders of the language groups involved, to carry out a joint review of the local situation in order to overcome the difficulties.

It developed that this move was well-timed and prompted serious reflection in Innsbruck and Vienna, where some misgivings were beginning to be harbored over the turn of events; some of the leaders of the German-language minority in the Alto Adige were noting signs of local concern over the consequences of the extremist policy that was being pursued.

[2]

For the first time, the Italian note of September 18 contained an explicit reference in an international communication to a domestic project reviewing the problems of the Alto Adige with the participation of representatives of the populations involved. The interministerial decree setting up the review commission under consideration, later called the Commission of 19, and including the German-speaking deputies in the Italian Parliament as well as some representatives of the *Südtiroler Volkspartei,* was dated September 1, 1961. It originated, however, from the wish of the Italian government again to offer the people of the Alto Adige that exchange of views already offered them by De Gasperi on the eve of the Paris Peace Conference and at the time rejected under Austrian pressure, based on the hope of a modification of the Brenner frontier. The experience of the talks between Rome and Vienna had made things considerably worse rather than better, and Italy now sought to return to a method which in the years immediately following the liberation of Italy had enabled it to introduce a whole series of measures aimed at protecting the minority group of German origin. This was the idea of the minister of the interior, Scelba, and it was favorably received in the Alto Adige.

On September 12, the commission held its first meeting at the Viminale. Scelba delivered an important address. He made several points that are worth noting and repeated statements he had made earlier on June 18, 1961, at Bolzano to the mayors, local officials, and representatives of industry and commerce in the province, and on June 22, to the Chamber of Deputies during the debate on his ministry's budget. The first point was that local interests were in harmony with national interests. Second, he officially expressed the Italian government's intention not "to confuse the German-speaking population of the province of Bolzano with the terrorists."[29] Nevertheless, "respect for democratic practice does not limit itself to the rejection of violence, but calls for cooperation—within the limits of each person's possibilities—in discouraging violent elements."[30]

A third fundamental principle concerned the inviolability of the Brenner frontier:

It is indisputable that the foundation of the De Gasperi–Gruber agreement rested on the moral obligation to consider the question of the frontier between the two states as definitely closed.[31] The directives followed (i.e., by the Italian government) can be synthesized in the words: intangibility of the frontiers of the state. . . .[32]
I am deeply convinced that if everyone, in and outside the Alto Adige, will accept once and for all that the Brenner frontier is inviolable and hence that the German-speaking language group of the Alto Adige is destined to continue to live within the Italian borders . . . then preconceived notions should give place to serious discussion and reasoned solutions.[33]

Equally important was his statement referring to the frank and sincere recognition of possible weaknesses in the present structure and of the possibility of remedying them.

Even admitting that the statute may not achieve maximum autonomy and that there may have been shortcomings in its practical application, we cannot overlook what has been done and achieved.[34] Nor can one deny, or underestimate, the efforts made by the central government to seek a solution, albeit gradually, to the problems inherent in the development of an autonomous local government and in the economic and cultural progress of the province of Bolzano.[35] The basic concepts of the Italian position are of course known . . . and may be summed up as . . . the will to entertain in the best good faith any proposal aimed at the removal of shortcomings—if there have been any—in the application of the De Gasperi–Gruber agreement and at achieving, within the present constitutional framework, an increase in the powers of local self-government.[36] Indeed, for this very reason we do not find it beneath the dignity of the state and the authority of government to discuss with political and local government leaders of the province of Bolzano, the interests of the people they represent. . . . It is because we consider citizens of German language as Italian citizens, on an equal footing with all other Italian citizens, that we believe it our duty to listen to their suggestions, to accept their offers of collaboration.[37]

As to the aims and limits of such improvements, the Italian government's position was stated as follows:

The legitimate ambition of preserving the heritage of one's language and of one's own particular cultural traditions has no connection with the attempts to transform the province of Bolzano into a sort of family holding and to violate the natural evolution of things, nor does it justify a proud isolation from the life of the state in which one lives.[38] The government rejects any proposal—aimed openly or covertly or even as part of a long-term approach—to sever the province of Bolzano from the ties which render it an integral part of the Italian state.[39]
As to the future development of the province of Bolzano, I believe that the doctrine that everything centers on ensuring protection of the rights of the

German minority is mistaken ... the Alto Adige is not only inhabited by German-speaking citizens but also by those who speak Italian ... the very integration of the industrial sector with the agrarian and tourist economy achieved by Italy, stands as the basis for the prosperity of the region. The Italian government cannot ignore this reality. ... It appears to me that the moment has arrived to make an effort to jettison the policy of support for this unnatural division and for the German-speaking group to abandon its fear of pursuing a common goal with the Italian-speaking population living in the Alto Adige.[40] Just as the right of protection of the ethnic and cultural heritage of minorities condemns any act or artifice impairing such heritage, so, and by the same token, does it condemn any act hindering civilized coexistence and progress.[41]

The liberal and realistic stand taken by the most qualified member of the Italian government made a certain impression. It was also accompanied by the solemn declaration that: "In carrying out its task, the Commission (i.e., Commission of 19) is entirely free, not being bound by previous undertakings of any sort, since these do not exist, nor by any preconceived plans."

In effect, this amounted to reconfirmation of the policy already laid down by the government at the first Austro-Italian meeting at Milan. The measures then contemplated for improving the statute of the German-speaking minority in the Alto Adige were directly linked to termination of the international controversy, but, as a purely domestic undertaking, it was proposed to study the measures that would be required in collaboration with representative elements of the minority: a method which was, in any case, in full accord with the Paris Agreement. However, both as a matter of domestic and of international concern, it had been decided to propose new liberal measures. It was this policy that received approval in Parliament.

[3]

The U.N. debate[42] was opened in the Special Political Committee with a speech by Kreisky on November 15, 1961. He began by stating that Austria did not seek revision of the Brenner frontier (he quoted in full, however, his own earlier statements on self-determination), but merely a full autonomous status for the province of Bolzano. Since the bilateral negotiations had produced no results, the Vienna government had proposed to seek a peaceful method of settling the controversy without, however, receiving a prompt reply from Italy. Hence the new recourse to the United Nations. The Austrian Foreign Minister then gave the reasons which he believed favored the selection of the commission of inquiry. Rejecting the charges of Austrian responsibility for the terrorism and stating that he was ready to receive an international commission of inquiry on Austrian territory to look into those charges, Kreisky concluded by emphasizing the urgent need to find a solution and thanked the United Nations for the opportunity afforded a small power to put forward its views.

While outwardly moderate, this statement by the Minister, containing only one new element, namely, the proposal that an international commission of inquiry operate also in Austria to investigage Vienna's possible responsibility for the demonstrations, was in effect uncompromising.

Segni replied the following day, November 16. The Italian Minister began by pointing out that the U.N. General Assembly resolution of the previous year had categorically rejected Austria's thesis seeking to attain modification of existing agreements and had stipulated that the proposed Austro-Italian negotiations should be limited to the application of the De Gasperi–Gruber agreement. Kreisky's proposals in Milan, Klagenfurt, and Zurich, as indeed now his speech before the Special Political Committee, completely ignored such limitations. Segni went on to give his government's view of the talks in the three cities and specifically challenged Kreisky's allegation that Italian delay in replying to Vienna's note on July 4 had forced Austria on July 18 to put the Alto Adige question once again on the U.N. agenda. Segni then outlined the reasons which led him to maintain that the Austrian government was guilty of negligence and had given moral support to the outrages. He explained the political and historical origins of the Commission of 19, its composition, and its purpose. Upon the completion of its work, the commission was to make a report to the government, which would constitute the basis for the final decisions to be adopted by Italy. In his view, the constructive approach and democratic spirit behind the decision to set up the Commission of 19 deserved recognition. On the other hand, in order to enable the commission to carry out its work, a favorable atmosphere would have to be created. Should this occur, and the commission, therefore, be in a position to put forward reasonable proposals in a reasonable form, the Italian government would be encouraged to take the necessary decisions to solve the Austro-Italian controversy once and for all.

Segni also explained why Italy believed that the period of bilateral negotiations was not at an end and pointed to the reasons why the proposed commission of inquiry could in no case serve as the appropriate "peaceful method." Here it was not a question of determining the existence or not of certain facts, but rather one of deciding which of two conflicting interpretations of the Paris Agreement was the correct one. Segni's words had a positive effect, though it should be noted that they contained the first announcement by Italy to the United Nations of the establishment of the Commission of 19 to study the problems.

Kreisky replied to the Italian Foreign Minister on November 21. In Vienna's view there was little to be gained by discussing—as Segni had done—the origins of the U.N. resolution. What was important was to secure the German-speaking minority appropriate conditions for the protection of their national heritage and way of life. What Austria sought was precisely the application of the Paris Agreement, and, in Kreisky's view, what had occurred since 1946 nullified the objectives of the agreement itself. The Italian offers carried no guarantee. At the same time, it was quite clear that the object of the De Gasperi–Gruber agreement certainly had not been to set up an autonomous region in the Trentino.

As to the Commission of 19, while welcoming the fact that it had been set up, Kreisky was not fully satisfied either as to its composition—initially projected on the basis of an equal representation and later changed to an Italian-speaking majority—or as to its terms of reference. Moreover, what action would be taken once its report was submitted? Austria did not look with enthusiasm on the proposed reference to the International Court, primarily for the delay this would involve but also because he did not see why one side should propose a single "peaceful method" and the other be held to accept it.

This was the second time that Austria explicitly referred to a query she had already raised at the Zurich meeting, a possible guarantee of any concessions that Italy might make in favor of the Alto Adige population. The subject that was later to become so important was hardly touched upon and did not take the form of a request in the proper sense of the word.

After Kreisky, Martino spoke for Italy. In his opinion, Austria's principal intent was to keep the Alto Adige question open. Kreisky's denial that he sought a frontier revision was contradicted by his behavior as well as that of his government. Martino then spoke of the terrorism, pointing out the ambiguous nature of Austrian official condemnations and listing equivocal phrases used by public spokesmen. Such outrages were in no way in keeping with the spirit of paragraph 3 of the U.N. Resolution. Italy wished to see the matter closed with a definitive ruling such as only the International Court of Justice could give.

The delegates from Argentina, Iran, Lebanon, Mali, Panama, Indonesia, and Mexico then took their turns at the rostrum. They were all, though with varying arguments, in favor of the continuation of the bilateral talks.

Discussion in the Special Political Committee was resumed on the morning of November 22. The first speaker was the delegate of Peru, who was followed by those of Yemen, France, the U.S.A., Cambodia, Greece, Colombia, the Republic of China, and Chile. These also all supported the Italian point of view. The delegate of Afghanistan, on the other hand, perhaps recalling his own country's claim to territory along the Pakistan border, took a position favorable to Austria.

The Cypriot delegate spoke next and offered a draft resolution jointly with India and Indonesia. Paragraph 1 of this document called upon the two parties to continue their efforts to reach an understanding on the basis of the Paris Agreement, in accordance with the U.N. resolution of October 31, 1960. The second paragraph recommended that the parties agree, should the talks fail, on the selection of bodies or persons who could assist in promoting application of the same resolution. The third paragraph recommended that the parties involved abstain from any action liable to compromise their friendly relations.

This unsatisfactory proposal was turned down peremptorily by the Italian delegate, Martino, who merely stated for the moment that there was no cause to amend last year's resolution.

In a night session on November 22, the committee was addressed by the delegates of Dahomey, the Philippines, Guatemala, Turkey, Yugoslavia, Spain, Liberia, Uruguay, Brazil, Ceylon, and Ecuador, who all expressed themselves in terms similar to those of the large majority of their colleagues who had spoken on the issue.

Kreisky then took the floor. Perhaps he had not expected the draft resolution submitted by Cyprus, India, and Indonesia and so restricted himself to thanking previous speakers for their statements, which, in fact, had hardly been in support of his claim since a considerable majority favored Italy's case.

Segni followed and spoke at length both in defense of Italy's case and to give reasons behind his delegation's rejection of the new draft resolution. The committee was favorably impressed by the five points he made. The preamble of the new draft resolution, he said, referred to the negotiations held between January and July and to negotiations which had been abortive. The truth was that negotiations had not been confined to this period and it was premature to say they had failed. The question at issue did not consist of seeking a solution that was "peaceful and just," but in applying the Paris Agreement. Further, if Austria and Italy had not reached a direct agreement on this subject, how could they possibly be expected to agree on trusting a third party with the role of a mediator? Nor was it a question of *continuing* to avoid acts likely to affect relations between the two countries, but of avoiding such acts purely and simply, for otherwise the wording would have offered encouragement to the terrorists. Moreover, there were two new developments: the setting up of the Commission of 19 and the resumption of Austro-Italian contacts; both of these were promising. Italy, consequently, remained faithful to the 1960 resolution, which it considered as being still in force.

This speech marked the close of the general discussion, which ended on a note clearly favorable to Italy. At the same time, the specific mention of the Commission of 19 in the course of the debate was of fundamental importance in securing the acceptance of Italy's arguments for the continuation of bilateral talks under paragraph 1 of the 1960 resolution. However, this also entailed calling the attention of the United Nations to the commission's work and especially to its conclusions.

During the vote the following morning, Kreisky again sought to bring up the issue in an attempt to redress the balance. But it was too late. His was a bitter and resentful speech that was in no way helpful to the Austrian case. At one point he stated that he had proof that the Italian police had resorted to atrocious methods of torture, comparable only to those of the Nazis and Fascists. At another, he reiterated his often expressed judgment that the ideal statute for the German minority was the one provided by Finland for the Swedes of the Aaland Islands, overlooking the great and varied differences between the two cases. Segni then replied, denying in no uncertain terms the charges of torture of German-speaking inhabitants of the Alto Adige by the Italian police.

The effect of Segni's statement the previous night brought quick results. The coauthors of the draft resolution were themselves influenced by it, and when the Australian delegate proposed a short suspension of the debate, the representatives of Cyprus, India, and Indonesia agreed on presentation of a new text as follows:

The General Assembly:
Recalling its resolution of the previous year;
having taken note with satisfaction of the negotiations taking place between the two parties;
having also taken note that the dispute had not been resolved;
invites the two parties to continue their efforts to find a solution in accordance with paragraphs 1, 2, and 3 of the above mentioned resolution.

This new draft was promptly supported by Argentina, Chile, Guatemala, Ireland, Peru, Sweden, U.A.R., and Yemen. Within a few minutes, after Segni had rejected a suggestion by the delegate of Ceylon to suppress the reference to paragraph 3, the new draft was adopted unanimously by the Special Political Committee and likewise unanimously endorsed by the General Assembly in its meeting on November 30, 1961.

The second debate in the United Nations on the question came to a close with an endorsement of the Italian arguments. Rome had maintained that bilateral talks were not yet exhausted, and the new resolution urged their continuation. Vienna had sought to make use of the tension created by the violence, but the United Nations had confirmed that the controversy turned on interpretation of the Paris Agreement and had dropped the proposal for a commission of inquiry. Certainly there were also limits to the possibilities of Italian action in the United Nations, but these were distinctly less than those confronting Austria. Kreisky must have understood that if he still wished to achieve his aim to amend the De Gasperi—Gruber agreement, he would have to seek new ways, and this is precisely what he tried to do during the years that followed.

[4]

Deliberations between Vienna and Rome were resumed on January 25, 1962, in the form of a long note from the Italian Foreign Ministry in which, based on the evidence given at the trial held in Graz on December 6—8, 1961,[43] attention was drawn to the direct and indirect responsibilities of the Vienna government for the demonstrations. In particular, it was confirmed at the trial that: (a) terrorist training courses had been organized by Austrian citizens on Austrian territory; (b) explosives of Austrian origin had been smuggled into Italy by Austrian citizens for use in the outrages; (c) Austrian citizens had personally taken part in carrying out the attacks on Italian territory; and (d) the Austrian authorities—and in particular the ministers of the interior and of justice—had long been aware of these illegal activities. The note went on to state that: (a) the three principal defendants were members of the Bund; (b) it was at a meeting of the Bund that it was decided to smuggle explosives into Italy; (c) terrorist training courses were held on behalf of the Bund; (d) German-speaking Italian citizens were given political indoctrination on the premises of the Bund and instructed on how to act if arrested by the Italian police.

All this amounted to a rejection of the Austrian idea that terrorist activities were merely the result of the alleged exasperation of the German-speaking inhabitants of the Alto Adige. The terrorist activities had, on the contrary, been organized on Austrian territory, and were also the result of a long and slanderous campaign to instill hatred for Italy. Therefore, the Italian government was once more obliged to request the Austrian government to: (a) take steps to prevent the operation of Austrian organizations fomenting activities hostile to the major leaders involved; (b) put an end to the campaign of venomous incitement against Italy, disassociating from it, first and foremost, members of the federal government and its executive organs; (c) take adequate measures to prevent the operation of Austrian organizations fomenting activities hostile to Italy; (d) abide by the applicable rules of international law; (e) conform with paragraph 3 of the U.N. resolution of October 21, 1960; and (f) keep the Italian government informed of the results of the inquiries carried out in Austria.

On January 27, 1962, the Austrian Embassy in Rome returned the note, stating that it contained a series of inaccuracies: it was couched in terms that strongly contrast with the tone normally used in exchanges between sovereign states; it did not take into account the steps already taken by the Austrian government nor of the moderation the latter had shown in the matter of the treatment accorded members of the Alto Adige who were taken into preventive custody.[44] To this the Italian Foreign Ministry replied on the same day,[45] pointing out that (a) the accusation of "inaccuracies" was left generic and undocumented; (b) that the tone adopted by the Italian note did not differ from that of earlier ones, and Austria had not indicated in what respect it conflicted with established international usage; (c) account had been taken of the measures adopted by the Austrian federal government; (d) far from showing moderation, a widespread campaign had been started against Italy based on slanderous assertions and inaccuracies; (e) contrary to the Austrian charge, the Italian note was aimed at clarifying the spirit of paragraph 3 of the U.N. resolution referred to. As a consequence, the Italian Ministry of Foreign Affairs in its turn, rejected the note presented by the Austrian Embassy in Rome.

Two days later, the Austrian Embassy in Rome replied[46] that the Italian note dealt with matters already discussed at the United Nations, ignoring the fact that the circumstances emerging from the Graz trial were something quite new. Consequently, the Viennese government did not see the wisdom of opening a new discussion.

It was perhaps unavoidable that after the unilateral termination of talks at Zurich, the sharp debates in New York and the Austrian disappointment over the failure of its U.N. move, the renewal of contacts between Rome and Vienna should reflect the difficulties of resuming negotiations. However, gradually the attitude began to prevail in Austria that, at least for the time being, no advantage was to be gained from pushing things too far. After some further written skirmishes, followed a short while later by another exchange of notes on matters already raised by the two sides,[47] the Austrian government stated on March 8, 1962, that it was "ready to resume as soon as possible the negotiations interrupted some time ago and aimed at a solution to the problem of the South Tyrol."[48]

The Italian Embassy in Vienna replied to the Austrian memorandum on March 27, 1962.[49] This reply stated that Italy was firmly convinced of the common interest in overcoming all difficulties between the two governments concerning the implementation of the Paris Agreement (this, and not "the problem of Süd Tyrol" being the accurate definition of the subject of disagreement). At the same time, precisely in order to further these results and in line with paragraph 3 of the U.N. resolution, it seemed desirable to Italy that Austria carefully avoid any action that might disturb friendly relations between the two countries and also give serious study to the information received from Italy on this subject. The Italian government was, in any event, "always ready to examine the situation with the Austrian government by holding talks directed toward a solution to the difficulties between them as defined above."

During this time, there were two factors that prompted the delay in the proceedings: first, the continued tension between the two countries,[50] and second, the fact that the Commission of 19 was at work. Without some reduction in tension, it was useless to reopen the talks with any real hope of success. At the same time, while the Foreign Ministry in Rome took great care to avoid giving the Commission of 19 any kind of an international character, no matter how minute, it could not be overlooked that its existence had been announced to the United Nations, where it was considered an event of political importance. Nor could it be ignored that any proposal made by the commission would have considerable influence both upon the stand taken by the Italian government and on that of the leaders of the German-speaking language group.

The Austrian government took no exception to the Italian Foreign Ministry's note and replied in a memorandum dated April 10, 1962,[51] that it had noted its contents with interest. With reference to the point raised in the last paragraph of the communication, the Austrian government asked to be informed as soon as possible as to when the Italian government would be ready to resume talks and went on to propose a meeting between the two foreign ministers.

On April 27, 1962, the Italian ambassador to Vienna, Enrico Martino, orally informed the Austrian director for political affairs, Minister Waldheim, that Rome preferred to await the results of the work of the Commission of 19 before fixing a date for the meeting of the two foreign ministers.[52] This proposal, which was at the same time logical and a possible source of uncertainty and disadvantage, was at first neither accepted nor entirely rejected by Vienna.

On May 22, 1962, the Austrian Ministry of Foreign Affairs pointed out in a note to the Italian Embassy that the Austrian government had patiently awaited results from the Commission of 19, results which for months had been given as imminent. Although the Austrian government, the memorandum continued, had for its part done its utmost to create an atmosphere of calm to assist the commission in its work, the repeated delay in completion had given rise to some concern in Austria. Nor could the Austrian government conceal that it had received no official indication as to the progress made by the commission, whose work should, it felt, be expedited. In conclusion, though appreciating Italy's desire to avoid prejudicing the work of the Commission of 19, Austria insisted on the necessity to reschedule the bilateral talks at the ministerial level as soon as possible.

The personal position of the Austrian Foreign Minister was not an easy one. On the one hand, he sought to give some satisfaction—at least of a formal nature—to public opinion in his own country through an immediate meeting with the new Italian foreign minister, Piccioni;[53] on the other, he was the first to appreciate how useful it would be if Vienna could in some way make use of the findings of the commission as a means of side-tracking the limitations imposed upon the Austro-Italian negotiations by the United Nations in seeking a solution "to the differences between the two governments over the interpretation of the Paris agreement."

The official reply of the Italian Foreign Ministry to Kreisky's note of May 22, 1962, was delivered on June 13.[54] This note recalled Italy's favorable attitude to the resumption of bilateral talks and then tackled the delicate question of the commission as follows:

> The Italian government has constantly been inspired by the firm desire to meet the legitimate claims of the German-speaking Italian population of the province of Bolzano, and this desire has not been affected by the various phases of the controversy with the Austrian government. Among other things, this desire has led to introducing, as a domestic measure, a joint review by those concerned with the principal problems involved in order to pin-point every possible means of improving the local situation and of overcoming the existing difficulties. This examination, conducted entirely as a domestic affair, may resort to criteria which are not subject to international involvement. On the other hand, since under given circumstances this review may lead to results that show that an international controversy no longer has reasonable grounds on which to survive, it has so far been considered preferable to avoid any step which might be likely to have an adverse effect upon these promising developments: and the Austrian government had indicated that it shared this legitimate concern.
>
> However, in view of the Austrian request to reschedule the talks in the near future, Italy was prepared to consider: . . . a meeting of the two Foreign Ministers, in Venice, in the month of July, subject to adequate preparation through diplomatic channels in order to ensure the most favorable conditions for its successful outcome.

Preparations for the Venice meeting were not easy and showed that Kreisky was either uncertain as to the best line to follow or under pressure from conflicting interests.

An Austrian memorandum of June 18, 1962,[55] proposed that the meeting could consider the following points: (a) briefing of the Austrian delegation by Italy on the internal steps previously taken toward solving the problem; (b) implementation of the U.N. resolution; (c) general questions, such as tourism, etc.

The Austrian move to internationalize as far as possible the work of the Commission of 19 was not limited to a request for official information from the Italian government to the Austrian delegation, but appeared even clearer in a passage in the memorandum intended to illustrate what Kreisky understood "fulfillment of the U.N. resolution" to mean.

The Italian government would send a note to the Secretary General of the U.N., referring to the relevant U.N. resolutions passed to date, and indicating it was endeavoring to seek a solution to the problem under domestic law, in line with those resolutions. . . . Should the proposed note be sent by the Rome government to the Secretary General of the United Nations, the Austrian government, after receiving adequate information from the Italian government, would in turn address a note to the Secretary General to state it had taken note of the Italian government's communication as to its internal efforts to settle the controversy, and would also express its own hope that the final outcome of the steps taken within Italy should form the basis of an agreement between the two states as provided for under the U.N. resolutions.

In an effort to render this move more acceptable, Kreisky was prepared to limit the size of the two delegations to a minimum, which in practice meant that the Tyrolese would not be invited.

The Italian reply was given on July 19, in the form of a memorandum[56] from the Italian Embassy in Vienna, which began by pointing out that according to the U.N. resolution, the bilateral talks were to cover disagreement over the application of the Paris Agreement. The note went on:

The points at issue for this purpose are those already identified in earlier phases of the talks. Among them, the Italian domestic survey which is referred to, evidently has no place. Whatever the outcome of such a survey and its possible results and consequences, it is clear that the work under way is purely a domestic matter carried out according to domestic considerations. Such activities cannot, therefore, become the subject of a communication either to the Austrian government or to the Secretary General of the U.N.

The Italian government was, at the same time, in agreement with the composition of the two delegations as proposed by Austria.

Vienna's reaction was immediate and clearly aimed at threatening a return to the rigid position it maintained at the Zurich talks. On July 20, a memorandum[57] from the Ministry of Foreign Affairs set down the agenda of the meeting between the two foreign ministers as follows: (1) general exchange of views on the "problem of the South Tyrol"; (2) in fulfillment of the two U.N. resolutions, discussion of (a) the language problem, (b) persons exercising the right of option, (c) the employment of "Südtiroler" in state or state-controlled positions, (d) low-cost housing, (e) cultural matters, (f) education matters, (g) employment, (h) right of residence, (i) the economic powers of the province of Bolzano, (h) right of residence, (i) the economic powers of the province of Bolzano, [no j, k] (l) agriculture and forestry, (m) commerce, (n) credit, industry, mining, tourism, hotel industry, public works, traffic, (o) legislation by the province of Bolzano on the organization of public administration, (p) fiscal and financial powers of the province of Bolzano.

The Italian reply was prompt, submitted in the form of a memorandum by the Italian Embassy in Vienna on July 25.[58] It began by emphasizing that the subject under discussion between the two governments was the controversy over the application of the Paris Agreement. It then pointed out that the subjects proposed by Austria were not a simple list of questions, but rather a list which, in practice, would tend to jeopardize the solutions to be sought; for this reason it appeared unsuitable as an agenda. The Italian government was convinced that it had carried out the Paris Agreement, but had declared itself willing to adopt suitable measures—within the present constitutional framework of the state and the region—in favor of the German-speaking population of the province of Bolzano in certain specified fields, in order finally to settle the controversy with the Austrian government. Italy was at all times willing to renew these offers and to continue bilateral talks.

As may be seen, the approach to the discussion on paragraph 1 of the U.N. resolution initiated by Segni at Milan was now confirmed by Piccioni. In order to settle the international controversy, Italy once more declared itself willing to adopt measures in favor of the German-speaking population of the province of Bolzano, renewing earlier offers, and to continue bilateral negotiations.

In order not to delay the proposed meeting by further discussion on its agenda, Kreisky decided to reply to the memorandum of the Italian Embassy on the same day, promptly dropping his previous proposal.[59] The new agenda was stream-lined to read: (1) discussion on application of the Paris Agreement of September 5, 1946; (2) discussion on application of resolutions 1497 and 1661 of the General Assembly of the United Nations; (3) exchange of views on other matters involving bilateral relations between Austria and Italy. Agreement between Rome and Vienna on this text was immediate. Kreisky and Piccioni, therefore, met in Venice on July 31.

Piccioni offered Kreisky the following alternative: either to resume talks where they were dropped at Zurich, or await the outcome of the work of the Commission of 19. Kreisky agreed to wait, but sought agreement to bring up for discussion between the two ministers the fate of proposals that might be advanced by members from the Alto Adige on the Commission of 19 but turned down by the commission as a whole. The Austrian suggestion was unsuccessful, since Piccioni had from the beginning declined to discuss the work of the commission. It was agreed, however, to hold another meeting between the two in the autumn. Kreisky also raised the question of the stand to be taken by the two countries in the United Nations. Piccioni suggested that when the heads of the two delegations made their statements in the general debate before the General Assembly they should confine themselves to mentioning the progress made. This Italian proposal was similarly accepted. The Austrian Foreign Minister then brought up the problem of the visas required on Austrian passports and his Italian counterpart agreed to review the matter. One or two minor matters were also raised, without producing anything more than an agreement to examine them carefully.

A new conciliatory spirit appeared indeed to inspire the Austrian delegation at Venice, as evidenced by the official communiqué issued at the end of the meeting.[60] Without much hesitation, Kreisky had agreed to await the outcome of the Commission of 19. His attempt to capitalize on all new proposals which the commission should make in favor of the population of the Alto Adige and then to negotiate from a position of strength those minority proposals that should be rejected, was abandoned after Piccioni had described such a method as "over-powering." For the first time, at this meeting, the Austrian delegation had not been accompanied by "Tyrolese experts," and there even seemed to be a lull in terrorist activities. Both sides appeared to be trying to reduce the tension and so Piccioni accepted the advice of some of his counselors to abolish the visa requirement and proceeded forthwith to do so.

As agreed upon in Venice, the Austrian government did not request inclusion of the question of the German-speaking language group in the Alto Adige on the agenda of the XVII U.N. General Assembly. Nevertheless, Kreisky's speech, delivered on September 25, 1962[61] during the general debate, did not lack a polemical tinge. He stated that the decision not to request the inclusion of the subject on the agenda had not been met with general approval in Austria and that the two U.N. resolutions had not been carried out. According to Kreisky, it had been agreed in Venice to examine at a further meeting between the two ministers the result attained by the Commission of 19, once Rome had decided what action to take as a result. In subsequent negotiations an effort would be made to solve any question that might still have been left open by the internal Italian Commission. In any case, in his view, only "a broad solution could be of lasting value."

This speech was rather revealing. Delivered at a time when tension between Rome and Vienna appeared to have substantially ebbed, it not only contained inaccuracies, but had also deferred to a considerable extent to extremist views. If, in Venice, Kreisky's line of action aiming at a substantive revision of the Paris Agreement had not appeared very evident, his speech at the United Nations revealed such a direction decidedly more clearly.

In his rejoinder during the general debate on September 28, Piccioni confirmed the stand taken by Italy during the earlier debates in 1960 and 1961. Italy recognized its international commitments, but would in no event or form accept any request for their revision. At Venice, it had merely been agreed to continue bilateral talks directed toward reaching a satisfactory solution. Moreover, the Austro-Italian controversy should also be viewed practically and clearly apart from the grave international problems confronting the world community that represented the main concern of the U.N. General Assembly.[62] Piccioni's statement gave rise to much discussion within the Austrian delegation, which, only after several hours' debate and in view of a possible and more detailed Italian rejoinder to Kreisky's speech, chose not to reply.

A renewed wave of demonstrations in the Alto Adige had led to a break in the promising atmosphere created at Venice. These attacks coincided with new general elections scheduled to be held in Austria on November 18. The two governments also stated their positions in press releases both dated November 5, 1962,[63] and these in effect opened a new phase of tension between Rome and Vienna.

[5]

The exchange of notes between Rome and Vienna during the long period of time necessary for the formation of the new Austrian cabinet, although frequent,[64] did not signal an immediate deterioration in relations between the two capitals. As soon as Chancellor Gorbach and Kreisky had both been confirmed in their offices and had officially resumed their posts, the Italian ambassador in Vienna, Enrico Martino, approached them on the subject of Italy's willingness to resume bilateral talks as soon as possible, a point already referred to by the chancellor himself in his policy speech delivered on April 3, 1963.

On April 9, a *note verbale* from the Austrian Embassy in Rome[65] formally communicated Vienna's request for a prompt resumption of talks between the two countries. Unfortunately, the note was sent when general elections in Italy were impending, and the elections were followed by a period of uncertainty as to the fate of Fanfani's administration.

The additional delay caused by Italian ministerial and parliamentary events lasted some time, and it was not until July 12—that is, immediately after the vote of confidence in Leone's administration—that the Italian Embassy in Vienna again officially took up, in the form of a *note verbale,*[66] the question of resuming Austro-Italian bilateral talks. The Italian government confirmed its support for a meeting between the two foreign ministers, but pointed out that its usefulness depended on its likely contribution to the talks as a whole, while its failure could adversely affect the entire situation. As a result, Italy believed it necessary to prepare the ground with care and was ready to do so in cooperation with Austria. With this in mind, two alternatives were put forward: either to let the two ministers decide on the guidelines for a meeting of experts to study the Italian proposals made at Zurich, or to hold a meeting of the experts of the two delegations before the meeting between the two ministers themselves.

The Austrian reply in the form of a proposal for a meeting in Rome of experts charged with drafting the agenda for the proposed meeting of the two foreign ministers to be subsequently held in Salzburg was favorably received by the Italian Foreign Ministry. As a result, the Austrian director of political affairs, Minister Waldheim, came to the Italian capital on July 29–30.

The striking coincidence between the departure of Minister Waldheim from Vienna and a new violent outbreak of terrorism in the Alto Adige may long remain a mystery. The natural suspicion of a connection between the two events does arise, especially since something very similar had happened on the eve of the Zurich meeting. Indeed, a little over a year later, an apparent connection led the governments of Rome and Vienna to agree that meetings between representatives of the two foreign ministeries should be held in secret.

Throughout August 1963, relations between Italy and Austria failed to improve. Two factors were responsible for this: continued outrages on Italian territory and a violent anti-Italian campaign in Austria following a decision by the Court in Trent to acquit members of the Italian military police charged with mistreatment of political detainees from the Alto Adige.[67] Throughout this period it seemed that extremist elements had definitively gained the upper hand in Austria and that a policy of calculated provocation was deliberately being followed. If marked inefficiency was shown by the Austrian police in preventing the frontier from being crossed by terrorists was not sufficiently surprising, [68] public statements by leading figures such as Chancellor Gorbach, Minister Kreisky, Under-Secretary Steiner, and various members of the Tyrolese regional government against the Italian police exceeded all bounds. If Vienna could prove its allegations of torture by the Italian police, there was no shortage of international bodies to which these matters could be referred, but it had no right to publicly insult the courts and administrative authorities of a neighboring state.

In the light of this situation, Leone's cabinet decided to defer the proposed Salzburg meeting. The decision was first announced verbally by the Italian government and then, in a note dated August 31,[69] attention was drawn to the situation caused by terrorist activities and the Austrian press campaign. The suggestion was made to hold the meeting in September in New York, where the two ministers would be attending the XVIII U.N. General Assembly. Should this not be suitable, the alternative was a meeting in October.

In its reply, in a note of September 7,[70] the Austrian Foreign Minister stated that it was a mistake to stress the activities of a few terrorists, which were condemned in the clearest manner by both government and public opinion in Austria. To do so would permit the terrorists to block meetings between the two foreign ministers whenever they wished. At the same time, while the proposal for a meeting in New York was declined, the Austrian government held it essential to fix a date forthwith and suggested any day between October 15–18. The Italian government accepted the proposal in a note on September 13,[71] at the same time emphasizing that the delay was not due to Italy. Such acceptance, it was added, was given, "provided that a recurrence of the violence should not render the meeting inadvisable."

In a *note verbale* dated September 24,[72] from the Austrian Embassy in Rome, Vienna stated that it took note with satisfaction that Italy accepted the Austrian suggestion to hold a meeting between the two ministers during October. At the same time, the Austrian government stated that it could not accept the reservation made by Italy and that further comment was unnecessary. It pointed out that it was unable to accept the condition on the reopening of the talks, since it felt that it was inadvisable to allow a few terrorists to influence the date of the meeting between the two ministers, especially since compliance with the condition lay beyond the Austrian sphere of control. Vienna, moreover, considered that the United Nations had enjoined the two parties to reopen their talks unconditionally.

These arguments were received with mixed feelings in Rome, where it could not be overlooked that the U.N. resolution contained three paragraphs. While the first of these had called upon the parties to resume talks, the third required the parties in the meantime to refrain from any act capable of harming the friendly relations between them. It was hardly possible to envisage applying only the first part and ignoring the rest of the resolution. In any case, the Austrian note also conveyed an impression of what Kreisky's line of approach would be during the forthcoming debate at the XVIII U.N. General Assembly.

Kreisky made his statement at the United Nations headquarters on September 26.[73] Couched in apparently moderate terms, it was decidely intransigent in substance. His statement emphasized that it was because of the United Nations that Italy had agreed to hold talks with Austria on the problem of the South Tyrol, but that the United Nations had not pointed to any specific "peaceful method" of solution in case such talks broke down. In his view, the most important fact was that the United Nations resolutions had solemnly confirmed the right of the South Tyrol minority to full equality of rights with the Italian-speaking population. Giving his own version of the sequence of events, he then blamed the difficulties raised by the Italians for the failure of his efforts to hold a meeting between the two ministers; Austria had been prepared to negotiate even during the period in which its cabinet was still being formed. In his opinion, continuation of terrorist activities could not justify the stand taken by Italy and, since the press in Austria was free, his government could not be held responsible for its attitude. Responsible Austrian authorities had always acted promptly upon being informed of any connections between Austria and terrorist activities in the South Tyrol. *Moreover, in his view, it was a universally accepted principle that, in cases of a political nature, assistance in enforcing a domestic law could not be tendered another state.* Both he and the Chancellor had always rejected recourse to terror and violence, and if, during the two years which had elapsed since the U.N. resolutions, "greater efforts to keep the talks going had been made by all those involved, the atmosphere would have been less strained." *Two years before, he had drawn attention to the fact that the Austrian government possessed proof of South Tyrol detainees being tortured by Italian police,* but despite the moderation shown by Austria, the Italian authorities had not reacted as the situation demanded. Austria was entitled to bring up matters concerning human rights and reserved its right to submit the question of the Italian tortures to the appropriate organs of the United Nations and the Council of Europe.

Piccioni spoke the next day and reviewed the reasons which he believed had blocked a meeting of the two ministers. The proposed composition of the Austrian delegation scheduled to attend the Salzburg meeting had indicated that the meeting envisaged was of a different type than those held in Venice and New York, hence the Italian request for a short delay. It was true that following the elections of November 18, the Austrian government had remained in office on a caretaker basis until April 1963, but the Italian preference to deal with a government vested with the authority of the new Parliament was hardly surprising.

The Italian government crisis had then followed, but the proposal to resume bilateral talks had been made the very day Leone's cabinet had received its vote of confidence from Parliament. Resumption of preparations for the meeting between the two foreign ministers had coincided with a renewal of terrorist activities, while the absence of any effective action by Austria to prevent the movement of terrorists and their arms into Italy had not only produced an unfavorable atmosphere, but appeared to conflict both with Article 9 of the State Treaty of Vienna and with paragraph 3 of the U.N. resolutions. Besides, Italy had suggested a meeting between the two ministers in New York. Had this offer not been turned down, bilateral talks would already have been resumed, and the Italian desire to negotiate would have been effectively met. Kreisky's remark that he had proof of the use of torture was rejected summarily, and the charges brought against the Italian judges were compared with the similar ones made in connection with the Fundres trial, charges that the Council of Europe had disposed of only a few days earlier, declaring them unfounded. In the meantime, the Commission of 19 had practically completed its work and the resultant domestic measures should eliminate the causes of disagreement over interpretation of the Paris Agreement. In any event and unless an attempt was made to heighten tension between the two countries, Piccioni confirmed that he was willing to meet Kreisky during the month of October.

The following day Kreisky availed himself of his right to reply to bring further charges. He was followed at the rostrum by Piccioni, who simply and fully denied such charges and, after again indicating his willingness to meet Kreisky in October, said he saw no purpose in spending any more of the assembly's time on the matter.

These lively public exchanges, in which the Austrian Minister's wish to accommodate the view of some Tyrolese extremists can hardly be said to have succeeded in the face of Piccioni's opposition, were followed by a much calmer interval. Kreisky, Steiner, and Waldheim had some very frank exchanges of opinions with a member of the Italian delegation in New York, thus paving the way for the now imminent Austro-Italian meeting.

Agreement between Rome and Vienna was on this occasion rapid, and so Kreisky and Piccioni met in Geneva on October 23.

These events presaged equally turbulent waters for the scheduled meeting at Geneva, and this forecast was reinforced by a not entirely orthodox incident occurring a few hours before discussions were scheduled to start. Kreisky asked Piccioni to permit two observers to attend the meeting, namely, former Under-Secretary Gschnitzer and Dr. Stadlmayer, whom, he assured him, he had found unexpectedly on the spot.

The Geneva meeting took place in the well-known Alabama room in the town hall and consisted of three sessions, of which one was reserved for the ministers and their closest advisors exclusively. At the start of the first, and plenary, meeting, Piccioni opened by making the position of the Italian government unmistakably clear. Italy remained prepared to resume talks on the application of the Paris Agreement at the point at which they had been abandoned at Zurich. At the same time, it was expected that the Commission of 19 was about to complete its tasks. The Italian government would give serious consideration to the proposals made to it, but it wished to make it quite clear that it did not propose to discuss with Kreisky any increase in existing international commitments. The point at issue between the two countries was the interpretation of the De Gasperi—Gruber agreement, and any addition to the subject matter under discussion at the international level was to be considered excluded. Moreover, it would clearly not be possible for the Italian government to submit to Parliament proposals that had been rejected by an advisory commission after years of study.

Piccioni's words were clear and firm, but Kreisky did not yield, seeking to draw the Italian Minister into making concessions to the Austrian position. Kreisky, in fact, sought to rewrite and revise the Paris Agreement of September 5, 1946, in respect to those few but delicate questions put forward by the German-speaking language group which the Commission of 19 had firmly rejected (all the remaining proposals had been unanimously accepted, or at least adopted against only a few nay votes). While the Austrian Foreign Minister's arguments failed to breach the Italian position, Piccioni's firm opening words likewise met no clear acceptance.

However, the Geneva meeting helped reduce the tension between Austria and Italy. Kreisky now needed above all to persuade his friends and political opponents at home to have confidence in him, and the last thing he wanted was to be accused of doing nothing when faced with allegations of Italian delaying tactics. The most unexpected event in Geneva was the contact established between the members of the Italian regional government, Messrs. Wallnöfer and Zechtl. At the opening of the first plenary session, Kreisky took care to disassociate them from the two "observers" whom he did not even mention in presenting the Austrian delegation. The new head of the Tyrolese regional government was considered a moderate, and during private discussions with a member of the Italian delegation in the presence of the Austrian Ambassador to Rome and the Italian Ambassador to Vienna, he indicated his understanding of the frank and full exposé of the Italian view made to him. An atmosphere of mutual confidence resulted, which made it possible for Wallnöfer to attend the closed session between the two ministers and their immediate advisors. It became clear that Italy had no objection to the participation of the Tyrolese themselves in the talks.

In conclusion, at the Geneva meeting it was agreed that the two ministers would again meet once the Italian government had assumed a position on the report of the Commission of 19, and that this would be arranged speedily because of the importance of the question.

Contrary to forecasts, the Commission of 19 did not complete its work immediately. Indeed, the completion of its report took up so much time that it was not finalized and signed until April 1964. The atmosphere created at Geneva, however, endured, except for a brief hiatus caused by the anti-Italian press campaign over the opening in Milan on December 9, 1963, of the trial of 143 persons (Italian, Austrian, and one German) charged with committing acts against the security of the state.[74]

In the meantime, Moro's first cabinet had been formed and its program drawn up on November 23, between the four coalition parties of the center-left government, explicitly covered the problem of the Alto Adige. This part of the program read as follows: "As to the Alto Adige, the government, while respecting Italy's rights, supports the just and peaceful co-existence of the Italian, German and Ladin speaking populations, drawing *inter alia* upon the recommendations of the Commission of 19 to insure peace and mutual trust in the area."

This was the first time that the Alto Adige question had been explicitly mentioned in a policy statement by the government, but the circumstances fully justified it. Respect for Italy's rights was clearly underlined, but the final goal was likewise solemnly expressed. The Commission of 19's recommendations would be a notable but not exclusive guide to ensuring just and peaceful coexistence between the various population groups. All who were involved had reason to be satisfied and hopeful.

During this period the new Italian foreign minister, Saragat, could confidently meet Kreisky in Paris in December 1963, when a meeting of the Council of Europe was being held in the French capital, prior to a ministerial session on NATO. During this discussion, the two parties repeated the ideas they had expressed at Geneva over awaiting the outcome of the work of the Commission of 19.

[6]

A brief look at the work of the Commission of 19 is completely relative and worthwhile.

Meeting under the chairmanship of Paolo Rossi, a member of the Chamber of Deputies known for the breadth of his views, the commission turned to its basic task of promoting serious discussion between leading representatives of the German-speaking language group and members of Parliament, as well as Italian experts on the Alto Adige question. Holding more than two hundred sessions, meetings of subcommittees, visits on the spot, and hearing evidence from spokesmen of all the interests involved, the commission discussed all of the aspects of the question. From this careful examination, a series of proposed legislative and other measures were prepared, directed toward providing

useful elements for a definitive solution to the problems that concern the linguistic groups in the Alto Adige. The Commission is of the opinion that to the extent to which the appropriate constitutional bodies take action along the lines thus inspired, and the extent to which the people of the Alto Adige accept the measures freely, and with a sense of responsibility and dedication, a comprehensive solution of the Alto Adige question can be realized, in an atmosphere of renewed confidence and loyalty to the interests of the country, interests common to every citizen.[75]

The commission, in effect, freely adopted all those proposals put forward by representatives of the German-speaking language group which, in its opinion, did not imperil the security of the state. However, it cannot be denied that some of the commission's suggestions received a mixed reception in Rome, where doubts were raised as to whether all of them were in practice compatible with the maintenance of the sovereignty of the Italian state.[76] Some of the suggestions were approved during the regrettable absence of a number of members of the Italian-speaking group, so that they were, in practice, proposals adopted by a majority made up of German members. On the other hand, it should be acknowledged that the German-speaking group did not attempt to jeopardize the structure of the present region of the Trentino–Alto Adige, but was guided by a more directly practical approach, concentrating its efforts on extending the autonomous powers of the province of Bolzano.

Understandably, even within these limits, not all of the major requests presented by the German group were accepted, four of relative importance were actually turned down. It should be stressed that among the difficulties arising from the commission's proposals and quite apart from their far-reaching nature, stood the basic requirement that the Italian state had to satisfy itself as to the loyalty of the beneficiaries of the proposed reforms. This implied careful and thorough reflection before the reforms themselves could be entertained.

It should also be mentioned that the commission envisaged adoption of a greater number of measures than that foreseen by those not engaged in the commission's work. Moreover, the far-reaching nature of the proposals gave rise to difficulties that could not be easily overcome. For example, some of them, from a purely technical point of view could be adopted only through constitutional legislation, which requires a two-thirds majority in Parliament. Bypassing details which are not directly pertinent in a study of diplomatic history, it is sufficient to mention that the concesssions made by the majority on the commission to the minority were indeed numerous. The commission dealt with 54 questions; 30 of these were considered by the German-speaking group as "essential" for autonomy, 22 as "important" for the same reason, and 2 were considered as "secondary." Final adoption by the government of the commission's recommendations would have resolved 41 of the above questions, 9 partially solved, and only 4 unsolved.

These figures alone seem sufficient to show the extent of the conciliatory effort made by the Italian-speaking[77] members of the commission. Perhaps a drawback in the commission's final report, from an Italian point of view, was the absence of a clear and explicit declaration that the proposals it contained encompassed all the requests of the German-speaking group.

To remedy this weakness, it was decided to seek the *Südtiroler Volkspartei's* public and solemn acceptance of the specific measures proposed unilaterally by the Italian government. Furthermore, this procedure reflected the letter as well as the spirit of the De Gasperi—Gruber agreement. This problem could, on the other hand, also be easily resolved by the choice of appropriate wording in the agreement terminating the international controversy. Once it was agreed that the De Gasperi—Gruber agreement had been fulfilled, the Viennese government would have no further ground to intervene.

The proposals put forward by the Commission of 19 constituted a point of departure from which the Italian government intended, of its own accord, to adopt a series of measures designed to further improve the status of the German-speaking population of the Alto Adige. These concessions were above and beyond anything contemplated in the De Gasperi—Gruber agreement. In any case, adoption of some or all of the proposals would of necessity improve the position of the German-speaking group and would consequently bring with it a gradual dissipation of the controversy between Italy and Austria.

Chapter VIII

The Austro-Italian
Controversy after the Report
of the Commission of 19

[1] Austro-Italian contacts resumed following submission of the Commission of 19 report. The Kreisky–Saragat meeting in Geneva, May 25, 1964.   [2] Work of the Austro-Italian Commission of Experts. First, second, and third meeting of this commission: June 22–27, July 8–15, and August 31 to September 5, 1964.   [3] The Kreisky–Saragat meeting of September 7–8, 1964. Fourth and fifth meetings of the Austro-Italian Commission of Experts, September 28–October 3, and October 21–25, 1964. Action taken by the Council of Europe. [4] Confidential meetings in London, November 1964. The Saragat–Kreisky meeting in Paris, December 16, 1964.   [5] Consultations between Austria and the Alto Adige. The critical position taken by the *Südtiroler Volkspartei*. Formal rejection by Kreisky on March 30, 1965 of the comprehensive outline of approach to a settlement developed in Paris.

[1]

As soon as the Commission of 19 had submitted its report to the government, on April 10, 1964, Austria called for a new meeting between the two foreign ministers. The request was based on the understanding reached at Geneva, though a new meeting could hardly be conclusive, since the Italian government would require some time to study and formulate decisions based on the commission's proposals.

In seeking this immediate renewal of direct Austro-Italian contacts, Vienna appeared to have two purposes: one on an international level, to hold talks with Italy in view of the negotiations in Brussels for Austria's entry into the Common Market, and one domestic, to show some positive result to satisfy Tyrolese pressures in the *Volkspartei*. Perhaps, Vienna's real design may have been to resume talks with Rome so as to compromise the report of the Commission of 19's leading to a purely Italian domestic solution of the status of the German-speaking inhabitants of the Alto Adige.

Italy accepted the Austrian request, both to emphasize her own intention of fulfilling the U.N. resolutions and to discover whether, for the reasons noted above, the Austrian government would find it possible to assume a more constructive attitude than in the past. Italy was also encouraged by what Kreisky had privately led Saragat to believe in Paris on December 12, 1963, regarding the firmer determination of the Viennese cabinet to mitigate the controversy as a means of discouraging Austrian and even German nationalists and neo-Nazis. It was agreed that the two foreign ministers would meet in Geneva on May 25, 1964.

This meeting between Saragat and Kreisky[1] served primarily to make it clear to Austria that Italy had no intention of abandoning its contention that the international instrument upon which the Italo-Austrian controversy pivoted was and must remain the Paris Agreement. As for the application of this agreement, Italy reiterated her belief that it had been applied in its entirety, while Austria continued to maintain that Italy had not fully implemented it. This difference in approach, as Saragat pointed out at the time, did not need to affect the desired solution to the controversy, since a wording could be found to safeguard the legal stand maintained by each side.

Saragat stressed the domestic nature of the proceedings and rulings of the Commission of 19 and, consequently, of the measures which the government might decide to adopt in favor of the inhabitants of the Alto Adige. The basic principle underlying any such measures would be the protection of the three population groups involved, but in no case an improvement in the living conditions and development of one group at the expense of the others.

Saragat's elucidation of the prerequisites which Italy felt were essential to the success of a new round of Austro-Italian negotiations led Kreisky to express the hope for a compromise, both as to the means of settling the controversy and as to the measures to be taken by the Italian government. Kreisky believed that once the two governments had agreed to seek a solution that would satisfy their differing view on the meaning of the Paris Agreement, it would be advisable to set up a bipartite commission of experts to review in detail all aspects of the controversy. This commission would report its findings to the two ministers and a new meeting would be arranged for them to decide on what steps should then be taken.

Italy agreed to accept this Austrian proposal. Through the new commission's work, it would be possible to determine if and under what conditions the Viennese government would be prepared to formally acknowledge closure of the international controversy in such a way as to enable the two governments to inform the United Nations that it had been settled.

This explanation identified the scope within which the Commission of Experts eventually worked and explains why there was no reference to internationalizing the proposals of the Commission of 19.[2] The task of the Commission of Experts was to examine the findings of the Commission of 19 within the general framework of the Alto Adige question. Though Italy was in no way disposed to discuss with Austria the domestic measures which its government might adopt, she favored the idea of exploring, at the technical level, the possible conditions on which the Viennese government might be willing to definitively settle the controversy.

Another reason for accepting the Austrian suggestion was the hope that this decision would lead to a reduction in the tension between the two countries. This tension had increased as a result of the bombing incidents in 1963, which had signaled a new phase; the target was no longer solely Italian property but apparently also members of the armed forces and police in the region. Moreover, by indicating that it was prepared to examine at a technical level a whole series of internal measures directed at satisfying the majority of the claims along the lines proposed by the Commission of 19, Italy might discourage the Austrian extremists.

Italian acceptance of the proposal was also encouraged by Kreisky's hint that, emulating the action of the Alto Adige group within the Commission of 19, it might be possible for Austria, in principle, to withdraw its previous condition requiring transformation of the province of Bolzano into a region. Before accepting the Austrian proposal, however, Saragat indicated his firm opposition to the possible creation of a bipartite Austro-Italian commission to examine future controversies, as suggested by Kreisky. On the other hand, Saragat pointed out that the Italian government might subscribe to instituting, as a domestic matter, suitable procedures that would enable the leaders of the Alto Adige to retain their contacts with the government in Rome.

The results of the meeting in Geneva indicated a substantial narrowing of the gap between the positions of the two parties. Austria demonstrated an awareness that the occasion was of real historic significance since, with the submission of the report by the Commission of 19, the Italian government was ready to examine the proposals that could lead to the adoption of a wide series of measures advantageous to the Tyrolese. It was also apparent that the Austrian government was aware of the dangers inherent in the nationalist and neo-Nazi ferment across the border. Kreisky appeared still under the spell of the *Südtiroler Volkspartei* regarding a possible termination to the controversy, but he did emphasize his confidence that, should the Italian government accord full consideration to the results of the Commission of 19, his attitude was subject to change, especially if the door were left open to renewed talks at the internal level on certain points which, in the eyes of Vienna and Bolzano, had been left unresolved.[3]

[2]

The task of the bipartite Commission of Experts, in accordance with the agreement reached at Geneva on May 25, was primarily to provide data and evaluation for appraisal by the two ministers. They would then decide whether or not there existed a real possibility of reaching an agreement on the application of the Paris Agreement. Should such a possibility appear not to exist, the two ministers would then decide whether there should be further talks devoted to determining the common choice of the "peaceful method" of settling the controversy, as the U.N. resolutions recommended.

The brief for the Italian delegation to the bipartite Commission of Experts was discussed at a confidential ministerial meeting, which decided that they should carry out an exploratory operation within the following terms of reference:

a) It remained the Italian government's opinion that the controversy was strictly limited to the interpretation and application of the Paris Agreement.

b) The Italian government also continued to uphold its belief that it had fulfilled the agreement, both by the readmission into the Alto Adige of 200,000 persons who had exercised an option to return, and by the adoption of an important program of legal provisions covering the various areas.

c) The Italian government likewise maintained its position that the statute of the Trentino–Alto Adige region was in conformity with the obligations accepted under the Paris Agreement.

The Italian commission was also to stress at the outset that the Rome government had agreed to the meeting of a bipartite Austro-Italian Commission of Experts, since it believed that the internal measures it could adopt might eliminate the controversy and lead to a complete understanding with the Austrian government.

The Italian experts were authorized to propose to their opposite colleagues that the commission carry out two parallel reviews: the first would concentrate on formal means of settling the controversy and the second would examine those internal measures which the Italian government might take favoring the Alto Adige inhabitants, measures which the Austrian government could consider sufficient to "stamp the bill paid-in-full" (to use Kreisky's words) in connection with the Paris Agreement.

As to the formal means of settling the dispute, the Italian experts were to submit a program of measures which, while safeguarding the Italian position legally that the Paris Agreement had already been implemented, would have been sufficient to settle the Italo-Austrian controversy.

As to the internal measures that the Italian government should choose to adopt, the Italian experts were to point out that while the controversy concerned only the Paris Agreement already implemented by the Italian government, they could in their talks with the Austrian experts, for example, draw attention to the proposals of the Commission of 19. However, in certain sectors, no concessions were to be made.[4]

At the first meeting of the bipartite Austro-Italian Commission of Experts in Geneva, June 22–27, 1964, the Austrians accepted the Italian proposals to carry out two separate reviews, but the point of departure of the two delegations on the two reviews was completely different.

As to the first one, according to the Austrian delegation, the final instrument settling the dispute should be a bilateral agreement, a procedure that would have involved a rewriting and broadening of the De Gasperi–Gruber agreement. This was unacceptable to Italy, since:

a) The Austrian *locus standi* would have been widened to include the status of the German-speaking inhabitants of the province of Bolzano, in all probability giving rise to new disputes on the interpretation and application of these new measures;

b) Italy would implicitly have admitted that it had not fulfilled its obligations under the Paris Agreement.

The Italian delegation, on the other hand, made it clear from the start that to be acceptable to both sides any definitive solution must fulfill the following two conditions:

a) each party should be in a position to maintain its own legal interpretation of the Paris Agreement;

b) termination of the dispute should not impose upon Italy international obligations greater than or different from those arising out of the Paris Agreement.

In the Italian delegation's view, therefore, the De Gasperi–Gruber agreement was to remain the sole international instrument upon which the dispute could be discussed. The termination of the controversy should be effected by a series of measures, primarily internal in character, taken one after another in a predetermined order and regrouped under the expression "operational calendar."

Notwithstanding this difference in approach, however, even at the first session a few interesting common denominators could be noted. The Austrians, in fact, agreed that the solution could be sought in a series of measures, rather than in a single act; insisting, however, that these measures in their entirety should constitute a binding international bilateral agreement. A similar understanding could be noted as to the number and nature of the measures called for. At the same time, they again presented the request, already clearly rejected by Saragat at Geneva,[5] that among the measures taken to close the dispute be included the establishment of a mixed Austro-Italian commission (without binding powers) whose task would be to periodically review the evolution of the Alto Adige Question.

This request was also firmly rejected by the Italian delegation, inasmuch as it plainly tended to perpetuate rather than end the dispute.

The second review concentrated principally on the points dealt with by the Commission of 19. The Italian delegation made it clear from the beginning that no reference to the proposals drawn up by the Commission of 19 implied that the matter fell under the De Gasperi–Gruber agreement and had, therefore, an international *locus standi,* or, even less, that it constituted an admission by Italy that such agreement might in any way be "improved" or "completed."

As to the examination of the proposals advanced by the Alto Adige German-speaking representation and studied by the Commission of 19, it was agreed at Geneva to consider all of these proposals except those adopted uananimously and these, in turn, would be selected on the basis of criteria suggested by Italy. This procedure was followed notwithstanding an attempt by Austria to include only the "open questions," i.e., those not accepted by the Italian members of the Commission of 19 and thus rejected by the commission itself.

It was also agreed, upon a suggestion by Italy, to adopt the following distinctions, bearing in mind the experience of the Commission of 19:

a) proposals adopted by a majority of the commission in plenary session;
b) proposals voted by the subcommission;
c) other proposals or requests by Italy or Austria.

In order to emphasize that the work of the Commission of 19 was merely considered as suggestive, it was proposed by Italy and agreed to, that the proposals contained in these categories should not be examined automatically on the basis of the proportion of votes received, as originally requested by the Austrian delegation, but should rather be considered one by one on their own merits. Italy also stressed that the relevant discussions should take into account the existing constitutional requirements, the interests of the state as a whole, and the need to insure that the region retain adequate powers to enable it to function.

The proposals presented under one or another of the agreed upon headings numbered 110, including 36 which, because they had been adopted unanimously by the Commission of 19, were not discussed again.[6]

The two reviews of the formal steps required to end the dispute and of the pro-Alto Adige measures to be taken by the Italian government continued on their parallel courses during the two subsequent meetings of the Commission of Experts held on July 8–15 and on August 31–September 5.

In substance, the position of the two sides remained unchanged, although some progress was made on a few points.

In an effort to overcome the differences in the review of the formal measures required to terminate the dispute, at the second meeting a short questionnaire was drafted for submission to the two ministers at their next meeting. From the views expressed on this item by both sides, however, the distance between them was still considerable. In particular, Italy favored a final unilateral measure, while Austrian continued to seek a bilateral agreement.

As to the internal measures to be taken by Italy, agreement in principle was reached on some 70 proposals of the 110 listed, on the lines proposed by the Commission of 19. The remaining 40 proposals were classified in 6 groups as follows:

1) Economic matters
2) Administrative matters
3) Social and cultural matters
4) Justice and the enforcement of law and order
5) Education
6) Labor and employment

The third session was devoted to economic matters and educaton. These were areas of special study along lines occasionally differing from those foreseen by the Commission of 19. However, the 40 proposals were still outstanding, even though a number of single points had been carefully studied and broad agreement upon them achieved. On September 4 an Italian meeting at the ministerial

level again examined the situation, confirming that the points originally presented were nonnegotiable and, at the same time, approving the formal measures
by which it was hoped to terminate the dispute.[7]

The first three meetings of the bipartite Commission of Experts had narrowed
the area of disagreement and established an initial rapprochement between the
positions represented by the two delegations.

[3]

Although the results of the first three sessions of the bipartite Commission of
Experts were far from providing a basis for a final solution to the dispute, the
Austrians insisted that the new meeting between the two foreign ministers be
held forthwith. Actually, the Austrian Socialist party was already in the throes
of a crisis that was to lead, in September, to the resignation of the minister of
the interior, Olah, and it seemed fairly obvious that Kreisky wished to give proof
to his own constituents of how keenly the Socialists were seeking a solution to
the Alto Adige problem.

It is also now known from Ritschel's book[8] that a secret meeting was held at
Spittal on the Drava on August 22, attended by Kreisky; Under-Secretary
Bobleter; the new director of political affairs, Minister Haymerle; Minister
Kirschlager; the head of the Tyrolese regional government, Landeshauptmann
Wallnöfern; a member of the regional Diet, Zechtl; the *Landesamtsdirektor* of
the Tyrol, Kathrein; Dr. Stadlmayer, Dr. Senn of Innsbruck; Professor Ermacora;
member of Parliament Riesenfeld, and the Italian members of Parliament for the
Alto Adige, Messrs. Saxl, Dietl, Mitterdorfer, Vaja, Benedikter, Brugger, and
Zelger. According to Ritschel's account, Kreisky stated that Italy was now
beginning to reason. There was no further talk of having already applied the
Paris Agreement, it was said only that discussion of the interpretation of the De
Gasperi–Gruber agreement was at an end. Austrian could take up negotiations
again at any time.[9] He thus appeared to have overlooked the details of what had
happened at the Geneva meetings where the Italian delegation had firmly
repeated its intention not to modify or affect in any way Italy's previously
determined official stand, i.e., that the De Gasperi–Gruber agreement had
already been fully implemented. It was under these circumstances that the
Austrian Foreign Minister felt induced to seek a new meeting at the ministerial
level.

At the same time, the fact that the Italian delegation had reported a better
atmosphere during the discussion encouraged Italy to hope that a new meeting
of the two ministers might overcome, at least in part, the obstacles still
hampering the negotiations. Italy also wanted to avoid giving the impression that
it might have abandoned its intention of seeking a solution to the international
dispute through direct contacts with the Austrian government, as a result of the
renewed outbreak of terrorism. This outbreak started on August 28, during the
meeting of the third session of the bipartite Commission of Experts and, for the
first time, a member of the Italian armed forces had been killed.[10]

The new meeting between the two ministers also appealed to Rome in that it would give Saragat the opportunity of pointing out to Kreisky in the clearest possible manner the need for the Austrian government to cooperate more effectively in preventing terrorist activites in the Alto Adige. Such an action by Saragat would certainly be aided by the recent sentencing by the Milan Criminal Court on July 16 in the trial against 91 persons accused of terrorist activities, among whom were four Austrian citizens. This verdict had been favorably received by responsible members of the Austrian press and by the public at large, which had appreciated the correct and equitable handling of the trial. As a matter of fact, Saragat, in precise terms, called attention to the responsibilities of the Viennese government in connection with the violence in his opening statement at the new meeting held at Geneva, September 7–8, a meeting of particular importance in the development of the Austro-Italian contacts.[11]

Kreisky appeared to be cognizant of the advisability of accepting the Italian proposal regarding the first review undertaken by the commission, a proposal based on the two fundamental principles regarding the safeguarding of each side's legal position and the absence of new international obligations for Italy. His intention may also have been to obtain further assurance and as many concessions as possible on the substantive matters in the second review.

Modifying his previous stand, Kreisky agreed that a formal end to the dispute could be achieved through a series of primarily unilateral measures, as suggested by Italy. However, a key factor in Kreisky's solution was an Austro-Italian agreement to set up a court of arbitration whose jurisdiction would extend to all disputes between the two countries.

The idea of an arbitration agreement leading to the creation of a court with binding powers to decide exclusively "according to the law," which had not been ruled out by Italy as a possible choice of a "peaceful method," met with Italian acceptance, subject to detailed consideration of all aspects of the matter (composition of the court arbitration, jurisdiction, etc.), to be carried out once Austria had submitted details of a draft agreement.

Italy, in fact, could not expect Austria to "stamp the bill paid-in-full" without giving Vienna at least temporary reasurrances. It was also expedient not to rule out the possibility of such a procedure, even though it might increase the already considerable difficulties anticipated in obtaining parliamentary approval of the proposed comprehensive outline of approach to a solution of the dispute.

At this time, Kreisky also raised the question about the political risk he would entail by agreeing to call the dispute closed *immediately after* a statement was made by the Italian Prime Minister to Parliament setting out the internal measures that Italy proposed to take as a unilateral act to further improve the status of the German-speaking citizens in the Alto Adige. He reasoned that such a statement would of necessity be opportune *before* the required legislation had been formally approved and enforced. According to the record of the proceedings published by Ritschel,[12] Kreisky is quoted as having said: "The members of Parliament of the two coalition parties forming the government—I am less afraid of the Opposition than of the coalition members—will ask me: 'What guarantee to do you bring us that will give us the certainty that what has now been promised by the Italian government will in fact be carried out? Or what do you bring us in its stead?' "

To this question Ritschel states that Saragat replied that Austria had not one guarantee, but four. The first would consist of the court designated by the agreement, legally charged to interpret the Paris Agreement on all future disputes. The second would be found in the record of the proceedings of the Italian Parliament and, particularly, in the policy statement made by the Prime Minister and its consequent approval by Parliament. A third guarantee could be found in the communciation made to the United Nations that the international dispute had been ended. The fourth would consist in the establishment of an internal consultative body representing the government and the Alto Adige minority.

Clearly, not even Saragat's able arguments could entirely cover the risk that after termination of the international dispute, albeit following a simple majority vote approving the Italian Prime Minister's policy statement, the qualified majority required for constitutional amendments might not approve certain of the measures. Kreisky's remarks indicated he was prepared to adhere in principle to the Italian proposal not to enter into a new international agreement and at the same time, they appeared to merit further consideration by the members of the Italian delegation present.

As to the internal measures which the Italian government could consider adopting, both ministers set forth their views on the more controversial issues, noting certain possible convergencies, particularly with respect to educational matters. Kreisky also placed weight on the economic and social sector, where the Austrians felt that certain measures were essential to improve the development of the autonomous powers of the province of Bolzano. At the same time, Saragat pointed out in his reply that there were constitutional and administrative problems on which the Italian government could make no concessions.

Some further progress appeared possible along the lines that Austria would accept the fact that Italy could not make concessions, especially in the administrative sphere and the enforcement of law and order, in return for which Italy would recognize the possibility of making certain other concessions to the German-language group in the Alto Adige, particularly in the economic field.

At the end of the meeting, the two ministers approved the work carried out to date by the bipartite Commission of Experts and instructed it to carry out the following tasks:

a) preparation of draft texts of the formal measures to terminate the controversy, upon whose nature and number agreement had been reached;

b) review of the forty questions remaining unresolved, taking into account both Kreisky's requests regarding the economic sector, and Saragat's specific mention of certain constitutional and administrative problems.

As a result of the meeting in Geneva and the instructions issued by the foreign ministers on that occasion, the Commission of Experts held a fourth and fifth session, September 28–October 3 and October 21–25, 1964.

As to the formal means of terminating the dispute, the experts drew up a first draft of the following documents, containing in some cases alternative clauses:

a) Statement by the Italian government to Parliament;
b) Statement by the Austrian government to the Austrian Parliament;
c) Procedural agreement for setting up a court of arbitration;
d) Communication from the Italian government to the United Nations;
e) Communication from the Austrian government to the United Nations.

An examination of these acts, all unilateral except for the procedural agreement under (c), shows that Austria had now adhered to the Italian approach, although she made several attempts here and there to introduce some features that deviated from it. The Austrian draft communication to the United Nations prepared by the Austrian experts sought to provide an international anchor for the Italian domestic legislation, listing the Italian enactments and giving, in an appendix, a detailed reference to each. The Italian experts rejected the proposal.

Furthermore, the Austrian experts requested that the list of measures to be taken independently by the Italian government should be sent through the United Nations Secretary General to every member of the United Nations. Finally, they urged that in the agreement, under (c), a series of provisions should be included for setting up a special permanent Austro-Italian conciliation commission. These requests were likewise firmly rejected by Italy.

Austria's main effort at "internationalization" rested on document (c) (procedural agreement for setting up a court of arbitration), with particular emphasis on the jurisdiction to be given to the court. Italy proposed that it should be empowered to rule, according to law, on disputes arising out of bilateral treaties between Italy and Austria, wherever these could not be settled through diplomatic channels. Austria also sought to have referred to the court all questions that had "a direct connection" with a contractual engagement, and even those "indirectly" connected with it, in addition to matters arising out of the results of negotiations conducted at the request of the U.N. General Assembly (Resolution 1947 [XV] and 1661 [XVI]). In effect, the Austrian experts wanted the jurisdiction of the court not only exercised according to *law* but also according to equity and fact. All these attempts were rejected.

Of the forty questions regarding proposed measures to be taken by the Italian government on which no decision had been reached during the third session, the experts succeeded in agreeing on 22 of them during the fourth session; the remaining 18, however, continued to remain open even after the fifth session. The Austrian government appeared determined to keep some of the most important claims in reserve, so as to bring pressure to bear in favor of its own proposals regarding the form and method of bringing the dispute to an end.

The 18 questions on which no agreement could be reached at the technical level covered a range of subjects: matters affecting economy, public administration, cultural and social policies, the courts and enforcement of law and order, schools, and labor. Sixteen of the points related to an increase in the autonomous powers of the province of Bolzano and 2 related to guarantees for the German-speaking population.

The work of the bipartite Commission of Experts undoubtedly provided an opportunity for a more detailed study of the complex material under review. The cumulative result of every session saw some progress in the task of reconciling the respective points of view. At the same time, differences between the two parties did emerge and remained unresolved at the expert level even by the end of the fifth session.

Examination of the position at the conclusion of the fifth session clearly shows that it envisaged the formal steps to terminate the dispute as a series of unilateral acts combined with an agreement providing for a peaceful method of settling possible future controversies between the two countries.

In other words, the proposed system matched the measures to be taken unilaterally by the Italian government to an agreement which, at the same time and backed by a declaration by Austria that the dispute was at an end, established the body that would adjudicate exclusively on the basis of the Paris Agreement, whether this had been applied in full or not. The heterogeneous nature of this combination of two different systems of terminating the dispute (by internal action and by an agreed definition of a "peaceful method"), was part and parcel of the series of measures foreseen by the proposals drawn up by Italy. This was made clear by the fact that the Italians on the bipartite Commission of Experts had never ruled out the possibility that the legal body to be designated as the "peaceful method" might be the International Court of Justice at The Hague, in line with the earlier proposals made by Italy on various occasions to the Austrian government and in the United Nations.

From Austria's point of view, however, the system proposed by Italy presented several substantial disadvantages. First, Vienna might fear that once the Austrian government declared the dispute closed after the Italian government's proposed unilateral declaration of policy before Parliament, her legal position would be weakened in the event of an appeal to the adjudicating body. However, this hypothesis is based fundamentally on an unjustified and unhistorical interpretation of Article 2 of the De Gasperi–Gruber agreement. According to this version, the 1946 agreement envisaged the establishment of a real independent region as such and not simply a province having an autonomy of a regional nature.

Second, as already pointed out, the system proposed by Italy clearly did not offer the Austrian government the guaranteed certainty that the measures announced in Parliament by the head of the Italian government would actually be approved and put into effect. Since the court of arbitration would only be entitled to rule on points of law and within the terms of the De Gasperi–Gruber agreement, it followed that a pronouncement on its part that Italy had actually fulfilled the terms of the agreement would deprive Austria of any further possibility of requiring Italy to carry out the measures that she had announced.

Finally, there was always the possibility, or at least the Austrians thought so, that Italy might feel it to be to her advantage to use an appeal to the court of arbitration as a means of postponing the application of the promised changes.

These were the considerations Austria confronted and they are, at least to some extent, understandable. At the same time, Italy's reluctance to concede Austria's demands on most of the 18 questions still to be settled is equally comprehensible.

Another factor of which Italy was aware, in her attempt to overcome the difficulties that had arisen at the expert level, was the meeting in Strasbourg on November 7, 1964, of the Sub-commission on the Alto Adige of the Consultative Assembly of the Council of Europe. At its conclusion, a communiqué was issued in which, despite Bettiol's reservations, reference was made to the imminent conclusion of a "new agreement" between Italy and Austria, which would end the controversy over the application of the De Gasperi–Gruber agreement.[13]

Attention has already been drawn to Austria's policy of associating the Council of Europe more closely with the Alto Adige question. This was clearly an effort to "internationalize" the matter further in a two-fold move adopting both legal and political arguments.

The Austrian legal contention had hinged on charges of irregularity in the trial held in Italy over the Fundres case. Austria here had failed to win her case when the Committee of Ministers accepted the recommendation of the European Commission for Human Rights, which had found that Italy had in no way violated the European Convention on Human Rights.

The Austrian government's political battle in the Council of Europe was fought out in the Subcommission for the Alto Adige, set up by the Consultative Assembly on September 5, 1961, on the proposal of the Belgian president of the senate, Struye, who was elected its chairman. Struye's motivation had been Italy's opposition to any discussion in the Assembly of the Alto Adige problem and the various phases of the Austro-Italian dispute.

Since it had been organized, the subcommission had met at almost every session of the Consultative Assembly. Its line of approach to the Alto Adige problem had not always been in accord with Italy's legal viewpoint. Italy could not silently ignore the reference to a "new agreement" between herself and Austria, contained in the communiqué that the Subcommission for the Alto Adige had circulated at the end of its meeting on November 7. The Italian Ambassador in Brussels drew Struye's attention to the fact that the Italian government had no intention of rewriting or amplifying the Paris Agreement and, therefore, did not propose to reach any "new agreement" with Austria.

[4]

Taking all the above factors into consideration, the Italian government decided to try to arrive at a formula encompassing the already described outline of approach to a solution of the dispute between the two countries. Confidential meetings began in London for this purpose in November 1964.

These confidential meetings did not take place to the accompaniment of terrorist bombs, as had been a normal feature of any publicized Austro-Italian meeting. Nor were there any of the traditional press statements in which the Austrian and Tyrolese leaders were perhaps often depicted as heroes defending their fatherland, which, in practice, only served to commit them with even greater intransigence to the positions they had adopted. The new approach now actually presented the possibility of broad and full discussion on the settlement of the dispute.

The two main objects of the discussion in London were: (a) the form that the termination of the dispute would take. A formula was visualized that would empower the proposed court of arbitration, for a limited period, to insure that the measures that the Italian government planned to announce in Parliament were carried out, without either government abandoning its own legal interpretation. An exchange of notes between the two governments would permit the court to ascertain *factually and within a limited period* (four years), whether the measures announced by the Italian government had or had not been put into effect. The result was that Italy could no longer insist that possible future Austro-Italian legal disputes should be referred to The Hague Court, since the latter's statute did not allow it to undertake this type of investigation.

Other difficulties remained and among these was securing Italian parliamentary approval. At the same time, the joint conciliation commission proposed by Austria and her attempt to increase international control, implicit in her draft communication to the United Nations, fell by the wayside. This line of approach was closely tied to Austria's agreement to declare the dispute at an end *immediately* after the Italian government had announced the measures it proposed adopting, and *before* they had been approved by the Italian Parliament. This plan gave rise to much speculation at that time. The suggestion, however, that the plan would internationalize the measures themselves has no solid basis in fact. Such a circumstance, apart from the court of arbitration having only the right to ascertain strictly factual matters, is ruled out by the *very existence of the time limit, the shortest necessary for the passage of all the new legislation and the publication of the new regulations.* By the time that all the constitutional and other measures could be approved, and the regulations that would put them into effect published, the four years would almost certainly have passed, and even the period allowed for ascertaining the actual situation would have expired.

b) the measures to be independently adopted by the Italian government for the benefit of the German-speaking group of the Alto Adige would correspond to those agreed to by the Commission of Experts during its five sessions (92 of the 110 questions contained in the report issued by the Committee of 19) for the purpose of bringing the international dispute to an end. As for the 18 questions to which the experts had been unable to find a solution, they would be solved along the lines suggested by the Italian experts. Thus, of the 110 questions considered, 88 would be settled along the lines laid down by the Commission of 19; 8, none of which was considered likely to risk Italy's national integrity, would be settled along even broader lines; 10 more restrictively; and 4 in an entirely different way.

On the whole, compared with the solutions proposed by the Commission of 19, those now envisioned would be more generous to local demands in social and educational matters and less flexible in matters of administration and police. As to the economy of the province of Bolzano, the terms agreed to in London were not very different from those proposed by the Commission of 19.

The confidential meetings could be characterized as having rendered possible the drafting of an outline of approach toward a settlement that took greater account of Italy's requirements and, at the same time, respected the tenor of the proposals made by the Commission of 19.

The number and order of the various procedural steps to be followed were also agreed upon during the course of the confidential talks, while a few less important points were left open for decision at a subsequent meeting of the two foreign ministers.

In conclusion, it can be said that at the Geneva meeting of September 7–8, 1964, it was Kreisky who had made concessions over the proposed method of formally ending the dispute, so that he could concentrate his efforts on seeking further major, and chiefly economic, concessions for the population of the Alto Adige. At this fairly advanced stage of the negotiations in London, a new formula was also suggested as a basis for settlement, which insofar as ending the dispute, met Austria's most pressing requirements within clearly defined limits and subject to a time limit. At the same time, with reference to the measures to be taken unilaterally by the Italian government toward ending the international dispute, most of Italy's requirements were met. It was emphasized by Italian representatives to their Austrian colleagues that the steps foreseen in formally closing the international dispute, and the measures to be adopted independently by Italy, were all strictly interrelated and concurrent, and that as a result the agreement now basically reached regarding the outline of approach toward a solution, was all-encompassing.

A cabinet committee meeting on December 11, 1964, under the chairmanship of the Prime Minister, approved the draft plan for ending the dispute as outlined at the confidential meetings in London and authorized Saragat to make certain further suggestions for resolving the situation, with a view to achieving an over-all, definitive settlement on the outline of approach as mentioned above.

It was agreed that, in accordance with the two U.N. resolutions, the two ministers could meet in Paris in December, since both had to be present there for meetings of other international organizations (NATO and the Council of Europe). This meeting took place on December 16.

The Paris talks, in which Saragat[14] kept himself strictly within the limits approved by the cabinet committee, were not as decisive as might have been desired. Kreisky tried to avoid an immediate commitment. Whereas there could be said to be a wide area of agreement about the method of ending the dispute with respect to measures which the Italian government intended to take independently, Austria sought to reopen discussion on all eighteen of the points left unsettled after the fifth meeting of the Commission of Experts. Faced with Italy's firm opposition, Kreisky asked that the possibility of a settlement based on the suggestions already put forward be studied, provided further concessions on the following points were included: (a) residence; (b) deployment of labor; (c) vocational training; (d) industry and industrial development; (e) credit.

Saragat at once and unequivocally declined to contemplate further negotiations on these matters. Kreisky countered that Austria was not ready to make a final decision and that he would, therefore, have to report to his government on the results achieved in the negotiations. The Austrian Minister stated that as a result of the work achieved over the past six months an area of agreement had been reached which went far beyond what could have been imagined at any time during the previous years. This could only strengthen Austria's desire to bring the dispute to an end. For his part, he would use all his influence with the appropriate bodies in Austria in an effort to overcome the remaining resistance to a solution of the dispute on the basis of what had been developed.[15] He would be in a position to reply on or about January 10, 1965.

Much has been said and written about this Paris meeting on December 16, in Italy as well as in Austria, and some of the views expressed were based on the version given by Kreisky. It, therefore, seems pertinent to emphasize some vital points. First, Saragat adhered closely to the precisely detailed instructions given him by the cabinet committee on December 11. Second, the draft outline of approach toward a solution that Italy submitted was all-encompassing, i.e., it needed to be considered in its entirety. This, therefore, ruled out the possibility of agreeing to the part referring to the method of ending the international dispute, while rejecting the measures Italy was to take independently in favor of the German-speaking group in the Alto Adige. Third, the formula devised to safeguard Austria as the result of an *immediate* declaration of the termination of the international dispute *before* the measures announced by the Italian Prime Minister to the Italian Parliament had entered into force, was only temporary and was designed only to ascertain matters of fact, and would in no way entail internationalization of such measures. Fourth, in exchange for this temporary and de facto safeguard against the political risk she ran, Austria would have to abandon her claims concerning the 18 points still left unsolved.

Kreisky, at least in public, has consistently kept quiet about these circumstances. At the same time, Ritschel, who has had access to the minutes of the Paris meeting, has in his commentary dwelled at length on the part of the discussion dealing with the termination of the international controversy, but has devoted only very perfunctory attention to the part of the talks devoted to the measures the Italian government proposed adopting. This constitutes a rather typical example of a one-sided presentation.[16] Those in Italy who were aware of how the negotiations really went were unable to correct this version, for the matter was still an official secret. Now that Ritschel has published his book, this is no longer the case.

[5]

The Austrian government was able to take advantage of a number of circumstances to delay making its reply regarding the conclusions of the Paris meeting of December 16. A meeting between Kreisky and the S.V.P. leaders did not take place until January 9, 1965.[17]

The results of this meeting were almost entirely negative, since the Alto Adige representatives maintained that the internal measures announced by the Italian government under the proposed plan for ending the dispute did not guarantee the province of Bolzano sufficient extension of its autonomous powers. It was decided to examine the problem again at a further meeting between Kreisky and the Alto Adige representatives, after the latter had intervened, on the internal level, with the Italian-speaking members of Parliament from the province of Bolzano and the leaders of the parties in the government.

Consequently, Austria sent a purely preliminary reply to the Italian government on the subject of the conclusions reached in Paris. It underlined the difficulties encountered with the Alto Adige leaders and at the same time proposed a further meeting between the two foreign ministers or, alternatively, their representatives.

Italy replied that she was firmly convinced that a new meeting between the two foreign ministers or their representatives could be constructive and useful only insofar as it was based on Austria's taking a definite position on the Paris meeting of December 16, 1964.

After the meetings scheduled by the S.V.P. leaders on January 9, Kreisky again met the leaders of the S.V.P. and representatives of the Tyrol government in Innsbruck on March 28, 1965.[18] Here it was decided to continue to press, both within Italy and internationally between Italy and Austria, for further concessions of autonomy to the province of Bolzano, with the aim of gaining a more generous settlement than the one envisaged in the draft outline of approach for ending the dispute discussed by the two foreign ministers in Paris. Finally, on March 30, 1965, the Vienna government communicated to Italy its reply to the draft proposals discussed at the Paris meeting.[19] The reply consisted of a request to reopen negotiations on 13 points, all connected with extending the autonomous powers of the province of Bolzano and already included in the 18 points left unsettled at the end of the fifth meeting of the bipartite Commission of Experts. With respect to the internal unilateral measures, Austria's reply was a decided step backward in the negotiations, even as reflected by Kreisky's own statements at the Paris meeting on December 16.[20]

An examination of the joint stand assumed by Austria and the Alto Adige with reference to the development of the negotiations, makes it clear that Vienna and Bolzano endorsed the results achieved at the confidential meetings in London. But, at the same time, they wanted Italy to concede all the requests they made concerning the internal measures to be independently taken by the Italian government. This would destroy the over-all plan which was the compromise worked out in London.

It is very doubtful whether, in deciding to tender this reply, Kreisky acted in his country's interest. From what it has been possible to subsequently learn, however, it appears that he had supported the plan discussed in Paris, but had been defeated by the leaders from the Alto Adige. Even he had become a victim of Vienna's policy of giving the Tyrol and the Alto Adige the final say on the subject of Austro-Italian relations. But Kreisky bears direct responsibility for one fundamental omission: on January 9 and March 28, 1965, he failed to draw the attention of his audience at Innsbruck to the fact that the draft outline of approach discussed in Paris was an *all-embracing* once, which precluded the possibility of accepting one part and rejecting the other. It may be that this omission resulted from his conviction that he would succeed in obtaining Italy's consent to abandon the principle of the all-inclusive character of the outlined solution, but facts were destined to contradict him in full. Hence his public statements were not in keeping with the true history of the negotiations. It may have been as a result of Kreisky's omission that the leaders of the S.V.P. were guilty of excessive optimism about the possibility of successfully forcing Rome's hand. The only good thing to come out of Austria's reply was that direct discussions between the S.V.P. and the Italian government were resumed.

Austria's response to the outline discussed in Paris was certain to create an unfavorable impression on the Italians. However, since it would always be useful to further consider the entire problem, it was decided to reply to the effect that Austria's new demands were so far reaching that they required another detailed review by the ministers. The Italian government could only consider another meeting of minister's representatives after this review had taken place. The Italian reply was sent on April 8, 1965.[21]

Chapter IX

Developments from July 1965
to January 1967

[1] Contacts resumed: meeting between officials of the Italian and Austrian Foreign Ministries in London, July 18–29, 1965. The meeting at Klagenfurt on August 5, 1965, between representatives from Austria, the Tyrol, and the Alto Adige. The meeting between Moro and Klaus in the Trentino, August 26, 1965. Further meeting at Innsbruck on September 11, between representatives from Austria, the Tyrol, and the Alto Adige. Semiofficial contacts: talks with Kreisky at Fiumicino, October 5, 1965 and at New York, October 11–12, 1965. [2] The Austrian government crisis, October 23, 1965. Meeting of officials of the Italian and Austrian Foreign Ministries in London, November 25, 1965. Talks between Saragat, Moro, and Klaus, and Kreisky. The Austrian memorandum of February 22, 1966. [3] The formation of a single-party Austrian government, April 19, 1966. Meeting between Fanfani and Toncic at Strasbourg, May 4, 1966. Meeting between officials of the Italian and Austrian Foreign Ministries in London, May 25–26, 1966. Further meetings between these officials at Montreux, June 16–18 and in London, July 18–20. [4] Meetings of the S.V.P. in Bolzano, August 29–September 1, 1966 to examine the proposals put forward in London on July 18–20, 1966. Debate in the Italian Parliament on the Alto Adige, September 12–22, 1966. [5] The problem of terrorism: Italy's note to Austria, October 6, 1966; Austrian reply, December 5, 1966; and Italian counter-reply, January 21, 1967. [6] Speeches by Toncic and Piccioni before the XXI U.N. General Assembly, October 5 and 13, 1966. Talks between Moro and Magnago about the "clarifications" requested by the S.V.P. Reply on the points made by Magnago, January 21, 1967.

[1]

Following the meeting in Paris on December 16, 1964, important domestic political developments took place in both Italy and Austria.

In Italy, Foreign Minister Saragat was elected president of the republic on December 28, 1964. As a result, Prime Minister Moro, after confirmation of his government by the head of state, reshuffled his cabinet, appointing the former Prime Minister Fanfani as foreign minister. The new Italian cabinet received its vote of confidence in the Chamber of Deputies March 9–12, 1965, and in the Senate, March 16–18, 1965. In this vote, the deputies from the Alto Adige abstained. They indicated, however, through Dr. Karl Mitterdorfer, that they

207

supported in spirit those who voted for the government, and expressed the hope that a final solution of the South Tyrol question was near at hand.[1]

In Austria the presidential elections took place on May 23, 1965, resulting in the victory of the Socialist candidate, Jonas. The postwar tradition of regularly electing a Socialist to the post was thus maintained. Jonas's victory was not followed by changes in the political equilibrium in Austria, even though he had obtained only 60,000 votes more than his rival, Gorbach, and this served to reassure those voters who had feared a move of the *Volkspartei* to the right. Nor did the latter's failure at the polls appear to have any serious effect on its adherents.

The negative stand taken by Austria on March 30, 1965, had undoubtedly weakened Italo-Austrian rapprochement. This had already been pointed out to the Austrian government and was again referred to by Fanfani when he met the Austrian under-secretary for foreign affairs, Bobleter, at a session of the Ministerial Committee of the Council of Europe at Strasbourg on May 3, 1965. Austria, however, for some time continued to insist on a stand which pointed to the Viennese government's failure to take into account the encompassing character of the proposals examined in Paris on December 16, 1964.[2] Vienna, in fact, wanted to consider resolved only those dealing with the procedural means of terminating the dispute, insisting that Italy accept all of its demands and adding new ones concerning the substance of the issues involved, namely, those measures which the Italian government intended to adopt on its own account in favor of the German-speaking group of the Alto Adige. These were obviously designed to improve the latter's situation and, at the same time, serve as a means of resolving the international dispute with Austria over the application of the De Gasperi–Gruber agreement. This was tantamount to rejecting the inclusive nature of the compromise worked out in the confidential meetings held in London during November and December 1964.

Following a number of Austrian proposals to resume bilateral talks, the Italian government was able to reply on July 2, 1965, that it was in no way opposed to this, but that it was essential that such meetings be based on assumptions different from those underlying the previous round, which had ended unsuccessfully on March 30, following Austria's rejection of the proposals offered at that time. Italy was prompted to agree primarily to continue to contribute to the peaceful coexistence of different ethnic groups and to the improvement of conditions for the population of the Alto Adige in the spirit of the U.N. resolutions. The new talks were subsequently scheduled for July 28–29 in London.

These conversations between officials of the Italian and Austrian Foreign Ministries, opened a new phase in Austro-Italian contacts and extended over five meetings held between July 1965 and July 1966.[3]

The first meeting was of an exploratory nature. There was a review of the situation that had emerged after the series of declarations by Austria following December 16, 1964.

Italy emphasized that Austria's reply of March 30, 1964, could only be interpreted negatively, since it disavowed the entire logic governing the earlier confidential meetings in London, which had sought a compromise solution based on a balance between procedural and substantive measures for resolving the dispute. Thus, it followed that any new attempt to settle this international dispute over application of the De Gasperi–Gruber agreement should start where it had been left at the close of the fifth meeting of the Committee of Experts held in Geneva on October 21–25, 1964. With this in mind, Italy's representatives also emphasized that an agreement could only be reached on a formula that would provide for abandoning the temporary procedure for de facto recognition of entry into force of the measures adopted by the Italian government favoring the German elements in the Alto Adige, originally envisaged at the Paris meeting on December 16, 1964, while, on the other hand, opening the way for possible concessions advantageous to the province of Bolzano. In this connection, Italy also indicated that a new formula for an Austrian "receipt" might be sought in order to reduce any risk incurred by the Viennese government in agreeing to declare the international dispute at an end before the Italian Parliament had sanctioned the proposals presented by the Italian Prime Minister. The Italian government could also look into the possibility of making some further concessions within the framework of the 18 points remaining open after the fifth meeting of the Committee of Experts, which were to have been settled in the manner requested by Italy in line with proposals reviewed at the Saragat–Kreisky meeting in Paris. Finally, some amendment might be accepted on the clauses referring to points already covered by the earlier proposals.

Italy's stand on the delineation of the talks apparently caused some surprise among the Austrian officials, who sought to reopen discussions on the basis of the proposals they had presented on March 30, 1965, or failing this, on the basis of the Paris proposals, with possible amendments on the budget of the province of Bolzano, and, in any case, with the indication of a clause covering revision of the proposed agreements.

Confronted by the rigid position taken by the Italian representatives who opposed such proposals as conflicting with the very basis of the earlier and continuing talks, the Austrians noted the Italian stand and indicated that they would communicate the reaction of the Austrian government at a later date.

Indeed, it develops that immediately following these London conversations, a meeting was called at Klagenfurt on August 5 between representatives of Austria, the Tyrol, and the Alto Adige in order to discuss the Italian position. Austria was represented by Kreisky and Kirschlager, the Tyrol by Wallnöfer and Kathrein, and the Alto Adige by Magnago, Pupp, Mitterdorfer, Benedikter, Brugger, Volgger, and Atz, secretary of the S.V.P. According to Ritschel's account,[4] Kirschslager reported on the London meeting. Kreisky then reported that Fanfani's appointment had changed the situation, since he believed the new Italian Foreign Minister was more particularly interested in domestic matters than in foreign policy.[5] Kirschlager felt that Italy had been forceful and categorical, especially on two points. First, when Italy indicated that she could not accept amendments to the Paris proposals once they had already been rejected by Austria and the German-speaking group of the South Tyrol, the Paris proposals represented the high-water mark of the concessions she was prepared to make. Second, when Italy declined to leave any question pending, for she would consider doing so a real drawback, since the Italian Parliament was prepared to approve nothing less than a definitive solution. Kreisky admitted, in effect, that he had believed in the possibility of further negotiations. At that time (he was probably referring to the two first meetings at Innsbruck in January and March) he had said that the most significant achievement was the international guarantee, but he had left the South Tyrol representatives free to see if they could obtain more. Currently, his impression was that the Italian position had stiffened. Toward the end of the meeting, Kreisky spoke again and his statements quite clearly indicated that he sought to blame North and South Tyrol for not having accepted, at Innsbruck on January 8, 1965, the comprehensive solution presented in Paris on the preceding December 16, and for failing to take advantage of the concessions made by Italy.[6]

The Austrian government redoubled its efforts by making contact at various levels to try and get Italy to alter its position. Vienna now sought, in fact, to return to the solution suggested in Paris on December 16 as a means of ending the international dispute over application of the De Gasperi–Gruber agreement. At the same time, she was attempting to obtain further major concessions in the legislative powers to be granted to the province of Bolzano.

Against this background and with these proposals in mind, the Austrian chancellor, Klaus, requested a meeting with Prime Minister Moro. A suitable occasion presented itself on August 26, 1965, while Moro was spending a brief summer holiday in the Trentino. An unofficial and strictly private discussion took place and consisted of a frank and broad exchange of views and proposals on various problems of general interest, including that of the Alto Adige. The Italian Prime Minister also took this occasion to clearly and explicitly repeat his government's policy as it was defined by public statements made before the Italian Parliament and other occasions.[7]

By a striking coincidence a most serious act of terrorism took place in the Alto Adige almost simultaneously with this meeting, in which two Italian *carabinieri* lost their lives. Once back in Austria, Klaus sent Moro a telegram expressing his sincere regret for the incident and condemning terrorism in a manner notably more emphatic and explicit than ever before.[8]

Following the position statements by the Italians to Klaus, another meeting was held at Innsbruck on September 11 between spokesmen for Austria, the Tyrol, and the Alto Adige. Kreisky, Lowenthal, Haymerle, and Kirschlager were present for Austria, Wallnöfer, Hetzenauer, Zechtl, Mader, Kathrein, Stadlmayer, Gschnitzer, Ermacora, Senn for the Tyrol and Magnago, Pupp, Sax, Vaja, Benedikter, Brugger, and Atz for the Alto Adige.[9] According to Ritschel, the meeting sought to mollify the already manifest disagreements which had emerged at Klagenfurt between Kreisky and the spokesmen of the Tyrol and the Alto Adige. The firmness shown by the Italian Foreign Ministry officials at the London meeting on the means of ending the international dispute over application of the De Gasperi–Gruber agreement had apparently had a strong effect. Ritschel's report conveys the clear impression that both the Austrian federal authorities and the spokesmen of the Tyrol were disturbed by the Italian intransigence and were prepared to show a certain elasticity as the price for resuming contacts. However, Austrian demands remained unaltered: an international guarantee to be accompanied by further measures advantageous to the German-speaking inhabitants of the Alto Adige.

This all took place while Kreisky was still Austrian minister of foreign affairs, but neither at this stage of the negotiations nor during those immediately following was there the least trace of Kreisky's repeated, open, and much publicized statements to the press, that he had obtained striking concessions from Italy.

In the meantime, terrorist activites continued to accelerate. A new serious incident took place on the night of September 13 against the *Alpini* barracks at the Reschen Pass. A firm protest was delivered two days later to the Austrian Foreign Ministry by the Italian Chargé d'Affaires in Vienna and the customary words of condemnation were expressed in the reply. To this, on September 18, Wallnöfer, Landeshauptmann of the Tyrol, added that he would welcome a solution to the problem of the South Tyrol.[10]

This situation was again discussed on October 5, by Kreisky and the Italian director of the Political Department in the Foreign Ministry, Gaja, at the Rome airport at Fiumicino, where the former stopped for a few hours on his way to New York. During this conversation,[11] Kreisky expressed his personal views on the difficulties that the Austrian government supposedly encountered in suppressing terrorist activities: not only were the length and nature of the frontier an obstacle but the terrorists only passed through the Tyrol on their way from other territories. As to the Italo-Austrian dispute, Kreisky stated that his efforts to persuade the spokesmen of the South Tyrol to accept the inclusive solution examined in Paris had not met with success, due in particular to the weakness of Magnago's position.

The position of the Austrian *Volkspartei* was also uncertain, he stated, and the Socialist party that favored a negotiated solution could not alone assume responsibility for it. All of these factors led him to take a very pessimistic view of the situation. If an agreement was to be reached, Kreisky felt, Italy would have to show magnanimity by trusting the German-speaking group of the South Tyrol and accepting the so-called international guarantee of the proposed bilateral agreements. Kreisky believed it would be useful if the Italian government made direct contact with the S.V.P. in order to find acceptable solutions to the main points still outstanding: approval of the provincial budget, and concessions in the spheres of industry, credit, police, and labor placement. The Austrian Foreign Minister concluded by saying that it would be preferable to avoid a situation in which his government would again have to seek recourse before the United Nations, possibly with a new case based on the request for self-determination, a situation that might develop under pressure from the extremists.

Ambassador Gaja immediately pointed out that the situation that had recently developed was one in which a series of terrorist attacks on Italian territory had been carried out by persons who came from Austria and had again found refuge there. This was in conflict with international law and not in keeping with good-neighbor relations. It was time that steps were taken by Vienna to prevent a repetition of such attacks. As to the Austro-Italian dispute itself, Italy had always been willing to resume meetings between representatives of the two Foreign Ministries in order to seek an acceptable solution on the basis established at the last meeting in London. It had, however, to be emphasized once again that a reference to a Court of Arbitration was no longer relevant, because of the stand taken in recent months by spokesmen of both the Alto Adige and Austria regarding the inclusive solution presented in Paris on December 16, 1964. Any subsequent negotiations would, therefore, have to be based on assumptions that were no longer the same as those earlier applicable in this context. Thereupon, a whole series of points describing the Italian government policy was repeated to the Austrian Foreign Minister, of which he should already have been aware.

Kreisky's attitude was unchanged when he spoke on October 11 with a member of the Italian U.N. delegation in New York during the XX U.N. General Assembly. At that time, Kreisky was informed of Italy's desire for a new meeting between officials of the two Ministries of Foreign Affairs. It was also pointed out that Italy's position remained the one outlined at the last meeting in July. Kreisky replied that although he took note of this, at the same time he still wished to insist on the need both to give Austria some form of international guarantee on the measures which the Italian government proposed to adopt unilaterally and to broaden the legislative powers of the province of Bolzano. Basically, the Austrian Foreign Minister maintained the same position that he had assumed at Fiumicino Airport. He also sought to point to dangers inherent in the proposals advanced in London by the Italian representatives, letting it be understood that should the Austrian "receipt" be put off and not immediately follow the Italian government's declaration to the Rome Parliament, it might never be given due to extremist pressures preventing the Austrian government from fulfilling such an undertaking.

On October 12, Kreisky spoke before the XX General Assembly of the United Nations. His reference to the South Tyrol question was couched in such moderate terms,[12] that Italy saw no need to use her right to reply. The basic optimism shown by the Austrian Foreign Minister in his handling of the South Tyrol question before the United Nations on this occasion was significant, coming as it did after his conversations with Italian officials, who had set forth once again the position of the Italian government.

On the day after Kreisky's statement to the United Nations, the Italian Prime

Minister spoke on the Alto Adige in the Chamber of Deputies in Rome during the absence of the Foreign Minister, who chaired the XX U.N. General Assembly in New York. In this speech, Moro dwelt at length on his meeting with Chancellor Klaus and all other major aspects of the question. Important points made by the Italian Prime Minister are included in the following verbatim extracts:

In general, by defending frontiers which have been established by treaty, we contribute to the peace of Europe and of the world, *since every alteration in the status quo can only mean a threat of war.* By respecting and guaranteeing the autonomy of the minorities in the Alto Adige, we fulfill a requirement of our Constitution and further strengthen confidence, peace and tranquillity. By seeking to maintain good and constructive relations with Austria, within the limits of our national dignity and legitimate interests, we do what is required by both our national needs and those of cooperation between peoples. Our position on the Alto Adige is laid down in the government's program where it is stated that, while fully respecting Italy's rights, the government intends to further the just and peaceful co-existence of the Italian and German-speaking populations, as well as the Ladins, among other things by the early application of the recommendations of the Commission of 19, so as to insure confidence and tranquillity in the region.

As to the remarks made by one deputy on the purely domestic nature of the Alto Adige question, may I recall a point I made in my reply during the debate on the vote of confidence in the Chamber: It is a mistake to maintain that by setting up the Commission of 19, the Italo-Austrian dispute has ceased to be a matter of international concern. On November 30, 1961, the United Nations General Assembly gave unanimous approval to a resolution which stated that it noted with satisfaction that talks were in progress between the two parties so as to reach a direct solution, or in its absence, to seek appropriate peaceful means of resolving the dispute, requesting them, in addition, to abstain from any act which might jeopardize the friendly relations between them. I wish in any case to reassure Parliament in view of the current talks with Austria, which we hope will reach a rapid and fruitful solution, that we have not abandoned—nor do we intend to abandon—our oft repeated point of view as to the implementation by Italy of the De Gasperi–Gruber agreement. I wish also to repeat that termination of the dispute must not involve Italy in international obligations going beyond those arising out of the Paris Agreement itself.

The talks that have taken place since this Government has been in power have been based upon these principles and directed towards these objectives. Such talks continue . . . in the hope, which we sincerely share, that they reach a positive solution which will make it possible for all the language groups in the Alto Adige to live together in conditions of mutual trust and respect.

As the Minister of the Interior has here had occasion to point out, all of our energies, backed by every necessary means, are being used to combat outbreaks of terrorism. A complete security network is permanently on the alert and was strengthened last summer in the high mountain areas by posting guards at Alpine refuge posts. Moreover, the number of incidents which have been prevented or neutralized testifies to the efficiency of these security arrangements. Through such criminal acts the terrorists seek to re-kindle and fan the embers of discord, to provoke disorders and prevent peace, but their crimes have only resulted in the indignation of the inhabitants of the area and in condemnation by every civilized man of conscience.

The firm intention of the Italian government not to allow itself to be diverted from its own policy of seeking a peaceful solution to the dispute with Austria over application of the Paris Agreement of September 5, 1946, including direct talks with the Austrian government, presupposes that the latter—as the Italian government has clearly and repeatedly stated—seeks every possible means at all times to avoid taking stands, decisions, or measures which might contribute to and encourage, even indirectly, the irresponsible action of the terrorists. In this connection, with reference to the demonstrations at Innsbruck on the anniversary of the transfer of the Alto Adige to Italy, we pointed out to the Austrian government that demonstrations of this kind could in no way contribute to the improvement of relations between the two countries. Italy's determination to reach a solution to the Italo-Austrian dispute over the Alto Adige in addition presupposes that the Vienna government collaborate with all the energy at its disposal in the prevention and suppression of acts which, by their nature and the aims of those responsible for them, provide no guarantee for the maintenance of good relations between the two countries.

It has also been asked whether the government should not denounce the Paris Agreement of September 5, 1946, in view of the outrages in the Alto Adige. One should remember that the Paris Agreement contains two elements. On the one hand, it provides for granting the German-speaking group of the province of Bolzano autonomous legislative and executive powers—of a regional character—within the area concerned. On the other hand, it implicitly re-emphasizes the fact that the province of Bolzano lies in Italy. Throughout the dispute with Austria over application of the Paris Agreement, Italy has always maintained that she had fulfilled in every way her obligations arising out of it. The fact that during the Austro-Italian dispute it was possible to refer to a legal text such as the agreement of September 5, 1946, is not to be under-estimated. Likewise, the fact that the UN resolutions referring to the dispute and requiring the two parties to negotiate a solution to it make specific reference to the De Gasperi–Gruber agreement, and the legal nature of the dispute are also precise elements which must not be overlooked. Moreover, by its very reference to the Paris Agreement of September 5, 1946, the Austrian government has again recognized Italian sovereignty over the province of Bolzano. Under such conditions, to denounce the Agreement—quite apart from its effect upon our own policy in the United Nations—and although this would leave unchanged our position and our obligation to the inhabitants of the Alto Adige, it would bring with it no improvement for Italy with respect to the problems of the Alto Adige.[13]

These statements are important because they publicly reconfirmed the Italian government's stand that "termination of the dispute must not involve Italy in international obligations going beyond those arising out of the Paris Agreement itself." This implied implicitly and explicitly the exclusion of any international guarantee in the new measures. Also, the Italian Prime Minister explained the relationship between the proposals of the Commission of 19 and the solution to the Italo-Austrian dispute over application of the Paris Agreement. Further, his explicit condemnation of the outrages and of the Vienna government's responsibility in the matter was put in terms deserving the latter's most serious attention. He clearly and forthrightly explained the positive aspects of the De Gasperi–Gruber agreement, which implicitly stressed Austrian recognition of the Brenner frontier. This last statement was particularly addressed to those who repeated, more or less intentionally, the argument advanced by Kreisky, or, more accurately, coming from the Tyrol, to the effect that the Paris Agreement of September 5, 1946 only imposed obligations upon Italy and, therefore, did not require their being fulfilled by Austria.

[2]

On October 23, 1965, a new development occurred that affected the progress of the talks between the Italian and Austrian governments: a political crisis in Austria resulted in new elections being scheduled for March 6, 1966. Since formation of a new government after the elections might be difficult and lengthy, it seemed likely that until early in May the government would be handicapped in its conduct at the talks, both because of its provisional nature and because of the lack of unity among the parties, which was at the roots of the crisis itself. However, Italy considered it advisable to continue the talks, even though no solution to the dispute could likely be reached as long as there was only an interim government in Austria.

As a result, representatives of the two Foreign Ministries met in London on November 25, 1965.[14] The Italian delegates reiterated their government's view that a solution to the international dispute over application of the De Gasperi–Gruber agreement could only be reached on the basis of fresh proposals regarding both procedural and substantive aspects of the problem.

As to procedure, the two parties could turn their attention to a solution based upon elimination of Austria's vulnerability in tendering a "receipt" before the Italian Parliament had approved the proposed legislation on autonomy, including both ordinary and constitutional legislation. At the same time, a number of *internal* guarantees could be developed for the German-speaking group. First, these could take the form of a declaration of policy, which the Italian Parliament was to approve, concerning the measures it was to adopt in favor of this group. Second, a special internal liaison body could be created for the study of local problems, consisting of representatives of the province of Bolzano and of the Ministry of the Interior or of the Prime Minister's office. Third, formal provision could be made for the participation of the chairman of the provincial council (Giunta Provinciale) of the province at cabinet meetings concerning the province (as already obtained for the chairmen of the other regions). As for the so-called international guarantee repeatedly requested by Austria, this could only take the form of acknowledging the jurisdiction of the International Court of The Hague on exclusively legal questions regarding any future dispute between Rome and Vienna over application of the De Gasperi–Gruber agreement.

With reference to substantive issues at stake, Italy confirmed its government's favorable attitude on the points developed at the five meetings of the executive committee in Geneva, subject to a reservation over the ethnic proportionality clause affecting public offices, which needed further examination. As to the 18 points remaining unresolved after those meetings and which, under the working solution discussed in Paris were to have been settled on the basis of the Italian suggestions exclusively, it was proposed to further discuss only those eight that Austria and the Alto Adige had considered vital.

From the Austrian side, the internal guarantee suggestion found some approval. Her representatives pointed out, however, that their government did not intend to abandon the request for an international guarantee in the form of a special arbitral body. The problem would, they maintained, lose its importance should the province of Bolzano be raised to the status of an autonomous region. On the substantive questions, the Austrian representatives accepted the Italian proposal to examine the eight points considered "vital," hoping for a small extension of this. At the end of the session, a new meeting was tentatively proposed for the end of January 1966.

As had been customary on previous occasions, the outcome of this meeting between officials of the two Foreign Ministries was the subject of a meeting between spokesmen of Austria, the Tyrol, and the Alto Adige, held in Vienna shortly afterward. For Austria, Kreisky and Bobleter attended; for the Tyrol, Wallnöfer, Kathrein, and Gschnitzer; for the Alto Adige, Magnago, Mitterdorfer, and Benedikter. Based on the minutes of the meeting made available to him, Ritschel[15] has given a full and detailed account of the proceedings, but it appears that there was no doubt concerning the position taken by the Italian government. The statements made by officials of the Italian Foreign Ministry had been noted and understood. Nevertheless, it appears that this had no affect on the intentions of the representatives in attendance, who continued in their determination to pursue their requests.

A few days after the London meeting, Klaus went to the United States on a visit planned sometime earlier, and spoke before the U.N. General Assembly on December 1. His statement contained a short reference to the question of the South Tyrol, repeating Austria's firm intention of settling the dispute with Italy through negotiations carried out in the spirit of the U.N. Charter.[16]

Immediately after this visit to the United States, the Austrian Chancellor came to Rome with Kreisky to attend the closing session of Vatican Council II. On December 7, he met with the Italian President and Prime Minister Moro. At the meeting, a detailed exchange of views took place on the subject of the Alto Adige.[17] As to the substantive aspects of the negotiations, Klaus and Kreisky proposed to work out practical solutions for the matters still unresolved. As to procedural aspects, they emphasized the need to agree on machinery to ensure application of the results achieved by the negotiations themselves. In replying to the first point, the Italians pointed to a need to achieve a balance between the various pertinent interests and points of view. Therefore, solutions must be found that were capable of satisfying all linguistic groups in the Alto Adige. On the procedural point, Italy did not rule out the need for a body empowered to resolve any disagreements that might arise over application of the Paris Agreement, but pointed to the need for careful study of the choice of that body.

The Austrians' line of thinking on the procedural aspects was clarified on

February 22, 1966, when the government officially informed Rome that with reference to the "international guarantee," it supported reaching an agreement on the basis of the proposals examined in Paris on December 16, 1964. Austria added that should this proposal not be acceptable to the Italian government, another type of guarantee would need to be studied, one that was both "real and effective."[18] In the same communication, the Austrians indicated that they were awaiting further details of the measures proposed by Italy concerning the South Tyrol, adding that should future Austro-Italian talks not reach agreement on any one of them, Austria would have no objection to their being left open, provided Italy agreed to their review at a later date.

Therefore, notwithstanding the explicit and unconditional refusal of officials of the Italian Foreign Ministry to discuss such a proposal, first presented by Austria in London on July 28, 1965, and in spite of conversations with Kreisky at Fiumicino, New York, and Rome in which he had repeatedly heard the same reply that was given by Italy in London on November 25, 1965, the Austrian Foreign Minister returned to the same proposal, one which would have left the Alto Adige question permanently unsettled.

The Italian Foreign Ministry immediately replied that as to the so-called international guarantee, Italy was still of the same opinion that it expressed at the last London meeting. Regarding the questions of substance under discussion in the Italo-Austrian talks, Italy could not accept the proposal made by Vienna, since—as the Austrian government knew—the goal of the Italian government was to reach a final, inclusive solution of the dispute.

A few days later, on March 3, following an Italian cabinet crisis, Prime Minister Moro made the following remarks on the Alto Adige in his statement of policy to the Senate and Chamber of Deputies:

As to the Alto Adige, the government will further the just and peaceful coexistence of the inhabitants of Italian and German language and the Ladins, within the framework of Italy's rights. In order to ensure confidence and tranquillity in the region, the government intends to adopt the recommendations of the Commission of 19 and to apply them in such a way as to satisfy the legitimate expectations of all linguistic groups in the Alto Adige and contribute to resolving the dispute with Austria via an understanding in accordance with the recommendation of the United Nations. While safeguarding the integrity of the Italian state, which is not open to discussion, the government will make every effort to protect the legitimate interests of the minorities in the Alto Adige, at the same time respecting the equally legitimate interests of the Italian-speaking population living in the area. These population groups need to live side by side in a democratic society which fully respects the sovereignty of the Italian state and be backed by reliable guarantees furthering the understanding required for new progress in all fields within the spirit of the Constitution. All those in the region must devote themselves to the attainment of this goal, while the government will carry out its own task, consulting where appropriate all population groups concerned.[19]

At the conclusion of the debate on the vote of confidence to his third cabinet, Moro made the following additional statement:

In this Chamber of Parliament as well, the problems of the Alto Adige have been discussed and opposing objections expressed. These objections are, however, unfounded when confronted with the policy of the government, which aims at safeguarding the integrity of the state and Italy's rights while at the same time seeking, through appropriate measures, to bring about a more satisfactory way of life for the German- and Ladin-speaking minorities in the Alto Adige, while preserving the rights of the Italian-speaking population in the area. Though convinced that it has fulfilled its obligations under the De Gasperi–Gruber agreement, the government intends to utilize in promoting these aims, the findings of the Commission of 19. Acting on its own initiative and under its own powers, the government will introduce measures to further the peaceful coexistence of the peoples of the Alto Adige within the autonomy authorized by the Constitution and by a more effective application of it. In carrying out this policy, its difficulties and pitfalls are clear to all, the government intends to examine the possibility of resolving unilaterally the dispute that has arisen between Italy and Austria and regarding which the UN has invited the parties to negotiate. Following meetings at different levels and despite an unsatisfactory Austrian reply, suitable steps are now being sought which will be capable of resolving the problems of autonomy in the best possible manner, and of settling the present dispute. Time has not and will not be lost, but all does not depend on us. Acting in the spirit of the Constitution and indisputable integrity, the Italian state will protect and further the well-being of its minorities, with the assurance that it can lose no prestige by the democratic implementation of this policy.[20]

The approach followed by the Italian government was thus confirmed and clarified regarding its aim of settling the Italo-Austrian dispute, and the relationship between that aim and the application of the recommendations of the Commission of 19.

[3]

The political crisis in Austria that had started on October 23, 1965, came to an end on April 18, 1966, with the formation, for the first time in twenty years, of a government represented exclusively by a single party, the *Volks partei*. In the new cabinet, headed again by Chancellor Klaus, the minister of foreign affairs was Toncic-Sorinj, who until then had been vice-chairman of the Political Commission of the Consultative Assembly of the Council of Europe and a member of its subsidiary body on the Alto Adige. Carl Bobleter remained in the post of under-secretary in the Ministry of Foreign Affairs. Another interesting element was the return to the Austrian cabinet of Karl Gruber, the man who had signed, with De Gasperi, the Paris Agreement of September 5, 1946, as under-secretary in the Office of the Chancellor.

In his policy statement to the Austrian Parliament on April 20, 1966,[21] Chancellor Klaus referred to the South Tyrol problem, pointing out that Austria had done everything in its power to reach an agreement with Italy. Klaus concluded his remarks on this subject by appealing to the Italian government to "press on" to overcome the "small" difference still existent. There was no doubt from this policy statement that the new government intended to continue discussions with Italy even in the new situation that resulted in the Socialist party becoming the opposition, with the government's majority reduced to a minimum.[22]

Immediately following formation of the new cabinet, the Austrian government requested Italy to reopen talks between officials of the Ministries of Foreign Affairs or at any other level that Italy might suggest. Toncic made the same request to Fanfani when they met at Strasbourg on May 4, 1966, during a meeting of the Council of Europe.[23] He confirmed his government's wish to resume the talks in an atmosphere of restored confidence. In turn, Fanfani drew Toncic's specific attention to the obstacles that lay in the path of restoring a tranquil atmosphere, namely, the various unfortunate moves by Austria (public petitions in that country favoring the Alto Adige, participation by Austrian politicians and members of the government in ceremonies in the Alto Adige, without or with inadequate notice to the Italian authorities, etc.). As to the substance of the talks for resolving the Alto Adige dispute, Fanfani confirmed that the Italian government could not accept any form of international guarantees over execution of the new measures it might unilaterally take to meet further the aspirations of the inhabitants of the Alto Adige and to put an end to the international dispute. Fanfani's firm stand on a fundamental issue of the negotiations certainly did not induce Toncic to nourish any illusions.

However, in compliance with a request by Toncic, a meeting between representatives of the two Foreign Ministries took place in London on May 25 and 26, 1966.[24] Again Italy indicated the need to nominate the International Court at The Hague as the judicial body competent to decide on the basis of international law any future dispute arising between the two parties concerning the application of existing treaties. The Italian government was prepared to examine the possibility of domestic guarantees, such as the establishment of an internal liaison body linking the government with representatives of the province of Bolzano, as well as the participation of the chairman of the Provincial Council of Bolzano (Giunta Provinciale) at cabinet meetings during which specific questions were to be discussed regarding the province. As to the substantive issues at stake in the Austro-Italian talks, that is, the measures that the Italians proposed to adopt unilaterally, the Italian representatives had been instructed to inform their Austrian counterparts that Rome was prepared to examine the possibility of discussing the ten questions still unresolved, in an effort to seek new solutions that were mutually acceptable. Italy also offered a new formula for solving the matter of the "ethnic proportionality in the employment of personnel in public offices in the province of Bolzano" (specifically foreseen by the De Gasperi–Gruber agreement). This formula was drafted to improve the application of a principle already in practice, more effectively than what had been proposed by the Commission of 19. Finally, Italy indicated to the Austrians that the government was considering the immediate adoption of a series of measures favoring the German ethnic group in the Alto Adige (including three that dealt with matters considered of major importance and as yet unresolved).

The Austrian representatives promptly pointed out that their government could consider the new basis for a solution to be satisfactory only if guarantees of an international character were added to the domestic guarantees planned by Italy. As to the specific issue of granting jurisdiction in the matter of the treaty to the International Court of Justice at The Hague, the Austrian representatives recalled that Vienna had previously publicly indicated that such a choice was not acceptable. However, the Austrians hinted at a possible alternative solution which, if agreed to by Italy, might conceivably lead to Vienna's acceptance of the Italian proposal regarding the selection of The Hague Court. The alternative solution based on the following: first, recognition of the validity of the Treaty of Friendship, Conciliation and Jurisdictional Arrangements signed by Italy and Austria on February 6, 1930;[25] second, withdrawal of the reservations made by Italy when signing the European Convention for the Pacific Regulation of Disputes, at Strasbourg on April 29, 1957;[26] third, acceptance of a clause giving retroactive effect to this European Convention (amending Art. 27 to cover disputes arising out of treaties—such as the De Gasperi–Gruber agreement—signed prior to the Strasbourg Convention, which applied in general only to treaties signed after April 29, 1957) and providing for bilateral negotiations to reconcile differences before having recourse to the court. As to the Italian measures to assist the German-speaking group of South Tyrol, although the Austrians indicated that these were not yet sufficiently far-reaching to satisfy their government, they gave the impression that a compromise regarding many of the matters still unresolved was possible. They agreed to provide the Italian government with more comprehensive comments on these matters and on any further measures that Italy was prepared to introduce unilaterally.

The Italian representatives replied by pointing out that it would be meaningful to fix a date for a further meeting between officials of the two Ministries of Foreign Affairs only if the Austrians were prepared to discuss, in principle, the suggested new proposals, that is, the possible choice of the International Court of Justice as the competent judicial body and the solution for the substantive matters as yet unresolved. Only a few minor residual concrete points might be left open for solution at the political level at a possible final meeting between the two heads of government, the two Foreign Ministers, or all four.

Ritschel does not say whether or not this session was followed by the usual meeting between representatives of Austria, the Tyrol, and the Alto Adige, nor does he give any indication of the reactions in those Austrian governmental circles primarily concerned.

In any event, the Austrian Foreign Ministry renewed its request to Italy for a further meeting between representatives of the two Ministries. The request was accompanied by an invitation to the Italian government to take another step forward in connection with the internal measures to be instituted by the Italian government unilaterally with respect to the issues still unresolved. Since it raised no other points, the request was understandably interpreted in Rome as an agreement to proceed in the manner suggested in London, and as such, was accepted.

The new meeting between the representatives took place at Montreux, June 16–18, 1966.[27] Italy sought to reduce the area of disagreement on both procedural and substantive points in such a way as to leave, at most, only two or three matters still open, which could then be left for review at a later date, specifically, at the tentatively projected top level political meeting. As to the procedural issue, the Italian representatives informed their Austrian colleagues that their government accepted the proposal to amend Article 27 of the Strasbourg Convention, giving it retroactive effect to include the Paris Agreement of September 5, 1946. As to the substantive issues, Italy sought to reduce to a minimum the points still unresolved.

In this way, on the opening day of the Montreux meeting, the Italian delegates followed a line that would make it possible to bring the positions of the two sides closer together, while not deviating from Italy's stand on fundamental legal principles at all stages of the dispute with Austria. In the same manner, Italy's desire to promptly put into effect the measures adopted regarding the Alto Adige, confirmed that its constant aim was the peaceful coexistence and development of the people in the Alto Adige.

Although these considerations could have signaled the first major breakthrough in the new series of Italo-Austrian talks following Austrian rejection of the proposals examined in Paris on December 16, 1964, unfortunately they brought no immediate results. This was because the Austrian representatives indicated that the entire package of new solutions proposed in London was still under review by a group of political representatives from Austria and the South Tyrol, together with expert advisers who were preparing their comments and counterproposals. All that the Austrian officials were in a position to say at the moment was that it did not appear at first glance that the newly proposed solutions offered a sufficient basis for terminating the dispute. In the eyes of the Austrian representatives, the measures suggested for the advancement of the German-speaking citizens were more or less the same as those examined in Paris on December 16, 1964, and the procedural part of the new proposals seemed to indicate that the Italian government had not modified its 1961 position.

To these preliminary Austrian reactions, it was not difficult for the Italian officials to reply that the new proposals actually represented a distinctly substantial step closer to Austria's position. It was pointed out that as to the possible domestic measures to be taken by Italy, the Italian government had authorized its representatives to consider solutions which as a whole went far beyond those examined in Paris in December 1964. The Austrian comment that the Italian suggestions regarding procedural aspects of terminating the dispute were, in effect, the same as those proposed by Italy in 1961 was not supported by the facts. In 1961 the Commission of 19 had only just been established and the Italian government had not yet declared its readiness to entertain the introduction of an important package of measures in favor of the population of the Alto Adige. Such a circumstance could not but clearly distinguish the Italian position in 1966 from that of 1961, when the commission had been just set up.

Immediately after the close of the Montreux encounter, at which the Italian delegation pointed out that a new meeting would be valueless should the approach suggested by the Italian government not be accepted, the customary meeting took place between spokesmen from Austria, the Tyrol, and the Alto Adige to review the results of the latest talks. This time, the meeting took place in Vienna on June 24, 1966. Austria was represented by Toncic, Bobleter, Lowenthal, Haymerle, and Kirschlager, the Tyrol by Wallnöfer, Zechtl, Kathrein, Stadlmayer, Gschnitzer, and Ermacora, the Alto Adige by Magnago, Mitterdorfer, Dietl, and Pupp.[28] Again there was the usual polarization of the moderates and the extremists, resulting, as usual, in giving the Austrian representatives instructions that Italy had repeatedly stated she was unable to accept.

Following the Montreux conversations, the Austrian Foreign Minister sent a letter to his Italian counterpart on June 28, 1966, and in view of the appeal that the document contained, the Italian government decided to agree to another meeting between officials of the two Foreign Ministries.

This meeting took place in London on July 18–20, 1966.[29] Italy's representatives informed the Austrians that further substantive matters could only be discussed if the Italian proposal concerning the International Court at The Hague as the jurisdictional authority was accepted. In this event, and should the discussion prove entirely successful, it could pave the way for a high-level political meeting. In other words, only when all outstanding questions—including the matters remaining unresolved concerning the internal measures proposed to be taken unilaterally by Italy—had been resolved would it be possible to reach a final political decision, possibly at a high-level meeting. This decision would be only tantamount to ratification of an agreement that had been reached beforehand at the level of experts by officials of the two governments.

As to the Austrian request for preliminary Italo-Austrian contacts prior to a possible reference of the dispute to The Hague Court, the Italian officials indicated that this might be acceptable to the Italian government, provided these contacts met the following conditions: they were to take place only when recourse had been had to the International Court of Justice; they were to form part of the proceedings of the court; they were to be strictly legal in character and must not give rise to any special mechanism or one that would be permanent. The Italian representatives then set out their case on the following lines: joint review of problems still outstanding in order to determine the presence or absence of a concrete basis for a mutually satisfactory solution to the dispute. Thus, Italy once again had set forth her government's position in terms that were clear and concise with respect to both procedural and substantive issues.

With Italy's position once again plainly stated, the Austrian representatives indicated that Vienna was trying to avoid accepting the new proposals regarding procedure, that is, the recognition of the jurisdictional court. Austria even requested that Italy undertake, through a unilateral declaration, valid *juris gentium,* to submit to The Hague Court the measures it was anticipating for the German-speaking group of the South Tyrol, and proposed the creation of a joint Austro-Italian commission for the purpose of reviewing the progressive application of such measures for a period of five years.

Italy's representatives stated that such proposals were quite unacceptable. They pointed out that in this new situation, whereby Italy accepted postponement of the "paid-in-full receipt" from Austria until the proposed measures had actually come into force, the latest Italian proposals could clearly be viewed at least as favorable to Austria as those considered in Paris on December 16, 1964. Indeed, some form of guarantee by Austria to Italy would now seem to be required.

As to the substantive issues at stake, the Austrian officials raised no basic objections to the proposals offered by their Italian colleagues, though making some observations on the matter of a "provincial budget" and on the subject of "residence." At the end of the meeting, the Austrian representatives promised they would reply in writing to Rome on the Italian proposals before the end of July.

These London talks marked the end of another phase in the negotiations, since, for the second time, a package deal for settling the dispute had been proposed, one on which it was necessary for the Austrian government to take a stand.

Meanwhile, a series of meetings continued in Italy between representatives of the S.V.P. and the government, in which the individual ministers concerned with the projected measures to be taken unilaterally by Italy had contacts with German-speaking Alto Adige spokesmen. These contacts took place without the representatives of the Alto Adige having to also discuss their problems at Innsbruck and Vienna. Moreover, they came within the spirit of the De Gasperi–Gruber agreement, which under Article 2 provided for consultation "with local representative German-speaking elements" in determining the framework within which the proposed autonomy was to be achieved and this logically also applied to a revision of the autonomous powers. These internal talks received additional impetus from the fact that immediately after the London meeting, the Austrian government publicly declared through its spokesmen[30] that before reaching a decision regarding the proposals made by Italy in London for a package deal to end the dispute, it intended to consult the S.V.P., declaring that its own decision here would depend on that of the German-speaking group of the South Tyrol. This resulted in the S.V.P. being able to take official notice of the contents of the "package" covering the premises for ending the dispute. It could, therefore, submit the package to its own internal policy bodies for review, and it could also request further details from the Italian government in the course of its contacts with it.

[4]

The plan of approach toward settlement of the Italo-Austrian dispute was examined by the S.V.P. at two meetings, both held at Bolzano: the first, by the Central Committee on August 26, 1966, and the second, by the directors of the *Südtiroler Volkspartei,* August 29–September 1, 1966. Both meetings were presided over by Dr. Silvius Magnago, chairman of the S.V.P.[31] The fact that these meetings had been immediately preceded by intense discussion at Innsbruck between leaders of the S.V.P. and senior representatives of the Tyrolese government and that Chancellor Klaus,[32] in the Tyrol on official business, was also present, seems to indicate the importance that both Austria and the Tyrol attributed to the stand about to be taken by the S.V.P. on the proposals outlined at London.

Both the discussions held in the S.V.P. Central Committee and those that followed in the meeting of its directorate were detailed and exhaustive. They covered every single point involved in the substantive issues at stake and, in the procedural aspects, were aimed at giving Bolzano's support to Vienna and Innsbruck on the subject of the so-called "international guarantee" for the measures contemplated by the Italian government. Despite lively opposition from a number of extremists, at the end of the meeting of the party directors, a majority headed by Magnago agreed on issuing a communiqué which, while not rejecting the London proposals, stated that the S.V.P. considered it essential to obtain considerable additional information from the Italian government on a number of points, among them the one on an "effective international guarantee." The communiqué concluded by stating that the Central Committee and the directors of the S.V.P. had decided, subject to the prerequisite of obtaining additional information from Rome, to recommend acceptance of the results obtained in the Austro-Italian talks. As to the requirement of additional information, the communiqué added that the Chairman of the S.V.P. was requested to take the necessary steps with the proper authorities in Rome.

In a press conference held after these meetings, Magnano was asked to explain the exact meaning of the "information" to be requested from Rome. He replied that this was not supposed to include the request for new concessions from the government, inferring that the requisite information was not such as to destroy the general equilibrium of the government's position as set out in London by the representatives of its Foreign Ministry. Magnago's comments implied that the requests concerned the need for a "clarification" of the Italian position.

The emphasis given by the S.V.P. to the so-called "international guarantee" question gave the impression that the party supported Austria in wanting Italy to discuss some additional clause, albeit within the framework of the choice of the International Court of Justice as the competent judicial body. Indeed, the Italian representatives at London had not minced words on this point: Italy was unable to accept extension of the right of jurisdiction of the International Court over any domestic measures it carried out unilaterally.

For some time observers in Italy had been noting the attacks against the

Austrian government's policy, particularly by the former foreign minister, Kreisky. His attacks were directed against the possibility of an agreement between Italy and Austria which, in its procedural aspects, would provide for recourse to The Hague Court. On more than one occasion, Kreisky had urged the single-party cabinet headed by Klaus not to accept what the Socialist former minister described as "an Italian offer substantially less than that of December 1964," nimbly overlooking the fact that it was he who, as Austrian foreign minister, had rejected the inclusive solution that was proposed.[33] In other words, the Austrian Socialists were presenting the question of an international guarantee as one of fundamental importance, perhaps because they believed that the series of internal measures contemplated by Italy might make the possibility of an understanding between Rome and Vienna a reality. To prevent this, unrealistic demands were made of the government and it was considered expedient for this same purpose to throw the entire Austrian Catholic party into a crisis.

In the Alto Adige, both the new Socialist party headed by Jenny,[34] and a number of leading figures in the S.V.P. took the same position. All this, when added to the moves made by certain groups in the Tyrol, explains the emphasis laid by the Central Committee and the directors of the S.V.P., in their analysis of the requests for clarification that the party made to the government, on Bolzano's wish for an "effective international guarantee," without wishing or being able to specify exactly what sort of guarantees were sought. However, neither the difficulties faced by the Austrian cabinet in the Socialist opposition, nor the position of some groups in the S.V.P. and in Jenny's new party seemed at that time sufficiently serious to insinuate that Bolzano was already prepared to reopen the question of the jurisdiction of The Hague Court on the substantive issues involved and to go so far as to seek to extend it to cover the proposed future internal Italian measures as well.

In September an important debate on the Alto Adige was held in both the Italian Chamber of Deputies and in the Senate. Numerous questions were raised by representatives of all political parties as a result of the new and serious demonstrations that were taking place there[35] and the press reports on the examination being carried out by the S.V.P. of Italy's proposals.

A review of the Italian government's proposals by representatives of the German-speaking minority had been foreseen by the De Gasperi–Gruber agreement in connection with the subject of regional autonomy. However, it was also an important governmental prerequisite to avoid committing itself to making certain concessions before ascertaining whether the proposed internal measures were capable of settling the international dispute. For this very reason, the Italian government avoided discussing in too great a detail the concrete measures it would take. At the same time, it seemed desirable to obtain the explicit sanction of Parliament on the eve of this possibly decisive phase of the negotiations, though Italian policy regarding the Italo-Austrian talks had on several earlier occasions received parliamentary support.

The debate in the Chamber of Deputies was opened on September 12, 1966, by the minister of the interior, Taviani. His speech dealt with the means and methods employed to combat terrorism and the overall action taken by the government in the Alto Adige, not only to quell but also to prevent terrorist outbreaks.[36] The Minister's speech was followed by a long and detailed statement by the Prime Minister, who used the occasion to place before Parliament the main issues involved in the Alto Adige question. As to the policy followed by the Italian government toward Austria, Moro made the following remarks:

I should start by pointing out that it is the view of the government that the autonomous powers of the province of Bolzano and their possible extension are domestic matters to be decided by us *inter alia* in the light of the findings of the Commission of 19. On the other hand, in its final recommendations, the commission had not clearly indicated what measures should be adopted. The explanation may be sought in the numerous reservations put forward by one side or the other with respect both to the proposals which were adopted and those which were rejected by the majority. Moreover, since the commission's recommendations are not binding upon the government, the government itself must seek out all those elements needed to assist it in reaching a mature and balanced solution. Foremost among these is the possibility of effectively resolving the Italo-Austrian dispute over the application and interpretation of the De Gasperi–Gruber agreement and the extent to which local linguistic groups are satisfied and their legitimate interests protected.

Once these elements are finally at our disposal, which it is believed will be soon, and in the light of the results which could follow from them and the reactions noted in the talks which have been taking place, the government intends to place before Parliament the whole body of measures, designed with particular reference to the work carried out by the Commission of 19, which could be adopted. It is also clear that any new powers granted to the province of Bolzano will be extended to the province of Trento.

In the talks which have taken place so far, and which have used as reference material the studies referred to, the Italian representatives had instructions to work within the following mandate:

1) There should be no difficulty in carrying out any measures put forward unanimously by the Commission of 19. Thirty-six proposals of various types are involved here and they do not in general imply a change in the present powers of the province of Bolzano.

2) As to the measures approved by a majority vote in the Commission of 19, the question of whether or not they should be carried out would depend upon the extent of the majority they obtained and, to an even greater extent, upon the overall interests of the state, upon the need to take into due account the legal structure of other bodies, and upon their possible effects on the coexistence of the various legal language groups involved. In the light of these considerations, a careful study was made of the possibility of widening the powers of the two provinces of Trent and Bolzano. No objection was seen, in principle, to the transfer from the region to the province of matters primarily of local interests, concerning local services, cultural matters and the development of certain sectors of the economy. Particular attention was also given to the proposals made by the Commission of 19 concerning the educational system and employment in public offices. In both cases, solutions are foreseen which are based on new conceptions, though governed by the same overall aims underlined in the commission's report.

3) Following this approach, certain individual proposals have been set aside (for example, the one concerning juries, which would have involved making the selection of each jury depend upon the ethnic proportionality factor as determined by the language group of the accused) while at the same time, certain measures have been taken into consideration which were not proposed by the Commission of 19. Included here are related subjects which it appeared best to entrust to a single autonomous body.

This notwithstanding, the government gave instructions for the following points to be strictly observed at the talks:

1) Retention of the Trentino–Alto Adige region with all of its regional powers, to serve as a framework which could insure uniformity among the various regional organs (communes, local government bodies, fire-fighting services, local public banks, public assistance and welfare bodies, health and hospital services). In addition to these powers, the region would maintain intact its other powers of a specifically governmental nature. It should be pointed out here that the region is not merely to be retained as a formal structure as has been said by some, but rather, as a substantive body, for the government believes that it has, as presently set up, a useful function to fulfill, above all in the harmonious development of all the peoples in the provinces of Trent and Bolzano.

2) Retention by the State of all powers essential to national security and social harmony. For this reason, no suggestion whatever may be entertained of a transfer of powers with respect to police, change of residence and allocation of labor.

3) A series of guarantees is anticipated directed essentially toward protecting, within each province, the various minority language groups and toward ensuring full equality of all citizens before the law together with the most equitable and correct exercise of autonomous powers.

Since this is a matter of particular importance to our Italian-speaking fellow citizens in the Alto Adige, I would like to list, by way of example, the most important and basic of these guarantees:

a) Provision has been made for each section of the budget of the province of Bolzano to be voted on separately by each language group. German-speaking and Italian-speaking, represented in the Provincial Council. Where a majority is not attained in both groups, the sections of the budget involved are to be submitted to an arbitration commission appointed by the council itself;

b) A majority of Counsellors forming a language group may request a vote to be taken by language groups with the council, wherever a draft measure be held to violate the equality before the law of all citizens whatever their group;

c) Should such a request not be granted, the language group not obtaining satisfaction has the right to appeal to the Constitutional Court;

d) Provision has been made for an appeal to be made to an administrative tribunal in cases where administrative measures taken by local bodies are considered to have violated the principles of equality between members of different language groups;

e) Each language group has the right to be represented on the municipal executive body when it has at least two representatives on the Communal Council.

I would point out further, that in examining the possibility of a transfer of powers, the situation of a minority group at the provincial level has always been born in mind, provision being accordingly made for the following:

1) in the field of employment and training, the legislative powers of the province would be limited to those of a supplementary nature;

2) once a right of precedence to employment vacancies is included in the statute of autonomy for residents of the province of Bolzano, further distinctions based on language group or length of residence will be dropped;

3) directors of employment exchanges will be appointed by the state, after consultation with the chairman of the provincial executive body and the mayors of the communes concerned;

4) with the transfer to the provinces of Trent and Bolzano of the regional powers regarding industrial development, sums set aside for this purpose in the national budget under industrial promotion legislation will be distributed with an agreement between the state and the province affected;

5) the use of funds set aside by the province of Bolzano for welfare, public assistance and cultural purposes, will be linked directly to the needs of each language group, as well as to their numerical size;

6) in appointing extraordinary supervisory bodies, the province is required to nominate their members from the language group providing the majority of counselors from the local administrations it has suspended;

7) when emergency suspension and replacement orders are due to reasons of public security or concern communes whose inhabitants exceed 20,000 persons, they are to be made exclusively by the state.

Finally, it will be recalled that the mayors of all communes in the province are government officials and as such come under the various organs of the State responsible for the services they administer. As to the maintenance of contact with the inhabitants of the Alto Adige, it is the government's view that they are essential for the smooth development and peaceful coexistence of the local populations. For this purpose, the government believes it advisable to make provision in the future for such contacts to be made normally in various forms, but principally through a consultative body forming part of the domestic administration of the state.

Aside from the domestic aspects of the problem which I have just dealt with, it will be recalled that there is also an international dispute between Italy and Austria over interpretation and application of the De Gasperi–Gruber agreement. On this point, the government has always held that a legal question is involved and that it would be extremely useful to have a judicial body which could decide the issue according to the law. As early as 1961, therefore, we proposed to Austria the submission of the dispute over interpretation and application of the De Gasperi–Gruber agreement to a decision by the International Court at The Hague. In the absence of an agreement on this point the dispute is still unresolved.

When the solution expected at Paris in December 1964, did not materialize, Italy insisted on the need to appoint the International Court of Justice as the judicial body competent to decide the question of interpretation of the Paris Agreement of 1946 according to international law. Indeed, this Court is in every way qualified to act as a judicial body in all disputes. It is the principal judicial organ of the United Nations, whose members are *ipso facto* parties to the Statute of the Court. By its very nature, it is the international judicial organ to which all members of the United Nations can have recourse in disputes regarding: interpretation of a treaty, any disagreement over a point of international law, the existence of facts which would involve violation of international undertakings, and the nature and extent of damages due for any such violation.

It will also be recalled that the U.N. resolutions of 1960 specified The Hague Court among the peaceful means of settlement foreseen by the U.N. Charter to which Italy and Austria could have recourse to resolve the dispute. The Hague Court is also recognized by the Strasbourg Convention, ratified in part by Italy, as the appropriate judicial body for hearing disputes between the nations of Europe. It would only be necessary to extend its coverage to include agreements entered into since 1945.

By recognizing, through an appropriate international declaration, the specific competence of the International Court of Justice, both Italy and Austria could submit to it any legal dispute originating from any bilateral agreement in force between them, in conformity with the general tendency towards achieving a system of European law. The Hague Court would thus become the international judicial body having overall jurisdiction for all disputes between Italy and Austria, as it already has been for disputes between European states since 1960.

Both the composition and procedure of The Hague Court eliminate the opinion expressed by some that recourse to The Hague Court would involve a "humiliating" Italo-Austrian condominium over the Alto Adige. The acceptance of the court's jurisdiction excludes new political claims. Choice of the International Court also represents an effective guarantee for all, since its decisions have greater effect than any other international judicial finding or arbitral award, the U.N. charter also providing that the Security Council may intervene to enforce the court's decisions.

It may then be concluded that recourse to the world's highest judicial body—for its prestigious traditions, its place in the most modern system of European public law, for its very high repute and for the prospects these offer in the enforcement of its decisions—constitutes the best "guarantee" of the De Gasperi—Gruber agreement, if by the word "guarantee" is understood an international guarantee that an agreement will be carried out. Lastly, I would like to emphasize that in pressing for this solution, the government has taken into particular account the fact that Parliament, when giving its approval to the line taken by the Italian delegation to the U.N. in 1960 and 1961, formally took a position in favor of the International Court of Justice.

Apart from appointing The Hague Court as the judicial body to which the parties may have recourse for interpretation and application of the De Gasperi—Gruber agreement, the proposed solution now under examination for putting an end to the Austro-Italian dispute likewise provides for a full declaration of complete satisfaction to be announced by the Austrian government upon approval of the Italian proposals, which would become operative once the measures announced by Italy in favor of the German-speaking group of the Alto Adige have been carried out. The actual declaration to be made by Austria that the dispute is at an end, will not therefore, as some have maintained, be left to the discretion of the Austrian government, but rather follow automatically, from an action already taken, when Italy will have actually carried out the measures planned. The fact that the Austrian declaration terminating the controversy is to become operative when the dispute will no longer have any basis in fact, renders unnecessary the request for any further "guarantees" from Italy on the subject of the measures themselves, other than those represented by the possibility of having recourse to The Hague Court over the application and interpretation of the De Gasperi—Gruber agreement.

I would finally like to emphasize the point that the government has not yet entered into any agreement, and now, today, after informing this body of the various aspects of the question, waits on Parliament to confirm, if it so desires, the mandate it gave earlier concerning implementation of the proposals contained in the final report of the Commission of 19, and the continuation of the international talks aimed at terminating the Italo-Austrian dispute over application and interpretation of the De Gasperi—Gruber agreement.

Should Parliament approve the policy outlined above, the government proposes to draw up the appropriate draft legislation and other measures needed to implement, to the extent considered just and equitable, the solutions put forward by the Commission of 19. At the same time, the government will proceed with the talks with Vienna, for the purpose, among others, of reaching a specific agreement on referring possible disputes to The Hague Court.[37]

Immediately after this statement by the Italian Prime Minister, a lively debate followed in the Chamber of Deputies, in which all parties took part. The opposition on the extreme right demanded suspension of all contacts with Austria as long as terrorist outbreaks continued. The opposition from the extreme left, tended to link the causes of the events in the Alto Adige with the wider problem of final recognition by Italy of the present German frontiers. Many deputies pointed to the absolute necessity to request the Austrian government to take concrete action against terrorism and to collaborate with Italy in so doing.

In his summation at the close of the debate on September 15, Prime Minister Moro stated:

> The problem which we have been discussing confronts us in all its gravity. Strong feelings and apprehension are justified. But now we have a line of approach to follow which has emerged stronger and more effective as the result of our exchange of ideas. It does not lead to a rapid solution of our difficulties, but it leads clearly in the right direction. It is a firm and just approach which may well bring us more slowly to our goal than we would like, but it will doubtlessly lead us there, and in so doing contribute to a smoother functioning of Italian politics. We must not let ourselves be unduly disturbed, nor let events overwhelm us. We must face them calmly and bring them gradually under control in line with our hopes and the needs of the country. Combating terrorism calls for firmness, without tying our hands. Firmness is required, also, in our dealings with other countries on cooperative measures against violence and on resolving the international dispute. Firmness is likewise demanded in the defense of our frontiers and of the unity and integrity of the Italian state.
>
> But justice is also called for, as is respect, and as is the will to use the whole apparatus of democratic life to acknowledge the rights of individuals and of groups. This is not incompatible with unity of the nation, but on the contrary, it prepares the ground for it and makes its realization possible. Neither is this incompatible with tranquillity and peace for the entire collectivity which makes up the nation, but on the contrary, it determines and achieves the calm self-confidence of groups and individuals.[38]

The government's policy was overwhelmingly approved by the Chamber of Deputies on a motion presented by the majority parties.[39] As a result of this vote, the government received a renewed mandate to continue its efforts to reach a solution of the international dispute along the lines previously followed. The only new element introduced into the motion approved by the Chamber concerned the requested "agreement of representatives of the populations involved" to the "proposed measures to be carried out unilaterally by the state."

The Senate discussed the Alto Adige question on September 21–22, 1966. Here also, the debates were lively, with senators of all political persuasions taking part.

The Prime Minister spoke again to the Senate in reply to the various speakers who took part in the debate. Given the very short lapse of time since the similar debate in the Chamber of Deputies, Moro repeated to the Senate substantially the same exposition of the situation that he had earlier made to the Chamber.[40] Since several speakers had expressed concern over the status of the Italian-speaking group in the Alto Adige should the autonomous powers of the province of Bolzano be extended, he dealt in detail with the guarantees anticipated for them, guarantees which were such as to insure the effective equality before the law of all language groups in the area. The Prime Minister also presented his ideas on the much debated problem of the so-called "international guarantee," stating as follows:

I now come to a delicate point of great importance, which has recently been raised repeatedly by Austria, namely, that of the so-called international guarantee. Now, if by guarantee one understands the fulfillment of a treaty to which we are a party, then we too are in favor of this guarantee, since a state such as Italy would certainly not violate its international undertakings. We support it in particular since such a guarantee ensures the inviolability of the law, the scrupulous fulfillment of reciprocal obligations and the rejection of unfounded claims. Had there been in the past a competent international judicial body, the dispute over application of the De Gasperi—Gruber agreement would long since have been resolved without the grave and tragic events of the last few years.

But one can only guarantee that to which one is entitled, not something which goes beyond one's rights, not an extension of the De Gasperi—Gruber agreement, which we could not accept. There is no doubt, and I believe this is recognized by Austria too, that the reciprocal obligations incumbent upon Italy and Austria stem exclusively from the De Gasperi—Gruber agreement. Austria's rights are those foreseen by the Paris Agreement, and Austria can only ask for a guarantee with respect to the Paris Agreement. The true rights of the two parties would be guaranteed by conferring jurisdiction upon a suitable judicial body. And this would be an important event, a step forward which we ourselves would welcome, since it would bring clarity and certainty to Italo-Austrian relations.

Establishment of a judicial body empowered to decide according to international law would provide the effective guarantee sought by Rome and Vienna. Other machinery and procedures mentioned by Austria have nothing to do with a guarantee, but on the contrary would risk extending rather than extinguishing the causes of disagreement. These proposals have, in general, the effect of shifting the dispute from the legal sphere, to which it belongs, to one of politics or equity; from the certainty of decisions, to the uncertainty of requests. They substitute demands for rights; in other words, they limitlessly extend the De Gasperi—Gruber agreement, radically altering both its spirit and its meaning. We are firmly opposed to such a proposal, which is quite unacceptable to us.[41]

The Italian Prime Minister also requested the Senate to give its fullest support to the government's action and, in particular, its authorization to continue the talks with Austria so as to seek an end to the dispute. By a large majority, the Senate then approved a motion similar in form and substance to that previously voted by the Chamber of Deputies.

[5]

The debates held in the Italian Parliament confirmed once again that it was essential to have the effective collaboration of the Austrian authorities in order to successfully combat terrorism, especially regarding effective methods of control and prevention on Austrian territory. Senators and deputies of different parties drew attention to the necessity of obtaining effective action from the Austrian government, which in the past had replied to many Italian requests by assurances, the implementation of which was inadequate, to collaborate with Italy, particularly through close cooperation between the Italian and Austrian police.

The Italian government had made it clear, through statements made by the Prime Minister during and at the close of the debate, that it fully concurred in the necessity for making every possible démarche to help stamp out terrorism, recognizing that it would be difficult to achieve this result through the efforts, albeit unremitting, of Italy alone. It was essential that the terrorists no longer harbor the belief that the various steps and measures taken by the Austrian government were such as would not seriously interfere with the planning of terroristic activities on Austrian territory. Above all, it was indispensable that the terrorists no longer feel that their backs were protected when they had crossed the Italian frontier, that it was easy to return into Austria and there find welcome asylum and protection.

Vienna had been cognizant of these claims for some time. But, as a result of these parliamentary debates and the numerous terrorist outbreaks that continued both during and following them, the Italian government decided to send a new *note verbale* to Vienna. The Italian note, dispatched to Vienna on October 6, opened by describing the long and unremitting action carried out by Italy to further the peaceful coexistence of the inhabitants of the Alto Adige and to conform with the covenant in the U.N. resolutions of 1960 and 1961. The note also recounted the details of the numerous domestic measures that had been taken, leading to a series of enactments and orders regarding the province of Bolzano.

As to the international aspects of the question, the note stated that Italy had fully carried out the U.N. resolutions, with particular emphasis on the invitation that they contained to reopen negotiations with the Austrian government to find a solution to the disagreements regarding the application of the De Gasperi–Gruber agreement. The many meetings that had taken place between the Italian and Austrian officials and ministers, during the period 1961–66, pointed most clearly to Italy's having entirely complied with the requests in the U.N. resolutions.

The note went on to review those aspects of the terrorist demonstrations which clearly indicated that their perpetrators had the advantage of tactical bases in Austria as well as support and encouragement in their activities. They had complete freedom of action there, to the extent of giving interviews to foreign newspapers and on television stations and were encouraged by well-

known extremist organizations.[42] In addition, numerous slogans on walls, distribution of anti-Italian pamphlets, frequent "pro-South Tyrol" financial drives
throughout the Tyrol, Styria, and other parts of Austria for nebulous cultural
and welfare purposes, and the undisturbed activities of extremist organizations
confirmed the obvious failure of the Austrian authorities to prevent and eliminate the real hotbeds of terrorism. The note concluded with a request by the
Italian government that a whole series of measures be taken by Austria to deal
with the situation.[43]

Two months later, that is, not until December 5, 1966, two days after another
Italian note on terrorist activities had been handed to Vienna,[44] Austria replied
to the Italian *note verbale*. The Austrian reply, after several introductory
remarks, referred to the Italian note's stressing that the Austrian government had
not fulfilled the recommendation set out in the third part of U.N. Resolution
1947 (XV), which had called upon the two parties to abstain from any act that
might compromise the friendly relations between them. Rejecting the Italian
charges relating to terrorism, the note stated that, on the contrary, these
accusations "had been made indiscriminately against Austria, in a manner
difficult to reconcile with the spirit of the U.N. resolution."

The Austrian note then drew the Italian government's attention to the
"solemn" condemnations of the terrorist outbreaks expressed by the Austrian
government, and emphasized that, in accordance with the Declaration of the
Rights of Man and Austrian law, they had applied all the means at their disposal
against these outrages.

The note went on to reply to the Italian reference to statements made before
Parliament by the Austrian minister of the interior, Hetznauer. It stated that
these statements referred exclusively to recent months, following the enactment
of the Austrian measures tightening frontier control. It confirmed the Minister's
remarks about the alleged difficulties in combating terrorism because of the
absence of detailed information from Italy. There followed a list of interventions
by the Austrian police against terrorists, mostly stemming from the South Tyrol,
as well as a list of seven persons found guilty of terrorist acts from 1961 to 1965,
testimony that the Italian note erred in stating that trials of terrorists in Austria
usually ended in acquittals. In reply to the accusation that Austrian authorities
tolerated propaganda for and defense of terrorism, the Austrian note pointed
out that criminal proceedings had been initiated against Burger and Kienesberger
with reference to statements they had made on German television and in Italian
newspapers.

The Austrian note added that, while the government of Austria had in word
and deed fulfilled the U.N. recommendation regarding abstention from any act
capable of disturbing friendly relations between the two countries, it did not
deny the usefulness of cooperation between the police of the two countries in
dealing with terrorism. Consequently, it had already taken certain measures and
was prepared to take others in line with the findings of the Italo-Austrian
Committee of Experts, in order to frame a common plan to prevent and suppress
terrorist outrages. The note concluded by stating that the only remedy for

terrorism was the elimination of its causes; that is, by finding a satisfactory solution to the Austro-Italian dispute, for which purpose the Austrian government would continue to work.

The Austrian reply to the charges leveled against it by the Italian government on the question of terrorism in the Alto Adige was basically negative, as could have been anticipated, given the stand regularly taken by Vienna regarding its own responsibilities in this matter. The reply did, however, contain isolated positive elements, such as Austria's declared intention to promote effective cooperation between Italian and Austrian security forces. But the Austrian reply also gave the general impression, apart from Vienna's unconcealed embarrassment, that the Austrian government sought to elude the specific Italian charges, both by claiming to disassociate itself from the terrorist outbreaks and by broadening the discussion to cover its direct and indirect causes.

The Italian government, therefore, felt it necessary to refute a number of Vienna's arguments. Great stress had been placed on legal subtleties, but no tangible proof had been submitted of the Austrian government's innocence. Furthermore, it contained some observations that could not be left unanswered if the Italian authorities wished to avoid the impression that Vienna's unsubstantiated arguments had convinced them. The main points involved in the Austrian note were:

a) The defense—albeit partial—of the statement made by Minister Hetzenauer regarding lack of collaboration by Italy in combating terrorism.

b) A whole series of statements designed to counter the Italian charges of Austria's lack of effort to suppress the organization on Austrian territory of terroristic activities in the Alto Adige, not through reference to specific incidents, but by simple denials of responsibility or by legal or procedural arguments that only indicated Austria's intention to tolerate terrorism, if not, indeed to foster it.

The Italian government's reply to Austria's note was forwarded on January 21, 1967. It pointed out that the claims advanced in their note, that the terrorist outbreaks had their origin and primary cause in Italian territory, in no way reflected the facts. In support, the Italian note cited a series of recent events in Austria that testified that Austria was primarily responsible for the planning and execution of terrorist outbreaks in the Alto Adige. The Italian note then described as unfounded the charge that the Italian police did not immediately inform the Austrian authorities of the details of terrorist demonstrations. As to the claim that the terrorists always acted as individuals, the note recalled that, in fact, they had never lacked support and encouragement from influential Austrian political figures.

[6]

The XXI U.N. General Assembly had opened on September 18, 1966.

Considering the status of the Italo-Austrian talks, Italy did not believe it was the appropriate time to report to the Assembly on developments in the Alto

Adige question. Italy was also guided by the conviction that, due to the continuing outbreaks of terrorism in the Alto Adige, an Italian statement to the United Nations could not exclude clear and detailed accusations against the Austrian government. This, in turn, could only lead to a further deterioration in relations between the two countries during a delicate phase of the Italo-Austrian talks. On the other hand, Italy was concerned that Toncic, the Austrian foreign minister, would find it difficult, for domestic political reasons, to avoid keeping U.N. interest in the Alto Adige alive.

In fact, on October 5, Toncic made a statement to the General Assembly which contained passages alluding to the Alto Adige.[45] The Austrian Foreign Minister recalled that negotiations carried out following the 1961 U.N. resolution had led to a gradual reduction of the areas of disagreement, reaching by 1964 a point which could be called "promising." Critical of the use of violence, which Austria continued to condemn with firmness, Toncic stated that the talks, resumed after 1964, concentrated on matters still unresolved and that "considerable" progress had been made, even if some important matters still remained outstanding. Toncic then recalled the good faith shown by the Italians and stated that he was confident that every effort would be made to overcome the last remaining hurdles. The Austrian Foreign Minister concluded by stating that there was reason to anticipate a satisfactory solution to the dispute in the near future, one that would give the minority that "security which reflected the ideals and aims" of the United Nations.

Toncic's statement clearly could not find as far-reaching and optimistic an echo in the address by the head of the Italian delegation, Piccioni, before the same Assembly. This was motivated by the renewal of terrorism, to which reference had to be made in the United Nations if only as a consequence of the debate on the Alto Adige in the Italian Parliament.

In his statement to the General Assembly on October 13,[46] Piccioni clearly identified the obstacles that the outbreaks of terrorism had raised toward a satisfactory agreement over the Alto Adige. He hoped that the condemnation expressed by Toncic would be "followed" by concrete steps designed to prevent events which could damage the two countries' mutual relations and expressed confidence that the "Austrian government would accept his request to cooperate in removing the grave obstacle represented by terrorism to the continuation of friendly relations between Italy and Austria."

The previous day, Toncic had forwarded a personal message to the Italian foreign minister, Fanfani, which closed by expressing the hope that Italy would appreciate Austria's gesture in not replying to Piccioni's intervention, and that she would show a "constructive and friendly spirit" in the final phase of the bilateral talks that were about to take place.

As has been noted, the motions voted by the Italian Parliament following the debate on the Alto Adige contained *inter alia* a reference to the government's need to obtain the agreement of the representatives of the inhabitants of the Alto Adige to the new draft proposals regarding the Austro-Italian dispute. The policy directors of the S.V.P. had requested Magnago, during the meetings held at Bolzano August 27–September 1, to contact the Italian government regarding the content of the proposals presented at the last meeting of the representatives of the two Foreign Ministries in London July 18–20, 1966.

However, a short while later, Magnago was able to go to Rome, where he was received by Prime Minister Moro, on October 20. Magnago explained orally to the Prime Minister the nature of the "clarification" requested by the S.V.P. In mid-November, the S.V.P. followed this with a written request for "clarifications" to the Prime Minister's office.

The S.V.P.'s communication, taken as a whole, showed a number of negative aspects. Among them was the question of the so-called international guarantee on which Vienna, Innsbruck, and Bolzano had insisted from the beginning of the talks, but which Italy had always rejected. Such a request also appeared to seek to reopen a number of issues that had been already dealt with and, simultaneously, to present some new ones. As to the specific request of the "international guarantee," its acceptance would have involved abandoning the basic Italian thesis by which the De Gasperi–Gruber agreement was the sole international instrument on which the Italo-Austrian dispute hinged, already repeatedly stressed by Italy.

A careful review of the requests for clarification clearly divulged that the motivating spirit raised considerable doubts as to the real prospect of their contributing to a solution, whether they reflected the convictions of Magnago personally or those of extremist groups within the S.V.P. who had forced his hand. Furthermore, the method chosen by the representatives of the German-speaking group was identical to the one that had been followed by Vienna in March 1965, regarding the draft proposals for settling the controversy examined in Paris on December 16, 1964. It will be recalled, in fact, that instead of stating clearly its acceptance or rejection of the Paris proposals in March 1965, the Austrian government had sought to reopen discussion on all those points on which the Austrian viewpoint had been rejected, while treating as final the Italian concessions which had been advanced as part of an overall compromise.

The representatives of the German-speaking group had not wished to reject outright the Italian proposals but, rather, to submit a long list of requests, some of them new. By taking this initiative, they probably believed that the Italian government either would have to reject them (in this case assuming responsibility for the failure of that phase of the talks), or to accept some of them, allowing the talks to continue and thereby giving Magnago a better foothold at the starting line. Given this premise, the talks would clearly have concerned only those requests which had not yet been accepted.

In a comparison of the Austrian reply of March 30, 1965, with the present S.V.P. stand, the latter appeared even more negative. The reason for this was that it did not confine itself to requests regarding substantive issues (as did Vienna's reply) but also included requests which Italy could not accept without abandoning her legal interpretation of the De Gasperi–Gruber agreement. The document also contained demands that sustained the suspicion that they were directed toward indefinitely postponing a definitive conclusion to the dispute.

For all these reasons, the "requests for clarification" presented by Magnago were very carefully reviewed by the interministerial committee. As a result of this long and detailed scrutiny, Prime Minister Moro was handed a detailed brief on the proposed replies. Moro delivered the government's considerations of the S.V.P.'s request for clarifications to Magnago on January 21, 1967, during a long conversation in which he elaborated on the government's position regarding each individual point.

Chapter X

On the Way toward
Settlement

[1] The stand taken by Austria and the S.V.P. on the Italian proposals of July 1966. Terrorist activities increase;   [2] Contacts continue, the guarantee question.   [3] The Paris meeting of July 25, 1969;   [4] Consultation with the ethnic groups, the fourth special congress of the S.V.P. The meeting between Moro and Waldheim in Copenhagen on November 30, 1969;   [5] Green light to a settlement of a question.

[1]

The new phase in Italo-Austrian contacts was opened in April 1965, but it had not yielded any major results by the beginning of 1967, with the exception of the second Italian proposal for an inclusive understanding, presented at the London meeting on July 18–22, 1966. Before making its reply, the Austrian government solicited the opinion of the S.V.P., which in turn was awaiting completion of the examination of the "clarifications" which had been elicited from the Italian government and which Prime Minister Moro transmitted on January 21, 1967.

The details provided by Moro on the measures that the government proposed to take in favor of the Alto Adige, took into account some of the doubts raised by the S.V.P. during the preceding autumn. As for the procedural aspects of the proposed settlement, Moro could do no more than repeat the statements he had made on the subject of the international guarantee to the Chamber of Deputies and the Senate four months before.

On March 23, 1967, the S.V.P. Executive Committee recommended that its next party convention should accept the proposed measures as understood in the light of the clarifications received, but also inferred that the greater degree of autonomy achieved was not considered to be entirely satisfactory. At the same time, the recommendation invited Italy and Austria to agree on the question of

---

This chapter, added by the editor, is a short chronicle of the events which took place between January 1967, and December 1969, and serves to update this account of the Alto Adige question; see also, Pietro Pastorelli, "I rapporti italo-austriaci dall' accordo De Gasperi-Gruber alle intese più recenti, 1946–1969," in *Rivista di Studi Politici Internazionali* 40, no. 2 (Florence, 1973): 199–229.

the international guarantee, reserving the right to the party's convention to render its final judgment on the effectiveness of such a guarantee.

A month later, Austria replied to Italy's proposals of July 1966. Vienna indicated that, in general, it sanctioned the proposed measures for the Alto Adige, but believed that a further meeting was necessary on the procedural aspect, to discuss the guarantee question and to recommend some changes. The reply itself suggested that these modifications were intended to develop a new bilateral agreement between the two countries so as to provide the proposed measures with that very type of international guarantee rejected by Italy.

In order to resolve the differences that emerged from the Austrian reply, the Italian government indicated its full willingness to accept the suggestion of a further meeting between representatives of the two Foreign Ministries and this, in fact, took place in London on June 19–20, 1967. On the main point at issue, the meeting was only informative in nature. The Austrian representatives illustrated the changes they wished to introduce in the procedural aspect of the steps to be taken to settle the controversy; their Italian counterparts emphasized the need not to modify the very basis of the talks carried on since 1964. As already established, this premise rested on two assumptions: the search for a solution not affecting the views of the two sides as to the application of the De Gasperi–Gruber agreement and, at the same time, not involving rights or obligations differing from or going beyond those derived from the agreement.

The principal events during the month of June 1967, however, concerned the terrorist activities. On June 1, a court at Linz acquitted a group of terrorists, all self-confessed, headed by Nobert Burger. Both the court's hearings, in which terrorism was pictured as the most concrete means of pursuing the struggle, and its sentence of acquittal were interpreted in extremist circles as affirmations of approval of their criminal activities.

On June 20, the Austrian television presented a program on terrorism that justified recourse to violence in a subjective presentation of the Alto Adige situation. During this program, not only Burger and the other acquitted terrorists made an appearance, but official representatives of all the Austrian parties as well.

On June 25, four Italian soldiers were killed in a terrorist assault on the customs post of Cima Vallona. This episode, the most serious in what was already a long series of attacks, produced the strongest reaction in Italy. A vigorous debate followed in the Italian Parliament, covering in detail all aspects of the Alto Adige question and Austro-Italian relations. For its part, the Austrian government condemned terrorism in general, but sought to minimize the matter. Moreover, this Austrian stand was consistent with that taken by Vienna a few days earlier in its reply to the Italian note of January 21, 1967, in which Italy had requested more effective preventive and punitive action against the terrorists. The Austrian reply, delivered on June 16, stated that Austria was a state governed by laws, which could not resort to arbitrary measures, and that she could apply only her own penal code. This, in turn, was in full conformity with international standards and was scrupulously applied in cases of subversive activities carried out by its own citizens on the territory of a neighboring state.

Faced with such a stand, the Italian government concluded that it was indispensable to firmly warn Austria that "Italy's agreement to Austria's possible association with the Common Market was dependent on the demonstrable capacity of the Austrian government to combat terrorism with appropriate preventive and punitive measures."[1] This decision was put into effect forthwith.

As Prime Minister Moro stated in Parliament, the reasons that led to this decision were based on the fact that the EEC (European Economic Community) had been set up "to increase progressive and peaceful cooperation between member countries" and, as such, presupposed that these countries based their relations on sentiments of friendship and collaboration. Naturally, such a requirement should apply also to countries requesting association with the EEC. Therefore, Italy believed that the time had come to request the Austrian government "to reflect upon the need to put an end to a policy which, by confining itself to mere verbal condemnation, did not effectively discourage terrorist activities against Italy but rather conflicted with the expressed wish to cooperate with Italy and the EEC, a collaboration which implied sentiments of real friendship and solidarity."[2]

The Austrian government attempted to use this condition imposed by Italy on Austria's entry into the EEC as a threat that applied pressure on the efforts being made toward a settlement of the Alto Adige question. The Italian Prime Minister replied: "We have linked together the encouragement to terrorism and the requested association with the EEC; it has, therefore, no connection with the De Gasperi–Gruber agreement, but solely with the failure of the Austrian government to prevent and punish terrorism within its borders."[3]

Thus, the Italian government continued to follow its consistent policy of not permitting terrorist activities to block the search for a solution of the Alto Adige question, the very thing the terrorists were trying to do. Confirmation of this had been given in the parliamentary debates. At that time, Moro gave a general review of the measures for the Alto Adige which the Italian government proposed to put into effect, adding further details relating to the talks underway with Austria. He rejected the opposition's proposals to break off those contacts or even to denounce the De Gasperi–Gruber agreement. At the close of his statement, Moro requested and obtained from the Italian Parliament authorization to continue the policy already approved on September 15, 1966, placing the government in a position to continue the talks as soon as circumstances permitted.

Notwithstanding a number of measures introduced by Austria, the most important of which was the announcement that the frontier with Italy would be guarded by special detachments of regular troops and not by the police alone, the summer of 1967 ended with two additional deaths resulting from a bomb explosion in the Trent station. This prompted the Italian government to again urge Austria to effectively collaborate in combating terrorism; if necessary, by means of new legislation if the existing laws were inadequate.

[2]

In the autumn of 1967, the Alto Adige question again became the object of discussions between the two countries, focusing on the draft settlement put forward by Italy in July 1966.

On October 21, the S.V.P. Executive Committee adopted a new resolution which referred to the opinion it had expressed in its meeting of March 23, concerning the measures proposed by the Italian government and the clarifications given regarding them. It noted that Italy and Austria had not followed up on the suggestion it had then addressed to them to agree upon procedures for effecting a settlement of the dispute. Repeating its suggestion, the new recommendation now added that by the expression "effective international guarantee" the S.V.P. understood "a system guaranteeing execution of the measures contemplated in the package deal."[4]

The Italian government had made known its views on this subject on several occasions. Most recently, the Italian Prime Minister had repeated these in his statement to the Chamber of Deputies on July 27, 1967, where he had declared:

Austria has sought to give the need for a guarantee a meaning and an expanded interpretation which are not acceptable, since they conflict with the principles that the two governments agreed upon in 1964 as a basis for seeking a solution to this dispute. Indeed, by insisting on certain forms of guarantee, the Austrian government seems, in effect, to request the internationalization of our actions and internal measures. This would involve our abandoning our point of view and accepting that of Austria regarding the fulfillment of the De Gasperi–Gruber agreement. For us, where application of the De Gasperi–Gruber agreement is involved, the Hague Court will handle any future disputes. But, if by the request for an international guarantee something is sought that goes beyond the 1946 agreement, we must reply negatively.

In compliance with the vote taken by Parliament at that time, on November 9, 1967, the Italian government resolved to pursue contacts with Austria, via an exchange of views on the procedural aspects of the proposed settlement and, in particular, on the timing of the various unilateral acts to be taken by Italy and by Austria which together formed the settlement. Following this decision, two meetings were held in London between representatives of the two Foreign Ministries, on November 17–19, and on December 6–7, 1967. Contacts then continued through normal diplomatic channels as well, and these led to some progress.

In 1968, Toncic-Sorinj was replaced as Austrian foreign minister by Kurt Waldheim, a career diplomat. As spring approached, Italo-Austrian contacts slowed down, since general elections were scheduled in Italy for May 19, 1968. As soon as the new Italian government was formed, Prime Minister Leone, in his policy statement speech to Parliament on July 5, repeated his intention to pursue in the Alto Adige the same line of his predecessors, "maintaining for such purpose appropriate contacts with the Austrian government" in the conviction that "in democratic Italy, citizens of different languages could peacefully live together and prosper with full respect for national sovereignty," and that "friendly relations between neighboring countries could always be assured."

Meetings between representatives of the two Foreign Ministries were resumed, prompted in part by Austria's wish[5] to have further detailed discussions on the Alto Adige question with the new Italian government. These meetings took place in Paris on July 24—25 and September 9—10,[6] in New York on October 12, and again in Paris on November 28—29 and December 14, 1968. The exchange of views on procedural aspects of the proposed settlement allowed a solution to be anticipated for the not too distant future, Austria having indicated that it would be prepared to drop the stand it had previously taken on the subject of the international guarantee. However, this change was achieved only slowly and step by step, and even after these meetings the Austrian government still sought to obtain under one guise or another the internationalization of the measures contemplated by Italy.

In any case, confirmation came from two separate sources that the Italo-Austrian contacts were heading toward positive results. These were the discussions between the two foreign ministers, Medici and Waldheim, at Geneva on September 4, 1968, during the Conference of Non-Nuclear Powers, and the fact that it appeared possible to get the S.V.P. to review in practice, if not to abandon in principle, the decision it had taken in October 1967, on the subject of an international guarantee.

Confirmation of the progress achieved in the Austro-Italian meetings during the second part of 1968, also appeared in Italian Prime Minister Rumor's speech to Parliament, presenting the new center-left coalition government. Rumor stated that he hoped to be able to submit to Parliament shortly an all-encompassing proposal for the solution of the Alto Adige question. At the same time, he announced that the various groups involved in the Trentino—Alto Adige region would be consulted on the proposals through their representatives. As to the international aspect of the problem, Rumor stated that the Italian government proposed to maintain "the policy of straighforward talks with the Austrian government in order to find a peaceful solution to the dispute over interpretation of the De Gasperi—Gruber agreement."

It was clear from what the Prime Minister stated, that if it was premature to say that the Italo-Austrian contacts had achieved their purpose, they had, in fact, reached the point where consultation with the various ethnic groups in the Alto Adige could be envisaged.

[3]

A new meeting between representatives of the two Foreign Ministries took place at Geneva on January 30—31, 1969. Reviewing the situation in a statement made to the Italian Senate on February 25, Foreign Minister Nenni declared:

The solution at present under examination in Rome and Vienna foresees a timetable for the steps to be taken, that is to say, a list of the measures to be carried out independently by each party, as for example, the communications to be made to the UN in connection with the General Assembly's earlier recommendations. The timetable also provides for the signing of an agreement between the two countries, recognizing that the jurisdiction of The Hague Court also extends to disputes over interpretation of the De Gasperi–Gruber agreement, which remains the sole treaty legally binding in these issues. The measures which the Italian government will propose to Parliament are of an independent and unilateral character. Nevertheless, it is foreseen that once these measures have been put into effect, the Austrian government will also issue a statement indicating that the international dispute is to be considered settled.

On May 13, 1969, the two foreign ministers, Nenni and Waldheim, met at Strasbourg during a meeting of the Council of Europe. Without elaborating on the substance of the problem, given the nature of the meeting, they reviewed the points still under discussion, agreeing on the need to make every effort to reach a solution, since the desired objectives were already in sight.

What in fact was taking more time than anticipated were the unofficial contacts with representatives of the S.V.P. in order to carry out the final consultation, envisaged by the vote of the Italian Parliament in September 1966 and aimed at securing the S.V.P.'s approval of the proposed measures. Given their internal character, these contacts were carried out by the Prime Minister and involved reexamination of each single measure to be put into effect. This was labeled the "re-reading of the package deal."

On June 25, 1969, the ministerial committee working on the problem arrived at its conclusions and authorized contacts with Austria in order to finalize the timetable and to dispose of other matters remaining open.

On July 25, another meeting took place between representatives of the two Foreign Ministries, the tenth of the series, producing an identity of views between the two governments on the content and timing of the 18 points to be implemented. It was agreed that Italy and Austria, through a meeting at the foreign minister level, should declare their wish to reach a settlement in the dispute. It also appeared desirable, before starting to implement the measures established in the timetable, that the exchanges of views on the terrorist issue should be terminated by an official statement by the Austrian government.

At the technical level, the long series of meetings dealing with the proposed inclusive solution of the dispute presented at London on July 18–20, 1966, were now completed. All was in readiness for a political decision by the two governments, once the ethnic groups had indicated their agreement with the solutions envisaged.

[4]

The Italian government crisis in July 1969 was no obstacle in this final political phase of the question. Indeed, it augured well for the important decisions to be taken that the government, still headed by Rumor, again included Foreign Minister Moro, who, while holding that portfolio from December 1963 to June 1968, had more than anyone else worked for a solution of the Alto Adige question.

In his policy statement to the Italian Parliament on August 8, 1969, Rumor declared that the matter was already in its final stages and that the government would, therefore, quickly seek to achieve those political aims which the preceding government had pursued in line with the intent of Parliament. The government, Rumor concluded, was confident that within a reasonable period of time it would be in a position to submit to Parliament its proposals for a solution of the entire problem.

Once the reply to the points which emerged from the "re-reading of the package deal" had been submitted to the S.V.P., on September 25, 1969, the formal consulation with the ethnic groups took place. Their representatives, and, in particular, those of the S.V.P., were called upon to give their approval both of the proposed measures and of the schedule for their application.[7] In connection with the timetable, it will be recalled that this represented a mere chronological sequence of the steps that the Italian and Austrian governments proposed to take, each for that part which concerned it, in order to be able to state that the dispute had been settled. The representatives of the population groups involved were, in effect, called upon to express their views on the overall solution put forward by the Italian government.

Understandably, full and detailed discussions took place within the Executive Committee of the S.V.P., since it had to recommend a decision to the next party convention which would bind the party for a long period. They had to make a final choice between the policy of dissatisfaction and isolation entered upon during the mid-1950s, and one of collaboration and becoming a part of Italian public life. The motion finally adopted was not without reservations as to the solutions proposed and cautious references to the future, but it concluded by inviting the party convention to approve both the package deal and the timetable.

A month later, on November 22, 1969, the 4th Special Congress of the S.V.P. voted, by a 52 percent majority, a resolution stating:

The Congress decides: (a) that its approval covers only the package deal whose text (together with the clarifications given thereto) forms the object of the present recommendation; (b) that it is perfectly clear that Austria will issue the proposed declaration stating that the dispute is settled only when, in the opinion of the South Tyrol representatives, the package deal has been fully carried out, it being clearly understood that this in no way involves renouncing the rights laid down and foreseen by the Paris Agreement.

The meaning of such a conclusion is rendered even more lucid by the preliminary paragraphs of the same resolution. These stated that the Congress declared it considered the measures proposed as "acts implementing the Paris Agreements," though they did not include "all those powers essential for the achievement of real and proper autonomy." For this reason, the Congress expressed the hope that "in a new relationship of mutual understanding between the state and the population group involved," Italy, "by introducing further measures to implement the Paris Agreement," takes into due account "the requests of the South Tyrol representatives which had not been accepted."

After obtaining the approval of the other population groups concerned, the Italian government decided to give its approval to the proposed meeting between the two foreign ministers, Moro and Waldheim.

This meeting took place at Copenhagen on November 30, 1969. It opened with an exchange of statements on individual points in the timetable, with Waldheim repeating that Austria's declaration that the dispute had been settled was exclusively a matter for the Austrian government, which would take into account for that purpose all data at its disposal in order to arrive at its conclusions. The ministers took note of the existence of "the basis necessary for initiating action designed to carry out the Italian measures in favor of the province of Bolzano and thereby arrive at a settlement of the current dispute between Italy and Austria." The two ministers, according to the communiqué issued at the end of the meeting, "expressed their conviction that with the implementation of the measures foreseen, a new period of constructive cooperation would start both in the Alto Adige and in Italo-Austrian relations."

To complete the Copenhagen meeting, the Austrian Chancellor, replying on the following day to a question concerning terrorism, stated that the federal government and the Austrian people had a sincere desire to live in peace and friendship with all countries, above all with neighboring countries. The Chancellor continued:

... in the past, in connection with the problem of the South Tyrol, irresponsible elements have carried out activities which, to our profound regret, have caused loss of life and damage to property. As strongly as I can, I repeat that we condemn recourse to violence as a political instrument. The competent Austrian authorities will continue to take action, in accordance with domestic law, against any recourse to violence or terrorist activities. . . . The Austrian federal government is convinced that this decision will help to eliminate the tensions and differences in opinion still existing between Austria and Italy and to consolidate the foundations for renewed confidence and friendly collaboration.

For its part, the Italian government, taking note of this declaration and of the gradual disappearance of terrorist activities during the recent months, gave instructions to its representative to the forthcoming ministerial meeting of the European Economic Community, scheduled to be held in Brussels on December 9, to withdraw Italy's reservations to Austria's request for association with the EEC, made in June 1967.

[5]

On December 2, 1969, the series of measures scheduled in the timetable began to be implemented, with the initialing at Vienna of the agreement amending, with reference to relations between Italy and Austria, Article 27 (a) of the European Convention for the Pacific Settlement of Disputes.

On the following day, the Italian Prime Minister outlined before Parliament the settlement of the Alto Adige question which his government contemplated. After referring to its origins and principal developments, Rumor proceeded as follows:

The Committee of 19 studying the Alto Adige problem finished its task in 1964, drawing up a detailed report which was submitted to ministers and members of Parliament. Taking carefully into account the conclusions which this committee reached after long, detailed and laudable work and an accurate analysis of the question of the powers of the province of Bolzano and the coexistence of Italian citizens of various language groups residing there, the government now intends to meet in the largest possible measure the wishes of the peoples of the Alto Adige, in such a way as to improve their economic, social and cultural environment. The Italian government has, therefore, decided, in the free exercise of its sovereignty, to implement concrete measures aimed at insuring the peaceful coexistence and development of the various linguistic groups residing in the Alto Adige.

Toward this end, the government declares its intention to present to Parliament within 45 days the draft constitutional law, and, within one year, the draft ordinary laws required to carry out the measures envisaged, in particular, to broaden within the framework of the Trentino-Alto Adige region, the legislative and administrative powers of the province of Bolzano.

The government will request a discussion of these draft laws, to be treated by the Chambers as a matter of urgency, and is confident that Parliament, aware of the exceptional importance of the problem as well as of this historic occasion, will consider the measures and cast its vote with the expediency that the circumstances require.

Using its own powers, the government further undertakes to issue the necessary regulations within two years of approval of the above mentioned constitutional legislation.

The list of measures which it intends to carry out is contained in the document which has been distributed simultaneously to members of the Senate and the Chamber of Deputies. This document is to be considered an integral part of this statement.

The government has also decided to set up a study commission, composed of members belonging to the three language groups and open, as required, to local officials, the periodic examination of matters regarding the province of Bolzano, as stated in the document just referred to.

The government is confident that the position of the Alto Adige will be improved by the gamut of measures proposed.

The government confirms its view that it has already applied the Paris Agreement of September 5, 1946. The measures which the government now has the honor to put into effect are the result of its own free decision and emphasize our sincere democratic conception of the relations between the state and all its ethnic groups. Moreover, taking into account these measures, the government believes that the dispute between Italy and Austria over the application of the Paris Agreement, will lose its *raison d'être* and its substance. In addition, in order to prevent good relations between the two countries from being marred by disputes, we have negotiated an agreement which applies Chapter I of the European Convention for the Pacific Settlement of Disputes, with respect to relations between Italy and Austria, to disputes over interpretation and application of bilateral agreements in force between the two countries, even where such disputes regard facts or situations ante-dating the entry into force of that Convention between the two states. Once this agreement has been signed, the government will submit it to Parliament for ratification and authorization. The government is also of the opinion that it has also acted effectively to reach the objectives set out in the U.N. General Assembly Recommendations No. 1947 (XV) and 1661 (XVI).

After a detailed review of the 137 measures for the Alto Adige contained in the government's proposals, Rumor concluded his statement by repeating the criteria which guided the government in its action:

The inviolable nature of our frontiers is beyond discussion. For whosoever insists on the thesis of autodetermination, we repeat that our frontier is on the Brenner, consecrated by the sacrifice of over 600,000 lives and by solemn recognition through international treaties. The proposed measures are an expression of inalienable Italian sovereignty and have and will have domestic and independent character.

Italy and Austria had concluded no new agreement since the De Gasperi–Gruber treaty, except the instrument just initialed which I have here described regarding recourse to The Hague Court. Italy and Austria, each on its own account and at the appropriate time, are to initiate, after the meeting between the two foreign ministers, a series of unilateral and independent actions which upon their completion will lead to a declaration by the Austrian government that the dispute has been settled.

Prime Minister Rumor concluded by detailing the various measures foreseen in the timetable.

In the debate that followed, representatives of all parties spoke. In favor were the Christian Democrats (DC), the other parties of the center-left coalition: the Socialists (PSI and PSU) and the Republicans (PRI), as well as the S.V.P. Three opposition parties abstained: the Liberals (PLI), the Communists (PCI), and the left-wing Socialists (PSIUP). Only the Italian Social Movement (MSI) and the Monarchists opposed the measures. The Chamber of Deputies approved the Prime Minister's statement by a vote of 269 to 26, with 88 abstentions.

Chancellor Klaus's statement to the Nationalrat on the following December 15, found no such broad consensus. After reviewing the principal stages of the dispute from Austria's point of view, Klaus stated, in the substantive part of his speech:

On December 3, 1969, the Italian government stated before its Parliament that within 45 days it would present the text of the draft constitutional law and within one year the text of the ordinary laws which would notably extend the powers of autonomy of the province of Bolzano.

The Italian government went on to state that it would request discussion of the texts under the procedure for urgent measures, and expressed the hope that Parliament, aware of the exceptional importance of the problem and the historic nature of the occasion, would deliberate the measures with the expediency required.

The Italian government further decided, acting under its own powers, to publish the necessary implementing regulations within two years of approval of the above constitutional law.

Details of the measures, which Italy has announced its intention of putting into effect, are contained in a document distributed to members of the Italian Parliament and form an integral part of the government's statement. A translation of the list accompanies the statement of the federal government. The Austrian government notes that the Italian measures are taken under the Paris Agreement. According to the Italian government, on the other hand, the proposed measures are the result of its independent decision and do not come under the Paris Agreement with which that government maintains it has already complied, a view which the Austrian government has always rejected. The federal government also wishes to point out that during the XV U.N. General Assembly it, for its own part, maintained the point of view that the Treaty of Paris could only be carried out by the granting of substantial regional autonomy. Each party stated that it wished to safeguard its own legal interpretation.

The Austrian federal government awaits fulfillment of the measures listed by the Italian government in its statement of December 3, 1969, within the time limits indicated and in a spirit of understanding for the wishes of the German-speaking group of the Alto Adige.

In this context, the Austrian federal government states that once the measures listed in the appendix to the document submitted have been carried out, that is to say, the constitutional law, the ordinary laws, and the necessary regulations, it will declare that the dispute existing between Austria and Italy, as outlined in the above-mentioned U.N. General Assembly Recommendations, be considered settled.

It is the intention of the Austrian government, in connection with the U.N. General Assembly Recommendations 1947 (XV) and 1661 (XVI) to inform the United Nations of all that has been stated here.

During the course of the Austro-Italian talks, an agreement was also negotiated to extend the provisions of Chapter I of the European Convention for the Pacific Settlement of Disputes, with respect to relations between Austria and Italy, to disputes over interpretation and application of bilateral agreements in force between the two countries, even where such disputes regard facts or situations ante-dating the entry into force of that convention between the two states.

On the understanding that approval of the constitutional provisions, the ordinary laws and the consequent regulations set out in the statement made by the Italian government on December 3, 1969, will be completed within the period of time therein indicated, that is, foreseeably within a total period of approximately four years, the Austrian government will abstain, during this time, from bringing up the South Tyrol problem before any international body.

The federal government is of the opinion that by means of such measures the greatest possible effort will have been made in the interests of the German-speaking population of the South Tyrol to achieve the peaceful coexistence of the various language groups of the South Tyrol and the friendly development of relations between Austria and Italy.

During the discussion on the Austrian Chancellor's statement, the Socialist opposition presented an amendment requesting extension of the jurisdiction of The Hague Court, already agreed upon, to cover possible disputes arising out of implementation of the measures included in the package deal. Put to a vote, the amendment was rejected by 83 votes, all from the *Volkspartei,* against 79,

including 73 Social-democrats and 6 National-Liberals. The same majority approved Klaus's statement.

With the votes of the two Parliaments, an important step was taken toward
resolving the Italo-Austrian dispute over application of the De Gasperi–Gruber
agreement.

Chapter Notes

NOTES TO INTRODUCTION

1. See Introduction, p. x.

2. See Mario Toscano, *Appunti sulla questione dell' Alto Adige* (Rome: Edizioni Ricerche, 1961). This volume containts notes from Professor Toscano's lectures compiled by his assistants, Professors Franca Puppo, Gian Luca Andrè, and Pietro Pastorelli.

3. Mario Tuscano, "Il problema dell'Alto Adige alla XV Assemblea Generale dell'ONU" in *Nuova Antologia*, December, 1960; Mario Toscano, "Il problema dell'Alto Adige dal 1960 al 1964" in *Nuova Antologia*, March 1964.

4. Karl Heinz Ritschel, *Diplomatie um Südtirol. Politische Hintergrunde eines europaischen Versagens* (Stuttgart: Seewald Verlag, 1966), with the words, "As described for the first time from secret documentary sources" printed on the dustjacket.

5. No one on the other side of the border seems to know, as has been officially stated, where such records are to be found, but, doubtless, the right thing would be for these to be returned to their owners.

The Bolzano and Trent State Archives have been purged not only of the papers contained in the Tolomei records but also of many other documents testifying as to how "Germanization" in the Alto Adige was enforced in the sixteenth century; for instance, Italians were not allowed to own real estate in Bolzano. On this subject see, *Alto Adige. Alcuni documenti del passato* (Bergamo: Istituto Italiano di Arti Grafiche, 1942), 3 vols.

NOTES TO CHAPTER I

1. "Traité de paix entre Sa Majesté l'Empereur d'Allemagne et d'Autriche et Sa Majesté l'Empereur des Français Roi d'Italie signé à Presbourg le 26 décembre 1805," in George Frederic De Martens, *Supplément au Recueil des principaux traités* (Goettingen: Dietrich, 1808), IV, pp. 212–20.

2. "Traité conclu entre Sa Majesté l'Empereur des Français et Sa Majesté le Roi de Bavière pour l'exécution du traité de Vienne du 14 octobre 1809, signé à Paris le 28 février 1810," in George Frederic De Martens, *Supplément au Recueil des principaux traités* (Goettingen: Dieterich, 1824), IV, pp. 16–21. Article III of this treaty provided that: "His Majesty the King of Bavaria cedes in total sovereignty and property to His Majesty the Emperor and King such parts of the Italian Tyrol as shall be chosen by His Imperial Majesty. These portions of the Tyrol will have to be respectively contiguous, and in a position of proximity and ease of access to the Kingdom of Italy and to the Illyrian provinces and comprise a population of between 280,000 and 300,000 persons. Italian and Bavarian commissioners will be appointed within fifteen days from the exchange of the instruments of ratification of the present Act and charged with the task of tracing the precise limits of the territories ceded and of marking their boundaries."

In connection with the drawing of the new boundary line see also: "Lettres patentes du Roi de Bavière en date du 23 juin 1810 portant les cessions de la Bavière dans le Tyrol, en exécution de l'art. 3 du Traitè avec la France du 28 février 1810," in George Frederic De Martens, *Nouveau Recueil de traités* (Goettingen: Dieterich, 1820), IV, pp. 30–32.

The expression "Italian Tyrol" merits comment, used as it is to indicate both the Alto Adige and the Trentino. In the second half of the nineteenth century Austria not only refused to use the historical term *Trentino* but also refused to recognize the term *Italian Tyrol*. Interesting details in this connection are published in Augusto Sandonà, *L'irredentismo nelle lotte politiche e nelle contese diplomatiche italo-austriache, 1866–1882* (Bologna: Zanichelli, 1932), I, pp. 6–7, note 3.

3. "Convention entre Sa Majesté Impériale d'Autriche et Sa Majesté le Roi de Bavière signé à Paris le 3 juin 1814," in George Frederic De Mertens, *Nouveau Recueil de traités* (Goettingen: Dieterich, 1887), II, pp. 18–23.

4. "Acte du Congrès de Vienne, signé le 9 juin 1815, Acte principal," in *ibid.*, II, pp. 379–432, Article 93.

5. Marc Lengerau, *La Question du Tyrol du Sud* (Paris: Centre de documentation universitaire, 1960), p. 13.

6. *Ibid.*, pp. 18–19.

7. See the minutes of the Austrian cabinet meeting held on November 12, 1866 and chaired by the Emperor Francis Joseph, in *Haus, Hof-und Staatsarchiv* (Wein: Politisches Archiv), Ministeratsprotokolle, M.R.Z. 108.

8. Di Sangiuliano to Tittoni and Carlotti, telegram, September 25, 1914, in *I documenti diplomatici italiani* (Rome: Libreria dello Stato, 1952 et seg.), 5th Series, I.D. 803, hereinafter cited as *I.D.*

9. Tittoni to Di Sangiuliano, telegrams, September 27, 28, 1914, in *ibid.*, DD. 826 and 834; Carlotti to Di Sangiuliano, September 28, 1914, *ibid.*, D. 827.

10. Hermann Oncken, *Die Rheinpolitik des Kaisers Napolean III 1863-1870 und der Ursprung des Krieges von 1870–1871* (Stuttgart, 1926), III, pp. 59–134; *Les origines diplomatiques de la guerre de 1870–1871. Recueil de documents publié par le Ministère des Affaires Etrangères* (Paris: Imprimerie Nationale, 1928), XXII, pp. 415–33, and XXIII, pp. 359–409.

11. Nigra to Visconti Venosta, personal letter, July 16, 1870, in *I.D.*, 1st Series, XIII, D. 178.

12. Menabrea's report to Lanza and to Visconti Venosta (for submission to King Victor Emanuel II), *ibid.*, D. 253. The enclosure attached to the report is published as a separate document. *Ibid.*, D. 265.

13. Regarding the circumstances in which the Italian northern frontier was defined in 1866, see, Sandonà, *L'Irredentismo*, pp. 5-35 and *Documenti presentati al Parlamento dal Ministro degli Affari Esteri il 21 dicembre 1866* (Florence: Eredi Botta, 1866), pp. 631–866.

14. Antonio Salandra, *L'Intervento* (Milan: Mondadori, 1930), pp. 156–60.

15. The text of this document may be found in Mario Toscano, "Il negoziato di Londra del 1915," in *Nuova Antologia*, November 1967.

16. See also Tittoni's letter to Prime Minister Nitti, July 13, 1919, in Paolo Alatri, *Nitti, D'Annunzio e la Questione Adriatica (1918–1920)* (Milan: Feltrinelli, 1959), p. 83.

17. On these negotiations, see Mario Toscano, *Il Patto di Londra* (Bologna: Zanichelli, 1934), and Mario Toscano, "Rivelazioni e nuovi documenti sul negoziato di Londra per l'ingresso dell'Italia nella prima guerra mondiale," in *Nuova Antologia*, August, September, October, November 1965.

18. For the text of the Treaty of London see *Senato del Regno, Documento diplomatico communicato alla Presidenza dal Ministro degli Affari Esteri (Scialoja) il 5 marzo 1920, Accordo di Londra del 26 aprile 1915* (Rome: Senato del Regno d'Italia, 1920).

19. Sonnino to Avarna, Italian ambassador to Vienna, telegram, April 8, 1915, in *Libro Verde 1915*, submitted to Parliament, May 20, 1915, D. 64; Salandra, *L'Intervento*, pp. 118–20.

20. On April 16, 1915, Ambassador Avarna telegraphed the text of the Austrian memorandum to Sonnino and this telegram was published in *Libro Verde 1915, ibid.*, D. 71. Perhaps insufficient attention has been paid in Italy to documents that came to light after the two world wars, which reveal the real spirit underlying even the limited territorial offers made by Austria. In this connection Leo Valiani, *La dissoluzione dell' Austria-Ungheria* (Milan: Il Saggiatore, 1966), pp. 118–19, points out that the French had decoded and communicated to Ambassador Tittoni a telegram from the Berlin government to the German Embassies in Rome and Vienna. The telegram expressed the hope that "Austria accede to the Italian demands seeing that, after all, once victorious, Austria could well be in a position to take back what she had granted." Other decoded telegrams referred to the offer made by Pope Benedict XV, on May 9, 1915, through the Austrian ambassador to the Vatican, Schoenburg, that the Holy See guarantee the implementation, at the end of the war, of such undertakings as Austria should enter into with Italy. The Austrian ambassador

in Berlin, Prince Hohenlohe, had in reply telegraphed to Vienna on May 11, 1915, that "if, with regard to certain concessions made, we are to make a mental reservation extending as far as contemplating our regaining possession of what we have been obliged to yield–this being a circumstance of which Prince Schoenburg is evidently unaware–then it is indeed unthinkable that the concessions we have made should even be covered by a Papal guarantee."

21. On the subject of these negotiations see Mario Toscano, *Gli accordi di S. Giovanni di Moriana* (Milan: Giuffrè, 1936).

22. See memorandum of the *Inquiry* of December 22, 1917, in *Foreign Relations of the United States, The Paris Peace Conference* (Washington: United States Government Printing Office, 1942–47), I, p. 50, hereafter cited as *FRUS.* A new memorandum, based on the earlier one, but amplified and revised, was submitted to Wilson on January 2, 1918. Lawrence E. Gelfand, *The Inquiry, American Preparations for Peace, 1917–1919* (New Haven: Yale University Press, 1963), p. 136. It is worth noting that in March 1918 a member of the *Inquiry,* Ellen Churchill Semple, completed a study on the problem of the Austro-Italian frontier, reaching the conclusion that the Italian request for a frontier at the Brenner Pass was fully justified because it reflected the essential safety requirements inasmuch as "Any Austrian force invading Italy has only to drop down into Italy. On the other hand, an Italian invasion of Austria would mean literally an "uphill battle." *Ibid.,* p. 222.

23. Charles Seymour, "Woodrow Wilson and Self-Determination in the Tyrol," in *The Virginia Quarterly Review,* Autumn 1962, p. 571, notes that Wilson did not make it clear what he really meant by this formula, which was so generic as to render varying solutions possible, depending on whether ethnic, linguistic, historical, or topographical factors were followed in tracing the line of demarcation.

24. Sonnino to Macchi di Cellere, telegram, January 12, 1918, in the Historical Record Collection of the Italian Foreign Ministry, herein and hereafter cited as *ASMEI;* Macchi di Cellere to Sonnino, telegrams, January 14, 21, and 23, 1918, in *ASMEI;* see also Lansing to Wilson, letter, January 25, 1918, in *FRUS, The Lansing Papers,* II, pp. 89–90; Wilson to Lansing, letter, January 29, 1918, *ibid.,* p. 94.

25. Luigi Aldrovandi Marescotti, *Guerra Diplomatica* (Milan: Mondadori, 1937), pp. 190–92 (meetings of the Supreme Interallied Council on October 29 and 30, 1918). Seymour commented as follows on Sonnino's declarations: "It was never entirely clear whether this reservation which Sonnino had read, almost *sotto voce,* but which had never been debated, could be regarded as formally valid. It certainly lacked the emphasis of the reservations upon reparations and the freedom of the seas. Wilson himself later agreed that the reservation might be accepted in the formal sense. It made little difference to him. He expected the Peace Conference to recognise the validity of his principles and he was prepared to see to it that they were effectively implemented." Seymour, "Woodrow Wilson and Self-Determination," p. 574. On this point see also, Ray Stannard Baker, *Woodrow Wilson and World Settlement* (New York: Doubleday, 1922), II, p. 133. However, Orlando notes in his memoirs that, in his conversations with Wilson, the latter always recognized that the Italian government had never pledged itself as regards Point IX. Vittorio Emanuele Orlando, *Memorie* (Milan: Rizzoli, 1960) p. 404, note; p. 424, note.

26. The text of the armistice with Austria of November 3, 1918 is in *FRUS, The Paris Peace Conference,* II, pp. 175–82.

27. House to Lansing, telegram, October 29, 1918, in *FRUS,* 1918, Supplement I, I, pp. 405–13.

28. Wilson to House, telegram, October 30, 1918, in *FRUS, ibid.,* p. 421.

29. The text of the *Inquiry* report is quoted in René Albrecht-Carrié, *Italy at the Paris Peace Conference* (New York: Columbia University Press, 1938), pp. 364–69, D. 16.

30. V. Iustus, *Macchi di Cellere all'ambasciata di Washington: Memorie e testimonianze* (Florence: Bemporad, 1921), pp. 183–86.

31. On Wilson's contacts with the Italian delegation on the eve of the Peace Conference, see Seymour, "Woodrow Wilson and Self-Determination," pp. 580–81.

32. The text of the memorandum is quoted in full in Amedeo Giannini, *Documenti per la Storia dei rapporti fra Italia e Jugoslavia* (Rome: Istituto per l'Europa Orientale, 1934), pp. 13–35.

33. Wilson to Orlando, memorandum, April 14, 1919, in Albrecht-Carriè, *Italy at the Paris Peace Conference*, p. 45, D. 36.

34. Perhaps inadvertently, here Sidney Mezes used an adjective which, in an historical context, was not inappropriate. He, in fact, suggested the concession to the German-speaking minority of an "autonomy" which in 1891 the Diet of Innsbruck had refused in the case of the Italian Trentino. See Gaetano Salvemini, *Mussolini Diplomatico* (Bari: Laterza, 1952), p. 439. It should also be recalled that on August 3, 1917 the same Diet of Innsbruck confirmed such a position by voting a resolution proposed by Deputy Toggenburg. Among other things, this resolution stated that "national autonomy of peoples, within the limits of the single countries of the Crown, is to be rejected as a matter of principle." *Archivio per l'Alto Adige*, 1923, I, p. 805. It should also be noted that on Ascension Day, 1918, the German People's Diet met at Vitipeno and unanimously approved a motion including: "2. With respect to Italy, national boundaries more suitable for the defense of the Tyrol and Austria, and annexation to Austria of former German territories such as the thirteen municipalities (Comuni), the seven municipalities and the townships of Bladen, Zahre, Schoenfeld, and Tischlwang. *Besides this, a rectification of boundaries with the cession to Austria of the upper valleys of the Adda and the Oglio as far as the southern shore of Lake Garda and the southern edge of the Alps of Venetia and the Friuli. Further, abundant compensation to cover war costs. . . . 4. German to be the only official language, fostering the unity of the state. The idea of setting up Slav states to the north and south to be rejected. . . . 5. Unity and indivisibility of the Tyrol from Kufstein to the Verona gorges; rejection of any degree of autonomy for the southern portion of this territory, that is to say, for the so-called 'Italian Tyrol'.* 6. No quarter to be given in the struggle against Italian irredentism, to be conducted primarily via the safeguarding and strengthening of Germanism in the southern Tyrol and the expulsion of all irredentist elements, so that the Italian Tyrol may at last become an Austrian land. . . . *9. Installation of a German Bishop in the diocese of Trent, and the diocesan clergy to be educated as good Tyrolese and pro-Germans. 10. Complete transformation of the educational pattern in the Italian Tyrol with the institution of the mandatory teaching of German and the teachers and youth to be educated in accordance with patriotic Tyrolese and pro-German sentiments."*

35. Mezes to House, letter, March 16, 1919, in Albrecht-Carriè, *Italy at the Paris Peace Conference*, p. 241, D. 26.

36. Douglas Johnson to House, letter, March 17, 1919, *ibid.*, p. 423, D. 27.

37. Minutes of the meeting of the Council of Four on April 19, 1919, in *FRUS, Paris Peace Conference*, V, pp. 80 et seq. Paul Mantoux, *Les deliberations du Conseil des Quatre* (Paris: Editions du Centre Nationale de la réchèrche scientifique, 1955) I, pp. 277–91; Aldrovandi Marescotti, *Guerra Diplomatica*, pp. 221–39.

38. The minutes of the meeting of the Council of Four, on May 29, 1919, in *FRUS, Paris Peace Conference*, II, pp. 102, 103–14; Aldrovandi Marescotti, *Guerra Diplomatica*, pp. 438–48. According to Orlando, *Memorie*, p. 438, President Wilson, on that day, behaved like a real arbiter and neither Lloyd George nor Clemenceau ventured to say a word.

39. The Tyrolese Diet, transformed into the National Council on December 16, 1918, after the provincial elections, sent twenty-eight deputies to the Diet at Innsbruck. In March 1919, eight Tyrolese were also elected to the National Assembly in Vienna, which, in turn, expressed the wish that the Tyrol should remain united with the new Austrian state. Later, on May 3, the Tyrolese Diet declared itself ready to transform the Tyrol into a neutral republic provided the unity of the Tyrol was maintained. Lengerau, *La Question du Tyrol du Sud*, p. 25.

40. The Austrian delegation's memorandum of June 16, 1919 in Nina Almond and Ralph Lutz, *The Treaty of St. Germain* (Stanford: Stanford University Press, 1935), pp. 350–53.

41. It should be noted that according to apparently sound evidence it was during the Paris Peace Conference that a group of the leading representatives of the Innsbruck Diet made the offer of the County of Tyrol to the King of Italy, rather than see their region dismembered. Nothing came of the offer, since Italy was not seeking to rule foreign territories. The episode is described in Pietro Stoppani, "Il Re d'Italia, conte del Tirolo: ricordi della prima conferenza della pace," in *La Martinella di Milano, 1964*, Fasc. I–II, pp. 20–30. The episode is also mentioned in a report of July 4, 1919 by General Badoglio,

which refers to a communication received from the head of the military armistice mission in Vienna, General Segrè. The communication stated that, "From conversations sought by members of the Carinthian government it would seem that Carinthia and Salzburg desire a confederate constitution with the Tyrol under an Italian protectorate. *A similar tendency exists in the Tyrol, on condition that the Alto Adige forms an integral part of the Tyrol.*" Paolo Alatri, *Nitti, D'Annunzio e la questione Adriatica, 1918–1920*, p. 83, note 116.

42. Counterproposals of the Austrian delegation, July 10, 1919, in Almond and Lutz, *The Treaty of St. Germain*, pp. 299–309.

43. Statement of the Austrian Delegation, August 9, 1919, in *ibid.,* pp. 310–25.

44. Reply of the Allied and Associated Powers to the Austrian statement on the question of the Austro-Italian border, September 2, 1919, in *ibid.,* pp. 358–59.

45. *Atti Parlamentari:* Camera dei Deputati, Legislature XXIV, prima sessione (Session of July 9, 1919), p. 19058.

46. The text of Foreign Minister Tittoni's statement reads as follows: "Let the populations of a different nationality who are united to us know that we abhor every notion of oppression or denationalization; that their language and cultural institutions will be respected; that their administrative representatives will enjoy full rights in our liberal and democratic legislation; that their political representatives will receive a cordial welcome in the Italian Parliament whose members will listen with due attention when they speak in the name of the peoples they represent.

"We can assure the people of the Alto Adige that they will never know a police regime of persecution and arbitrary action such as the one to which Italians in Julian and Tridentine Venetia were subjected for many years by the imperial government of Austria.

"We ask this people to clasp the hand which we offer them in brotherly friendship. Besides, both from them and from the Germans over the border, in the Tyrol, in Carinthia, and in Styria, unanimous praise has greeted our soldiers who, with their correct, disciplined, and humane behavior, have everywhere won admiration and respect." *Ibid.,* Sessione 1913–1919, XIX, p. 21303. The passage from King Victor Emmanuel III's address reads as follows: "The new lands united to Italy require solutions to new problems. Our tradition of liberty must point the way to these with the greatest regard for local autonomies and traditions. No effort or sacrifice must be spared in order that, after the inevitable uncertainties of the initial adjustment, the return of those lands to their natural and national unity causes no regression or diminution of their well-being." *Ibid.,* Sessione 1919–20, I, p. xii.

47. The text of the letter of resignation dated December 28, 1918, with explicit reference to the London Treaty, is in Leonida Bissolati, *La politica estera dell'Italia dal 1819 al 1920* (Milan: Treves, 1923), p. 406.

48. See *Atti Parlamentari*, Sessione 1913–19, XVIII, p. 19324.

NOTES TO CHAPTER II

1. As noted in the Introduction, this study is devoted exclusively to the diplomatic history of the Alto Adige question. Yet, even in a work of this nature certain internal developments have some bearing on the central theme and must be considered, albeit briefly.

2. See "Comando Prima Armata. Governatorato di Trento. Affari Civili. Relazione sulla attività svolta dal Governatorato di Trento dal 4 novembre al 19 dicembre 1918," p. 9, in *Archivio Centrale di Stato,* Carte Credaro, file IV/30, pp. 120–21.

3. "Comando Prima Armata. Governatorato di Trento. Relazione sull' attività svolta dal Governatorato di Trento dal 1 maggio al 31 luglio 1919," in *Archivio Centrale di Stato,* Carte Credaro, file IV/30, p. 145.

4. *Ibid.,* pp. 171–72.

5. *Ibid.,* p. 117.

6. The text of the treaty is also contained in *R. Ministero Degli Affari Esteri, Trattati e Convenzioni fra il Regno d'Italia e gli altri stati* (Rome: Tipografia del Ministero degli Affari Esteri, 1931), XXIV, pp. 419–702. The Brenner frontier is treated in article 27, paragraph 2. Article 78 contemplated the right of option for Austrian citizenship. Wide use was made of this provision. As late as 1939–as noted in a later chapter–those who had availed

themselves of the option formed the core of the ten thousand Austrian citizens residing in the Alto Adige, where, under the same article 78, they were allowed to retain possession of their property.

7. Letter, Credaro to Nitti, October 11, 1919, in *Archivio Centrale di Stato,* Carte Credaro, bundle O.

8. In this proposal, autonomy was requested for the Alto Adige from Salorno to as far north as the Brenner Pass, including the Italian valleys of Non and Fiemme and the Ladin territories. Also requested were the creation of a provincial council for educational and agricultural matters, the inclusion of the German part of the then diocese of Trent in the diocese of Bressanone, exemption of the Alto Adige population from military service, and the noninterference of the Italian government in the internal affairs of the Alto Adige, such as in the schools, churches, and local administration. In return, Italy's right to maintain small garrisons in the Alto Adige would be recognized. "La riscossa del germanismo," in *Archivio per l'Alto Adige, 1919,* p. 645.

9. For the text of this project see Giuseppe A. Borgese, *L'Alto Adige contro l'Italia* (Milan: Treves, 1921).

10. On April 12, 1920 an agreement between Italy and Austria for the application of the Treaty of St. Germain was signed, whereby Italy pledged to use her rights, granted under the economic and financial clauses of the peace treaty, "in a conciliatory spirit while taking into account the difficulties of Austria's economic and financial situation," and to give her diplomatic support to Austria in all that concerned territorial integrity and admission to the League of Nations.

11. The king said: "I extend my greetings to the representatives of the new lands, freely elected by the industrious people who enlarge and strengthen Italy. Here, in the National Assembly, which has added to its numbers to welcome them, they will find the Roman tradition that moulds diverse laws and a variety of cultures into a unity that is never bondage, one that is alive and continuous." *Atti Parlamentari, Camera dei Deputati, Sessione 1921, Discussioni,* I, pp. ix–xiii.

12. The text of Mussolini's speech to the Chamber on June 21, 1921 is in E. and D. Susmel, eds., *Opera Omnia di Benito Mussolini* (Florence: La Fenice, 1956), XVI, pp. 431–46. Hereafter cited as Mussolini, *Opera.*

13. De Gasperi's speech of June 24, 1921 is in *Atti Parlamentari, Camera dei Deputati, Sessione 1921, Discussioni,* I, pp. 206–10.

14. The province of Trent, including the neighboring districts of Merano and Bolzano, was organized by royal decree published in the official gazette on January 30, 1923. This decree was preceded by one establishing the province of Trieste and published in the official gazette, January 24, 1923. The fact that the posts of the two special commissioners for Venetia Julia and Venezia Tridentina, established in 1919, were eliminated almost simultaneously seems to reflect an early and general Italian desire to normalize the situation in the "liberated territories" as a whole, rather than any intention to persecute the people of the Alto Adige. It should also be noted that the creation of the province of Trent took place a full six months before the Tolomei program was put into effect.

15. This section is based on the research undertaken by Professor Pietro Pastorelli.

16. See also, Report of the Italian Minister to Vienna, Chiaramonte Bordonaro, April 13, 1925, in *I.D.,* Series VII, III, D. 799.

17. See also, cable from the Italian Consul General in Innsbruck, March 16, 1925, in *ibid.,* D. 765.

18. Herriot, in outlining French objections to Stresemann's proposals, listed "the failure of Germany to renounce annexation of Austria and claims on the Italian Tyrol." Chamberlain replied, that in his opinion, "Even if Germany had not renounced Anschluss, she laid no claims to the Italian Tyrol." Italian ambassador to London, Della Torretta, telegram, March 11, 1925, in *ibid.,* D. 757. As confirmed later, Chamberlain's unequivocal reply was based on what had been learned in earlier contacts between London and Berlin.

19. Romano Avezzana to Mussolini, courier telegram, March 4, 1925, in *Ibid.,* D. 743.

20. Mussolini to Della Torretta, telegram, March 14, 1925, *Ibid.,* D. 761. A few days later the British ambassador in Berlin, Lord D'Abernon, still unaware of Chamberlain's clarification, asked his Italian colleague, de Bosdari, what the Italian government's reaction would be in the event of the annexation of Austria by Germany. De Bosdari avoided

replying and put Palazzo Chigi on its guard in the event D'Abernon had spoken to Stresemann about Anschluss "as possible compensation for concessions made by Germany in the Rhine Pact." De Bosdari, telegram, March 24, 1925, in *ibid.*, D. 772. This warning did not cause any real alarm at Palazzo Chigi offset as it was at the end of March when Besnard, the French ambassador to Rome, officially made the French position known, that is, that the French government regarded respect for the peace treaties ranking above everything else. Besnard also warmly agreed with the statement made to him by the secretary general of the Italian Foreign Office, Contarini, that "To allow Austria the possibility of uniting with Germany was tantamount to agreeing to the loss of the fruits of the 1918 victory." Besnard to Contarini, letter, March 28, 1925 in *ibid.*, D. 778. Finally, early in April, Chamberlain gave assurances that he had never discussed the question of Austria with the Berlin government and that his only reference to it had been made to Herriot, as was known in Rome. Della Torretta to Mussolini, telegram, April 2, 1925 in *ibid.*, D. 797. This denial completely reassured Mussolini.

21. De Bosdari to Mussolini, telegram, May 8, 1925, in *ibid.*, D. 846.

22. Mussolini to De Bosdari, telegram, May 14, 1925, no. 104, in *ASMEI.*

23. The official version of Mussolini's remarks was first oral and then immediately appeared in the press. It was later altered to read: "One must not, gentlemen, guarantee the frontier on the Rhine alone, thereby weakening the guarantee on the Brenner."

24. Mussolini to De Bosdari, telegram, May 30, 1925, in *I. D.*, Series VII, IV, D. 13.

25. Romano Avezzana to Mussolini, cables, June 3, 4, 1925, in *ibid.*, DD. 18, 19.

26. Mussolini to Della Torretta, Romano Avezzana, and Scialoja, telegram, June 8, 1925, in *ibid.*, D. 21.

27. Scialoja to Mussolini, telegram, June 10, 1925, in *ibid.*, DD. 28, 29.

28. Scialoja to Mussolini letter received June 14, 1925, in *ibid.*, D. 32.

29. Romano Avezzana to Mussolini, telegram, June 17, 1925 and Mussolini to Romano Avezzana, telegram, June 23, 1925, in *ibid.*, DD. 37, 42.

30. Mussolini to King Victor Emanuel III, telegram, July 17, 1925, in *ibid.*, D. 68.

31. Chiaramonte Bordonaro to Mussolini, courier telegram, June 27, 1925, in *ibid.*, D. 48.

32. Romano Avezzana to Mussolini, telegram, August 5, 1925, in *ibid.*, D. 88.

33. Chiaramonte Bordonaro to Mussolini, telegram, July 10, 1925, in *ibid.*, D. 61.

34. Della Torretta to Mussolini, telegram, August 13, 1925, in *ibid.*, D. 93.

35. Mussolini to Della Toretta, telegram, August 17, 1925, in *ibid.*, D. 95.

36. Della Torretta to Mussolini, telegram, August 26, 1925, in *ibid.*, D. 110.

37. Summonte to Mussolini, telegram, August 27, 1925, in *ibid.*, DD. 111, 112.

38. Mussolini to Romano Avezzana, telegram, September 14, 1925, in *ibid.*, D. 120.

39. Report of the counsellor of state, Amedeo Giannini, chief of the Treaties and Legal Department in the Italian Foreign Office, September 12, 1925, in *ibid.*, p. 90, note 1; Report of the head of the Treaties Office, Mniister Pasquale Sandicchi, September 12, 1925, *idem;* Scialoja to Mussolini, telegram, September 28, 1925, in *ibid.*, D. 132.

40. Chiaramonte Bordonaro to Mussolini, telegram, October 22, 1925, in *ibid.*, D. 160; Mussolini to Chiaramonte Bordonaro, telegram, December 30, 1925, in *ibid.*, D. 214.

41. On December 30, 1925, Mussolini wrote to Ambassador de Bosdari, noting that it was time to raise the problem openly with Stresemann: either he should stop the anti-Italian campaign, which had become extremely active, or else it would be clear that Germany was not interested in maintaining friendly relations with Italy. Mussolini to de Bosdari, telegram, December 30, 1925, in *ibid.*, D. 215.

42. Mussolini to de Bosdari, telegram, January 7, 1926, in *ibid.*, D. 218.

43. For the text see, *Le Temps,* February 9, 1926.

44. On this point see his statements to Ambassador de Bosdari, in *I.D.*, Series VII, IV, p. 158 note 1.

45. Mussolini, *Opera,* XXII, pp. 68–73.

46. For the text see, *Le Temps,* February 10, 1926.

47. The text of the speech delivered before the Senate on February 10, 1926 is in Mussolini, *Opera,* XXII, pp. 74–78.

48. After Mussolini's speech of February 6, 1926, the Tyrolese Diet asked the Vienna government to take the matter up with the League of Nations under articles 10 and 11 of

the Covenant. As soon as he received news of this, Mussolini explained to the Austrian minister in Rome, Egger-Moellwald, that his words on the presence of the Italian flag on the Brenner merely meant that Italy would not remain passive if the terms of the Treaty of St. Germain were broken by Anschluss. Nor would Italy recognize the League of Nations as in any way entitled to deal with the question. See Mussolini's note of February 10, 1926 in *ASMEI*. The following day Mussolini instructed Chiaramonte Bordonaro to peremptorily inform the Vienna government that Italy would consider an Austrian recourse to the League of Nations "as a hostile gesture." Mussolini to Chiaramonte Bordonaro, telegram, February 11, 1926, in *I.D.*, Series VII, IV, D. 243. On February 17, 1926 the Austrian chancellor, Rudolf Ramek, stated that following Mussolini's explanation to the Austrian Minister in Rome, the Austrian government had decided not to resort to the League of Nations, since there seemed to be no threat to the integrity of Austria. He also made it clear that, in any case, the league could not act on the situation in the Alto Adige, it being an Italian domestic problem. For Mussolini's reaction to Remak's speech see Mussolini to Chiaramonte Bordonaro, telegram, February 18, 1926, in *I.D.*, Series VII, IV, D. 246. On the entire question see Arnold Toynbee, *Survey of International Affairs, 1927* (London: Royal Institute of International Affairs, 1929), pp. 199–200.

49. The memorandum reporting this talk was prepared by Dr. Schüller and was sent to the Italian Foreign Minister and may be found in *ASMEI*.

50. It should be noted that this negotiation had had a precedent in the summer of 1922 when the Austrian republic was in grave economic straits. As recalled in Guarneri's memoirs [Felice Guarneri, *Battaglie economiche tra le due guerre* (Milan: Garzanti, 1953), I, pp. 93–95.], under these circumstances the Austrian chancellor, Seipel, submitted to the Italian government a formal proposal for a customs union between Italy and Austria as a solution to the economic chaos prevailing in his country. The proposal was received with mixed feelings in Italy. From a political standpoint, it was welcomed by the Foreign Ministry, and especially by Secretary General Contarini, who saw in the Customs Union a suitable instrument for finally putting an end to any attempt to reassemble into a unit the economic and political complex formed by the succession states to the Austro-Hungarian monarchy. At the same time, such an instrument would provide Italy with a dominant position in the *Danube Basin* and in the Balkans. On the other hand, the proposal was opposed by economic and manufacturing interests, which looked upon the union as a pure loss, both because of the overall burden that Italy would have had to assume and because Austria was a very small market endowed with few industries, which were, nevertheless, in competition with those of Italy. Italy would have offered such industries a wide market without receiving anything in return. Nonetheless, the objections of the experts were overruled in consideration of the political advantages offered by the proposal, inasmuch as the Customs Union would have constituted a solid guarantee against an Austro-German Anschluss. Negotiations reached a fairly advanced stage, but then had to be abandoned because of the opposition of France, who feared that the union would pave the way for an increase in Italian influence in the Danube basin and in the Balkans. Moreover, France, with the support of Czechoslovakia, sought to bring the problem of Austria's economic plight before the League of Nations. This action led to the Protocol on Austrian Reconstruction initialed at Geneva, October 4, 1922, whereby Austria was granted an international loan under the League's control and, in return, Austria agreed to maintain her independence vis-à-vis Germany, in accordance with the provisions of article 88 of the Treaty of St. Germain.

51. The same ordinance created the province of Gorizia when published in the official gazette on January 11, 1927. The principle of simultaneous action was thereby maintained, as had been observed in establishing the two special commissions for Venetia Julia and Venetia Tridentina in 1919 and the two provinces of Trieste and Trent in 1923.

52. In his Ascension Day speech of May 16, 1927, Mussolini made it clear that creation of the province of Bolzano did not constitute "a gift or a concession to the German-speaking inhabitants, and especially to the more impetuous ones beyond the Brenner" but that, on the contrary, its creation had been decided upon "so as to Italianize the region more quickly." For the text of this speech see, Mussolini *Opera*, XXII, p. 369. Later, on May 3, 1927, in a letter to the ambassador in Berlin, Aldrovandi, Mussolini explained the strong language in his speech by referring to "the misplaced and persistent campaign of most of the German press over the nonexistent problem of the Alto Adige" and by emphasizing

the deterioration of relations with Berlin due to the canceling of Stresemann's visit to Italy, in addition to the criticism in the German press of the recent Italo-Albanian Pact. Mussolini to Aldrovandi, letter, May 30, 1927, in *I.D.*, Series VII, V, D. 228.

53. In September 1927 Stresemann himself, in colloquy with Grandi in Geneva, informed the then Under-Secretary for Foreign Affairs that the reaction in Germany to the measures taken in the Alto Adige was serious enough to endanger Italo-German relations. Grandi to Mussolini, telegram, September 11, 1927, in *ibid.*, D. 408.

54. The text of Siepel's speech is published in the *Weiner Zeitung*, February 25, 1928.

55. For the text of the speech delivered to the chamber on March 3, 1928, see Mussolini, *Opera*, XXIII, pp. 116–23.

56. For the text of Seipel's message, see *I.D.*, Series VII, VI, D. 313. A résumé of Mussolini's interview, mentioned in Seipel's message, may be found in Mussolini, *Opera*, XXIII, pp. 135–36.

57. Mussolini's reply to Seipel was sent on May 18, 1928. For the text, see *I.D.*, Series VII, VI, D. 348.

58. Auriti to Mussolini, telegrams, July 7 and 15, 1928 and courier telegram, August 2, 1928, in *ibid.*, DD. 459, 480, 529.

59. Adolf Hitler, *Die Südtiroler Frage und das deutsche Bundnisproblem* (Munich: Eher, 1926).

60. Adolf Hitler, *La mia battaglia* (Milan: Bompiani, 1938), pp. 347–52.

61. Report of the Italian Consul General in Munich, November 18, 1932, n. 511/339, in *ASMEI*.

62. Pittalis to Mussolini, report, February 28, 1933, in *ASMEI*. Even Goering, during his meeting with Mussolini on November 7, 1933, declared that he "could give a most solemn pledge for the Chancellor, the government, and the German people that the question of the South Tyrol will never again be brought up by Germany." Minutes of the Mussolini–Goering conversations, November 7, 1933, in *ASMEI*.

63. See Von Hassell to Seebohm, letter, February 25, 1933, in *Documents on German Foreign Policy 1918–1945* (Washington: U.S. Government Printing Office, 1949), Series C, I, D. 40. Hereafter cited as *G.D.*

64. Preziosi from Vienna to Mussolini, telegram, March 7, 1933, N. 860 R, in *ASMEI*. It was later discovered that the acts of sabotage committed in Austria against Dollfuss's administration were organized in the Alto Adige by Nazi cells that had been established in the area as soon as the Nazis had taken over in Germany. The same cells were to organize the installation of the Nazi administration in the Alto Adige after September 8, 1943.

65. Ricciardi to Mussolini, telegram, February 3, 1933, in *ASMEI*.

66. Minutes of the February 7, 1933 conversation between Mussolini and Schüller, in *ASMEI*.

67. Minutes of Mussolini's conversation with the Austrian Chancellor, April 12, 1933, in *ASMEI*.

68. Suvich, Memorandum, April 25, 1933, in *ASMEI*.

69. Suvich, memorandum on the Riccione talks, August 19–20, 1933, in *ASMEI*.

70. Suvich, memorandum, in *ASMEI*.

71. Suvich, memoranda of April 10 and 14, 1934, in *ASMEI*.

72. Preziosi to Mussolini, dispatch, June 18, 1934, in *ASMEI*.

73. On his death-bed, Chancellor Dollfuss asked that Mussolini should take care of his family. After the Anschluss, Himmler appointed a commission to prepare a report on the events of July 25, 1934. This report is published in *Il giorno che uccisero Dollfuss* (Milan: Mondadori, 1967).

74. Minutes of the talks between Mussolini, Suvich, Schuschnigg, and Austrian Foreign Minister Berger, in *ASMEI*. In his memoirs, Schuschnigg, under the heading "Rome 1934–1935" quotes minutes that must refer to this conversation. From this it would appear that the Austrian Chancellor requested for the Alto Adige adequate teaching of German, suspension of the industrialization in the area promoted by Italy, subsidies to German cooperatives, and a pardon for political prisoners. Kurt von Schuschnigg, *Ein Requiem in Rot-Weiss-Rot* (Zurich: Amstutz, 1946).

75. Schuschnigg to Mussolini, letter, March 7, 1935, in *ASMEI*. Subsequently, both

Schuschnigg and Berger again expressed the same ideas in speaking with Preziosi in Vienna. Preziosi, dispatch, March 10, 1935, in *ASMEI.*

76. Minutes of the conversation between Mussolini and Starhemberg, April 19, 1935, in *ASMEI.*

77. Minutes of the Mussolini–Schuschnigg–Schmidt–Ciano talks in Galeazzo Ciano, *L'Europa verso la catastrofe* (Milan: Mondadori, 1948), pp. 165–75.

78. Minutes of the Mussolini–Goering conversations, January 15, 1937, in *ASMEI.*

79. Von Hassell, memorandum, January 16, 1937, in *G.D.*, Series D, I, D. 199.

80. The complete text of Magistrati's letter to Ciano quoting his conversation with Goering of April 21, 1938 in its entirety may be found in Mario Toscano, *Pagine di storia diplomatica contemporanea: Origini e vicende della seconda guerra mondiale* (Milan: Giuffrè, 1963), II, pp. 176–80.

NOTES TO CHAPTER III

1. *I.D.*, Series D. D. 352.

2. Galeazzo Ciano, *Diaro 1937–1938* (Bologna: Cappelli, 1948), entry for March 12, 1938. Hereafter cited as Ciano, *Diario.*

3. *Ibid.*

4. Ribbentrop to Hitler, letter, March 17, 1938, in *G.D.*, Series D, I, D. 396; Attolico to Ribbentrop, letter, March 17, 1938, in *ibid.*, D. 397. For Hitler's speech see Norman H. Baynes, ed., *The Speeches of Adolf Hitler, April 1922–August, 1939* (London: Oxford University Press, 1942), II, pp. 1428–36. Hereafter cited as Hitler, *Speeches.*

5. Ribbentrop note, March 7, 1938, in *G.D.*, Series D, I, D. 396.

6. Von Mackensen note, March 14, 1938, in *ibid.*, D. 383.

7. Von Weisäcker note, March 14, 1938, in *ibid.*, D. 384.

8. See Winfried Schmitz-Esser, "Hitler–Mussolini: das Südtiroler Abkommen von 1939," in *Aussenpolitik* (June 1966), pp. 401–02. Conrad Latour, *Südtirol und die Achse Berlin–Rom 1938–1945* (Stuttgart: Verlags-Anstalt, 1962), pp. 22–24.

9. For the text of Hitler's speech to the Reichstag, February 20, 1938, see, Hitler, *Speeches,* II, pp. 1376–1409.

10. Note of March 14, 1938, in *Austrian Press Agency.*

11. Ernst Von Weisäcker, *Erinnerungen* (Munich: List, 1950), p. 158.

12. Ciano, *Diario,* entry for April 3, 1938.

13. Renzetti, note, April 8, 1938, in Toscano, *Pagine di Storia Diplomatica,* II, pp. 170–71. The Gauleiter must have been the notorious Hofer.

14. Von Mackensen to Ribbentrop, telegram, April 18, 1938, in *G.D.*, Series D, I, D. 741.

15. Ciano, *Diario,* entry for April 17, 1938. The text of Ciano's letter to Magistrati is in Toscano, *Pagine di Storia Diplomatica,* II, pp. 173–74. See also Massimo Magistrati, *L'Italia a Berlino* (Milan: Mondadori, 1956), pp. 164–65.

16. Magistrati to Ciano, letter, August 2, 1938, in Toscano, *Pagine di Storia Diplomatica,* II, pp. 176–80.

17. Ciano, *Diario,* entry for April 24, 1938.

18. *Ibid.*, entry for April 30, 1938.

19. D. C. Watt, "An Earlier Model for the Pact of Steel. The Draft Treaties Exchanged between Germany and Italy during Hitler's Visit to Rome in May 1938," in *International Affairs,* April 1957, p. 196. Hereafter cited as Watt, "An Earlier Model."

20. Schmundt, memorandum, April 1938, in *G.D.*, Series D, II, D. 132.

21. Watt, "An Earlier Model," pp. 186–89.

22. *Ibid.*, pp. 189–90.

23. Von Weisäcker, *Erinnerungen,* p. 158.

24. Ribbentrop, note, May 20, 1938, in *G.D.*, Series D, I, D. 768.

25. Minutes of the meeting of May 19, 1938, chaired by the Foreign Minister, in *ibid.*, D. 767.

26. Mario Toscano, *The Origins of the Pact of Steel* (Baltimore: The Johns Hopkins Press, 1967), p. 24. Hereafter cited as Toscano, *Pact of Steel.*

27. *Ibid.*, pp. 27–29.

28. Ciano to Ribbentrop, letter, January 2, 1939, in Ciano, *L'Europa verso la catastrofe*, pp. 392–94.

29. Ciano, *Diario*, I, entry for January 2, 1939.

30. Toscano, *Pact of Steel*, p. 106, note 74.

31. On this conversation, see Attolico to Ciano, report, January 5, 1939, in *ibid.*, pp. 108–09; Ribbentrop, note, January 10, 1939, in *G.D.*, Series D, IV, D. 427.

32. Ciano, *Diario*, entry for January 7, 1939.

33. Ribbentrop, note, January 10, 1939, in *G.D.*, Series D, IV, D. 427.

34. The archives of the Italian Foreign Ministry contain more than thirty dispatches on the Alto Adige problem, sent during this period to the Italian Embassy in Berlin.

35. Von Weisäcker, memoranda, March 31 and April 1, 1939, in *G.D.*, Series D, VI, DD. 140, 143.

36. Heinburg, memorandum, April 5, 1939, in *ibid.*, D. 163.

37. Magistrati, *L'Italia a Berlino*, pp. 333–34.

38. *G.D.*, Series D, VI, D. 317, note 5.

39. The text is in Toscano, *The Pact of Steel*, p. 311.

40. The German minutes of the meeting dispel any doubt as to the accuracy of the Ciano report, reading as follows: "Count Ciano again expressed the desire of the Italian government that the 10,000 former Austrians in the South Tyrol, who were now Reich subjects and the source of constant unrest, should be evacuated. He emphasized that this was a special request from the Duce. The Reich Foreign Minister promised Count Ciano to give this request his favorable consideration." Ribbentrop, note, May 18, 1939, in *G.D.*, Series D, VI, D. 341.

41. The text is quoted in Attolico's telegram to Ciano, May 12, 1939, in Toscano, *Pact of Steel*, pp. 342–45.

42. Note, May 18, 1939, in *G.D.*, Series D, VI, D. 341.

43. Gaus, note, May 12, 1939, in *ibid.*, D. 371.

44. Attolico to Ciano, telegrams nos. 312, 313, May 12, 1939, in Toscano, *The Pact of Steel*, pp. 347–48.

45. *Ibid.*, p. 355.

46. Attolico to Ciano, phongram messages nos. 315, 316, May 13, 1939, in *ibid.*, p. 355.

47. *G.D.*, Series D, VI, D. 562.

48. *L'Alto Adige fra le due guerre* (Rome: I.C.S., 1961), pp. 45–46.

49. Woermann to Von Mackensen, telegram, June 24, 1939, in *G.D.*, Series D, VI, D. 562; Attolico to Ciano, telegram, June 24, 1939, in *I.D.*, Series VIII, XII, D. 334; Magistrati, *L'Italia a Berlino*, pp. 361–62.

50. On this point, see Junker, note, August 16, 1939, in *G.D.*, Series D, VII, D. 83.

51. On the discussions that took place between Rome and Berlin over the publication of a communiqué on the June 23, 1939 agreement, see the telegrams from Attolico to Ciano, July 3, 5, 7, 8, 1939, in *I.D.*, Series VIII, XII, DD. 454, 474, 475, 493, 509; Siegfried, note, July 6, 1939, in *G.D.*, Series D, VI, D. 624; Attolico to Ribbentrop, letter, July 7, 1939, in *ibid.*, D. 631; Von Weisäcker to Von Mackensen and Bene, July 10, 1939, in *ibid.*, D. 643; Woermann's telegram to Von Mackensen and Bene, July 14, 1939, in *ibid.*, D. 668.

52. Among other things, the article stated: "It is not a question of a compulsory exodus, or of exile, or of mass expulsion of the people of the Alto Adige, but rather one of calling back to the Reich the German citizens residing in the Alto Adige, in addition to the voluntary transfer to German territory of those Alto Adige people of German origin who desire it of their own free will . . . thanks to this clarifying agreement, those who have always demonstrated their loyalty to Italy and her institutions will remain and continue their fruitful work on their ancestral lands." "Chiarificazione," in *Athesia Augusta*, August 1939.

53. Romano, report, September 5, 1939, in *I.D.*, Series XI, I, D. 51; Pittalis, report, September 7, 1939, in *ibid.*, D. 84.

54. The Prefect of Bolzano published still another article to further clarify this position, which was carried and commented upon in all of the Italian papers—including those in the German language—and by the official news agency, Stefani. The article, among other things, included the following: "It is only obligatory for German citizens residing in the Alto Adige to return to the Reich, while those who are Italian citizens have been granted the option of

a completely free choice whether to remain in Italy as good citizens of the Kingdom or assume German citizenship and emigrate from their country of origin. Thus, German-speaking elements of the population are not compelled to change their citizenship, nor are any of them forced to abandon the Alto Adige, just as those who choose to remain loyal Italian citizens will not be sent to our lands overseas." Article in *Athesia Augusta,* October 1939.

The prefect, speaking on behalf of the government, subsequently repeated on more than one occasion that exercise of the option was completely voluntary and that inhabitants of the Alto Adige who remained in Italy would not be subject to restrictions of any sort. He stated this in public speeches at Appiano on October 20, 1939 and at Bressanone on November 1, 1939, and he repeated it for the last time at a meeting of the mayors of the Alto Adige on December 15, 1939 at Bolzano. The Italians desired only that the problem be resolved within the prescribed time.

55. On this point, see the comparative analysis of the Italo-German agreement on options in the Alto Adige and the German–Esthonian protocol contained in Attolico's report to Ciano, October 18, 1939, in *I.D.,* Series IX, I, D. 798.

56. Ciano to Attolico, telegrams, September 17, 1939, in *ibid.,* D. 267.

57. Attolico to Ciano, telegrams, October 3, 1939, in *ibid.,* DD. 580, 581.

58. *G.D.,* Series D, VIII, D. 244, note 3.

59. *Rules for the repatriation of German citizens and the emigration of German-speaking inhabitants from the Alto Adige to Germany,* October 21, 1939, in *I.D.,* Series IX, II, Appendix II.

60. *Ibid.,* D. 160; Ciano, *Diario,* entry for November 1939.

61. *Chiarimenti alle norme per il rimpatrio dei cittadini germanici e per l'emigrazione di allogeni tedeschi dall'Alto Adige in Germania,* November 17, 1939.

62. The text is in *I.D.,* Series IX, II, Appendix VI.

63. Winfried Schmitz-Esser, "Die Genesis des Hitler-Mussolini Abkommen von 1939," in Franz Huter, ed., *Südtirole, eine Frage des Europäischen Gewissens* (Munich: Oldenburg, 1965).

64. Franz Huter, "Option und Umsiedlung," in *ibid.,*

65. In a reply to a question on the subject, raised publicly by the then president of the Senate, Merzagora, on September 9, 1965, Silvius Magnago, head of the Südtiroler Volkspartei, wrote, on the following day, that in 1939 the German-speaking inhabitants of the Alto Adige had to choose between two evils, fascism and nazism. (The text of Magnago's letter is in Karl Heinz Ritschel, *Diplomatie um Sudtirol. Politische Hintergrunde eines europäischen Versagens (Erstmals dargestellt auf Grund der Geheimakten)* (Stuttgart: Seewald Verlag, 1966), pp. 529–30. Hereafter cited as Ritschel, *Diplomatie.)* This interpretation of the events is difficult to square with the facts, as is demonstrated by the evidence that very few out of the 82,000 German-speaking inhabitants of the Alto Adige who elected to remain in Italy joined the Fascist party. This interpretation also fails to take into account the important fact that the choice in favor of Germany was made when Hitler had already attacked Poland and was at war with the Western democracies, while Italy was not only "nonbelligerent" but had publicly announced her disagreement with Berlin in Ciano's speech in the Chamber of Fasces and Corporations on December 15, 1939. Mussolini had also drafted a letter in secret, which was sent to Hitler later, on January 5, 1940 (see text in *I.D.,* Series IX, III, D. 33), in which, for the first and last time, he informed the Führer of his approval of Ciano's speech, of the need to reestablish a Polish state, of his opposition to the attack on Finland and to Hitler's pro-Soviet policy, and of his readiness for compromise and peace, since the United States would not allow a complete overthrow of the democracies. In addition, Mussolini's words to Prince Starhemberg, quoted earlier, are worth recalling at this point. Mussolini had explained to his interlocutor that he could make no more concessions to the people of the Alto Adige because they were already practically all Nazis.

66. In the peace treaties concluded at the end of World War I, the right of options was based on the principles incorporated in Article 3 of the treaty concerning the recognition of Poland's independence and the protection of minorities and signed at Versailles, June 28, 1919. See Friedrich von Martens, *Nouveau Recueil général des traités* (Leipzig: Wiecher, 1927), Series III, XIII, p. 505: On this point, see also Mario Toscano, *Le minoranze di razza, di lingua, di religione nel diritto internazionale* (Turin: Bocca, 1931) and, especially, Mario

Toscano, "L'opzione della cittadinanza degli incapaci di agire nei recenti trattati di pace," in *Rivista di diritto internazionale*, 1935, nos. 3 and 4.

67. Bene to Ribbentrop, report, November 5, 1940, in *G.D.*, Series D, XI, D. 291.

68. Ciano, *Diario*, entries for June 30, July 6, and 13, 1941.

69. Von Mackensen to Von Ribbentrop, report, September 27, 1941, in *G.D.*, Series D, XIII, D. 362.

70. Ciano, *Diario*, entry for July 6, 1941.

71. Von Mackensen to Von Ribbentrop, telegram, August 2, 1941, in G.D., Series D, XIII, D. 279; Von Mackensen to Von Ribbentrop, September 27, 1941, in *ibid.*, D. 362.

72. In December the Reich High Commissioner for the South Tyrolese Resettlement wrote to Von Mackensen, noting that the problem of the transfer from the Alto Adige of the optants had then entered a static phase. Mayr-Kalkenberg to Von Mackensen, letter, December 4, 1941, in *ibid.*, D. 544.

73. It should be noted that this flow continued even after the war because it was supported by the French forces occupying Bavaria and because, until January 1, 1946, the Alto Adige was administered and garrisoned by American troops.

74. F. W. Deakin, *Storia della Repubblica di Salò* (Turin: Einaudi, 1962), pp. 602–03. Note Deakin's statements are based on German records.

75. B. H. Liddell Hart, ed., *The Rommel Papers* (London: Collins, 1953), p. 433.

76. Enzo Collotti, *L'amministrazione tedesca dell'Italia occupata* (Milan: Lerici, 1963), p. 62.

77. Louis P. Lochner, ed., *The Goebbels Papers* (London: Hamish Hamilton, 1948), pp. 345, 352, 356–57, 361, 362, 363–64, 379, and 383.

78. E. F. Moellhausen, *La carta perdente. Memorie diplomatiche, 26 luglio 1943–2 maggio 1945* (Rome: Sestante, 1948), pp. 390–91.

79. On this point, another German source, Dollmann's memoirs, is also worth noting. He writes, "From then on, after September 8, 1943, the Alto Adige became the object of a fierce conflict between Wolfe, Rahn, and Kesselring on the one side, and Hofer on the other, not for love of the Republic of Salò nor out of any delicate consideration for its hapless leader, but because of political and military pressures created by the events of the moment. Hofer, however, in agreement with Bormann, gradually and step by step applied a policy of extending the 'Kingdom of the Tyrol' beyond Trent and Belluno." *Had the Third Reich won the war, the Italian frontiers, given also the Duce's weakened position would have inevitably becomes those of 1914.* Eugenio Dollmann, *Roma nazista* (Milan: Longanesi, 1951), p. 123.

80. On this point, see Allen Dulles, *Secret Surrender* (New York: Harper and Row, 1966), pp. 158, 181, 215, 222–23, 225, and 227; Ferruccio Lanfranchi, *La resa degli ottocentomila* (Milan: Rizzoli, 1948), pp. 334–41, which quotes General Wolff's report clearly exposing Hofer's behavior. The last chapter of this book, entitled "How the Alto Adige was retained by Italy," also contains detail worth noting.

81. Deakin, *Storia della Repubblica di Salò,* pp. 532–51; 603–04; Collotti, *L'Amministrazione tedesca dell'Italia occupata,* p. 102.

82. Deakin, *Storia della Repubblica di Salò,* p. 603.

83. *Ibid.,* pp. 563–64.

84. *Ibid.,* p. 580.

85. Filippo Anfuso, *Da Palazzo Venezia al Lago di Garda* (Bologna: Cappelli, 1957), p. 378. Hereafter cited as Anfuso, *Da Palazzo Venezia.*

86. Anfuso to Mussolini, report, December 10, 1943, in Mario Toscano, "La controversia fra Salò e Berlino per l'occupazione nazista e per le decisioni annessionistiche di Hitler dell' Alto Adige e del Trentino nei documenti diplomatici della Repubblica Sociale Italiana" in *Storia e Politica* (1957), I, pp. 13-16. Hereafter cited as Toscano, "La controversia."

87. Among other things, the German ambassador to Salò, Rahn, had wired to Ribbentrop on October 19, 1943 that he had met Hofer and Rainer and had advised them to make public only the more important decisions regarding the conduct of the war, so as to "disguise" the annexation. Deakin, *Storia della Repubblica di Salò*, pp. 604–05. At the same time, Moellhausen mentions Rahn's attempts to bridle the two Gauleiters. Moellhausen, *La carte perdente*, p. 393.

88. Anfuso, *Da Palazzo Venezia*, p. 358; Moellhausen, *La carta perdente*, p. 394.

89. Cecchi to Anfuso, report, April 26, 1944, in Toscano, "La controversia," pp. 40–42.

90. Rahn to Ribbentrop, telegram, March 27, 1944, in Deakin, *Storia della Repubblica di Salò*, p. 666.

91. *Ibid.*, p. 669.

92. Mazzolini to Anfuso, letter, August 8, 1944, in Toscano, "La controversia," pp. 17–19.

93. Anfuso to Mazzolini, letter, August 23, 1944, in *ibid.*, p. 20.

94. Anfuso to Mussolini, report, November 18, 1944, in *ibid.*, pp. 36–38.

95. Anfuso to Mussolini, report, December 1, 1944, in *ibid.*, pp. 45–46.

96. "Punti di vista di resistenti sulla questione Alto-Atesina (1944–45)," in *Il movimento di Liberazione in Italia*, November 1951, pp. 3–9.

97. Collotti, *L'Amministrazione tedesca dell'Italia occupata*, p. 62.

98. Detailed information on what happened in Bolzano after the defeat of the German army in Italy may be found in Lanfranchi, *La resa degli ottocentomila*, pp. 333–35.

99. *Atrocities committed by Tyrolese Nazis after September 8, 1943.*

100. "Participation in the war on the side of Germany by Austrian and German-speaking Alto Atesini (South Tyrolese) after September 8, 1943 (Italian armistice)." Document number 4 attached to the *Aide Mémoire on the Question of the Italian Northern Frontier* presented by the Italian delegation at the Paris Peace Conference, February 1946.

NOTES TO CHAPTER IV

1. Expressed in a note, August 1943, by the British Ambassador to Washington to the State Department, in *FRUS, Diplomatic Papers, 1943*, I, p. 515. For earlier statements of the British viewpoint favoring the restoration of Austria see Robert E. Clute, *The International Legal Status of Austria, 1938–1955* (The Hague: Nijhoff, 1962), p. 47. On July 27, 1942 the State Department also issued a statement noting that the United States had never held the view that Austria had been legally absorbed by the Reich. *Ibid.* p. 47.

2. The text of the proposed declaration may be found in *FRUS, 1943*, I, pp. 516–17.

3. *Aide-mémoire* from the British Embassy in Washington to the State Department, August 28, 1943, in *ibid.*, pp. 515–16.

4. State Department to the British Embassy, October 9, 1943, in *ibid.*, pp. 549–50.

5. *Ibid.*, p. 550.

6. *Ibid.*, p. 704.

7. Minutes of the 7th session of the Tripartite Conference, October 25, 1943, in *ibid.*, p. 663.

8. Philip E. Moseley, "The Treaty with Austria," in *International Organization*, 1950, IV, pp. 219 and 227.

9. Text is in *FRUS, 1943*, I, p. 761.

10. Committee on Post-War Programs, memorandum, June 8, 1944, in *FRUS, 1944*, I, p. 441.

11. Alberto Tarchiani, *Dieci anni tra Roma e Washington* (Milan: Mondadori, 1955), p. 82.

12. On this point, see General Antoine Bethouart, *La bataille pour l'Autriche* (Paris: Presse de la Cité, 1966).

13. Tarchiani to President Truman, note, July 6, 1945, in *FRUS, The Conference of Berlin (Potsdam) 1945*, I, pp. 697–98. The relevant passage reads as follows: "The Brenner frontier line is the natural geographic and strategic border between the Italians and the Germans. A German minority resided within the borders of the Italian state. Not long ago this minority was given the option of choosing to remain in Italy or of emigrating to Germany. A part of them decided to leave and went to Nazi Germany. A substantial part of the alien population chose to remain in Italy."

14. "General Memorandum on the Italian Northern Frontier, August, 1945," in *The Austro-Italian Frontier*, part I: *Official Statements and other documents presented by the Italian Government to the Council of Foreign Ministers, February–June, 1946* (Rome: no date). Hereafter cited as *The Austro-Italian Frontier*.

15. De Gasperi to Byrnes, letter, August 22, 1945, in *The United States and Italy, 1936–1946* (Washington: U. S. Government Printing Office, 1946), pp. 167–68.

16. Byrnes to De Gasperi, letter, September 4, 1945, in *ibid.*, p. 171; see also, Tarchiani, *Dieci anni*, p. 91.

17. Ambassador Tarchiani was also received by President Truman and gave him an explanation of the Italian point of view on this and other questions concerning the peace treaty that might be considered in London. Tarchiani also gave Truman a brief printed "Summary of Italian views for an equitable solution of the principal questions that may be discussed at the London Peace Conference," which also noted that Italy was enacting in the Alto Adige, as well as in the Aosta Valley, and on behalf of her Slav minorities all democratic principles of individual and collective liberties." See *FRUS, 1945*, II, p. 107.

18. Ritschel, *Diplomatie*, p. 209. Representatives of the German-speaking inhabitants also presented an explicit request in a memorandum sent to the Allies during the summer. In it they asked that, while awaiting the desired union with Austria, full autonomy under the control of the allied troops should be conceded to the region. *L'Accordo De Gasperi–Gruber sull'Alto Adige* (Rome: Istituto Poligrafico dello Stato, 1958), p. 10.

19. It is revealing to note that the "Draft Heads of Treaty with Italy," prepared by the British delegation (*FRUS, 1945)*, II, p. 135), contained no clause referring to the Brenner frontier, this pointing to the British government's opinion that there was no need for this frontier to undergo any alteration.

20. Memorandum of the U.S. Delegation to the Council of Foreign Ministers, September 12, 1945, in *FRUS, 1945*, II, p. 134. It should be noted that the Soviet Union supported the American proposal. See memorandum of the Soviet Delegation to the Council of Foreign Ministers, September 12, 1945, in *ibid.*, p. 151.

21. *Ibid.*, p. 136.

22. Memorandum of the American Delegation to the Council of Foreign Ministers, September 12, 1945, in *ibid.*, p. 179.

23. Minutes of the 3rd Session of the Council of Foreign Ministers, September 14, 1945, in *ibid.*, p. 162. The decision taken by the Four read as follows: "The frontier with Austria will not be changed, subject to the decision to be reached by the Council on any case which Austria may present for minor rectifications in her favor." *Ibid.*, p. 462.

24. Nicolo Carandini, "Un Patto tra galantuomini," in *Il Mondo*, October 16, 1956. Hereafter cited as Carandini, "Patto."

25. These provisions regarded the introduction of primary schools in the mother-tongue and parification of language in public documents.

26. Ritschel, *Diplomatie*, p. 209.

27. *Il Popolo*, December 22, 1945.

28. Ritschel, *Diplomatie*, p. 209.

29. Michael Balfour and John Mair, *Survey of International Affairs, 1939–1946. Four Power Control in Germany and Austria, 1945–1946* (London, Oxford University Press, 1956), pp. 319–24; William B. Bader, *Austria between East and West, 1945–55* (Stanford; Stanford University Press, 1966), pp. 45–53.

30. *L'Accordo De Gasperi-Gruber*, p. 11. Gruber states that Austria never directly requested the return of the Alto Adige, but limited herself to proposing a plebiscite. See Karl Gruber, *Between Liberation and Liberty: Austria in the Post-War World* (London: Deutsch, 1955), p. 51. Hereafter cited as Gruber, *Between Liberation;* Carandini, "Patto."

31. *FRUS, The Conference of Berlin, 1945*, II, p. 1511.

32. *The Austro-Italian Frontier*, part I.

33. On this subject, see also the articles in *Die Furche*, March 2, 1946; *Vorarlberger Volksblatt*, February 21, 1946; *Neues Osterreich* Feburary 28, 1946.

34. Ritschel, *Diplomatie*, p. 203.

35. Carandini, "Patto."

36. *Ibid.*

37. *Ibid.*

38. Carandini, "Patto."

39. Nicolo Carandini, "L'Accordo di Parigi," in *Il Mondo*, April 17, 1962, Hereafter cited as Carandini, "L'Accordo."

40. Gruber, *Between Liberation*, p. 50.

41. *Ibid.*, p. 53. Consequently, Gruber's statement that this decision upset the principle of the inviolability of the northern Italian frontier and offered new possibilities to Austria is

less than accurate. As will be noted in greater detail below, it was not this decision but, instead, that of May 14, 1946 that offered new and unexpected opportunities to Austria.

42. *Ibid.,* pp. 53–54; *L'Accordo De Gasperi–Gruber sull'Alto Adige,* p. 12, Carandini, "Patto."

43. *The Austro-Italian Frontier, part I. Statement of the Italian delegate to the Council of Foreign Ministers, May 30, 1946.* To illustrate Carandini's statement, the Italian government, on June 1, 1946, presented to the council two additional *aides-mémoire.* In the first, Austria's claims to minor adjustments of the frontier were refuted (Additional memorandum A, *The Austrian Claims on the Pusteria and Upper Sarco Valleys*) and, in the second, the provisions made for the German-speaking group were outlined (Additional memorandum B, *Outline of the Measures taken by the Italian Government in favor of the German-speaking group in the Alto Adige*). For the texts of these two documents see, *The Austro-Italian Frontier,* parts I and II.

44. Gruber, *Between Liberation,* p. 66; Lothar Wimmer, *Zwischen Ballhausplatz und Downing Street* (Munich: Fromme, 1958), p. 94.

45. Gruber, *Between Liberation,* pp. 57–58.

46. *Ibid.,* p. 55.

47. Carandini, "Patto."

48. The resolution and the extracts from the Soviet minutes were quoted by Vishinsky in his speech at Luxembourg Palace on August 17. See Recueil des documents de la conference de Paris, 29 juillet–*15 octobre, 1946* (Paris: Imprimerie Nationale, no date), I, p. 359.

49. Carandini, "Patto."

50. *Parliamentary Debates,* House of Commons, Official Report, Fifth Series, CDXXVI, No. 183. For the debate see pp. 282–333; for Bevin's statement see pp. 327–328, and 333.

51. Bevin stated that the Tyrolese could be granted a hearing at the Peace Conference before twenty-one nations summoned to do more than simply approving the decisions of the four Great Powers. Note how Carandini emphasizes this point in "Patto."

52. *Recueil des documents de la Conference de Paris,* I, p. 230. Hereafter cited as *Recueil.*

53. The American proposal read as follows: "The State to which the territory is transferred shall take all measures necessary to secure to all persons within the territory, without distinction as to race, sex, language, or religion, the enjoyment of human rights and of the fundamental freedoms, including freedom of expression, of press and publication, of religious worship, of political opinion, and of public meeting." This proposal–reproducing in its entirety the first of the political clauses (Article 14) imposed on Italy–appears in the draft peace treaty with Italy as paragraph 4 of Article 13 under the heading simply of "United States Proposal"; it does not form a part of the agreed text. *Paris Peace Conference 1946: Selected Documents* (Washington: U.S. Government Printing Office, 1947), p. 85; *Recueil,* IV, p. 424.

54. *Recueil,* I, pp. 237–40.

55. *Ibid.,* p. 354.

56. *Ibid.,* pp. 354–59.

57. *Ibid.,* p. 360.

58. *Ibid.,* p. 363.

59. Gruber, *Between Liberation,* p. 66.

60. *Recueil,* I, pp. 382–87; Gruber, *Between Liberation* pp. 63–64.

61. "Memorandum: 'Observations on Article 10 of the draft peace treaty with Italy'," in *Paris Peace Conference 1946: Selected Documents,* pp. 185–87.

62. Carandini, "Patto"; Gruber, *Between Liberation,* pp. 66–67.

63. The Belgian delegation helped in the preparation of this *aide-mémoire* with its suggestion. Wimmer, *Zwischen Ballhausplatz und Downing Street,* p. 101.

64. "Proposal by the Austrian delegation concerning certain clauses in the draft peace treaty with Italy," in *Paris Peace Conference 1946: Selected Documents,* pp. 367–68.

65. Carandini, "Patto"; Gruber, *Between Liberation,* p. 67.

66. Gruber, *Between Liberation,* p. 68.

67. Carandini, "Patto"; Wimmer, *Zwischen Ballhausplatz und Downing Street,* p. 101.

68. The following are the five points mentioned by Gruber and are quoted in full from an appendix to the *aide-mémoire* submitted by Austria to the Peace Conference, in which it was declared that the Innocenti proposals were unacceptable to the South Tyrolese:

"1) Under this scheme the Southern Tyrol and the Trentino will form a joint autonomous area known as 'regional'. As a result, the South Tyroleans will, a priori, find themselves an obvious minority (200,000 against 500,000) in the proposed self-governing territory, to such an extent that it would no longer be possible to speak of autonomy for the South Tyrol and its inhabitants. Moreover, this scheme makes no provision at all for including in the regional area the old Tyrolese comunes which, at present, are part of the province of Belluno, namely, Cortina d'Ampezzo, Colle Santa Lucia, and Buchenstein.

"2) The plan offers no protection against the intrusion of Italians into the South Tyrol. On the contrary, Article 54 of the proposal deprives the autonomous territory of all possibility of hindering the settlement of persons foreign to the district.

"3) No guarantee is provided, regarding state officials or officials of the autonomous regional administration, that will insure to the South Tyrolese a proportional representation based on population. On the contrary, Article 29 provides that the new self-governing administration would have to take over the staff of the present provincial administration.

"4) There is no provision for uniform fiscal and police organization in the proposed self-governing territory despite the fact that this is indispensable to any real measure of self-government. All legislation dealing with taxes and fees—with the exception of provincial taxes, up to the present of minimal importance—is reserved to the state. Under Article 40 there will be a national police force in the self-governing territory, and the president of the area is only allowed to say how it will be used but has no power to decide its numerical strength, its composition, or the way in which it is recruited.

"5) Through the government representative appointed for the self-governing territory, the central government may, at any moment amend the Statute of the autonomous territory, or even suspend it, so that neither the extent nor the duration of this measure of self-government would seem to be guaranteed in any way whatsoever." "Statement on the Italian Plan for Self-Government," in *Paris Peace Conference, 1946: Selected Documents*, p. 378. Gruber's statement, recorded in Ritschel, *Diplomatie*, p. 246, that during the negotiations the Austrian Foreign Minister had no idea of the existence of Innocenti's proposals is, therefore, completely without foundation.

69. Carandini, "Patto."

70. *Ibid.*, and Carandini, "L'Accordo." The text herein is condensed.

71. Wimmer, *Zwischen Ballhausplatz und Downing Street*, p. 102.

72. All of the documents presented are printed in *Paris Peace Conference, 1946, Selected Documents*, pp. 367–88.

73. Wimmer's statement that Britain was pleased with the agreement is of interest here. Wimmer, *Zwischen Ballhausplatz und Downing Street*, p. 101; See also Gruber, *Between Liberation*, p. 71.

74. Wimmer, *Zwischen Ballhausplatz und Downing Street*, pp. 94–114 *passim.*

75. Negotiations were based on the English text, since the agreement, when reached, had to be presented to the conference in one of its official languages.

76. Text is in Carandini, "Una parola inglese e il traduttore tedesco," in *Il Mondo*, April 24, 1962. Hereafter cited as Carandini, "Parola."

77. *Ibid.*

78. Carandini, "Patto."

79. Carandini, "Parola."

80. For Gruber's offer, see Gruber, *Between Liberation*, p. 68.

81. The text is in Carandini, "Parola." Professor Weisgerber's philological disquisitions on the word *frame,* which Ritschel seems to consider important (Ritschel, *Diplomatie*, pp. 228–29), are irrelevant. For the purpose of interpreting the text, nothing is to be gained from a study of all of the possible meanings of the word; only the sense in which it was used by the negotiators is important. This can be deduced only from the minutes of the negotiations, marking the developments leading up to its introduction, and the meaning

given to the word by the negotiators at that moment. If a difference appears between this interpretation and that of the philologist, the only inference that can be drawn is that the negotiators were not masters of the English language. But that is another matter.

82. Gruber, *Between Liberation*, p. 68, provides the reasons for Austria's stand on this point. He also mentions the difficulties that were raised regarding the inclusion of the agreement in the Peace Treaty. It should be noted that Italy did not oppose the inclusion. However, Gruber does not state by whom such difficulties were raised.

83. *Ibid.,* pp. 62 and 69.

84. *Ibid.,* p. 69; Wimmer, *Zwischen Ballhausplatz und Downing Street,* pp. 102–03.

85. Gruber, *Between Liberation,* pp. 70–71.

86. De Gasperi and Gruber also exchanged letters that day on the subject of education. The portion of the letters common to both read: "With reference to sub-paragraph I (a) of the amended text of Article 10 of the Draft Peace Treaty with Italy, it is to be understood that the right to be taught in the mother-tongue will be subject to special regulations determining the minimum number of students required for the establishment of local mother-tongue teaching." The reference to Article 10 of the Draft Peace Treaty with Italy must be assessed in the light of the fact that the context in which the De Gasperi–Gruber agreement was to be considered by the Peace Conference had not yet been formulated.

87. Wimmer, *Zwischen Ballhausplatz und Downing Street,* pp. 103– 04.

88. *Recueil,* IV, p. 255.

89. Wimmer, *Zwischen Ballhausplatz und Downing Street,* pp. 106–07.

90. *Recueil,* II, p. 65. The committe numbered twenty, Norway not participating.

91. General Smuts said: "The Italian and Austrian delegations are to be congratulated on reaching a happy compromise, one which does them great honor and will probably remain one of the outstanding achievements of this conference. We congratulate the two delegations on this exceptionally satisfying solution, on this example of one method of dealing with human problems on this continent which is so racially divided." *Recueil,* IV, pp. 10–11. The New Zealand delegate, Mason, also emphasized that the agreement was one of the most important to be reached in the course of the conference. *Ibid.,* p. 70. Bevin, too, after describing the concern he felt at "leaving about 200,000 German-speaking people in Italy," felt obliged to express his satisfaction in seeing "the Italian Government doing everything in its power to safeguard the minority rights of the German-speaking South Tyrolese, responding in this way to criticisms suggesting that for ethnical reasons this region should be returned to Austria, despite the strength of the economic arguments in favor of maintaining its union with Italy." *Ibid.,* IV, pp. 44–45. These statements should be added to that made almost immediately by Secretary of State Byrnes, who, on September 8, 1946, wrote to De Gasperi as follows, "I have your letter of September 6, 1946 announcing the conclusion of an agreement between yourself and the Foreign Minister of Austria relating to the Upper Adige. I can most heartily welcome this development in the relations of two States which provides reassuring evidence that two nations, inspired with democratic principles and regard for the rights of peoples to have a voice in their affairs, can reach a mutually satisfactory adjustment of an old dispute.

"Other problems, arising from disputes between neighbors, are even now being laboriously considered by the Paris Conference, and your example of direct negotiation and friendly agreement with your neighbor, Austria, should be an inspiration to the delegates meeting in Paris.

"May I congratulate you on the successful outcome of the negotiations which you have so wisely directed."

92. *Ibid.,* pp. 88–89.; Wimmer, *Zwischen Ballhausplatz und Downing Street,* p. 109; Ritschel, *Diplomatie,* p. 232, repeats the mistake to be found in Herbert Miehsler, "Das Gruber-De Gasperi Abkommen und seine Auslegung," in Huter, ed., *Sudtirole,* p. 393, by stating that the number of votes in favor was 13. He clearly confused this vote with the one that took place on September 21 in the Political and Territorial Committee for Italy.

93. This was the final definitive text: "Article 10: (1) Italy will conclude agreements with Austria to ensure freedom of transit for both people and goods between northern and eastern Tyrol or shall confirm the existing agreements on the subjects. (2) The Allied and Associated Powers have taken note of these provisions (the text is contained in appendix

IV) on which the Austrian and Italian Governments reached agreement on September 5, 1946."

94. *Il Tempo,* September 8, 1946.

95. It should be noted that the Australian amendment mentioned above was discussed by the Political and Territorial Committee for Italy on September 21 and adopted by a vote of 14 to 6. However, on September 23, when Article 13, in its entirety, was put to a vote, it gained only 12 votes with 2 against and 6 abstentions. Brazil and Greece disassociated themselves from the majority for undisclosed reasons. *Recueil,* II, pp. 66 and 70. Put to a vote in the plenary assembly of the Peace Conference, Article 13 reacquired its majority and its adoption was recommended by a vote of 14 to 7. *Recueil,* IV, p. 90. Finally, the entire article (Article 19 in the final numbering) was accepted by the foreign ministers of the four Great Powers at their meeting in New York, but with a basic reservation introduced by the Soviet Union that deprived the article of its value. This reservation stated that all of the rights and freedoms mentioned in the article were guaranteed to the Italian minority, but in conformity with the constitution of the Yugoslav state.

96. *Le Monde,* September 20, 1946.

97. On September 24 it was Gruber's turn, in a letter to Von Guggenberg, to elaborate on the matters agreed upon between himself and De Gasperi. Gruber, *Between Liberation,* pp. 69–70. This letter is quoted *in extenso* in Ritschel, *Diplomatie,* pp. 228–29. It may be noted that the explanation that Gruber provides in this letter often reaches the maximum limit insofar as content and interpretation of the clauses contained in the agreement are concerned and, on occasion, he strays beyond into ambiguity.

98. Miehsler, *Das Gruber-De Gasperi Abkommen und seine Auslegung,* pp. 409 et seq.

99. *Tiroler Tagezeitung,* October 3, 1946.

100. This theory was contested by Professor Gschnitzer at a meeting of the U.N. Special Political Committee on October 20, 1960, when he maintained that the Paris agreement imposed obligations on Italy alone.

This Austrian legal view is also expounded in Herbert Miehsler, *Südtirol als Volkerrechts Problem* (Graz: Verlag Styria, 1962), and in Heinrich Siegler, "Neutralität Prosperität," in *Osterreichs Weg zu Souveränität* (Wien: Verlag Zeitarchiv, 1959).

NOTES TO CHAPTER V

1. *Volkszeitung,* September 22, 1947.

2. For the text of Article 5 of the *D.L.* n. 23 of February 2, 1948, see, *L'Accordo De Gasperi–Gruber sull'Alto Adige,* pp. 76–77.

3. Minutes of the conversations held between the Austrian and Italian delegations on the problem of the revision of the options, Rome, November 22, 1947, in Presidenza del Consiglio dei Ministri, *L'attuazione dell'accordo intervenuto a Parigi tra il governo italiano e il governo austriaco il 5 settembre 1946* (Rome: 1952), pp. 71–73.

4. *Ibid.,* p. 75.

5. Ministero degli Affair Esteri, *L'Alto Adige alla XV sessione dell' Assemblea delle Nazioni Unite* (Rome: Ministry of Foreign Affairs, 1961), p. 43. Hereafter cited as *L'Alto Adige alla XV sessione.*

6. See Chapter 4, section 9.

7. *L'alto Adige alla XV sessione,* p. 42.

8. *Ibid.;* Ritschel, *Diplomatie,* p. 225.

9. *L'Alto Adige alla XV sessione,* pp. 42–43.

10. Miehsler, *Das Gruber–De Gasperi Abkommen und seine Auslegung,* pp. 409–11.

11. Among them were former Prime Minister Ivanoe Bonomi, the future president of the Republic, Luigi Einaudi; the president of the Constitutional Court, Gaspare Ambrosini; the future foreign minister, Gaetano Martino, the future judge of the Constitutional Court, Costantino Mortati; the well-known professor of international and constitutional law, Tomaso Perassi, later to become vice-president of the Constitutional Court.

12. Alcide De Gasperi, *Discorsi politici* (Rome: Cinque Lune, 1956), I, p. 138. There is no clear explanation of why Ritschel, *Diplomatie,* p. 257, states that on that occasion De Gasperi said that the demand for autonomy for the Alto Adige alone would act to pave the

way for its annexation to Austria. Perhaps the author was led astray by the writings of others, because *De Gasperi never made this statement attributed to him,* even though there may have been times when he may have had some concerns of this kind. This may have been the case when, in reading a report from Vienna, he learned that Austrian pressure to have the options in Article 5 modified—as confided unofficially to the Italian political representative during a conversation at the Ballhaus—derived from the hope that this would save certain persons who, though compromised by their ties to Nazism, formed the ranking cadres of the major political organization in the Alto Adige.

13. Ritschel, *Diplomatie,* pp. 259–61.

14. For the origin of Gruber's letter, see Joseph Raffeneir, "Diario di 20 giorni," in *Regione Trentino-Alto Adige:* Quaderni di aggiornamenti, numero speciale-supplemento al no. 1 del 1968, p. 44.

15. Raffeneir noted in his diary (*ibid.,* p. 45) in the entry for January 7, 1948 as follows: "Erich Amonn and Dr. Tinzl reported on their visit to Vienna, from which they had just returned. The *Austrian Foreign Minister, Gruber,* has informed them that the Austrian government cannot lend us its support on the question of structure (that is to say, region in common with the Trentino or complete severence of the South Tyrol from the Trentino) but *desires that we consider ourselves satisfied with the solution wanted by the Italian government (two autonomous provinces within the framework of a single autonomous region).* Within the context of such a 'regional' solution, Vienna has worked out a series of 'essential demands' which the Austrian government would be prepared to support."

16. At the same time, it is to be noted that even in his *Reply to Critics* of 1961 Gruber avoided expressing himself in terms that actually conflicted with the obligations he knew he had assumed. See Ritschel, *Diplomatie,* pp. 238–47.

17. A fairly detailed account of such consultations may be found in Raffeneir's Diary.

18. *L'Accordo De-Gasperi–Gruber sull Alto Adige,* p. 143. The secretary of the other party in the Alto Adige, the Social Democrat Foglietti, also addressed a similar statement to Tomaso Perassi. See *L'Alto Adige alla XV sessione,* p. 44.

19. Miehsler, *Das Gruber–De Gasperi Abkommen und seine Auslegung,* pp. 410–11; Ritschel, *Diplomatie,* pp. 264 and 281.

20. *L'Accordo De Gasperi–Gruber sull'Alto Adige,* p. 73.

21. *L'Alto Adige alla XV sessione,* p. 43.

22. *Ibid.,* pp. 43–44.

23. *Ibid.,* pp. 126–27.

24. Miehsler, *Das Gruber–De Gasperi Abkommen und seine Auslegung,* p. 267, reports that Von Guggenberg himself affirmed in 1959 that everyone has a right to change his opinion, but facts cannot be altered.

25. *L'Alto Adige alla XV sessione,* pp. 91–92. Also published in *Dolomiten,* February 26, 1948.

26. The text of this law is also printed in *L'Accordo De Gasperi–Gruber sull'Alto Adige,* pp. 145–53.

27. For the text of the constitutional law, see, *ibid.,* pp. 123–41.

28. Josef DeFlorian, *Das Optantendekret* (Innsbruck: Sudtirolerverband, 1948).

29. *L'Accordo De Gasperi–Gruber sull'Alto Adige,* p. 81.

30. Kreisky's speech before the XIV session of the general assembly of the United Nations, September 25, 1959, in *Relazioni Internazionali, 1959,* XL, p. 1372.

31. "Final report on the conversations held between the Italian and Austrian delegations on the problem of the reoptions and concerning other questions relating to the reoptants, March 28, 1950; jointly drafted minutes constituting understanding reached between the Austrian and Italian delegations on certain questions touching on property affecting the reoptants from the Alto Adige, July 6, 1950; exchange of letters dated May 15, 1952 and of notes dated September 15 and 24, 1952, on the question of the transfer of assets of reoptants," in *L'attuazione dell'accordo intervenuto a Parigi tra il governo italiano e il governo austriaco il 5 settembre 1946,* pp. 77–81.

32. It is interesting to note that the number of those who reopted is considerably larger than the number (185,085) who had opted for Germany in 1939. This is explained by the fact that many of the young people had married in Austria and in Germany and had

children born outside of the Alto Adige. When the bill became law there were still 44,684 emigrants. The number of these refused citizenship was 4,106, of whom 3,442 were emigrants.

33. *L'Accordo De Gasperi–Gruber sull'Alto Adige,* pp. 93–94.

NOTES TO CHAPTER VI

1. For Prime Minister De Gasperi's speech, see *Alto Adige,* November 11, 1952.
2. See Gruber, *Between Liberation,* Chapter IV.
3. *Ibid.,* p. 61.
4. For the part of the speeches made on this occasion by Ebner and Guggenberg referring to the Alto Adige, see *Relazioni Internazionali,* December 19, 1953, no. 51, p. 1216.
5. The text of Grauss's speech can be found in *Relazioni Internazionali,* December 5, 1953, no. 49, p. 1184.
6. The motion read: "The governor of the Tyrol took a position in the Landtag today against the oppression of the people of the Alto Adige, remorselessly exercized by Italy in virtue of an absurd interpretation and application of the Treaty of Paris. The people of Innsbruck thank the governor for his determined stand. For their part they are not content to remain passive while their brothers in the Adige and Isarco valleys struggle for survival, but will strive to help them by every means available to a civilian population. First of all, they proclaim the existence of the right, time and again ignored, of the people of the South Tyrol to self-determination; the more so in that Italy claims the same right, as a natural right for Trieste. In any case, the people of Innsbruck call on the Austrian government to spare no effort to bring to an end the cold-blooded oppression of the people of the South Tyrol." *Ibid.,* p. 1185.
7. See *Relazioni Internazionali,* December 19, 1953, no. 52, pp. 1225–26 summarizing the speeches by Reimann, Koref, Ebenbichler, and Gschnitzer.
8. The speech is also published in *Relazioni Internazionali,* July 14, 1956, pp. 874–75.
9. "Memorandum dell'Ambasciata d'Italia a Vienna al ministro degli esteri austriaco in data 9 luglio 1956," in Ministero degli Affari Esteri, *Alto Adige. Documenti presentati al Parlamento Italiano dal ministro degli affari esteri, Segni, il 16 settembre 1960* (Rome: Tipografia riservata del Ministero degli Affari Esteri, 1960), D. 1. Hereafter cited as *Libro Verde,* 1960.
10. *"Memorandum del ministro degli affari esteri austriaco alla ambasciata d'Italia a Vienna in data 8 ottobre 1956,"* in *ibid.,* D.3.
11. Gschnitzer's speech is reproduced in *Relazioni Internazionali,* February 5, 1957, no. 5; *Libro Verde, 1960,* D. 4.
12. "Memorandum del Ministero degli Affari Esteri italiano all' Ambasciata d'Austria a Roma, 31 gennaio, 1957," in *Libro Verde, 1960,* D. 4.
13. "Memorandum del Ministero degli Affari Esteri austriaco all' ambasciata d'Italia a Vienna, 7 febbraio 1957," *ibid.,* D. 5.
14. "Memorandum del Ministero degli Affari Esteri italiano del 30 gennaio 1957," in *ibid.,* D. 6. Handed to the Austrian Chancellor by the Italian Ambassador in Vienna on February 9, 1957.
15. See *ibid.,* DD. 7,8,9,10.
16. "Ordine del giorno del 22 febbraio 1958 per le consultazioni italo-austriache ad alto livello," in *ibid.,* D. 13.
17. "Promemoria dell'ambasciata d'Italia a Vienna al Ministro degli Affari Esteri austriaco in data 21 luglio, 9 settembre, 1 ottobre, 29 ottobre 1 dicembre 1958 e 8 gennaio 1960," in *ibid.,* DD. 14, 15, 16, 17, 19, 21.
18. Kreisky's speech of September 21, 1959 before the U.N. General Assembly is reproduced in *Relazioni Internazionali,* October 3, 1959, no. 4D, p. 1371.
19. "Memorandum del Ministero degli Affari Esteri austriaco all' Ambasciata d'Italia a Vienna del 29 ottobre 1959," in *Libro Verde, 1960,* D. 18.
20. Gschnitzer's speech is reproduced in *Relazioni Internazionali,* December 19, 1959, no. 51, p. 1688.

21. "Lettera del President del Consiglio dei Ministri Italiano, On. Segni, al cancelliere federale austriaco, J. Raab, del 10 gennaio 1960," in *Libro Verde, 1960,* D. 22.

22. "Lettera del cancelliere federale austriaco, J. Raab, al presidente del consiglio italiano, On. Antonio Segni, del 26 gennaio 1960," in *ibid.,* D. 23.

23. "Promemoria del ministero degli affari esteri austriaco all' ambasciata d'Italia a Vienna del 4 maggio 1960," in *ibid.,* D. 26.

24. "Lettera del presidente del consiglio Tambroni al cancelliere federale Raab del 18 maggio 1960," in *ibid.,* D. 27.

25. Segni a Guidotti, istruzioni del 18 maggio 1960, in *ibid.,* D. 28.

26. "Lettera del cancelliere federale Raab al presidente del consiglio Tambroni del 18 giugno 1960," in *ibid.,* D. 31.

27. Lettera del presidente del consiglio Tambroni al cancelliere federale Raab dei 22 giugno 1960," in *ibid.,* D. 32.

28. Guidotti a Kreisky, lettera del 25 giugno 1960, in *ibid.,* D. 33.

29. Kreisky a Guidotti, lettera del 14 luglio 1960, in *ibid.,* D. 35. The reference here is to the project submitted by representatives from the Alto Adige in 1920, which has been discussed in Chapter II.

30. "Memoria esplicativa annessa alla lettera del ministro degli esteri Kreisky al segretario generale delle Nazioni Unite, Hammerskjold, del 23 giugno 1960," in *Libro Verde, 1960,* D. 34.

31. For the text of the speech by Martino on September 22, 1960, see *ibid.,* pp. 7–9.

32. For Martino's statement of September 23, 1960, see *ibid.,* pp. 13–14.

33. The text of Segni's speech is printed in *ibid.,* pp. 25–26.

34. Kreisky's speech is reproduced in *Relazioni Internazionali, 1960,* no. 41, p. 1318.

35. The text of the memorandum presented by the Italian delegation on October 12, 1960 is published in *L'Alto Adige alla XV sessione,* pp. 31–73.

36. Kreisky's speech of October 18, 1960 is also reproduced in *Relazioni Internazionali, 1960,* no. 44, pp. 1421–26.

37. The draft resolution presented by Austria on October 14, 1960 is reproduced in *L'Alto Adige alla XV sessione,* p. 157.

38. For the text of Segni's speech see, *ibid.,* pp. 83–96.

39. The text of Martino's comments is in *ibid.,* p. 107.

40. The text of Martino's statement is in *ibid.,* p. 107.

41. The text of the draft resolution presented by the Austrian delegation on October 25, 1960 can be found in *ibid.,* p. 158.

42. The draft resolution presented on October 25, 1960 by Argentina, Brazil, Paraguay, and Uruguay is in *ibid.,* p. 158.

43. The text of Martino's speech of October 25, 1960 is in *ibid.,* pp. 111–15.

44. See the text of Segni's speech of October 26, 1960, in *ibid.,* pp. 131–35.

45. For the text of the draft resolution, see *ibid.,* p. 160.

46. The text of Martino's speech is in *ibid.,* pp. 139–41.

47. The text of this resolution can be found in *ibid.,* p. 161.

48. For the text of Martino's speech of October 31, 1960, see *ibid.,* pp. 149–51.

49. For an Austrian version of the entire discussion on the Alto Adige at the XVth session of the U.N. General Assembly, see Ritschel, *Diplomatie,* pp. 333–63, although it takes the form of a narrative rather than an in depth evaluation of the events.

NOTES TO CHAPTER VII

1. For the text of the Italian note, see Ministry of Foreign Affairs, *Alto Adige. Documenti presentati al Parlamento Italiano dal Ministro degli Affari Esteri On. Segni il 19 settembre 1961* (Rome: Ministry of Foreign Affairs, 1961), D. 5. Hereafter cited as *Libro Verde, 1961.*

2. The text of the Austrian note is in *ibid.,* D.6.

3. The text of the official communiqué is given in *ibid.,* D. 24.

4. The text of the Milan communiqué is in *ibid.,* D. 13; for an Austrian account of the meeting, see Ritschel, *Diplomatie,* pp. 365–68.

5. For the text of Segni's speech, see *Atti Parlamentari*, III Legislatura, Discussioni, pp. 19091–102.

6. Kreisky's statement to the Austrian Parliament, February 9, 1961, is in *Relazioni Internazionali*, 1961, no. 7., pp. 205–06; Kreisky had previously held a press conference in Vienna on February 3, 1961 and for this text, see *ibid.*, p. 174. On February 9, Under-Secretary Gschnitzer also spoke in the *Nationalrat*, repeating the request for separate autonomous status for the province of Bolzano. For the text, see *ibid.*, pp. 206–07.

7. For the text, see *Libro Verde, 1961*, DD. 14 and 15.

8. For the text, see *ibid.*, D. 16.

9. For the text, see *ibid.*, D. 18.

10. See *ibid.*, DD. 19–22.

11. For the text, see *ibid.*, D. 25.

12. For the text of the official communiqué issued at Klagenfurt, see *ibid.*, D. 26; an Austrian account of the meeting is published in Ritschel, *Diplomatie*, pp. 370–71, which also includes the text of a long interview on the subject granted by Segni on June 11.

13. See *Libro Verde, 1961*, D. 29.

14. For the texts of Segni's statements, see *ibid.*, D. 30.

15. For the text of Kreisky's statements, see *ibid.*, D. 31.

16. The text of the *Zurich* communiqué is given in *ibid.*, D. 32. An Austrian account of the meeting is to be found in Ritschel, *Diplomatie*, pp. 376–80.

17. See the text in *Libro Verde, 1961*, D. 33. Compare with Ritschel, *Diplomatie*, p. 382.

18. See the text in *Libro Verde, 1961*, D. 34.

19. See, Ritschel, *Diplomatie*, pp. 380–82.

20. See the text in *Libro Verde, 1961*, D. 35. Compare with Ritschel, *Diplomatie*, pp. 382–83.

21. For the text, see *Libro Verde, 1961*, D. 37.

22. *Atti Parlamentari*, III Legislatura, Discussioni, p. 23014.

23. For the text, see *Libro Verde, 1961*, D. 41.

24. For the text, see *ibid.*, D. 43.

25. For the text of the final report, dated July 25, 1951, see *ibid.*, D. 42. The request was accompanied by an "explanatory memorandum."

26. For the text, see *ibid.*, D. 44.

27. For the text, see *ibid.*, D. 49.

28. For the text, see *ibid.*, D. 55.

29. From Scelba's already noted statement to the Chamber of Deputies on June 22, 1961.

30. From Scelba's speech at the Viminale on September 13, 1961 on the occasion of the inaugural meeting of the Commission of 19.

31. From the speech made at Bolzano on June 18, 1961 and noted above.

32. From the statement made to the Chamber of Deputies on June 22, 1961 and noted above.

33. From the above-mentioned speech at the Viminale, September 13, 1961.

34. From the speech at Bolzano, June 18, 1961 and noted above.

35. *Ibid.*

36. From the statement made to the Chamber of Deputies, June 22, 1961, and noted above.

37. *Ibid.*

38. *Ibid.*

39. From the speech at Bolzano, June 18, 1961 and already noted.

40. From the statement to the Chamber of Deputies, June 22, 1961 and noted above.

41. From the speech at the Viminale, September 13, 1961, noted above.

42. Full details of the debate extracted from the records of the United Nations may also be found in Ministry of Foreign Affairs, *Le Haut Adige à la XVI iéme Session de L'Assemblée Générale des Nations Unies. Discourses et documents* (Rome: Ministry of Foreign Affairs, 1962). See also, Ritschel, *Diplomatie*, pp. 392–95.

43. The court passed sentence in the Graz trial only on February 26, 1962, finding as

proven the existence of a terrorist organization. For the text of the Italian note verbale, see *Libro Verde, 1962,* D. 18.

44. For the text of the Austrian note, see *ibid.,* D. 19. For the text of these documents, see Ministry of Foreign Affairs, *Alto Adige. Documenti italiani ed austriaci dal 22 settembre 1961 al 28 settembre 1962* (Rome: Ministry of Foreign Affairs, 1962). Hereafter cited as *Libro Verde, 1962.*

45. *Ibid.,* D. 20.

46. *Ibid.,* D. 21. Referring to the points made in the Austrian note, Ritschel, *Diplomatie,* p. 397, complains that this note was not published in the Italian press at the time. Ritschel's position is understandable, since he has published a book based on confidential records of the meetings between the foreign ministers of Italy and Austria, and is perhaps unaware that such publications are not in keeping with diplomatic usage. However, he should appreciate that what would inevitably give rise to an exchange of polemics in the press, would simply not be conducive to promoting an agreement between Italy and Austria.

47. *Libro Verde, 1962,* DD. 22, 24, 26, 27.

48. For the text, see *ibid.,* D. 25.

49. For the text, see *ibid.,* D. 28.

50. See *ibid.,* DD. 29, 30, 31, 32, 34, 35, 36.

51. For the text, see *ibid.,* D. 33.

52. See *ibid.,* D. 37.

53. Piccioni had been appointed after Prime Minister Fanfani had been interim foreign minister for about a month subsequent to Segni's election as president of the republic.

54. For the text, see *ibid.,* D. 41.

55. For the text, see *ibid.,* D. 43.

56. For the text, see *ibid.,* D. 46.

57. For the text, see *ibid.,* D. 47.

58. For the text, see *ibid.,* D. 48.

59. For the text of the Austrian note, see ibid., D. 49.

60. For the text, see *Relazioni Internazionali, 1962,* p. 926.

61. For the text, see *ibid.,* pp. 1125–26.

62. For the text, see *ibid.,* pp. 1157–59.

63. See *ibid.,* pp. 1308–09. The Italian position on the Alto Adige was also stated by Piccioni in his address to the Chamber of Deputies on October 30, 1962, following the debate on the budget for the Ministry of Foreign Affairs. The portion of the address most directly concerning the problem under discussion here will be found in *ibid.,* p. 1336.

64. See *Documenti diplomatici sulla vertenza per l'Alto Adige (dal 5 novembre 1962 al 5 ottobre 1963)* (Rome: Ministry of Foreign Affairs, 1963), DD. 1–13. Hereafter cited as *Libro Verde, 63.*

65. For the text, see *ibid.,* D. 14.

66. For the text, see *ibid.,* D. 19.

67. For the Austrian view of the Trent trial, see Ritschel, *Diplomatie,* pp. 411–12.

68. On the subject, see *Libro Verde, 1963,* DD. 22, 24, 26, 28, 30–31, 33, 35, and 37.

69. For the text, see *ibid.,* D. 29.

70. For the text, see *ibid.,* D. 32.

71. For the text, see *ibid.,* D. 33.

72. For the text, see *ibid.,* D. 38.

73. The text is also in *Relazioni Internazionali, 1963,* p. 1356. Compare Ritschel, *Diplomatie,* pp. 423–24.

74. The Austrian view of the Milan trial is in Ritschel, *Diplomatie,* pp. 414–19.

75. See the text of the final report of the commission in *Relazioni Internazionali, 1964,* pp. 611–23. On the work of the commission and an Austrian evaluation of same, see Ritschel, *Diplomatie,* pp. 428–36.

76. It was precisely these that the Italian government excluded from the "package deal" offered to Vienna and Bolzano.

77. The final report of the Commission of 19 lists all of the proposals present by the German-speaking group that were rejected by the majority, as well as those proposed by a very small Italian-speaking group and likewise rejected.

NOTES TO CHAPTER VIII

1. Using the Austrian verbatim record, Ritschel, *Diplomatie,* pp. 437–43, reproduces almost without comment, a large part of the statements made by both sides. The official communiqué issued at the close of the meeting is reproduced in *Relazioni Internazionali, 1964,* p. 813.

2. Ritschel, *Diplomatie,* p. 441, reproduces from the Austrian record a positive and precise statement on this point made by the Italian side in the formal and official session in reply to the ambiguous phrases offered by Kreisky.

3. *Ibid.,* p. 337 et seq., p. 440 et seq. Ritschel writes that the primary importance of the Geneva meeting lay in the narrowing of the differences between the two sides noted there. He admits that Kreisky had believed it possible that the Austrian government would be willing to declare the Paris Agreement to have been carried out, once the recommendations of the Commission of 19, adopted unanimously or by majority vote, had been applied, and agreement had been reached on the questions still to be resolved.

4. The instructions received by the Italian experts may be inferred from the detailed reports sent to the Austrian and the Alto Adige press by corresponsdents in Geneva, to whom the Austrian experts frequently talked about what had been discussed.

5. See the minutes reproduced in Ritschel, *Diplomatie,* p. 441.

6. Reference is made to the communiqué issued on June 28, 1964 by Ritschel, *Diplomatie,* p. 445.

7. The question of the Alto Adige was repeatedly brought up during the debate on the vote of confidence on Moro's second cabinet. Speaking to the Senate on that occasion, the Prime Minister, on August 1, 1964, expressed the hope that the dispute would be settled. The text of the speech is in *Relazioni Internazionali, 1964,* p. 1099.

8. Ritschel, *Diplomatie,* p. 447.

9. *Ibid.,* p. 447. Ritschel comments that evidently there was disagreement on that occasion among the Alto Adige representatives. Kreisky is reported to have asked them—in order to obtain greater clarity and unity of approach—to promptly present a formula on which further talks with Italy could be based.

10. Another important event which took place during that week was the reorganization of the dioceses of Trent and Bressanone, decided upon by the Holy See after consultation with the Italian government. This reorganization not only met with local approval but also made it possible to better utilize the local priests. On this point, see *Osservatore Romano,* August 8, 1964 and Ritschel, *Diplomatie,* pp. 445–46. The matter had been the object of considerable study, not only in the Vatican, but by all concerned for many years, and the final decision was reached only after long and careful thought.

11. Almost all of the minutes of that meeting may be found in Ritschel, *Diplomatie,* pp. 449–53. The official communiqué is also in *Relazioni Internazionali,* 1964, p. 1192.

12. Ritschel, *Diplomatie,* p. 451.

13. On this episode, see *ibid.,* pp. 472–74.

14. A considerable part of the record of the statements made by Kreisky and Saragat is reproduced in *ibid.,* pp. 474–78.

15. *Ibid.,* pp. 479–96. Ritschel publishes a complete list of all of the Italian government's measures and proposals presented for ending the international dispute. His only omissions are indications of the *all-embracing* nature of the proposals and the interrelation between the two parts. This omission leads him to make severe and unjustified criticism of Italian diplomatic action in the period following the Paris meeting.

16. *Ibid.,* p. 478.

17. *Ibid.,* pp. 496–505, provides complete particulars on the ground covered and progress made by the meetings. On this occasion, too, it was possible for Ritschel to transcribe the contents of the minutes relating to portions of the statements made by the key participants, among them, Kreisky, Magnago, Gschnitzer, Dietl, Mitterdorfer, and Wallnofer.

18. For details, see *Ibid.,* p. 513.

19. The Austrian's Foreign Minister's telegram to Ambassador Loewenthal on this subject is dated March 28. Reproduced in *ibid.,* pp. 513–14.

20. Curiously enough, Ritschel omits this portion of the minutes of the meeting. See *ibid.*, p. 513.

21. The final paragraph of this concluding chapter has been deleted, since it is followed by an additional chapter. Nonetheless, it is perhaps pertinent here to add the final lines of this final paragraph written by Professor Toscano: "Italy's internal measures and international agreements may even be able to eliminate all of the existing area of friction and resolve the present international dispute. But this will not create a really positive, secure, and lasting structure until two closely interdependent conditions have been met, that is, until Austria, the Alto Adige, and the Tyrol eliminate their mental reservations and until Italy, as a result, abandons her mistrust. Every serious historian and honest citizen must hope that this day may soon arrive and be followed by an era of loyal understanding and fruitful cooperation among all peoples of the Alto Adige within the framework of a comprehending Europe."

NOTES TO CHAPTER IX

1. For the text of Mittersdorf's speech of March 12, 1965, see Ritschel, *Diplomatie*, pp. 512–13.

2. Typical in this respect was the speech by Kreisky at Rum near Innsbruck, May 9, 1965. For the text, see *ibid.*, pp. 516–17.

3. The minutes and findings of all five of these meetings may be found in *ibid.*, pp. 517–19; 540–42; 569–70, and 570–71.

4. *Ibid.*, pp. 521–25.

5. *Ibid.*, p. 522.

6. *Ibid.*, p. 523.

7. For the contents of this conversation, see the speeches made by Prime Minister Moro on October 13, 1965, in *Relazioni Internazionali, 1965*, pp. 1026–27.

8. See *Salzburger Nachrichten*, August 28, 1965.

9. For details, see Ritschel, *Diplomatie*, pp. 526–28.

10. *Ibid.*, pp. 530–31.

11. The Austrian report is summarized in *ibid.*, p. 533.

12. For the text, see *United Nations General Assembly A/PV*, October 12, 1965, pp. 2–20.

13. See also, *Relazioni Internazionali, 1965*, pp. 1026–27.

14. The greater part of the Austrian report of this meeting is in Ritschel, *Diplomatie*, pp. 540–42.

15. *Ibid.*, pp. 542–46.

16. For the text, see *ibid.*, p. 546.

17. See the full report in *ibid.*, pp. 547–48.

18. This was the origin of the phrase "effective guarantee" used in the Austrian proposals and later to appear in those of the Alto Adige and Vienna.

19. See also, *Relazioni Internazionali, 1966*, p. 271.

20. *Ibid.*, p. 303.

21. See the original text, in Josef Klaus, "Regierungseklärung, 1966," in *Dokumente unserer Zeit*, p. II. Immediately after this, at a press conference, the new Austrian Foreign Minister also indicated that, in his view, four avenues should be used to reach a settlement (domestic Italian action, agreement between the Italian and Austrian governments, the United Nations, and the Council of Europe).

22. It is of interest to note that at the same time that the break occured between the Volkspartei and the Socialist party in Austria, the SVP deputy for the Trentino–Alto Adige Diet, Jenny, was expelled from his party, and he formed a new group called the Socialist Progressive party.

23. Ritschel, *Diplomatie*, p. 557.

24. *Ibid.*, p. 568, provides the substance of the Austrian minutes of these meetings.

25. For the text, see Italian Ministry of Foreign Affairs, *Trattati e convenzioni tra il Regno d'Italia e gli Altri Stati* (Rome: 1934), pp. 252–69.

26. For the text, see also *Rivista di diritto internazionali, 1960*, pp. 355–63. It was ratified under Italian law, no. 411, March 23, 1958.

27. See the résumé of the Austrian minutes in Ritschel, *Diplomatie,* p. 569.

28. *Ibid.,* pp. 569–70.

29. See the report of the Austrian minutes in *ibid.,* pp. 570–71.

30. *Ibid.,* pp. 571–81.

31. In addition to the Italian press reports for the period, for some interesting details, see also, *ibid.,* pp. 582–84, 586.

32. *Ibid.,* pp. 582–84, 586.

33. In particular, see the text of Kreisky's statements made on August 25, 1966, in *ibid.,* p. 582.

34. See note 22 above.

35. On September 9, 1966, a terrorist attack was carried out against the barracks of the Guardie di Finanza (Customs Police) at Malga Sasso, killing three and wounding three. As Italian Prime Minister Moro noted in his speech of September 12, one of the victims, "a dramatic symbol of a common destiny in death as in life, was an Italian soldier from the German-speaking group."

36. For the text, see Camera dei Deputati, *IV Legislatura, Discussioni, 505* (afternoon session of September 12, 1966), pp. 25477 et seq.

37. See also, *Relazioni Internazionali, 1966,* pp. 973–79.

38. *Ibid.,* pp. 1003–06.

39. The substantive portion of the text reads as follows: "The Chamber, having heard a statement by the Government on the situation in the Alto Adige and on the steps taken to maintain public order and to introduce a program increasing the autonomy of the area, approves this statement: considering that the proposals of the Commission of 19, based on a most liberal approach to minorities, constitute an appropriate guide to measures necessary to guarantee peaceful and orderly development under conditions of equality for all and for every language group within the national boundaries, authorizes the Government to continue the approaches currently being made so that the proposed measures, to be implemented unilaterally by the State with the agreement of the representatives of the populations involved, will make it possible to resolve the dispute with Austria on the basis of total acceptance by both parties of the De Gasperi–Gruber agreement; and in order to finally suppress the criminal activities of the terrorists, binds the Government to seek and acquire concrete and effective collaboration from the Austrian Government and, insofar as it is concerned, from the Government of the German Federal Republic, a collaboration which the Chamber regards as a self-evident necessity and an obligation within the framework of European democratic solidarity, as well as essential to achieve the desired solution of the unresolved questions of the Alto Adige." *Relazioni Internazionali, 1966,* p. 1005.

40. For the text, see also, *ibid.,* pp. 1031–37.

41. *Ibid.,* pp. 1033–34.

42. Typical was an interview granted by the terrorist, Norbert Burger, quoted in full in Ritschel, *Diplomatie,* pp. 572–76.

43. On the same day, October 6, 1966, a note was handed to the German government by the Italian Embassy in Bonn, drawing the attention of the German authorities to the fact that certain aspects of the terrorist outrages in the Alto Adige would suggest that the perpetrators also enjoyed encouragement, bases, and financial support from within the territory of the German Federal Republic.

44. Based on information in the possession of the Italian police, an Italian note was sent to Vienna, December 3, 1966, providing documented information of the existence on Austrian territory of a number of terrorist bases, training centers, stores, and refuges. Specific reference was made to the criminal activities of the well-known terrorist, Burger, who had acquired arms, munitions, and explosives for use in illegal activities in the Alto Adige. It did not appear, the note continued, that the Austrian police dealt effectively with these activities. Moreover, the few charges brought against Austrian citizens involved in terrorist activities in the Alto Adige were restricted to the crime of "possession of explosives," without consideration of the origin and destination of such substances. As to the matter of the extremists from the Alto Adige, the note expressed the view that Austrian law undoubtedly required their expulsion, since, in any event, the activities of these terrorists were contrary to the interests of the Austrian state. Furthermore, adoption of measures by the Austrian government limiting length of stay in certain parts of Austria

and prohibiting residence in areas close to the Italian frontier would, in all likelihood, discourage terrorist activity. The note went on to mention that new terrorist outbreaks had occurred in Italy since Vienna had received the Italian note of October 6, 1966, outbreaks which could probably have been prevented had it been possible to achieve complete cooperation between the Italian and Austrian security forces in combating terrorism. Therefore, the Italian government reiterated the request it had earlier expressed in its note of October 6, 1966, to learn what concrete measures the Austrian authorities intended to adopt against those responsible for acts of terrorism, in line with the United Nations recommendations of 1959 and 1961.

The note concluded by stating that serious misgivings had developed in Italy as a result of the presentation to Chancellor Klaus of a memorandum by the *Union für Südtiroler,* revealing the avowed aim of annexing the province of Bolzano, and the reports in the press that the Chancellor had shown himself to be "very sympathetic" to these proposals. These misgivings were strengthened by the fact that the Austrian government had been repeatedly requested to take appropriate measures against these extremist organizations, whose real aims were very different from those stated in their statutes.

45. For the text, see U.N. General Assembly, *A/PV 1430,* October 5, 1966, pp. 41–60.
46. For the text, see *Relazioni Internazionali, 1966,* pp. 1125–26.

NOTES TO CHAPTER X

1. Moro's statement to the Chamber of Deputies, July 27, 1967.
2. *Ibid.*
3. *Ibid.*
4. This recommendation of the Executive Committee was approved by a large majority at the subsequent party congress held on December 2, 1967.
5. Speech by Chancellor Klaus in Graz, May 24, 1968 and the statement by Foreign Minister Waldheim before Parliament, June 28, 1968.
6. This was the last of these meetings attended by the author of this volume, who died a few days later in Rome.
7. The eighteen points included in the timetable were the following:
    1) Initialing of the agreement regarding amendment of Article 27 (a) of the European Convention for the Peaceful Settlement of Disputes with respect to relations between Italy and Austria.
    2) Amendment of Article 18 of the regulations issued under the Code of Police Laws and recognition of the legal entity of the "Associazione reduci e vittime di guerra altoatesine" and the "Südtiroler Alpenverein."
    3) Statement to be made by the Italian Prime Minister to Parliament, followed by vote of approval.
    4) Statement by the Austrian Chancellor to the Nationalrat, followed by vote of approval.
    5) Formulation and initiation of activities by the Italian committee charged with implementing the measures for the Alto Adige.
    6) Oral statements by the Italian and Austrian delegates to the U.N. General Assembly.
    7) First vote on the required Constitutional Law by the Senate and the Chamber of Deputies.
    8) Signature of the agreement mentioned under point 1.
    9) Vote by the Italian and Austrian parliaments on the law ratifying the agreement mentioned under point 1 and, simultaneously, the final vote on the required Italian Constitutional Law.
    10) Approval of the necessary Italian legislation of a nonconstitutional character.
    11) Publication of the regulations to be issued under the required Italian Constitutional Law.
    12) Publication of the decree transferring from the Trentino–Alto Adige region to the province of Bolzano the offices and staff responsible for the new powers of the province.
    13) Formal declaration by Austria that the dispute is settled, and exchange of ratifications of the agreement mentioned under point 1.

14) Italian diplomatic note recording receipt of the formal declaration by Austria that the dispute is settled.
15) Notification of the settlement of the dispute to the U.N. secretary general by the Italian and Austrian governments.
16) Notification of the agreement under point 1 to the registrar of the International Court of Justice by the Italian and Austrian governments.
17) Notification of the agreement under point 1 to the secretary general of the Council of Europe by the Italian and Austrian governments.
18) Possible conclusion of a treaty of friendship and cooperation between Italy and Austria.

Index

The Johns Hopkins University Press

This book was composed in Press Roman text and display type by The Composing Room from a design by Susan Bishop, and printed on 50-lb. Warren 1854 regular paper. It was printed and bound by Universal Lithographers, Inc.